T0366462

Knowledge, Sophistry, and Scientific Politics

Knowledge, Sophistry, and Scientific Politics

Plato's Dialogues
Theaetetus, Sophist, and Statesman

James M. Rhodes

St. Augustine's Press
South Bend, Indiana

Manufactured in the United States of America.

1 2 3 4 5 6   26 25 24 23 22 21 20

Library of Congress Cataloging in Publication Data
Names: Rhodes, James M., author.
Title: Knowledge, sophistry, and scientific politics : Plato's Dialogues :
Theaetetus, Sophist, and Statesman / James M. Rhodes.
Description: 1st [edition].
South Bend, Indiana : St. Augustines Press, 2016.
Includes bibliographical references and index.
Identifiers: LCCN 2016012559
ISBN 9781587314216 (clothbound : alk. paper)
Subjects: LCSH: Plato. Dialogues. Selections.
Plato. Theaetetus.
Plato.
Statesman.
Plato. Sophist.
Socrates.
Classification: LCC B395 .R46 2016
DDC 184--dc23 LC record available at

St. Augustine's Press
www.staugustine.net

For
Anne Marie
Jane, Pat, Dallas, and Sean
Maria and Alan

and to the memory of Gerhart Niemeyer

Table of Contents

PREFACE

This essay seeks to elucidate Plato's *Statesman*. The task demands study of the Platonic trilogy *Theaetetus-Sophist-Statesman* because the first two dialogues in the trio bear upon the meaning of the third. Brief looks at *Philebus* will also be necessary.

In *Wilhelm Meisters Wanderjahre*, Johann Wolfgang von Goethe wrote: "*Alles Gescheite ist schon gedacht worden. Man muss nur versuchen, es noch einmal zu denken*" (Everything intelligent [or sensible] has already been thought. One must only try to think it again.) Plato's thoughts were *gescheit*. By nature, they cannot be comprehended without being rethought. One begins to rethink Plato's thoughts by reading his dialogues carefully enough to become conscious of their subtle complexities and nuances and to let their drama and reasoning open one's soul to the realities that he envisages, especially the highest.

I adhere to definite principles that govern the right reading of Plato. I learned some of them from Eric Voegelin. He will not be cited often below because *Statesman* was written at a level beneath the philosophizing to which his concepts are relevant and because he overlooked glaring problems in the Eleatic dialogues. However, he has inspired my statement that the *telos* of Plato studies is an opening of the soul to the highest reality. This insight guides me. I learned more of the principles from Leo Strauss and his students. I think that their esotericism leads to occasional misconstructions of texts. That aside, they propose sound rules for careful reading. I try to heed their precepts, with no guarantee that I do this well.

The task of reading Plato is aided by study of his best commentators. I shall credit those who have helped me in my text. Even those with whom I disagree have helped enormously.

My work has been aided immeasurably by my conversations with Zdravko Planinc, who has taught me the Homeric characteristics of Plato's dialogues. Ruth Groff has read portions of my manuscript and has offered valuable suggestions. Special thanks go to Michael Fleet for helping me to finish Chapter 7 while I was ill, and for his many splendid suggestions. And, finally, thanks as well go to my friend Tilo Schabert, who, without realizing that he had done so, gave me the idea for this work.

In at least one respect, I depart from the tradition of Plato scholarship in this book. It has been customary from time out of mind to preface every reference to a Platonic dialogue with the word "the," as in "the *Republic*," "the *Symposium*," "the *Sophist*," etc. I do not believe that this practice is justified. Plato's works are plays. We do not speak of "the *Hamlet*," "the *Romeo and Juliet*," "the *Julius Caesar*," and so on. I have decided to drop the "the," referring, for example, to *Republic*, *Theaetetus*, *Sophist*, and *Statesman*, Plato's actual titles. At first, readers might find this annoying. However, I trust that, after a while, my new practice will seem as natural to them as it now does to me. Of course, all errors herein are my own.

1

ON READING PLATO

As a political scientist, I want to learn whether Plato's Statesman teaches us noble and useful things about politics. To do this, I must study Statesman and related dialogues properly, following sound rules for interpreting Plato. I shall state my understanding of these precepts, none of which are original with me.

The best rules for reading Plato are derived from his own statements about his writing and from considerations of the form of his writing. His remarks about his writing are found in his Seventh Letter. I have defended this epistle against the charge that it is a forgery in another place.[1] I do not need to repeat that argument here. As for the form of Plato's writing, everyone knows that it is dialogue.

In a section of the Seventh Letter often called "the philosophic digression," even though it probably is not a digression, Plato addresses himself to the claim of Dionysius II of Syracuse that he knew Plato's doctrines well enough to propagate improved versions of them as his own. Plato denies this. He asserts that it is impossible that Dionysius or other writers could know that about which he is serious (*peri ôn egô spoudazô*, 341c1–2),[2] either as auditors of his or of others or by themselves. They could grasp nothing of the matter. "For there is no writing of mine about these things nor will there ever be. For it is in no way a spoken thing like other lessons" (*hrêton gar oudamôs estin hôs alla mathêmata*, 341c5–6). These statements apparently mean that Plato never spoke or wrote serious doctrines. Plato seems to confirm the same thing of the protagonist of most of his dialogues, Socrates, when he makes Socrates say in Apology: "I never became the teacher of

---

1 James M. Rhodes, *Eros, Wisdom, and Silence: Plato's Erotic Dialogues*, ch. 3.ê.
2 I cite Plato in the usual way, in my text by Stephanus numbers.

anyone (*egô de didaskalos men oudenos pôpot egenomên*). I ask questions, and whoever wishes may answer and hear what I say. I never promised or gave any instruction to any of them" (33a5–b6).[3] Socrates also appears to confirm this in Theaetetus, maintaining that some people were improved by their conversations with him despite "learning nothing from me ever" (*par' emou oudev pôpote mathontes*, 150d6–7). He seems to confirm it again in Republic (518b–d) when he argues that education is not the practice of putting knowledge into souls like sight into blind eyes—which is what the transfer of doctrine qua verbal information would be—but rather a matter of turning the soul around so that it faces away from becoming (*gignomenou*) toward being (*to on*) and the brightest of being (*tou ontos to phanotaton*), the Good (*t'agathon*)—which would enable the soul to see eternal reality for itself without teaching it propositions.

If Plato never spoke or wrote anything about the serious things and if his Socrates never taught anything, it would appear that the first rule for interpreting Platonic dialogues is that we ought not to try to mine them for "Plato's theories." As Kenneth Sayre puts it, the right way to read them "is not as repositories of philosophic doctrine."[4] I think it safe to observe that Plato scholars, particularly but not only those in the field of analytic philosophy, tend to ignore this precept. They generally study Plato's dialogues with a view toward learning his "doctrine of _____." For example, Theaetetus, Sophist, and Statesman are viewed as "Plato's theory of knowledge," "Plato's ontology," and "Plato's final political teaching" (some say "Plato's mature methodological prescriptions"). Even Sayre lapses, finding doctrines in Plato's late works.[5]

Those who investigate "Plato's theories" will object to my first hermeneutic rule. Plato wrote volumes. Why, they will ask, would he have

3   Fowler's translation in the Loeb edition. I use Joe Sachs's readings if they are available, otherwise Loeb translations. I might alter Loeb texts slightly for greater clarity, as appropriate. If I use other translations, or if Plato's meanings are ambiguous or translations are controversial, I shall call this to readers' attention.

4   Kenneth M. Sayre, *Plato's Literary Garden: How to Read a Platonic Dialogue*, ix.

5   Sayre, *Plato's Late Ontology: A Riddle Resolved*, all, especially 96, and *Metaphysics and Myth in Plato's "Statesman,"* all.

knowingly filled up his thousands of pages with worthless dross? Why would he waste his time on a pointless activity? On the basis of these kinds of questions they would declare the idea that Plato proposed no serious teachings incredible and reject or ignore the Seventh Letter.

I answer that modern quests for doctrines misconceive Plato's philosophy.[6] Sayre does better when, having warned against treating the dialogues as doctrinal treatises, he advises seeing them "as interactions with a master philosopher that are carefully shaped to guide the attentive reader in a personal pursuit of philosophic understanding."[7] I think that it would be better yet to paraphrase Socrates and say that they are writings designed to enable souls to face being and the brightest of being, the Good. Given this, the dialogues would be far from worthless. So, instead of dismissing Plato's testimony about his writing, we should ask why he set out to guide readers to encounters with the Good without enunciating *mathêmata* and how he proposed to do that.

To begin to ascertain these things, we return to the Seventh Letter. Plato's explanation of why Dionysius II could not know that about which he is serious, partially quoted above, reads in full as follows:

> For there is no writing of mine about these things, nor will there ever be. For it is in no way a spoken thing like other lessons but, from many associations with (literally "from many beings with," *ek pollês sunousias*, 341c6) and living with (*suzên*, 341c7) the matter itself (*peri to pragma auto*, 341c7) it is brought to birth in the soul suddenly, as light that is given off by a leaping flame (*hoion apo puros pêdêsantos exaphthen phôs*, 341c7–d1).[8]

6   See Eric Voegelin on "the deformation of philosophy into doctrine" in Order and History, IV, *The Ecumenic Age*, 36ff. Index entries on deformation and deculturation in *The Collected Works of Eric Voegelin*, vol. 12. *Published Essays 1966–1985* are also helpful.
7   Sayre, *Plato's Literary Garden*, ix.
8   In the Cooper anthology, Glenn R. Morrow has "after long-continued intercourse between teacher and pupil, in joint pursuit of the subject" in place of "many beings with and living with the matter itself." Sayre, *Plato's Literary Garden*, xiv, wants to translate *pollês sunousias* as "many conversations," arguing that Plato often uses *sunousia* to signify dialectical conversation. These translations are not literal but they might catch Plato's meaning.

To unpack this, we first must ask what Plato means by saying of the object of his serious thought that "it is in no way a spoken thing like other lessons" (*hrêton gar oudamôs estin hôs alla mathêmata*).[9] Plato could be announcing any of three things: (1) that the serious realities can be described in words but not in propositions like those found in the other fields of study, (2) that there are secret doctrines about the serious realities that could be whispered to a trustworthy few but never revealed to the many, or (3) that these realities are ineffable. Stanley Rosen denies that Plato is declaring that his serious knowledge cannot be stated at all. He maintains that the myth of the cave in Republic is, or borders on, serious argument.[10] I think that all such reasoning fails for several reasons. To claim that anything in a dialogue is an instance of a serious statement is to ignore Plato's denial that he ever wrote one. (Rosen also slights the fact that the images of the sun, divided line, and cave are offered in lieu of a direct report of the highest *mathêmata*. These pictures are analogies that are as close as Socrates can fly toward the Good in his ascent on that occasion.) Such claims also miscarry because *oudamôs* normally means "absolutely not at all." Further, there is no way that Plato could affirm the impossibility of his doctrines being related to Dionysius II by others unless he never had broadcast them himself. This rules out interpretation number one. I think that the *oudamôs* and doubt that confidants could keep a secret under torture by the tyrant Dionysius II—a not unlikely prospect for anyone in Syracuse taught by Plato—also are fatal for reading number two. I infer that Plato cannot verbalize his serious insights because they are ineffable.

Why should Plato's serious *mathêmata* be ineffable? The impossibility of putting his knowledge into words must owe to its nature. Plato's cognition comes like a flash of light given off by a leaping flame. Together with his *hrêton gar oudamôs estin hôs alla mathêmata*, this is to declare that it comes to one not as propositional "good ideas" that could be reported verbally but as an experience analogous to being illuminated by a lightning bolt.[11]

9   For *hrêton gar oudamôs estin hôs alla mathêmata* Morrow has, "For this knowledge is not something that can be put into words like other sciences."

10   Stanley Rosen, *Plato's "Symposium,"* xliii.

11   This is not, as Rosen believes, an inference that flows from the subjective passion of the Christian individual, *Plato's Symposium*, lv. It is simply what Plato says.

This inference tallies with Socrates' reference in Republic to the soul's wordless look at the brightest of being and also with his tale of the philosophic soul's wordless gaze at the eternal realities in Phaedrus 247a ff. Plato is a mystic, a fact noticed by thinkers as disparate as Immanuel Kant, Gregory Vlastos, and Eric Voegelin.[12] We wonder what the serious things are and how we could attain to the illumination-like insight into them. Plato's probably autobiographical answer is that one acquires his serious knowledge from much being and living with the matter itself. What does that mean?

Plato seems to explain with a long, complicated illustration. He notes that three things are necessary to knowledge of each of the beings. The knowledge is fourth. The being itself, which is knowable and true, is fifth. First is the name (*onoma*), second the *logos* (here, definition or account), third the image (*eidôlon*), and fourth the knowledge (*epistêmê*). The circle provides an example. We have the name "circle." It has its *logos* (all points that are equidistant from a point). We make a perishable image of it (say with chalk on a blackboard) that is not the circle itself, which is not subject to decay. We acquire knowledge and intelligence and true opinion (*epistêmê kai nous alêthês te doxa*) about it, which are a whole that exists not in sounds or in bodily shapes but in souls and which accordingly is neither the name-*logos*-image complex nor the nature of the circle itself. Of all this, *nous* approaches the fifth most closely. The same holds true of everything else: geometric figures, color, the Good, the beautiful, the just, all bodies, all living creatures, and all ethical actions and passions of souls.

I interrupt Plato's explanation of what he means by being with and living with the matter itself to notice that he seems to have contradicted himself. He appears to have said that we can have knowledge of everything, including serious realities, that rests upon name, *logos*, and image and is stated in speech. This does not worry me. I believe that Plato does suppose that there is a sense in which we can attain to a verbal knowledge of all

12   Immanuel Kant, "Von einem neuerdings erhobenen vornehmen Ton in der Philosophie," 377–79; Gregory Vlastos, *Platonic Studies*, 52, 54, 63–64; Voegelin spoke of "mystic philosophers" in the volumes of *Order and History*. See also several essays in his *Collected Works*, vol. 12. Vlastos might have agreed with Kant in seeing Plato's mysticism as a philosophic vice.

things. However, in the light of what he says next, he does not contradict himself. He states that unless one grasps the four in a certain way, there will never be a partaking of perfect knowledge of the fifth (*oupote teleôs epistêmês tou pemptou metochos estai*, 342e1–2). So, there are two kinds of knowledge, the verbal fourth-level science that rests upon name, *logos*, and image and a different, perfect, serious knowledge of the fifth. Owing to "the weakness of *logoi*," the four attempt to express the quality of each thing no less than its being. However, "the soul seeks to know not the quality but the essence,"[13] so the four do not offer the soul what it wants, which might be well described as "the contact of the soul with the beings without mediation or the need for thinking."[14] For this and other reasons pertaining to the fluidity of names, *logoi*, and images, the nature of each of the four is "naturally defective" (*pephukuia phaulôs*). This makes the four easy to distort, mock, and seemingly refute, thus inspiring widespread confusion and contempt, and this, in turn, is why no one having *nous* would ever put the things observed by reason into words, especially not into the unchangeable words of writing. This reinforces the judgment that Plato warns that there never has been and never will be an oral lecture or a writing by him on the serious realities. As Sayre concludes, the advice given in 343a1–3 is "that no intelligent person would risk putting what he understands into language—into language (*logos*) of any sort—although written language is cited as particularly unreliable."[15] Still, Plato has asserted that unless one grasps the four in a certain way (*amôs*), one will never attain to the perfect knowledge of the fifth. The four are defective but we cannot reach the *telos* of philosophy without attending to them. We wonder why we need to consider them at all if they are so defective.

Plato's explanation of what he means by much being with and living with the matter itself resumes. It is by means of passing through all these [the four] (*dia pantôn autôn diagôgê*), up and down to each, that knowledge is engendered with difficulty, "good natured to good natured" (*eu pephukotos eu pephukoti*). There are two conditions of Plato's being with and living with here. The first is that there must be passing through the four up and down

---

13   Morrow's translation.

14   Seth Benardete, *The Being of the Beautiful*, I-161.

15   Sayre, "Plato's Dialogues in Light of the Seventh Letter," 95.

to each. I assume that this involves studying the four with the strictest logical rigor. This will not suffice to produce perfect knowledge of the fifth. The second condition seems to be that one must have a good nature to commune with good natures. A person whose nature is bad will never see (344a). So, there is and could be no such thing as an evil or immoral philosopher. Perhaps unethical people could be brilliant logicians, but Platonic philosophy transcends logic in the direction of the light.

What does passing through the four up and down to each entail? Plato says it is an effort to learn what is false and true about the whole of existence (*tês holês ousias*). One must engage in long study, examining and comparing names, logoi, visual sightings (*opseis*), and perceptions (*aisthêseis*) [our apprehensions of sensations and apparent facts by whatever means] with kindly tests (or refutations, *elegchois*), employing "questionings and answerings" devoid of envy.[16] It is "by such means, and hardly so, that there bursts out the light of intelligence and reason regarding each object in the mind of him who uses every effort of which mankind is capable."[17]

Why are the *elegchois* (tests or refutations), *elegchomena* (testings or refutings), and the questions and answers devoid of envy the necessary preludes to illumination? Before venturing a solution of this puzzle, we should notice that Plato has just listed the characteristic activities of Socrates. If the Seventh Letter is one of Plato's late products, written in his mid-seventies a few years before his death, it seems clear that he never renounced what we call the "Socratic method" of questioning and refuting. Now, to prevent misunderstanding of the need for this method, we must recall that the four are "naturally defective" owing to the weakness of *logoi*. Acquiring the perfect science therefore cannot be a matter of drawing logical inferences from our criticisms of the four, replacing inaccurate logoi with accurate ones. We must require tests and refutations of the four for another reason, to reach something that goes beyond a logical correctness that itself

16 Morrow has pupil and teacher asking and answering questions here. This is not in the text.

17 Morrow has "only then, when reason and knowledge are at the very extremity of human effort, can they illuminate the nature of any object." Post, in the Hamilton-Cairns anthology, has a more exuberant "flash of understanding blazes up, and the mind . . . is flooded with light." The difficult Greek speaks of *phronêsis* and nous in connection with the illuminating (*exelampse*).

is defective and incapable of giving the soul what it wants. What is it that we need to accomplish? I speculate that we all are immersed in the four, greatly impressed by their power and proud of our achievements of what is, after all, a sort of knowledge. We cannot reach philosophy's *telos* unless we challenge the four extensively because our minds are simultaneously overwhelmed, trapped, and delighted by them. *Elegchos* is needed to confront us with their inadequacy. It frees us from their grip by reducing us to an aporia (resourcelessness, bafflement) that comes with the realization that our best efforts regularly fall short. The *elegchos* must be gracious and devoid of envy because our egos are gratified by our accomplishments. If we do not overcome our pride, we will never realize that our science, although worthy, is unserious. So, the long investigations of the four, the questioning, the refuting, the aporia, the graciousness, and the subduing of envy are the right path to the illumination-like knowledge because they purify the soul, eliminating the hindrances that keep us in darkness. This purification will not produce the serious knowledge in our souls—the analogical illumination and the soul's contact with the beings still must come—but it will make us more capable of receiving it. Thus (if there is anyone sufficiently virtuous to continue), the second rule for reading Plato appears to be that we must follow the arguments of his speakers closely, appreciating the power of their premises and the cogency of their deductions but permitting ourselves to be led by a master philosopher to discoveries of flaws and dead ends that plunge us into aporia. This is the "certain way" in which the four must be grasped. It would seem from this reasoning that Plato had to write dialogues that were aporetic in one way or another as a matter of principle. I believe that this expectation is borne out by a quick synopsis of his major works. I suggest the following classification of the dialogues, which is too simple to stand detailed scrutiny but which will do for the present purpose.

The Explicitly, Entirely Aporetic. This cluster includes Ion, Laches, Lysis, Euthyphro, Charmides, Hippias I, Hippias II, Meno, Protagoras, Republic, book I, and Theaetetus. In this kind of work, a question is posed in either of two forms: "What is X?" or "Is X properly said to be Y?" Interlocutors of Socrates maintain one or more positions and are logically refuted. A correct answer is either not supplied or only hinted at.

The Refuting, Gratuitously Didactic, Implicitly Aporetic. This set contains Alcibiades I, Apology, Crito, and Gorgias. In these dialogues, Socrates either gently or harshly refutes people who hold sophistical, unjust, or otherwise unsalutary opinions. However, he also fills the voids thus created by urging better views on the interlocutors, stating moral imperatives that he claims to regard as valid (on this point, Leo Strauss and his students suspect him and Plato of irony). He advances his ethical opinions without trying to demonstrate their truth rigorously. His teachings acquire impressive auras of veracity by virtue of looking like inspiring alternatives to the morally unacceptable ideas that he has demolished (and, perhaps in Crito and Gorgias, by offering some partial proofs). Inasmuch as Socrates preaches positive doctrines in these works, my insistence that Plato never posits serious theories or *mathêmata* might be judged wrong. On the contrary, I would say that Plato dramatically implies that Socrates' affirmations are insufficiently grounded. Socrates trounces Alcibiades, Meletus, Crito, Gorgias, Polus, and Callias by beating them down logically. Except for Crito, who agrees for the sake of friendship, these characters are not really persuaded. They yield grudgingly like Thrasymachus in Republic, whom Socrates explicitly says is unrefuted, and they persist in their erroneous ways. Having portrayed results like these, Plato could not suppose that Socrates has imparted knowledge to the defeated interlocutors, who could not be truculent and fail to reform if they knew that Socrates was right. Plato appears rather to be indicating to us readers that more is needed to raise Socrates' sermons to the level of the perfect science of the fifth. I draw the same conclusion from the fact that Socrates' views are asserted gratuitously. So, while I agree that Socrates is urging ethical opinions that he presents as true on Alcibiades, Meletus, the Athenian jurors, Crito, Gorgias, Polus, and Callias, his preaching comes across not as *epistêmê* but as fourth-level *alêthês te doxa*—true belief—at best. We accordingly wonder whether his inspiring moral opinions are verified by his illumination.

The Extensively Reasoned, Didactic, Implicitly Aporetic. Falling into this category are Republic, Symposium, Phaedrus, Phaedo, Laws, and Philebus. In these works, Socrates and the Athenian stranger present fully elaborated and rigorously reasoned positive teachings. After his speech in Symposium, Socrates assures everyone that he is persuaded by the lecture of Diotima that he has recited (212b2). Near the ends of Republic and Phaedo, he urges his hearers to accept what he has said in order to fare well in this life and the next. Near the conclusion of Phaedrus, he tells Phaedrus to convert Lysias to the right sort of rhetoric that he has adumbrated. As Laws closes, the Athenian plans to help Kleinias and Megillus put his laws into effect. Philebus looks like the most scientifically reasoned of all Plato's dialogues. Thus, someone might say that here we have serious Platonic teaching. However, Plato indicates in numerous ways in the dialogues that the positive arguments are tentative, fourth-level *epistêmê kai nous alêthês te doxa* that are not fully proved. For example, John White correctly says of Republic that "it is full of questions that turn back upon themselves and answers that somehow cancel or contradict themselves" and that "Book X turns against and 'cancels' the unity of the Republic itself."[18] An illustration of his point is the fact that the tripartite soul of book IV that clinches the definition of justice as "doing one's own" is nullified by the argument in book X (611b) that the soul cannot be composed of parts. We are left to wonder whether justice is what Socrates has said it is. Close examination of the other dialogues always reveals similar oddities. Another example is that Socrates comments at Republic 382a–d that we tell myths because we do not know the truth about ancient things, making our "lies" as close to the truth as possible (thus raising the question of how we could do so if we do not know the truth that we hope to make our tales resemble). Republic, Symposium, Phaedrus, Phaedo, and Laws all bolster their arguments with myths. Further examples: Speaking of the Good in Republic 505d–e, Socrates says the "the soul divines that it is something but is at a loss about it and unable to get a sufficient grasp of just what it is."[19] Having flown as high as he could with the images of the sun, line, and cave, he comments at 518b6–7 that "a god, perhaps," knows whether what he has said is true. In Symposium, Alcibiades accuses Socrates of being a mocking Silenus and challenges Socrates to correct any falsehood that he utters, which Socrates does not explicitly do. In Phaedrus, Socrates characterizes the speech on the divine madness of love that he has delivered as a joke (265c–d). In Laws, from 963a to the end, the Athenian seems to make the validity of his entire argument hinge on a solution of the problem of the unity of the virtues, which is not attempted. Philebus ends with a reminder that the

18   John White, "Imitation," in Plato, *Republic*, trans. Joe Sachs, 323, 325.
19   Allan Bloom translation. The Sachs translation replaces "divines" with "has a sense."

argument is unfinished. Thus, while it is true that these dialogues offer positive teachings, I think that they once again rise only to the level of *epistêmê kai nous alêthês te doxa*. They are not the perfect knowledge. We wonder whether these teachings would be validated by an experience of the telos.

The Apparently Dogmatic. This class includes Timaeus, Sophist, and Statesman. A pair of new protagonists, Timaeus and the Eleatic stranger, offer a fully elaborated, tightly reasoned cosmology, an ontology, an analysis of sophistry, a discourse on method, and a political theory. The cosmology of Timaeus is said to be "the truth" (26d1) and "no invented myth" (26e4). At the end of Sophist, the Eleatic stranger praises his results as *t'alesthestata* (the most true, the greatest truth). At the close of Statesman, a speaker named Socrates calls the stranger's analysis of the king and statesman *kallista*, most beautiful. These are impressive endorsements. Therefore, my expectation of uniformly aporetic Platonic works might now be rejected as unfounded. However, it is too early to make that judgment. It is not obvious that the endorsers, who are characters in plays, speak for Plato. Also, the dialogues in question still need to be analyzed to see whether they are chock full of questions that turn back upon themselves and answers that somehow cancel or contradict themselves, dead ends, and self-refutations that readers are expected to discover for themselves. Leaving Timaeus out of account because analyzing it would take me too far afield,[20] it appears to me after several readings that Sophist and Statesman are so replete with discrepant elements that they tentatively must be judged unserious and aporetic. While the presentations of the Eleatic stranger might or might not be worthy of being regarded as fourth-level science—they claim to be the truest theories of metaphysics, cosmology, politics, and dialectical science—I still think that they will be seen to founder on various thought-provoking difficulties.

At this juncture, someone might wonder why Plato should bother to test one thesis after another extensively when he knows in advance that all will be disproved. Why not simply try to ascertain the truth? I think that in addition to preparing for the light Plato actually is attempting to discover the truth about the whole, as he has said. It is possible that every thesis with

20　But see Zdravko Planinc's critique of *Timaeus in Plato through Homer: Poetry and Philosophy in the Cosmological Dialogues.*

which he begins could be approved as either valid logic or useful rhetoric. Each of his dialogues should be seen as a thought experiment aimed at learning whether *logoi* "work" in either of two senses: that they help us understand a reality as well as human logical reason can, or that they can serve as foundations for a viable society even if they are compounds of truth, honest error, sophistry, and rhetoric, thus becoming "true" in a pragmatic way. In this connection, I perceive three sorts of theses that are subjected to the Socratic-Platonic elegchos. The first begins with a Socratic assumption that appears sound, for example, that it is efficient and best for people and elements of the soul to do only the tasks for which they are naturally suited. The premise is offered as a basis for answering a question of primary interest, such as "what is justice?" The partners to the conversation are led by seemingly credible logic to an apparently successful conclusion. Upon closer inspection, we are surprised to discover that their inspiring (but sometimes also shocking) result is riddled with problems. The second variety starts with an assumption that is clearly anti-Socratic and morally repugnant, such as "justice is the interest of the stronger" or "friendship is founded on utility" (*lysis*), but which nevertheless could explain the reality in question whether we like it or not. In the course of the dialogue, we are gratified to see the hypothesis thoroughly refuted but left unsure how to replace it with truth. In the third sort, apparently unassailable anti-Socratic premises are made the grounds of arguments that explicitly purport to explain different elements of reality most truly or beautifully. The reasoning is so powerful that excellent scholars believe that Timaeus, Sophist, and Statesman are Plato's serious teachings and crowning glories. However, to return to my tentative comment on the latter two dialogues just above, the Eleatic stranger appears to offer inadequate reasoning, precipitating us once again into aporia.

This preliminary assessment of the Eleatic dialogues as aporetic will elicit the objection that a rational Plato could not possibly have penned such long and intricate documents as Sophist and Statesman for the sole purpose of wrecking the theories that he writes into them. It will also be argued that what I take for anti-Socratic premises are commendable developments of Plato's thought and that what I interpret as insuperable difficulties in arguments are merely elements of pedagogical strategies that work out well by the ends of the dialogues. For the time being, I can let one author, Kenneth Sayre, stand for all those who might raise such objections.

As I noted above, Sayre surprisingly finds doctrines in Plato even though he has argued against doing so. It may be that he does this because, like other analytic philosophers, he holds that philosophers are "essentially logicians"[21] and he sees superior logic in the Eleatic dialogues. I have two replies. First, if Plato's works are necessarily aporetic owing to the nature of his philosophy, each must be just as long as needed to test its subject premises and reasoning fully. There are no legitimate grounds for the a priori assumption that the length and intricacy of a dialogue are relevant to the issue of whether it is aporetic. Theaetetus proves that. Of course, one may not decide a priori that a dialogue is aporetic either. My first and second rules for reading Plato—that we should not try to mine his writings for theories and that we should follow their logic closely, allowing them to guide us into aporia—might be all wrong, such that his works are full of serious doctrines that are intellectually satisfying. A final decision about that must await full analysis of the dialogues. So, let us say for now that my precepts are provisional, pending later testing. Second, assertions that Plato's ideas developed, that defective arguments in the Eleatic dialogues are repaired, and that Platonic philosophy is essentially logic are challengeable. They also must be evaluated by study of relevant passages, so I shall leave these matters in abeyance until later chapters.

I turn to the hermeneutic implications of Plato's dialogue form of writing. Leo Strauss makes the essential point: "One cannot separate the understanding of Plato's teaching from the understanding of the form in which it is presented. One must pay as much attention to the How as to the What. At any rate to begin with one must even pay greater attention to the 'form' than to the 'substance,' since the meaning of the 'substance' depends on the 'form.'"[22] Stanley Rosen adds that heeding this opinion constitutes "the minimum requirement for competency in a Plato scholar." I take these observations to heart. My third precept for interpreting Plato, learned from Strauss and stated in Rosen's language, is that we must recognize "the substantive importance of the dramatic structure of the dialogue."[23]

---

21 Sayre, *Plato's Analytic Method*, 37.
22 Leo Strauss, *The City and Man*, 52.
23 Rosen, *Plato's "Statesman,"* 193–94. I do not move from here to Strauss's esotericism.

Accepting this rule should cause no great difficulty. We all know that words acquire their meanings in real life partially from their circumstances and tones. A person says something. An interlocutor replies "Right!" in an enthusiastic cast of voice. We understand that the respondent agrees with the remark. Someone else says "Right!" in a sarcastic tone of voice. We promptly apprehend that this individual disagrees with the comment. In stage plays, nuances like these can be conveyed by the performers. However, if we had nothing but the text of speeches in a drama in which the enthusiastic and sarcastic "rights" were uttered, we would be tempted to think that the second person also agreed. We would grasp the second respondent's intended meaning only by inferring it from the totality of elements of the play. This, for example, is how we know what Antony really means in his oration on the murdered Caesar in Shakespeare. Platonic characters' speeches draw much of their meaning from their dramatic contexts. Dialogues are not systematic scientific treatises with univocal terms. They are plays and must be read as such.

How do we infer the meanings of statements and arguments of Platonic characters from the totality of elements of a dialogue? Well, we first ascertain the story line. We do so because we know that what the characters think and say must be understood as directed to the situations with which they are grappling and to what they hope to do about them. Sometimes the story of a Platonic drama extends over more than one work. Then we must follow the entire narrative to grasp what is happening in the dialogue under discussion. My fourth rule for reading Plato is that if there are multiple ways of comprehending a statement or argument, the best exegesis is the one that squares its logic with the story of the play or series of plays.

Platonic dialogues have long stretches of argument with no stage directions. How can we discern their story lines? I reply that we rely on Plato for the pointers that he offers. He endows most of his dialogues with dramatic settings that include clear references to the fictitious dates on which the depicted conversations occur. He presumably has a rational purpose for writing that way, which could only be this: He realizes that if his audiences know the real histories in which his plays are set, as educated Athenians will, and if they arrange the dialogues by their dramatic dates, they will grasp the situational contexts. This will enable them to perceive the matters to which the characters direct what they think and say. From there they can move to appreciation of how the characters' relationships to the contexts color the meanings of their speeches. Plato also uses allusions to the poets to frame his dramas and infuse them with meaning, much as Herman Melville employed the Christian Gospels in Billy Budd. My fifth rule for interpreting Plato is that if there are multiple ways of understanding a text, the best is that which takes account of the story indicated by its dramatic setting, dramatic date, and quotations of the poets.

It should be mentioned here that there are scholars who like to base exegeses of Plato on the dates of composition of his dialogues. My sixth precept for reading Plato is that this is to be avoided. When Platonic meanings are in dispute, the dialogue's story line, its dramatic setting, its dramatic date, and its select pieces of poetic evidence are relevant while dates of composition constitute no adequate foundation for an interpretation. I have two grounds for this rule. First, Plato contrived his stories, dramatic settings, dramatic dates, and bits of poetic evidence in the dialogues, thus deliberately providing us with clues to his intentions, while dates of composition do not represent the author's thinking. Many will retort that the dates of composition illuminate the development of Plato's ideas and that this is why they surely ought to trump dramatic details. However, as I indicated above, "development of Plato's ideas" arguments are debatable. Plato denies having published serious ideas that we could use as base lines for measuring development. Further, if "A" is found in one dialogue and a different "A'" in another, which does occur, this could be an artifact of drama or of logical testing. Inasmuch as the appearances of "A" and "A'" have multiple possible explanations, it must be proved that these phenomena imply development of Plato's ideas rather than one of the other options. Partisans of the development of ideas do not do this. They assume a priori that difference is development. Second, and worse for those who favor the dates of composition, we do not know those dates. Standard divisions of the dialogues into early, middle, and late depend on frequently conflicting assumptions about the relationships of Plato's varying idioms to periods of his life. Hence, they are tissues of circular speculation. Kenneth Dorter has done an excellent analysis of this subject, citing the (gratuitous) premises and deductions of the stylometrists. He decides that the dialogues marked "late" might really be late (I see good reasons for dating Theaetetus, Sophist, Statesman post-369 B.C.) but that one should base nothing of substance on this datum.[24] John M. Cooper has addressed the issue too, urging readers "not to undertake the study of Plato's works holding in mind the customary chronological groupings" and suggesting that it "is better to . . . concentrate on the literary and philosophical content of the works."[25] Catherine Zuckert has arrived at the same result.[26]

My sixth rule seems to be both well-founded in Plato's philosophic artistry and accepted by greatly respected scholars as well. Another part of the totality of elements of a play from which the meanings of arguments can be gleaned is the artistically created nature of each character. One must raise these questions about the dramatis personae: How does the playwright use them? What moral and intellectual make-ups and fictitious motives does he give them? What does he have them trying to achieve with their speeches? All this colors the import of what they say.

The protagonist in most Platonic dialogues is Socrates. Readers must ask whether Plato employs Socrates as his spokesman. The same question applies to all of Plato's protagonists and especially to the Eleatic stranger, the chief speaker in works that will occupy me here. Scholarly opinions about this issue range over a wide spectrum. Leo Strauss considers the proposition that "the spokesman par excellence of Plato is his revered teacher or friend Socrates." His response is that "we do not know what it means to be a spokesman for Plato; we do not even know whether there is such a thing as a spokesman for Plato." He also argues that: "The views of the author of a drama or dialogue must not, without previous proof, be identified with the views expressed by one or more of his characters, or with those agreed upon by all his characters or by his attractive characters."[27] So, without telling evidence, we may not claim that Socrates, the Eleatic stranger, and Plato's other protagonists are his spokesmen. Kenneth Sayre takes a middling and somewhat inconsistent position. He initially seems to agree with Strauss. He contends that it is an error "to assume that Plato endorses the conclusion of every argument he puts in the mouths of his

24 Kenneth Dorter, *Form and Good in Plato's Eleatic Dialogues: "The Parmenides, Theaetetus, Sophist, and Statesman,"* 4–9.

25 John M. Cooper, ed., *Plato: Complete Works*, xiv.

26 Catherine H. Zuckert, *Plato's Philosophers: The Coherence of the Dialogues*, 3–5.

27 Strauss, *The City and Man*, 50; Strauss, *Persecution and the Art of Writing*, 30.

main protagonists—akin to the mistake of assuming that every thesis affirmed by Socrates is espoused by Plato himself." However, he then suggests that we can have evidence "on some other basis that Plato did in fact accept (or reject) the thesis in question."[28] The other basis would have to be some pattern of characters' arguments, so Sayre's accord with Strauss is weakened. Eventually Sayre asserts that there are doctrines in Philebus, so the Socrates of that drama is well on his way to becoming a conduit of Plato's propositional teaching. However, Socrates' new status pales in comparison with that of the Eleatic stranger. Sayre maintains that the stranger is a better trained, more powerful thinker than Socrates, who must be retired as the leader of the dialogues because all he knows how to do is refute and he cannot guide anyone to the higher analytic logic of Forms that Plato finally has decided is the real work of philosophy.[29] Therefore, for Sayre, the Eleatic has become Plato's ultimate alter ego. At the other end of the spectrum from Strauss's, Gregory Vlastos never entertains our hermeneutic question. He takes it for granted that Socrates is Plato's "mouthpiece." He also invariably reports that it is "Plato" who is speaking whenever Socrates or the Eleatic stranger makes a remark.[30] Most of the renowned Plato scholars, including the early twentieth-century British dons and the subsequent analytic philosophers, seem to follow suit.[31]

To inquire whether Plato's protagonists are his spokesmen is to ask whether they are used to transmit his doctrines. I assume that we can answer "no" immediately if we are thinking about protagonists communicating Plato's serious insights because we already know that he has denied writing them down. Do Plato's characters relate his positions at this level? Here I repeat Strauss's point: the form of Plato's work is a truer guide to its meaning than our habitual expectations of philosophic writing. That is, we must acknowledge the equivalence of a Platonic dialogue to a drama. The opinions that a playwright puts in the mouths of his characters are not necessarily

---

28   Sayre, *Plato's Late Ontology: A Riddle Resolved*, 18–19.
29   Kenneth M. Sayre, *Plato's Analytic Method*, 154; *Plato's Literary Garden: How to Read a Platonic Dialogue*, 31; *Plato's Late Ontology: A Riddle Resolved*, 96, 190–93.
30   For example, Vlastos, *Platonic Studies*, 82, 117, and 270–317 on the stranger.
31   Regarding the analytic philosophers, see the authors in Vlastos (ed.), *Plato: A Collection of Critical Essays, I: Metaphysics and Epistemology*.

his own. So, as Strauss remarks, "If someone quotes a passage from the dialogues to prove that Plato held such and such a view, he acts about as reasonably as if he were to assert that according to Shakespeare life is a tale told by an idiot, full of sound and fury, signifying nothing." The more reasonable inference is that: "We hear Plato never. In none of his dialogues does Plato ever say anything. Hence we cannot know from them what Plato thought."[32] We do tend to believe that when Socrates makes morally uplifting comments he is stating Plato's actual opinions but, as Strauss has warned, we have no theoretical right to affirm that without proof. As Strauss slyly intimates, Thrasymachus could be the one who tells the truth in Republic.[33] Let us conclude, then, contra the lapsed Sayre, Vlastos, and others like them, that we cannot know that Plato taught any proposition or endorsed any argument at all. My seventh rule for reading Plato is that we must not treat his protagonists or any of his characters as spokesmen for his doctrines or beliefs. Instead, we must assume that he makes characters say what they say both to facilitate the testing and refutation of theses and for other purposes internal to the roles that he gives them in his plays.

We want to discover the dramatic motives that Plato gives Socrates and other characters. The cases must be handled separately. That of Socrates is the easiest. Socrates is employed to do exactly what we see him doing in the plays. We observe him acting as the tester and refuter of arguments and as the voice of moral imperatives that he presents as true. Probably he is used this way to prepare his fictitious interlocutors and Plato's audience for analogical illumination while teaching nothing serious of his or Plato's own. This assumption tallies with something that Plato makes Socrates say about himself. Socrates claims in Theaetetus to be a midwife who treats not bodies but souls when they are giving birth. He adds:

> [T]he greatest thing in our art is this: to have the power to put
> to the test in every way whether the thinking of the young man
> is giving birth to something that is an image and false, or to
> something that is generated and true. And since this at least

32 Strauss, *The City and Man*, 50.
33 Strauss, *The City and Man*, 74.

belongs to me just as it does to the midwives, that I am barren
of wisdom, and the very thing belongs to me that many people
have blamed me for before now, that I question others but answer nothing myself about anything on account of having nothing wise in me, what they blame me for is true. But the cause
of this is the following: the god (continuously) forces me to be
a midwife but (each time) prevents me from generating anything. . . . But those who associate with me . . . if the god permits them, improve to a wonderful extent . . . And this is
incandescently clear: that they do so despite learning nothing
from me ever, but by discovering and bringing forth many beautiful things out of themselves. The midwifing, however, the god
and I are responsible for (150b–d).[34]

So, besides making Socrates his tester of arguments, Plato gives him
the aim of helping students bring forth fair things that the god permits.
(It must be stressed that Socrates credits himself with delivering his students of fair things, contrary to Sayre's charge that all he can do is refute.)
My eighth precept for reading Plato is that we must regard Socrates as a
midwife who wants to do to us what he hopes to do to Theaetetus and other
young men. We should cooperate by embracing the hypotheses that he tests
(they might actually be ours) and by following his refutations, hoping that
our souls will bring forth beautiful things by the end of the process.

This rule has implications for the interpretation of Socrates' behavior.
Socrates regularly propounds theses, prompting scholars to regard the proclaimed notions as his or Plato's own. He also makes shockingly unsound
arguments, moving Gregory Vlastos, for example, to remark that Plato had
to "understand his own theory better" in order to avoid "quite gratuitous
errors."[35] He even tells lies without admitting that he has done so and he
indulges in deliberate sophisms and rhetorical ploys. Vlastos rejects this
observation about lies, sophisms, and rhetorical chicanery as the expedient

34 Sachs translation. The Fowler (Loeb), Levett-Burnyeat (in Cooper), Cornford
(in Hamilton-Cairns), and Jowett translations differ in details, all more or less
to the same effect.
35 Vlastos, *Platonic Studies*, 56.

of a scholar desperate to explain away Plato's mistakes. He especially disagrees with the suggestion that Socrates lies, arguing that "We are in the presence of a writer whom we know to be scrupulously truthful."[36]

All this looks different in the light of Plato's dramatic intentions. Not only is it a blunder, as Sayre holds, to assume that "every thesis affirmed by Socrates is espoused by Plato himself."[37] It also is erroneous to imagine that the character Socrates believes everything he affirms. When Socrates advances a proposition, he often is articulating the inchoate opinion of his interlocutor. He is pretending to accept it in order to test it, this being a feature of his irony. When Socrates makes a bad argument, we may assume that "Plato himself is aware of its logical deficiency."[38] Plato wants Socrates to examine not only the tidiest theories of which he can conceive but the reasoning that typically convinces the interlocutors (and the Athenians whose souls he hopes to save by writing). The same consideration applies to Socrates' sophisms and rhetorical appeals. In Plato's plays, as in real life, people victimized by sophists and base politicians are taken in by logical tricks and demagogic rhetoric. Plato employs Socrates to sound influential arguments on every logical-sophistical-rhetorical front. As for Plato's honesty, we must ask what obligation to truth he acknowledges. Plato probably does not adhere to fundamentalist or Kantian notions of scrupulosity. Rather, he seems to think that his prudential duty is to make Socrates move people toward visions of the highest truths by saying whatever he needs to say to prod their souls to turn. That certainly appears to be the attitude of a philosopher who makes Socrates talk about "useful lies" while insisting on the search for truth and denouncing "the lie in the soul" (Republic 389b, 413a, 414b–c, 459c, 485c–d, 535d–e). My ninth rule for reading Plato is that we must understand Socrates as both a tester/refuter and a gadfly who tailors his statements to the individual needs of his interlocutors, saying variously accurate, inaccurate, honest, and dishonest things to different people to goad them to go in the same direction, toward serious truth. If this precept is correct, it tallies with what Socrates says about the need for different kinds of speeches for different souls in Phaedrus (271c–272b).

36 Vlastos, *Platonic Studies*, 222–23, 283.
37 Sayre, *Plato's Late Ontology*, 18.
38 Sayre, *Plato's Late Ontology*, 19.

On the surfaces of his plays, Plato does not seem to use the Eleatic stranger or his other protagonists in the same manner as he employs Socrates. They are not testers and refuters but, rather, advocates. We thus see them engaged in a decidedly un-Socratic activity. Doubting that Plato has doctrinal spokesmen, I suspect that he is using the Eleatic and other protagonists in the same way that he uses Socrates' interlocutors, as foils for the arguments that he wants to test, and that their reasoning will fail to become the perfect knowledge. So, my tenth precept for reading Plato is that we must try to understand the Eleatic stranger and his other characters by inferring their moral and intellectual natures, their motives, and their plans from their speeches and roles in the plays, with the aim of learning whether my expectation is borne out.

It will be recalled that my third rule for interpreting Plato declares that we must recognize the substantive importance of the dramatic structure of a dialogue. This is to say that we have to understand the logic of Platonic arguments in light of the actions of the plays in which they are set. The relationship is reciprocal. We also have to square our readings of the stories of Plato's dialogues and the meanings of his characters' speeches with the logic of the arguments. Thus, my eleventh precept for studying Plato is that the logic and the drama must be used as checks on each other.

I said above that my first and second rules for interpreting Plato could be wrong and need to be verified by full analysis of the dialogues to which they are applied. This goes for my third precept and its corollaries, rules four through ten. As Vlastos and the other analytic philosophers appear to suppose, Plato's dramatic touches might be mere artistic fluff with no implications for the meanings of his arguments, his protagonists might be his spokesmen, and his works might reduce to logical treatises. My last nine rules therefore cannot be decreed a priori any more than the first two could be arbitrarily imposed. Like the first pair, they must be corroborated by study of the dialogues. What form could validation take? I submit that if my rules lead to a consistent and inherently reasonable interpretation, such a reading will be preferable to another that ignores Plato's comments on his writing and his dialogue form.

We are ready to begin the study of Plato's Statesman.

2

SOCRATES' STORY OF DEATH AND LIFE

If my rules for reading Plato are correct, students of his dialogues have five tasks. They must get the logic of the arguments and the meanings of the myths right. They must determine how the reasoning is valid and invalid and allow themselves to be plunged into bafflement. They must get the action of the plays and the characters of their personae right. They must understand the logic of the arguments in light of the drama. Conversely, they must interpret the drama in light of the logic. They must do all that in hope that Plato's flashes of leaping flame will come to them, or that Socrates' god will permit their souls to bring forth fair things. I begin my study of Statesman by concentrating on the third of these tasks. This chapter is a preliminary effort to get the action of the dialogue and the characters of its personae right.

Statesman—Politikos in Greek—is part of a trilogy: Theaetetus, Sophist, Statesman. The first two dialogues in the trio are foundations for the action and meaning of the third, so the three must be treated as a single drama. This observation is incomplete. Politikos actually belongs to a group of seven plays focused on the trial and death of Socrates. The series moves in a dramatic chronological circle that both begins and ends with Theaetetus. This dialogue has a main section set in 399 B.C., on the morning of Socrates' arraignment on charges of impiety and corrupting the young, which begins the circle, and a prologue set shortly after Athenian troops lost a battle near Corinth, either that of 394 or that of 369, in which Theaetetus was fatally wounded, which closes it. The other plays have the following dramatic order and dates: Euthyphro (later on the day of the arraignment); Sophist (the next morning); Statesman (right after Sophist); Apology of Socrates (the day of Socrates' trial); Crito (three days before Socrates' execution), and Phaedo (principal part: the day that Socrates dies;

prologue: a few months or years after Socrates' death). The circle closes when the prologue of Theaetetus moves from lamentations about the impending death of Theaetetus to memories of the fateful morning in 399. To understand any dialogue in the array fully, it would be best to analyze all seven together. However, this would be too much to attempt. Meanwhile, it is legitimate to study Theaetetus, Sophist, and Statesman separately because Plato presents them as a unified subset of the whole.[1]

Although I shall concentrate on Theaetetus, Sophist, and Politikos, it would be a serious error to miss the relevance that the scheme of the whole series has for the meaning of the trilogy. To get at this, I shall start with a bare-bones summary of each story. I shall also note the structure and mode of each work. With respect to structure, two of the plays, Theaetetus and Phaedo, have anamnestic prologues in which the characters recall Socrates' ordeal. The others lack prologues. With regard to mode, in the terminology of Leo Strauss, some of Plato's dramas are "narrated," with a storyteller recalling deeds and discussions that took place in the past, using expressions such as "I went down," "I said," and "He agreed." Others are "performed," meaning that they are composed as if to be acted like stage plays. In these dialogues, designated characters imitate live conversations, such that the texts read, for example: "Theo: According to yesterday's agreement, Socrates, we have come ourselves . . . ." All the dramas under consideration here are performed but Theaetetus and Phaedo have traces of narration that are not found in the others. It probably is significant that the plays that mark the beginning and end of Socrates' agony have anamnestic prologues and traces of narration while those in between do not. Here are my summaries:

Theaetetus (anamnestic prologue, performed, with a trace of narration). A short time after the Athenian defeat near Corinth, Eucleides and Terpsion, disciples of Socrates who were present at his death, meet in their native city of Megara. Eucleides reports that he has been with Theaetetus, who is dying of battle wounds and dysentery and is being carried back to Athens.

The two observe that Theaetetus has been praised for his courage,

---

1   I shall explain below why I do not include an eighth dialogue, Cratylus, in the series.

bewail his plight, and recall that Socrates had foretold celebrity for him. Terpsion asks Eucleides about his transcription of Socrates' account of a conversation that he had with Theaetetus a little before his death. They go to the home of Eucleides. Prior to having a slave read the text, Eucleides reports that he wrote up the discussion not as Socrates related it but as if Socrates were speaking with others, omitting annoying expressions such as "I said" and "He agreed." He transformed a dialogue narrated by Socrates into a performed one, which is why I argue that Theaetetus has traces of narration even though it is performed. In the script, Socrates visits the school of Theodorus, inquiring whether the illustrious geometer has any Athenian students who show promise in geometry or some other branch of philosophy. Theodorus recommends Theaetetus. Socrates tests the boy by asking him what *epistêmê* (knowledge or science) is. After a confused start, after interpreting the query as analogous to a geometry problem that he solved with his friend young Socrates, who is standing by, and after eliciting Socrates' claim to be a midwife, the lad defines *epistêmê* as perception. Socrates ties this account to a doctrine of the sophist Protagoras and criticizes it. Theodorus is dragooned into helping Theaetetus defend Protagoras. In the middle of the dialogue, Socrates engages Theodorus in a discussion about philosophers' troubles in law courts, the differences between philosophers and legal orators, and divine and atheistic patterns of life. His remarks in this ostensible digression call Protagorean political theory into question. Socrates then resumes the discussion of *epistêmê*. Protagoras is refuted, much to the chagrin of Theodorus, who bows out of the conversation. Theaetetus is left alone to reply to Socrates. All told, three definitions of *epistêmê* are drawn out of Theaetetus and fail to pass muster. What knowledge is remains a mystery, partially because Socrates affects to worry that false speech is impossible. At the end of the play, Socrates tells the company that he now must go to the porch of the king to respond to a lawsuit brought by Meletus. He requests that they all meet again the next morning.

Euthyphro (performed). Socrates happens to meet Euthyphro at the porch of the king. Euthyphro is astonished to see Socrates there. Socrates explains that Meletus has indicted him for corrupting the young, creating new gods, and not believing in the city's old gods. Euthyphro guesses that Socrates' talk about his daimon must have inspired the charge. He complains that he has troubles too. The Athenians ridicule him because he prophesies and voices innovative religious views in the assembly and because he now is prosecuting his father. The father had negligently killed a servant whom he was punishing for murder. Socrates is scandalized. He inquires whether Euthyphro does not fear that prosecuting his father for such a deed is unholy. Euthyphro scoffs that this question betrays ignorance about what the gods maintain regarding holiness and unholiness. Socrates proposes to become Euthyphro's pupil in order to learn the truth about piety and impiety. He feigns hope that such re-education will enable him to persuade Meletus to withdraw his suit, on the grounds that better information ensures better behavior. He asks Euthyphro what holiness is. Euthyphro answers that it is what he is doing now, for he is emulating an act of Zeus, who bound his father for devouring his children. Socrates retorts that he is being prosecuted because he does not believe such stories. He pushes Euthyphro to define holiness essentially. Euthyphro asserts that holiness is what is dear to the gods. However, it is established without much ado that Homer's deities disagree about what is dear. This difficulty proves insurmountable. For the rest of the dialogue, Euthyphro reasons in circles. When he is shown this, he accuses Socrates of being a Daedalus who sets his words in motion. He departs, with Socrates crying ironically that he has not learned doctrines that will save him from Meletus.

If Cratylus belonged to the series that I am considering, it would come next. Catherine Zuckert includes this dialogue in the array because Socrates reports that he had just spent a long time with Euthyphro and because Cratylus is "linked thematically" to Theaetetus and Sophist.[2] I disagree with her reasoning (although the issue is too minor for lengthy debate). Socrates says at 396d6 that he met Euthyphro *eôthen*, which Liddell and Scott translate as "from morn, at earliest dawn, at break of day." For Zuckert's time-line to work, Socrates' conversation with Theodorus and Theaetetus would have had to occur in the middle of the night. This would have been a most unlikely time for Theodorus to be holding school. I infer that Cratylus must take place on a date prior to that of Euthyphro and that Socrates is referring to a meeting that he had with Euthyphro at dawn on

2 Catherine H. Zuckert, *Plato's Philosophers: The Coherence of the Dialogues*, 650–52.

that unspecified day. Plato might well link Cratylus thematically with Theaetetus and Sophist. However, I think that Plato intends his use of *eôthen* to indicate that Cratylus is not part of the story of Socrates' trial and execution.

Sophist (performed). Socrates, Theodorus, Theaetetus, and young Socrates meet on the next morning. Theodorus has brought a stranger from Elea whom he introduces as quite a manly philosopher or quite a philosophic man, a follower of Parmenides and Zeno. Socrates asks if the stranger is some god, for Homer says that the gods, especially the god of strangers, go with the reverent and just, observing the hybristic and lawful deeds of men. Perhaps the stranger is a god come to refute them because they are worthless in logos. Theodorus denies that the stranger is either a god or contentious but he maintains that the stranger is divine qua philosopher. Socrates answers that philosophers are as hard to recognize as gods. He explains that real philosophers, as opposed to pretended ones, *phantazomenoi dia tên allôn agnoian epistrôphôsi poleas*. Fowler, in the Loeb edition, translates this as "appear disguised in all sorts of shapes thanks to the ignorance of the rest of mankind." Cornford, in the Hamilton-Cairns collection, has "appear, owing to the world's blindness, to wear all sorts of shapes." Nicholas White, in the Cooper anthology, writes "take on all sorts of different appearances just because of other people's ignorance." I think that Fowler's version is wrong and that Cornford's hits the bull's-eye. Although the middle participle *phantazomenoi* suggests that the philosophers engage in reflexive action, disguising themselves—a reading that many scholars accept—Plato's use of *dia* plus the accusative *agnoian* suggests that the participle could be passive, "being made to appear by the ignorance of others." As Mitchell Miller has it, then, the sense of the passage is that the ignorant many project appearances onto the genuine philosophers.[3]

In a tale about Socrates, who presumably is a real philosopher, it makes a colossal difference whether the real philosophers react to the ignorance of the many by disguising themselves or the many ignorantly perceive them in certain ways and project those appearances onto them. For reasons that will become clear in a moment, I think that we get Socrates' story right by hearing him make the latter claim, not the former.

3   Mitchell H. Miller, Jr., *The Philosopher in Plato's "Statesman,"* 9.

Socrates continues by noting that the real philosophers appear in their various shapes to be visiting cities beholding from on high the lives of those below. Sometimes they appear as *politikoi* (the plural of *politikos*) and at other times as sophists or as completely mad. We have another translation problem here, one regarding *politikoi*. Fowler, together with many others, has the genuine philosophers appearing (disguised) as "statesmen." This is one correct translation of *politikoi*, depending on the context in which the word appears. In the dialogue Politikos, the title of which traditionally is translated as Statesman, the Eleatic stranger clearly intends *politikos* to convey what modern Americans understand by "statesman"—someone wholly admirable. When the stranger uses the word, it normally should be translated as "statesman." However, in Plato, *politikos* is not always an honorific term. A glance at Brandwood's concordance[4] reveals some twenty occasions on which *politikos* means "politician" in one pejorative sense or another.[5] (To cite just one case, at Republic 489c4 Socrates applies *politikoi* to the present archons of Athens, likening them to the seditious sailors in his image of the ship who are not helmsmen in any true sense.) This makes it necessary to justify translating *politikoi* as "statesmen" in the comment by Socrates that is under consideration. No one ever undertakes a defense of this common practice.

I think that an examination of the context shows that the practice is indefensible and that Fowler's translation is wrong. The remark about philosophers judging ordinary people from on high is a reference to Aristophanes' image of Socrates in Clouds as an airborne sophist. Socrates is paraphrasing Aristophanes' accusation that he is a snob who looks down on others. Socrates professes respect for the Athenians in Apology. I infer that we have a case of the ignorant many projecting Aristophanes' perception onto philosophers. Assuming that the projection of negative appearances has constantly remained the subject of our passage, it seems to follow that Socrates' next words mean that the philosophers are seen by the ignorant

---

4   Leonard Brandwood, *A Word Index to Plato*, s.v. all the grammatical forms of politikos.

5   Examples are *Gorgias* 473e6, 484e1, 452e4, 513b8, 519b4, 519e2; *Phaedrus* 248d5, 257c5, 257e2, 258e1; *Republic* 426d5, 489c4, *Meno* 99d2, 100a1, *Apology* 21c4, 22a8, 22c8, 241a1; *Euthyphro* 2c8; *Laws* 693a6.

many as "politicians (pejorative), sophists, and madmen," with three consistent pejoratives instead of an unintelligible mixture of a positive with negatives. Translating Socrates' remark this way also appears to be justified by the fact that it would not make sense for philosophers worried about the ignorant many to "disguise themselves" either as statesmen or as politicians, let alone as sophists and madmen, all of whom are frequently targets of popular rage, whereas ignorant perceptions of the philosophers certainly would be uniformly negative. There is another point: Socrates could not "disguise" himself as a statesman because real philosophers are statesmen in his understanding of the terms. Therefore, I believe that to get our story right we must acknowledge that Socrates has said that owing to the ignorance of others, the real philosophers appear [are perceived] as presumptuous snobs and also variously as politicians (pejorative), sophists, and madmen. Sometimes, he adds, the people who appear in those ways are valued highly (one thinks of Protagoras, the darling of Pericles and his allies) but at other times they are viewed as worthless (as in Aristophanes' ridicule of Socrates). He then says that he would like to ask the stranger about sophist, *politikos*, philosopher. Do the names denote one kind (*genos*), two, or three?

The stranger agrees to discuss the matter and asserts that the names refer to three different types. Theodorus is struck by the coincidence that he and his party happen to have put a similar question to the stranger on their way to the meeting. The stranger gave no reply then but asserted that he had heard the topic analyzed thoroughly and has not forgotten what he heard. Socrates renews his request. He asks whether the stranger wishes to proceed by means of long speeches or dialogue. The stranger prefers long speeches but opts for dialogue if he can have a respondent who gives no trouble. Theaetetus is drafted as his interlocutor. The stranger evidently has found Theaetetus acceptably tractable. The boy's docility is not necessarily an intellectual virtue.

The stranger decides to begin with the sophist. He says that he and Theaetetus share the name "sophist" and that they must search and clarify by definition or argument (*logô*) what he is. He warns that the sophists are a difficult tribe to catch and asserts that they must be hunted. To teach Theaetetus how the hunt must be conducted, he proposes an example: defining the angler. This fisherman is hunted by means of diaeresis (continuous divisions of classes into two parts by cutting through middles, followed by summaries of the definitive halves). To start, the angler is defined as a *technitên*, a man who possesses and practices a *technê*, namely, hunting. His art is divided and subdivided until he has been hemmed in by the categories from which he has been excluded and confined with his list of phenomenal differences to a class that he occupies alone. The stranger likens this exercise to snaring the prey in a net of word devices (235b).

Having given his illustration, the stranger says that he has been surprised by an insight. The sophist, like the angler (and himself) is a hunter who has a characteristic *technê*. Now the hunters are hunting a hunter, striving to throw nets of verbal categories over him and his art. The stranger leads Theaetetus through several diaeresis, offering six (?) accounts of the sophist. He selects one of them as best and builds on it. The sophist is a contentious image-maker who paints word pictures of things that are not. An obstacle to accepting this account is Socrates' ostensible doubt in Theaetetus that false speech is possible. The sophist defends himself against the charge that he says what is not by hiding behind the claim that false speech is impossible. The stranger says that this problem involves a being of non-being. This paradox is investigated so extensively that scholars interpret Sophist as Plato's late ontology. The being of nonbeing is affirmed by a logical consideration of being, motion, rest, sameness, and otherness. Having demonstrated that we can speak intelligibly about the being of nonbeing, the stranger reconfirms his definition of the sophist as a maker of images of things that are not. He praises his own account as most true. Socrates has been silent throughout. At least one and probably more of the stranger's definitions apply to him. Thus, he has been implicitly portrayed as a sophist himself.

Statesman (performed). Socrates thanks Theodorus for his introductions to Theaetetus and the stranger. Theodorus replies that Socrates' gratitude will be three-fold when the statesman and philosopher have been defined too. Socrates is shocked to hear the great geometer say that. Theodorus has counted sophist, statesman, and philosopher as equals but their values differ more than the ratios of his *technê* can express. The embarrassed Theodorus admits the error. He vows to avenge himself on Socrates later and implores the stranger to continue. The stranger suggests that young Socrates should replace Theaetetus as interlocutor. Socrates agrees, for Theaetetus looks like him, young Socrates is his namesake, and he ought to get to know both of his "kin." Here, it might be apposite to remember that Socrates has portrayed himself as the only Athenian of his day who practices "the true *technê* of politics" (*alêthôs politikê technê*, Gorgias 521d). If his claim is just, this means that a boy who bears the name of Socrates and a lad who is the image of Socrates are being used by a man who insists on the efficacy of logos to distinguish the sophist from the true statesman/philosopher who is standing in their midst. Recalling the Seventh Letter, we wonder whether Plato is hinting that characters who, as it were, personify name, image, and logos necessarily will fail to discern the essences of sophist, statesman, and philosopher, thereby misunderstanding Socrates completely.

The stranger indicates that he will define the statesman by applying the method that he used on the sophist, *diaeresis*. He asks whether the *politikos* should be ranked among those who have an *epistêmê*. Young Socrates says yes, so this figure will have to be described in terms of the nature of his science. The stranger inquires whether the sciences should be cut in the same way as when they were examining the sophist. The boy is unsure. The stranger replies that there must be a different division. They must compel their souls to conceive of all sciences as either theoretical (*gnôstikên*) or practical (*praktikên*). On this basis, he leads young Socrates to a view of the *politikos* as a keeper of herds of piggish, featherless bipeds. The result worries him. Many false *politikoi* claim to be tenders of the herd, contesting the genuine king's authority. *Diaeresis* as practiced so far cannot settle the dispute. Thus, bifurcating *diaeresis* gives way to a succession of new methods: *poiêsis* (myth-making), paradigm construction, identification of means between excess and defect, and *diaeresis* that divides by joints rather than halves, nevertheless attempting to cut as close to two parts as possible.

The stranger first tries to repair his analysis by inventing a great myth. In his tale, periods in which human life proceeds as it does now alternate with times in which people under the rule of the god are born old from the earth and get younger and smaller until they vanish. The reverse people enjoy paradisiacal conditions while they live. The myth shows that the first *diaeresis* erred by confusing the *politikos* of the present age with the god of the opposite era. This convinces the stranger that they need to describe the manner of the present statesman's governance. However, he now begins to fret that he made his myth too long and used too much of its material. To get proper coloring and to explain great things it is necessary to employ a paradigm. To explain how a paradigm argument will work, it is necessary to supply a paradigm of paradigm, for which the stranger adduces the example of letters. This preparation accomplished, the stranger introduces weaving as the right paradigm of the *politikos* and launches upon a *diaeresis* of weaving. Then he worries that young Socrates will think that they have been rambling on at too great a length so he turns to analysis of excess and defect. This leads to identification of the mean between excess and defect as a measure of proper length and of all the arts. Ability to discern means is declared essential to statesmanship. After announcing that his whole exercise has aimed at making better dialecticians rather than defining the *politikos*, the stranger returns to the effort to understand this statesman. He switches from *diaeresis* that cuts classes in two to that which divides limb by limb. This leads him to the conclusion that statesmanship requires an *epistêmê*. This criterion is used to crowd out the pretenders to the statesman's throne and to classify unscientific *politikoi* as "the greatest sophists" and seditionists. The *politikos* finally is defined as a scientific weaver of the courageous and the moderate into a friendly unity. This conclusion is praised as most beautiful by "Socrates." The text does not make clear which Socrates has spoken.

The stranger's political science obviously differs greatly from Socrates' *alêthôs politikê technê*, which is practiced not on citizen bodies by giving public orders but on private individuals by *elegchos*. Although Socrates does not rule anybody, he still is a sort of present-day *politikos* who confesses that he knows nothing. Thus, just as he was implicitly portrayed as a sophist in the previous play, he is indirectly classified as an unscientific political meddler here. Hence, he has been made to look like one of the greatest sophists.

Apology of Socrates (performed). Socrates is on trial for his life. Meletus, Anytus, and Lyco have presented the prosecution's case. We were not present to hear their statements. We arrive when Socrates begins his defense. This apologia includes a cross-examination of Meletus, who is easily rebutted but to no avail. We come to a gap in the proceedings. Then we listen to Socrates' response to the verdict, in which he is expected to propose his penalty. After another lacuna, we hear Socrates' reaction to his death sentence.

Socrates defends himself by replying to two sets of accusers, the long-standing ones and the recent ones, the former being Aristophanes and the masses whom he has influenced and the latter being his present prosecutors. The first attackers have been slandering him for years with charges that he investigates things under the earth and in the heavens and that he also teaches others how to make the weaker argument the stronger, which implies that he is a sophist. These detractors have raised a prejudice against him that he does not believe he can overcome during his short time in the dock. The current prosecutors allege that he corrupts the young, does not believe in the gods of the polis, and makes new gods. Answering both groups, Socrates explains that in response to a question from Chaerophon, the Pythia at Delphi proclaimed Socrates the wisest of men. Socrates knew that he was not wise so he was at a loss to understand the oracle. He set out to learn what the god meant. He went to see *politikoi*, poets, and artisans, expecting to find thinkers wiser than himself. He discovered that these men thought that they knew what they did not know. This revealed that they were less wise than he, for he knew that he knew nothing. He inferred that the oracle meant to say that human wisdom is worthless. Meanwhile, he had been required to show his interlocutors that they did not know what they thought they knew, so that they were not wise. This had embarrassed and enraged them. Now Aristophanes' calumnies and the interlocutors' resentments have led to his prosecution on charges of which he is innocent. This misfortune was unavoidable, for he has been demonstrating the vanity of human wisdom to Athenians in obedience to the god's command and his *daimon* has not stopped him. He is not ashamed that his activities have endangered him, for the only question that a man of merit should consider is whether a contemplated deed is right or wrong. Like Achilles, who understood that he must die if he avenged Patroclus, he accepts his death. If the jury offers to acquit him on the condition that he leave off philosophizing, he will reply that he will never stop. He must obey the deity rather than human beings. This goads the jury into a furious uproar. Socrates says much more that I have omitted. My abbreviated summary will suffice for now.

When Socrates is convicted, Athenian custom expects him to propose a punishment that befits his offense. He suggests that, inasmuch as he only benefitted his fellow citizens by forcing them to examine their lives and strive for wisdom and virtue, he should be awarded maintenance for life in the prytaneum. This alienates more jurors. When Socrates is informed of his sentence, he says that it is a good thing. Death is either perpetual dreamless sleep, which would be fine, or a transition to another place where he will be received favorably by divine judges and have pleasurable occasion to converse with poets and heroes such as Homer and Odysseus. He is not angry with his killers, for no evil is befalling him. However, his successors and admirers will punish them. He goes to die and the jury to live. Only the god knows which lot is better.

Crito (performed). Crito has entered Socrates' prison cell silently before dawn and has discovered Socrates sleeping peacefully. He is amazed that a condemned man could be so calm. He announces bad news when Socrates awakens. The Athenian ship that takes the annual thank-offering to Delos (a sacrifice in payment for the salvation of Theseus and his comrades from the Minotaur) is at Sunium and returns to Athens today. Therefore, Socrates must die tomorrow. Socrates contradicts Crito. He asserts that a woman in white came to him in a dream, telling him that on the third day he will come to fertile Phthia. He will die the day after tomorrow. This moves Crito to beg Socrates to save himself. Crito and other friends can arrange an escape. They would happily bear the financial and political costs. Crito adduces reasons why Socrates should accept their offer and resist the evil being done to him. Socrates declines. He engages Crito in dialectic, forcing him to admit that one should perish rather than do wrong. Then he enters into a dialogue with personified laws of Athens, who contend that it would be wrong of Socrates to destroy them by escaping. Socrates agrees that these laws have done nothing but help him all his life and that he has implicitly contracted to obey them by not immigrating to another city. Therefore, he has no right to flout them when they demand his death. If he does it, the personified laws of Hades will not receive him kindly. The escape is off.

Phaedo (performed prologue, narrated main body). In the prologue, Echecrates asks Phaedo if he was there when Socrates drank the poison. He wonders too why so many days passed between the trial and the execution, who else attended it, and what Socrates said. Phaedo replies that he was there, that the execution was delayed owing to the legal requirement of ritual purity while the Delos ship was away on its mission, and that fourteen named comrades of Socrates and some others were present. Socrates was happy and was narrating a tale about pain and pleasure. Cebes interrupted by relaying a question from Evenus, who wondered why Socrates was writing poetry. Socrates said that he was reacting to a recurring dream in which he was commanded to practice music. He had always supposed that philosophy is the greatest music but now he was writing poems to be sure. Evenus was to be told this and urged to follow Socrates into death as soon as possible—but not to commit suicide, an impious deed. Simmias and Cebes asked Socrates what he meant by this. As recounted by Phaedo from here on—so that the dialogue becomes a performed narration—there ensued an inquiry into the immortality of the soul, the details of which I shall skip. It is enough to report that the conclusions seemed more plausible than certain. Socrates finished the quest with a myth in which souls purified by philosophy rise after biological death to fair abodes where they exist without bodies. Something like this being true, he said, people should pursue wisdom and virtue in this life and repeat such stories as if they were magic incantations. Socrates then made final dispositions of his affairs and died saying "Crito, we owe a cock to Asclepius. Make this offering and do not forget it."

This survey of the seven dialogues has been superficial. Still, I think it begins to show that the series tells a coherent story about Socrates, a tale with three simultaneous trajectories. The thesis that the seven dialogues tell this story, and that Theaetetus, Sophist, and Statesman constitute a major portion of it, will have to be confirmed by rigorous examinations of all the arguments and dramas. Here, pending such later verification, I can offer a preliminary outline of the course that I think the three-fold tale takes, concentrating on the trilogy that is my subject and paying minimal attention to the other plays.

The first trajectory that the series seems to trace is Socrates' descent into death, or what the Germans would call his Untergang (going under). The plays present vignettes associated with steps of Socrates' ordeal: indictment; arraignment; trial (with silencing, vilification, and conviction); death row; execution; and the slaying of the geometer who was his physical image and for whom he initially had philosophic hopes, which occurs in tandem with the routing of the Athenian army. Theaetetus, Euthyphro, Sophist, and Statesman also link the first four events in Socrates' descent with studies of the most important elements of Greek and Athenian culture: geometric science, Homeric piety, sophistry, and aristocratic political thought. I think that this scheme is so obviously systematic that Plato must have a theoretical purpose for it. There is a prima facie obligation to inquire what Plato means to achieve with this apparent program of the four dialogues.

My hypothesis is that in the initial plays of the series Plato connects incidents in Socrates' Untergang with cultural studies to illuminate the causes of Athens' debacle and Socrates' doom. Theaetetus associates the city's disaster with its rejection of philosophy. As for the execution of Socrates, Plato understands that it resulted from the hatred generated by Aristophanes and from the anger of powerful people who were embarrassed by being made to look like fools. However, these were proximate causes. They could not have had their fatal consequences if the Athenian culture had not been thoroughly anti-philosophical, so that the charges against Socrates could resonate with jurors and incite them to kill him. The four dramas explore the scientific, religious, sophistical, and political reasons why Socrates had to die, perhaps along with philosophy itself. (Plato could not know that Socratic thought would survive for centuries.) They do this musing by creating a fictitious history in which fundamental Athenian assumptions are examined and exposed as inimical to philosophy, deadly to Socrates, and erroneous, so that the cultural hostility to Socrates has been unjust. Here is a synopsis of the history that I think the plays present:

At the beginning of Theaetetus, Socrates already suspects that his death is imminent. He plainly wants to prolong the existence of philosophy by recruiting one more promising boy to his way of life. He goes to Theodorus's school because geometry is the *technê* closest to philosophy. An excellent student there could be the right lad, one who could be given a start and bequeathed to Plato or Ctesippus for further, long-term education. However, if such a boy exists, there are also factors in Greek geometric science that would militate against his conversion to philosophy and dispose him to condemn and resist Socrates personally. To wit:

Geometry begins with axioms suggested by inspections of drawings (example: parallel lines never intersect). Employing names, definitions, images, measurements, and calculations, it reasons from these premises to results viewed as science. Founded and built up as it is, it equates knowledge with perception and its implications. Theaetetus believes that something perceived is something known. However, this notion is incomplete at best and almost wholly false at worst. What is more troubling, the boy's teacher, Theodorus, was a friend of the sophist Protagoras and has been mixing his teaching of geometry with transmission of the sophist's notion of truth. This combination extends the equation of knowledge with perception beyond geometric figures and numbers to all being. Not only are perceptions of things like the behavior of parallel lines and commensurable numbers treated as proven knowledge but perceptions of all natures, all physical qualities, all virtues and vices, and all characters and actions of persons are thought infallible to boot. Greek geometric science thus supports the tendency of the many to assume the inerrancy of perception, with lethal consequences for people perceived as threats. Pursuant to his fictitious purpose (and Plato's analytic aim), Socrates therefore must try to show Theaetetus that his diet of pure, reasonable geometry and Theodorus's adulterated, sophistical, Protagorean teaching fails to attain to fully adequate cognition, stifles philosophic growth, and unjustly endangers men seen as dangerous. Accordingly, Socrates does two things. He criticizes Theaetetus's Protagorean idea of knowledge. In the middle of the dialogue, in an excursus that many erroneously interpret as a digression, he also attacks its political implications. The epistemological critique requires careful thought that gives the geometric understanding of science and Protagoras's extension of it to all things a fair hearing, allowing them to erect every possible defense, before rejecting them. This exercise does not demand a positive epistemology and Plato makes no effort to supply one. To the extent that the dialogue is an epistemological study, it has only a negative aim: it seeks to demonstrate that while Athenian science is partially to blame for the death of Socrates and the smothering of philosophy, it cannot justify its claim to be *epistêmê* because it has no idea what knowledge is. With regard to that issue, the dialogue is explicitly aporetic.

Socrates makes progress with Theaetetus, inducing him to recognize that he does not know. This encourages Socrates to request the meeting on the next day. However, Socrates has shown Theodorus up in front of his students. Theodorus has been truculent, giving off visible signs of feeling humiliated, deeply offended on behalf of his friend Protagoras, and grievously angered. In his pique, he has compared Socrates with mythical murderers and robbers.

Socrates proceeds to the king archon's office, where he must reply to the capital charge of impiety. As he will say later in Apology (35d), he believes in gods more than any of his accusers do. As we have seen in Euthyphro, he also claims that he is being prosecuted because he rejects unseemly stories about wars of the gods. He is truly pious. At court, he meets Euthyphro, a man whose motive for indicting his righteous father, that he must piously imitate Zeus, is impious. Meletus is a man much like Euthyphro. He has impiously accused the pious Socrates of capital crimes because Socrates disdains the mythical blasphemies. The fact that impious monsters such as Euthyphro and Meletus can prosecute pious men while Socrates will be tried demonstrates that Athenians understand their well-being as dependent on the pleasure of malevolent gods and view philosophic holiness as a threat that must be quashed. Socrates must expect death from Homeric believers. This is not to maintain that Plato has diagnosed a principled quarrel between poetry, religion, and faith on one side and philosophy on the other. His portrait of Socrates indicates that a wondering openness to divine reality unites with philosophy in opposition to corrupt religiosity, which is marked by dogmatic fundamentalism, power lust, and paranoia. Some scholars construe Socrates' professions of wondering faith as ironic. Right or wrong, their thesis distracts us from Plato's portrait of the evil of libido dominandi in religion.

Confronted by crowds of aggressive, paranoid fundamentalists, Socrates cannot expect to prolong the existence of philosophy by converting many. He goes to the next day's meeting with Theodorus and his pupils hoping to make Theaetetus more philosophic. However, just as Anytus was enraged by Socrates' critique of Themistocles and Pericles (Meno 93b–94e), Theodorus was angered by his attack on Protagoras and his science. When Socrates sees that Theodorus has the Eleatic stranger in tow, he suspects, probably rightly, that Theodorus has brought the newcomer to refute him. Scholars who heed Plato's drama go further, arguing that Theodorus has recruited the stranger to prosecute Socrates in a philosophic trial. The charge is that Socrates is a sophist who corrupts the young. Stanley Rosen writes: "[T]he stranger arrives at a definition of sophistry that is unmistakably intended to apply to Socrates. Socrates is a 'noble sophist' but a sophist nonetheless. . . . Socrates pretends to have no positive doctrines and spends much of his time in aporetic conversations with the future leaders of Athens [that] leave them prey to the twin wolves of cynicism and skepticism. . . . Socrates is guilty as charged."[6] Seth Benardete says: "Socrates' maieutics is a poor copy of the sophistic art noble by descent. . . . The stranger indicts Socrates: Socrates is unjust. He induces his own illness in others in order to cure them but he lacks the skill to cure whomever he has corrupted. Socrates is a noble failure."[7] Catherine Zuckert adds that: "In sum, the Eleatic charges in the Sophist, Socrates is a sophist who appears to be wise by refuting others but who, according to his own admission, knows nothing."[8] Mitchell Miller also thinks that Theaetetus, Sophist and Statesman together are "a distinctively philosophical version of Socrates' trial." Surprisingly, he contradicts the opinions just quoted, holding that Theodorus and the stranger are friends of Socrates rather than his accusers. His thesis seems dubious. One would expect "friends" of Socrates to state explicitly that the stranger's definitions of the sophist do not apply to him even though they seem to do so, perhaps explaining the distinctions between sophistry and Socratic philosophy in clarifying detail. Theodorus and the stranger take no such pains. Also, Miller advances his view despite the fact that he notices "a substantive antagonism between Theodorus and Socrates."[9] This makes his position awkward. However this issue must be resolved, it is agreed by the drama-sensitive commentators that Socrates is on trial. If this is the case, Socrates might well be silent in the Eleatic dialogues not because his replacement as protagonist by the stranger symbolizes some momentous change in Plato's thought but because the defendants in Athenian lawsuits are legally obliged to be quiet when the prosecution briefs are being presented.

I agree with the view that Socrates is on trial and that the Eleatic stranger is prosecuting him. I think that the beginning of Sophist constitutes the initial evidence for this judgment. We find Socrates waiting at the geometry school on the morning after his arraignment. Four people approach. Theodorus speaks first, saying: "According to yesterday's

6   Stanley Rosen, Plato's "Sophist," 24.
7   Benardete, The Being of the Beautiful, II-99.
8   Zuckert, Plato's Philosophers, 682. See also Jacob Howland, The Paradox of Political Philosophy: Socrates' Philosophic Trial.
9   Mitchell H. Miller, Jr., The Philosopher in Plato's "Statesman," 2–3.

agreement, Socrates, we have come ourselves, orderly (*kosmiôs*), and we bring also this stranger, by origin [or by birth] from Elea (*to men genos ex Eleas*), a comrade of those around Parmenides and Zeno, very much a philosophic man" (216a1–4).

This speech raises important questions. Why does Theodorus tell Socrates that he and his students have come "according to yesterday's agreement, *kosmiôs*"? Why does he assert that the stranger whom he has brought is "by genos from Elea" when it would suffice to declare that he is "from Elea?" Who or what is the stranger? How should we interpret Theodorus's description of him as "a comrade of those around Parmenides and Zeno, very much a philosophic man?"

I cannot prove that Theodorus's salutation is not a normal Hellenic [10] courtesy. However, I think rather that his language formally opens the philosophic prosecution of Socrates. When lawsuits in Athens are approved by the king archon at arraignment, prosecutors and defendants are ordered and consent to meet in court at specified times. I assume that Athenian customary law considers it *kosmiôs* to comply. So, Theodorus appears to regard his accord struck with Socrates post-Theaetetus as the equivalent of an arraignment agreement—hardly a "friendly" sentiment. Now, Theodorus has his own idea of what a philosopher is, which later analysis will show differs from that of Socrates. He is suing Socrates on behalf of the cosmic society of his "philosophers," not on behalf of Athens. To sue or to prosecute in a Greek society, one must be a citizen of that society by birth. Elea is the capital of philosophy. Theodorus is proving the right of the stranger, as an Eleatic by genos and a "philosopher," to act as Socrates' prosecutor and nominating him for the post. By calling the stranger very much a philosophic man, an associate of the circle around Parmenides and Zeno, Theodorus probably also is diminishing Socrates' rank, asserting that the stranger's philosophic credentials outweigh those of the sophist who unfairly took advantage of a philosophically unpracticed geometer yesterday.

Socrates seems to sense the legalistic cast of Theodorus's language and the challenge to his credentials. That is why he suggests that Theodorus has brought "some god" to refute "us who are worthless in logos." When Theodorus denies that the stranger is a deity or contentious but affirms

---

10   Cf. Zuckert, *Plato's Philosophers*, 682.

that he is divine qua philosopher, Socrates replies, as we have seen, that philosophers are as hard to recognize as gods, adding that he means "the not counterfeit but real philosophers" (*hoi mê plastôs all' ontôs philosophoi*). He thus alerts us to a very significant fact, that there is a difference between sham and real philosophy, prompting us to wonder about the criteria for the distinction. He does this as he speaks of the ignorance of the many projecting appearances onto philosophers. I think he is expressing the suspicion that the stranger is a fake philosopher who will join the ignorant mob in classifying him with politicians (pejorative), sophists, and madmen. Also, his suggestion that the stranger is Zeus Xenios in disguise accompanying the reverent and just to refute "us (*hêmas*, plural accusative) who are worthless in argument" is an urbane, polite expression that leaves open the identities of the reverent and just and those who are to be refuted. Socrates has exhibited a higher reverence. In the Seventh Letter (324e), Plato calls Socrates "the most just" man. I doubt that Plato would have portrayed Socrates as the unjust man of Rosen's and Benardete's guilty verdicts. It is much more likely that he makes the reverent, just Socrates include himself among the targets of the god to avoid giving offense and to acknowledge, as he always does, that he does not know and that he therefore must be easy to refute. If so, Socrates' use of the ambiguous "us" clearly is his warning that the unidentified reverent and just will be protected and that the anonymous persecutors of the reverent and just stand to be punished in the court of truth. Socrates is suggesting that Zeus Xenios is preparing to speak through the Eleatic to make him refute both his sponsor and himself. Theodorus and the stranger should beware.

Ultimately, the question of whether the stranger has come to prosecute or help Socrates will depend on the course the story takes. I expect that later exegesis will show that the dialogue depicts an attack by the stranger-prosecutor's sophistic "philosophy" on genuine philosophy. I also expect that the stranger will persuade Theaetetus to vote to convict Socrates of sophistry by getting him to accept his definitions. This is the result that would fit a series centered on the trial and death of Socrates. It would be Plato's dramatic explanation of how sophistry was partially responsible for the murder of Socrates.

When we read the beginning of Statesman, we wonder why Socrates thanks Theodorus for his introduction to Theaetetus and the stranger.

Contemporary scholars think it self-evident that Socrates is grateful for having been taught a powerful new philosophy that excels his own. This is the seemingly natural assumption. However, it is not the only possible interpretation and not clearly the right one. As we continue to test the hypothesis that Socrates is on philosophic trial in Sophist and probably in Statesman too, we are justified in looking for parallels between his criminal lawsuit and this process. In Apology, after Socrates has been convicted and again after he has been sentenced, he is allowed to speak and he behaves as if he is grateful for a good thing that has been done to him. What good thing? He has been made to realize that he must accept an unjust death to remain true to philosophy and to keep his soul worthy of the eternal reward that somehow awaits him. In Statesman, after he has been found guilty of sophistry in Sophist, Socrates is permitted to speak again. It seems likely that he thanks Theodorus here for a similar favor, that he has been taught that he must accept an even greater blow to save his soul, the misunderstanding, rejection, and perhaps even the extermination of his philosophy.

There is another parallel to consider. In Apology, after he has learned his biological fate, Socrates rebukes those who have voted for his execution but expresses a desire to converse with those who voted to acquit him. In the opening scenes of Statesman, where Socrates is allowed to speak for what might be the last time, he rebukes Theodorus for undervaluing true statesmanship and philosophy and expresses the wish to speak later with young Socrates, one of his "kin" who has not yet voted to condemn him. These parallels look like hints that Statesman is an extension of the philosophic lawsuit.

Statesman proceeds with the stranger's virtuoso display of methods, his initial definition of the *politikos*, his myth, his call for the use of paradigm and his illustration of paradigm with the example of letters, his appeal to the mean between excess and defect, his choice of weaving as the paradigm of statesmanship and his *diaeresis* of weaving, his *diaeresis* of statesmanship by joints rather than by halves, and his final account of statesmanship as a weaving of the moderate and the courageous into a bond of friendship. As he presents his arguments, the stranger seems to me to employ a dialectic and to develop a cosmology, a theology, an ethics, and a political theory that are un-Socratic. This inspires Catherine Zuckert to describe Statesman as a conflict between antagonistic views of the nature of philosophy, with

Socrates focused on a quest for a Good upon which the intelligibility of all things depends and the stranger confident that he has a science of the intelligibility of the whole premised on determinations of how things are the same and different. She concludes: "If the Eleatic is an exemplar of the dialectical science and thus of philosophy, as he suggests, then in his judgment Socrates cannot be a philosopher, even though the Eleatic is too urbane to say so explicitly. He contents himself with intimating that Socrates is a sophist . . ."[11] I concur in her opinion. The stranger's insinuation, together with his implication that Socrates meddles in politics unscientifically by practicing his *alêthôs politikê technê*, might expose Socrates to the punishment that the stranger decrees for materials unfit for use in political weaving. His reasoning convinces young Socrates. The boy is too impressed by the promise of a scientific politics that produces harmony and happiness, much as the Athenians were persuaded to adopt the policies of leaders who heeded the likes of Protagoras while promising conquest and prosperity. The stranger thus apparently secures another vote to condemn the real philosopher. So, Socrates' prediction in Gorgias (521e–522a) comes true literally in Plato's fiction just as it does figuratively in history: He is convicted by a jury of children. Like the result of Sophist, this would fit a series focused on the ordeal of Socrates. It would explain by dramatic means how Athenian political culture was behind the murder of Socrates. Of course, as I have been saying, the proof of this interpretive pudding must be in the eating. A complete exegesis of Sophist and Statesman will have to determine whether the arguments of those plays match this hypothesized story.

Socrates' fictitious conviction of sophistry and sedition in Sophist and Statesman sets the stage for the remaining dramatic steps of his Untergang in Apology, Crito, and Phaedo. These are adequately summarized above.

The second trajectory that Plato's dramatic series describes is Socrates' ascent from death to eternal life. As happens so frequently in Plato, the way down is the way up. With every step of his descent toward execution, Socrates reconciles himself more and more to it, relinquishing the hold that he and philosophy have on life and rising to a tranquil embrace of posthumous immortality. In Theaetetus he knows that he himself will die but thinks that he can contribute one more youth to the perpetuation of

---

11 Zuckert, *Plato's Philosophers*, 706.

philosophy. By the end of Politikos, when Theaetetus and young Socrates have convicted him, he obviously abandons this hope, for he requests no more meetings and he later prophesies to Eucleides that Theaetetus will be celebrated or talked about (*ellogimon*), which is not to say that he will become philosophic. Socrates probably already has given up his project by the end of Sophist. In parallel with Apology, he seems glad at the start of Statesman to have found that he must accept his cultural fate and rise to a higher fulfillment. At the close of Apology, Socrates muses that, if the myths are true, there will be pleasant philosophy after death, although only the deity knows whether death or life is superior. In Crito, he stops emphasizing this uncertainty, speculating that he will arrive in Hades after death and not be ill-received. In Phaedo, he tells a story to support a guess that souls purified by philosophy go to beautiful homes after departing from their bodies or, at least, that something like this is true, so that his tale should be repeated as an incantation from now on. His reservation makes us wonder whether he believes in immortality literally or in some figurative sense, one that represents some participation in eternity in the well-lived life here.[12] I do not know. Either way, Socrates finishes his ascent from death to life as he utters his famous last words, which indicate that he thinks he has become healthy.

The third trajectory that Plato's dramas track seems to be his own meditative-mythical spiritual voyage inside the soul of his hero Socrates along the down-up course of death and life. I am basing my concept of meditative-mythical spiritual travel on the work of Zdravko Planinc, which I have adapted to my own purposes in my own language. In Plato through Homer, Planinc argues that Homer was a poet-shaman whose consciousness meditatively transmigrated into the *psychê* of Odysseus as the hero sailed the axis mundi. Odysseus was a wily scoundrel but, as he faced terror after terror on his voyage, he rose toward the divine reality, becoming a finer man. Homer spiritually entered the experiences of Odysseus to face temptations symbolized by the ethical and physical dangers that plagued Odysseus. Planinc contends further that Plato adopts Homer's plan. Plato is a philosopher-

---

12 For profound analyses of this issue, see Eric Voegelin, "Immortality: Experience and Symbol," in *Collected Works*, vol. 12, and Jacob Klein, "Plato's Phaedo," in *Lectures and Essays*.

poet-shaman whose consciousness transmigrates into the *psychê* of Socrates, which in turn transmigrates into the *psychê* of Odysseus in Plato's plays. In Timaeus, Critias, and Phaedrus, Plato "refigures" tropes from the Odyssey, creating the dialogues as mimes of the myths. In spirit, he journeys with Socrates-Odysseus down toward Hades and up toward divine being. He does this not to make Socrates transmit doctrines but to overcome his own philosophic temptations in the person of Socrates-Odysseus.

With Planinc's kind permission, I shall avail myself of his insights for my analysis. In all of the seven dialogues centered on the last days of Socrates, Plato again refigures poetic tropes, making his plays mimes of the myths. His consciousness transmigrates into the soul of Socrates, which in turn transmigrates into the souls of mythical Hellenic characters. Plato goes with the Socrates-heroes down toward spiritual death and up toward spiritual life, facing philosophic temptations that threaten to snare and imprison his soul. The proof that Plato again is behaving as a philosopher-poet-shaman consists in sometimes explicit, sometimes implicit allusions to Homer and other poets that he embeds in his texts.

I shall begin to illustrate this reading with a brief sketch of the ascending branch of Plato's meditative-mythical journey. In Apology, Socrates cites Achilles in explaining why he will not give up philosophizing to prevent his execution. Quitting his work to eliminate the risk of assassination must have been an option that occurred to Plato too. Achilles' divine mother warned him that he would surely die if he killed Hector. Achilles resolved to do so regardless of the certainty of his demise.[13] The philosopher-poet-shaman says that he must take the analogous stance. So, in this play, Socrates and Plato-Socrates have become Achilles embracing his risks to stay true to his mission.

In Crito, when Socrates reports his dream of a beautiful woman in white informing him that he will come to fertile Phthia in three days, he is paraphrasing Achilles' furious bluster to Odysseus. Achilles swears to let the Achaeans be massacred while he departs and reaches his home in Phthia three days hence with his plunder. His angry vow is frustrated. Achilles is killed at the end of that time.[14] Plato refigures the trope. Achilles' rage at

13   Homer, *Iliad*, xviii, 96, 98.
14   Homer, *Iliad*, ix, 363.

being cheated of a female captive presumably is replaced by the just anger of Plato-Socrates over Athens' perfidy toward the philosopher. Achilles' plan to deny the Achaeans his prowess and let them be slaughtered while he pursues safety and wealth is supplanted by Plato-Socrates' temptation to deprive Athens of philosophy, let its citizens go to blazes, and delight in private communion with the Good. The woman in white is a goddess, not the petulant warrior. She changes Achilles' pledge from a resolution to survive and reap material profit into a prophecy of imminent death in exchange for eternal life in blessedness. Her promise is right, not wrong. The subject of her prophecy is not the invincible fighter who will prevail in battle before being killed but the willing victim whose execution will be a victory. Thomas Payne contends that Plato-Socrates is Achilles resisting Agamemnon's envoys, who are personified by Crito.[15] Owing to the changes in the trope, I am a bit worried by this interpretation. I suggest instead that the soul of Plato-Socrates has become Odysseus hearing a divine promise of his homecoming. In either case, Achilles harvested death by going back on his decision, but Plato-Socrates wins eternal life by adhering to his.

In Phaedo, the question about the delay in Socrates' execution and the explanation about the thank-offering ship refer directly to the myth of Theseus and the Minotaur. Jacob Klein has shown that the scene of Socrates' death attended by nine named Athenians, five named disciples from other Hellenic cities, and anonymous Athenians replicates Theseus's dangerous adventure with nine young men, five girls, and a ship's crew. The winding argument is the labyrinth, Phaedo is Ariadne, and fear of death is the Minotaur with whom Socrates-Theseus duels.[16] I can add nothing to Klein's exegesis except to observe that the temptation that Plato-Socrates-Theseus faces down, the fear of death, is only the second greatest philosophic temptation. The first and worst is confronted earlier in Sophist and Statesman.

Turning now to the descending leg of the journey, Plato-Socrates appears in Theaetetus to be Odysseus on the second stop of his voyage after the sack of Troy, in the country of the lotus eaters. I gather this not from

15   Thomas Payne, "The Crito as Mythological Mime," *Interpretation* 11:1 (1983), 1–23.
16   Klein, "Plato's Phaedo."

quotations but from parallels. Odysseus, who always refers to his shipmates as his comrades, dispatches some of them into the interior of the land to learn what the inhabitants are like. These people are not hostile. They give the scouts lotus to eat, whereupon they lose their desire to return home. Odysseus has to drag them back to the ships, bind them to the benches, and escape. I think that Plato refigures this trope. The geometry school is the lotus country because those who gorge on the mathematics there become complacent, supposing that they have scaled the heights of human rational endeavor and that they can keep working on their plateau. Philosophers are strongly tempted to accept the certainties of mathematics as the perfect science that they seek. Two "comrades" of Plato-Socrates-Odysseus are already in the lotus land when he arrives, Theaetetus and young Socrates, the boys who are "kin" because they bear the image and name of Socrates. In an intellectual sense, they have become terminally comfortable there and Plato's soul could be snared too if he ate the geometric lotus. The two lads have to be dragged out of smug scientism and up towards their real philosophic home. The rescue initially succeeds in the case of Theaetetus (and perhaps in that of young Socrates) but it is thwarted by subsequent catastrophes, just as Odysseus ultimately loses all his men.

When Socrates goes to the porch of the king and meets Euthyphro, there are no allusions to Odysseus, Achilles, and Theseus. It might be argued that this scuttles my interpretation of Plato's seven-fold series as a poetic meditative-mythical psychic journey in which the philosopher vicariously confronts philosophic temptations. However, Euthyphro does not contradict my thesis at all. Dogmatic religious fundamentalism is the presumption that one knows the mind of God. This is one of the most dangerous temptations of the spirit, an enticement that can take philosophic forms, as witness Hegel. The temptation can be symbolized by the attempt of Talos, the apprentice of Daedalus, to fly to the sun, an effort that must result in the melting of the soul's wings and a plunge to a spiritual death. Like Talos, those who indulge their reckless pride justify themselves by construing the strength and sincerity of their convictions as their warrant. Plato's soul journeys with Socrates to meet Euthyphro, whose name implies good whole-heartedness or sincerity. Approaching this incarnation of sincerity dialectically, Plato-Socrates easily refutes Euthyphro's rationalizations of his presumption, thus resisting the temptation. However, like Talos, the sincere fundamentalist Euthyphro is unfazed by reason. His mind is closed so he persists in his dogmatism. Now, if Plato-Socrates is mastering this stubborn evil inclination of the spirit here, why is there no reference to Odysseus, Achilles, or Theseus? The answer is that Socrates explicitly claims Daedalus as his ancestor and actually becomes Daedalus in a way that Euthyphro senses but does not understand. Socrates is Daedalus not because he magically sets Euthyphro's words in motion but because he tries to warn Euthyphro away from the sun.

In the next episodes, Sophist and Statesman, the soul of Plato-Socrates has journeyed to a new scene in which two Homeric tropes have collapsed into one. The pleasantries addressed by Socrates to the Eleatic stranger are paraphrases of speeches in different books of the Odyssey.[17] In the first Homeric text, Odysseus petitions the Cyclops as a suppliant, requesting the generosity owing to strangers and warning him that Zeus, the avenger of suppliants and strangers, watches over them. In the second passage, Odysseus has returned to Ithaca and has dressed as a beggar. Antinous, the most powerful suitor of Penelope, has struck him. A youth tells Antinous that he ought not to have done that, for deities visit cities in all kinds of shapes, beholding the hubris and righteousness of men. So, Plato-Socrates has spiritually flown to a place that merges the country of the Cyclops with a not-yet-reclaimed Ithaca. We still must learn who he has become. Has he become Odysseus or the Cyclops and Antinous? Further, which of these figures does the Eleatic stranger impersonate? Let us attempt to find out by consulting the text. We must return to the opening scene of Sophist.

As we have seen, Theodorus keeps yesterday's agreement, arriving at his school with his two pupils and the stranger and telling Socrates that the Eleatic is very much a philosophic man. Socrates replies by asking whether Theodorus has not brought some god, for Homer says that the gods, and especially the god of strangers, go with reverent and just men beholding the hybristic and lawful deeds of mankind. Perhaps, he continues, the stranger has come to "refute us who are worthless in *logos*," acting as "a sort of god of refutation." The case apparently is open and shut. Socrates has imputed philosophic guilt to himself. Hence, the stranger is Zeus Xenios, the god of strangers, Theodorus is Odysseus, and Socrates is the

17 Homer, *Odyssey*, ix, 272; xvii, 485–87.

philosophic equivalent of Polyphemus, the lawless monster. In terms of the second Homeric passage, the stranger is Odysseus disguised as a god and Socrates is Antinous.[18] This time, it will be thought, my reading of the story of Plato's seven-fold series is well and truly sunk.

I reply that this interpretation is too hasty. Socrates has more to say. When Theodorus denies that the stranger is a god but nevertheless praises him as divine qua philosopher, Socrates, as we have noted, answers that the real philosophers—not the sham ones—appear in all kinds of shapes because of the ignorance of others. Socrates was quoting Homer when he first alluded to the stories of Odysseus and the Cyclops and Odysseus and Antinous but now he has spoken on his own authority about the real and fake philosophers. In doing this, he has reversed the roles of his original allusion, assuming the part of the anonymous youth in Ithaca. Thus, he has hinted to his interlocutors and Plato's readers that they are in a world in which things are not as they first appear. To ascertain the real, we must ask who is the true philosopher and who is truly reverent. I think it safe to assume that Socrates is the true philosopher and that he is more reverent and just than anyone. I therefore would expect Zeus Xenios to be accompanying Socrates to the school. Socrates, not the Eleatic, is the actual xenos, a guest of Theodorus who has the suppliant's right to petition for good treatment. Socrates has been ironic in hailing the stranger as a deity and in using the ambiguous "us" that strikes the unwary eye as a confession to being the counterpart of Polyphemus and Antinous. He has been urbanely warning Theodorus and the stranger not to carry out their plan to prosecute him as a sophist and a vile politician lest they incur the wrath of Zeus. Thus, he is the Odysseus who is in danger of being devoured by Polyphemus and struck down by Antinous. The stranger is Polyphemus/Antinous.

I can offer some additional dramatic reasons for favoring this interpretation. Socrates is the one who will be devalued by the stranger, just as Odysseus was degraded to the status of fool and enemy by Polyphemus and scorned as a useless burden on the earth by Antinous. It is not the other way around, with Socrates degrading the stranger. When Socrates asks for an account of sophist, politikos, philosopher, he is acting as a

---

18   Thus Benardete, *The Being of the Beautiful: "Plato's Theaetetus, Sophist, and Statesman,"* II.69.

suppliant and beggar, just as Odysseus did before Polyphemus and Antinous. The stranger asks for nothing. Further, Socrates' self-accusation, if it were serious, would not make sense in the context of the play. Socrates is speaking to Theodorus and the stranger. If the stranger has come to refute Socrates for horrors perpetrated in argument, these crimes would have to be actions about which Theodorus and the stranger knew and cared. The misdeeds also would have to resemble those of the Cyclops and Antinous. If the stranger were an angry Zeus Xenios, Socrates' felonies would have to be sins against the deity's law of hospitality. The atrocities of Socrates that would be both known and important to Theodorus and the stranger can be reduced to a short bill of particulars. Socrates subverted the Protagorean concept of geometric science and its application to human affairs, driving Theaetetus into aporia. He also has dabbled in politics unscientifically. Those crimes, if crimes they were, are unlike anything Polyphemus or Antinous did. Finally, the stranger simply looks like Polyphemus more than Socrates does. The Cyclops was an inveterate classifier, sorting cheeses into crates by kind and his sheep into pens by age. The stranger's science is almost wholly based on classification. Socrates classifies too but in ways that differ from those of the stranger, and his philosophy ultimately rests on other foundations. An additional point is that "Polyphemus" breaks down etymologically into the words for "much" and "speech." Often the word means "much spoken about, famous." However, Polyphemus also can mean "wordy" (cf. Liddell and Scott). Neither appellation makes much sense as applied to the monster, although the Cyclops does utter too many words to deadly effect, like the stranger. Calling Homer ironic, Eva Brann states flatly that "'Polyphemus' means 'wordy.'"[19] Her authority suffices for me. I believe that the drama suggests that the real name of the stranger is Polyphemus/Antinous.

What temptations is the soul of Plato-Socrates-Odysseus facing among the Cyclops and the suitors of Penelope? I think that the first is the urge to achieve intellectual power by turning philosophy into a sophistry that controls appearances by manipulating words. The second is the libido dominandi that aspires to achieve political mastery by the same means.

19 Eva Brann, *Homeric Moments: Clues to Delight in Reading the Odyssey and the Iliad*, 189.

These speculations will shock readers who regard the arguments of the Eleatic stranger as the highest achievements of philosophy. Again, I caution that my reading must be confirmed by a complete analysis of the arguments of the dialogues. I turn to a close study of Theaetetus.

3

THEAETETUS:
BOY-TESTING IN LOTUS LAND

What is the subject of Plato's Theaetetus? That is an easy question. The dialogue studies knowledge. However, the most prominent parts of the dialogue, its beginning, middle, and end, refer to the trial and death of Socrates—surely not by chance. Why? Our leading commentators, especially the analytic philosophers, appear to agree that Plato, outraged by the fate of Socrates, could not refrain from inserting philosophically irrelevant matter into one of his finest scientific works. Therefore, they sweep his obiter dicta under the rug, either with a few rueful, dismissive remarks or by ignoring them altogether. I think that Plato would say that this is to misunderstand philosophic relevance. He would tell us that he deliberately designed the surface of Theaetetus to indicate that the dialogue is both an investigation of knowledge for its own sake and a statement about a link between Hellenic *epistêmê* and the execution of Socrates. He would explain further that, on its deeper level, the dialogue is an analysis of the relationships among a society's concept of science, its genuine philosophers and great-souled youths, and its politics.[1] Together with the epistemology, these relationships *are* what is relevant. Plato's readers must try to grasp all of the pertinent elements at once. Let us begin where Plato does, with the story framed by his prologue.

The play opens with Eucleides meeting Terpsion in their home city of Megara. The two Megarians are former companions of Socrates who attended him during his last hours. Eucleides is also the master of the Megarian philosophic school, which according to Aristotle (*Metaphysics*

---

1   As far as I know, the only book about *Theaetetus* that perceives this intention of Plato's is Paul Stern, *Knowledge and Politics in Plato's "Theaetetus."*

1046b29–1047a7) held the absurd (*atopa*) doctrine that "there are no potentialities before things happen."[2] Eucleides tells Terpsion that he chanced upon Theaetetus near the harbor. Theaetetus is expiring of dysentery and wounds sustained in a battle near Corinth, probably that of 369 B.C., in which allied Athenian and Spartan armies were vanquished by a Theban force.[3] He is being carried home, having spurned Eucleides' urging to stop in Megara. Eucleides therefore went with him as far as Erineum. Terpsion exclaims: "What a man you say is in danger!" Eucleides answers that Theaetetus is *kalon te kai agathon* (beautiful and good, the Athenian appellation of an aristocratic gentleman), as proved by praises that he has heard of Theaetetus's conduct in the battle. Eucleides also recollects that shortly before his execution, Socrates met Theaetetus when Theaetetus was a *meirakion* (a term that Liddell and Scott translate as the "diminutive" of "lad"). When Socrates had been with him (*suggenomenos*) and spoken with him he greatly admired his nature. Eucleides wonders at the accuracy of Socrates' prophecy that Theaetetus would become *ellogimon* (much talked about, famous) if he survived to adulthood. His astonishment probably owes to his inability or unwillingness to comprehend the existence of a gifted student's potential that Socrates could have discerned.

Eucleides also reports that Socrates had related the content of his talk with Theaetetus to him. Terpsion asks if Eucleides can recount what was said. Eucleides cannot do that but he says that he wrote the conversation down at the time. Then he returned to Athens repeatedly and had Socrates fill lacunae. He pretty much has it all. The dramatic date of the play indicates that these meetings occurred in Socrates' cell while he was awaiting execution. Terpsion answers that he had meant to ask about the manuscript today. They go to Eucleides' home to view it. Eucleides explains that to avoid unspecified trouble in the writing, he eliminated annoying expressions such as "I said" and "he said," recasting Socrates' narrative as if people were speaking

2   The quotation is Joe Sachs's excellent succinct account of the teaching in his translation of Plato, *Theaetetus*, note 2 to 142c.

3   The battle to which the Megarians refer could have occurred either during the Corinthian War of 394 or the Theban War of 369. If it were the former, Theaetetus would be dead between ages eighteen and twenty, leaving him with insufficient time to do the geometric work that made him famous. Hence, it probably was the later war. This would date our trilogy to post-369.

(thus making it a "performed" piece). Eucleides orders a slave to read the text.

Does this prologue have philosophic relevance?[4] In this connection, what impresses me about the drama is that characters who deny potentiality juxtapose two premature deaths, those of Socrates and Theaetetus. Indeed, an astute Athenian might have noticed that they juxtapose four premature fatalities. The combat near Corinth was deadly both to Athens and to Hellas. Athens speedily recovered from its disastrous defeat of 404 in the Peloponnesian War. Within ten years, it was striving to reestablish its empire. Other cities were also vying for hegemony. All Hellas was drawn into a maelstrom of incessant warfare. Athens, Sparta, and Thebes fought for control of the Isthmus of Corinth. The Theban victory presaged the end of Athens as a great power. As Plato knew well (see Republic 469b–471b), internecine strife also made Hellas liable to foreign conquest. He would have regarded the battle near Corinth as a harbinger of that fate.

Assuming that Plato does not do things mindlessly, we must ask why he introduces his dialogue by artfully linking one consummated and three impending premature deaths of persons and polities, this in the speeches of intellectuals who deny potentiality. I can think of only one reason: Plato wants to suggest a pair of points subtly. First, there is a sense in which the coming three tragedies are effects of the original, realized one and all four are cases of potential snuffed out. Socrates had the potential to educate more philosophers and perhaps to make Athens more just had he not been murdered. If Socrates admired Theaetetus's nature, he would have hoped to make the boy philosophic. He had the potential to do that had he not been killed. Theaetetus had the potential to become a philosopher as well as a great geometer.

---

4   Among the leading modern commentators to whom I alluded above, the following fail to explore the prologue: Myles Burnyeat, *The Theaetetus of Plato*; John McDowell, translation of Plato, *Theaetetus*; Kenneth Sayre, *Plato's Analytic Method* and *Plato's Literary Garden*; John Cooper, *Plato's "Theaetetus"*; David Bostock, *Plato's "Theaetetus."* In *Reading Plato's* Theaetetus, Timothy Chappell notes that Cornford, Bostock, McDowell, and Burnyeat give 142a–145e short shrift. Chappell himself finds philosophic significance only after the prologue. For all these writers, it is as if nothing interesting happens until 145e, where Socrates asks his question about knowledge. Their answer to my question about the prologue must be no.

Had Socrates lived to educate him Theaetetus might have done that. However, the execution of Socrates left Theaetetus to be educated by Theodorus, who only made him into a geometer, and by the civic culture of Athens, which evidently made him into the type of "good citizen" who unreflectively fights for his city's dubious interests. (We do not learn that he openly undertook to condemn Athenian imperialism, as Socrates did; see Gorgias 517b–c.) By the day after his talk with Theaetetus (when the boy fell back under the sway of Theodorus and newly under that of the Eleatic stranger), Socrates foresaw this development. This is why he predicted only that Theaetetus would become famous and not that he would also become a philosopher. Of course, the boy became a very great geometer but he also became a soldier and was slain, so that his potential to do more great geometry also was extinguished. In death he became merely another broken cog in Athens's military machine, which might be why the specific praise that the Megarians thought to bestow on him made no mention of his mathematics, eulogizing him only in conventional political terms. Meanwhile, Athens had the potential to become a just city and to guide Hellas to a united peace had it sought wisdom and the rest of virtue instead of killing Socrates and waging imperialistic wars, and had it not steered potential philosophic leaders like Theaetetus into admired unphilosophic sciences and uncritical patriotism. Hellas was left mired in warfare. Second, if all this dramatization of loss of potential is Plato's preface to his analysis of *epistêmê*, the *epistêmê* about to be examined can be expected to have something to do with the loss. The prologue is philosophically relevant partially because it alerts us to think about the connection.[5]

A few more words about the prologue are in order. It is telling that Socrates chose to co-operate with Eucleides' writing project while awaiting execution. It seems likely that he did so because he intended the transcript of his conversation with Theaetetus as something like his last philosophic testament. If he did, it would follow that the document contains his legacy of advice about the right education of potentially philosophic youths, the

5 Paul Stern, in *Knowledge and Politics*, 15–23, argues that the philosophic relevance of the prologue is that the Megarian denial of potentiality touches on *the* problem of knowledge, the relationships among potentiality, nonbeing, and the being of wholes. This is a fruitful thesis but I think that the relevance starts where I have suggested, prior to the epistemological puzzles.

barriers to such education erected by unphilosophic sciences, and the political effects of those obstacles, which include threats to the lives of philosophers. This must be another part of any account of the philosophic relevance of the prologue and we must look for the anticipated lessons. However, this inference prompts a question. Why did Plato let the Megarians suggest his philosophic purposes? To frame the issue another way, why does Socrates entrust Eucleides with his testament? Plato and Socrates cannot have picked the Megarians because Eucleides and Terpsion were outstanding thinkers. Although Paul Stern is right to observe that their denial of potentiality was arguable,[6] Aristotle's judgment of the Megarians as absurd still seems to have been fair. The prologue also heaps Plato's implicit criticism on them. It was unconscionable that Eucleides stuck his text in a drawer for thirty years and that Terpsion took that long to ask for it, apparently on a random whim. Plato has depicted the Megarians as philosophically lackadaisical. He also has made Eucleides admit inadvertently that his poor memory prevented him from capturing everything that was said. We may assume that Eucleides also lost philosophic substance by changing the mode of Socrates' narrative, thus omitting trenchant observations that Socrates might have made together with the "I said" and "He agreed" expressions. Plato probably allows the Megarians to suggest his intentions because their histories and their physical location in Megara make his drama plausible and because their denial of potentiality symbolizes what he wishes to imply. Inside the play, Socrates probably gives his last testament to Eucleides because he understands that the record is being composed in Megara, where it will be safe from destruction by his enemies even if it is somewhat garbled. Tradition has it that Plato himself fled to Megara after Socrates was killed.

As the curtain rises on the main body of the drama, Socrates is in the school of Theodorus asking about Athenian students of geometry or any other sort of philosophy who might make a decent showing. This would appear to be a strange thing for a man to be doing when he is about to be indicted for capital offenses. It seems even more odd for him to be seeking out boys when one of the charges is that he corrupts the young. Socrates tells Theodorus that he is going about his normal activity. This is true. We read in Symposium that Socrates has been taught "the right method of boy loving" (211b) by

6   Stern, *Knowledge and Politics*, 15–23.

Diotima, that this is a matter of guiding good-looking and plain lads who are fair of soul up to visions of the ever-existing, essential, divine Beauty, and that he always searches for youths to educate. Hence, in Theaetetus, Socrates is persisting in his habitual work in the face of death. He must regard his mission today as urgent, for he knows that this is his last chance to recruit a promising youth to philosophy. Of course, he is perfectly aware that he will not be able to finish educating such a lad himself, but he has students like Plato whom he can trust to finish the work when he is gone.

The question that Socrates faced when he woke up on this fateful morning was where he could find a suitable boy on short notice. The Platonic Socrates did not have to puzzle over this problem for long. Legend has it that Plato admitted no one to his Academy who was not versed in geometry. In Republic, his Socrates analytically (but not by way of serious metaphysics) maps reality onto four sections of a divided line, two in an intelligible domain and two in a visible one (509d–511e). The higher level of the intelligible realm consists of forms (or ideas) and is known by an investigative process that ascends from hypotheses to a beginning, eschewing images and thinking with forms alone. What Socrates means by this is not clear. The lower intelligible level consists of numbers and geometric objects and is explored by reasoning from hypotheses down to conclusions, treating the odd and the even, geometrical shapes, and the three kinds of angles as known and using drawn images of lines, planes, and solids to facilitate understanding. This tier has an important place in Socrates' analytic hierarchy of being and its reasoning is indispensable. Pondering an education for philosopher kings in Republic, Socrates obtains Glaucon's agreement that geometry draws the soul to the contemplation of what always is, for it is itself a knowing of what always is (527b). So, geometry rightly done is a necessary preparation for philosophy even though it is only the prelude to dialectic (531d). Unfortunately, geometry is not done properly in Hellas. Geometers speak as if they were acting, talking about "squaring," "setting up against," "adding," and so on, whereas they should be focusing on knowing and turning their souls toward unchanging reality (527a–b). Nevertheless, Socrates evidently has decided today that a visit to a geometry school will give him the best odds of locating the right kind of boy. If he finds one, he can begin to turn his glances upward to eternal being and help him transcend geometry's intrinsic limitation, the need to descend from hypotheses to conclusions with the assistance of images.

Socrates initiates his search for a potentially philosophic youth with a lengthy speech:

> If I cared more about things in Cyrene, Theodorus, I'd ask you about things there and about the people, whether there are any of the local young people who pay attention to geometry or to any other sort of philosophy (*hê tina allên philosophian*). But as things are, I love them less than those who are here, and I'm more eager to know which of our young people are considered likely to make a decent showing. Now I myself look into these things to the limit of my power, and I question those others whom I see that the young people want to associate with. Not a few of them come around you, and with justice, for you are deserving of it both for other reasons and on account of geometry. So if you've happened upon anyone worthy of mention, I would hear the news with pleasure.[7]

A number of things about this oration are notable. It is stiffly formal. It seeks to excuse a lack of interest in the young people of Cyrene that might have offended Theodorus by invoking a chauvinistic patriotism that Hellenes tend to take for granted. It also avoids offending Theodorus by suppressing Socrates' principled ranking of geometry below philosophy. It explains Socrates' usual quest to Theodorus as if the latter previously had been unaware of it. It flatters Theodorus. I think that these facts tell us that Socrates and Theodorus have not been close friends or regular associates prior to this meeting. Close friends and regular associates would not need to be stiffly formal. They would not have to apologize for caring only about their own young. Neither would they need to walk on eggshells to avoid wounding each other's professional pride. They would already be cognizant of each other's ordinary business. One would not have to flatter the other to learn who his best students were. Thus, the previous relationship of the two must have been one resembling that between some of our

---

7   As noted in chapter one, I use Joe Sachs's translations when they are available. This quotation from *Theaetetus* and others above from *Republic* are Sachs translations.

modern distinguished professors who encounter each other at conferences, who interact with guarded civility, talking generally about scientific progress, and who have regarded each other differently, one having followed and appreciated the other's work and one having been aware of the other's reputation without deeming him or his work worthy of much attention.

Theodorus replies that he has a lad worthwhile for him to tell about and for Socrates to hear about. He says that if the boy were beautiful, he would greatly fear to identify him lest he be accused of desiring him. Theodorus evidently keeps a nervous eye on public opinion. He thinks, perhaps rightly, that no one would send a son to a tutor suspected of pederasty. His comments also betray the facts that he is ignorant of Socrates' views of homoeroticism and that he suspects that Socrates would inform on him for being sexually attracted to a student. This is yet another indication that he and Socrates have not been close friends or regular associates. But he can talk. The lad looks like Socrates so he is not handsome. Urging Socrates not to be angry, Theodorus "fearlessly" denigrates the boy's looks on the grounds that, like Socrates, he has a snub nose and bulging eyes. His "fearlessness" probably reflects confidence that he can speak authoritatively about beauty. Socrates does not take umbrage at this description of his countenance. However, by his tactlessness, Theodorus has just invited blunt pronouncements of verities that offend him. Socrates will fearlessly utter such truths. Theodorus will not be as unaffected as Socrates.

Theodorus goes on to praise his nominee. The lad is amazingly good-natured. More than nearly anyone, he is *eumathê* (well-learning), gentle, and courageous. Theodorus would not have supposed that this could happen, for he does not see it [in others]. Usually, sharp, quick people with good memories have rapid mood swings. They are carried about like ships without ballast, more maniacal than brave. The weighty types are poor learners and forgetful. Unlike those two prevalent sorts, this boy advances toward learning and seeking smoothly and surely like a quietly flowing stream of oil. It is astounding that the lad could accomplish so much at his age.

Theodorus's praises of his student reveal some of his own traits. He does not credit what he cannot see. He dislikes intellectual agility that cannot be focused on a goal because it reacts to every stimulus. He likes intelligence that relentlessly pursues an aim. One could interpret this to mean that he embraces the freedom of a soul that makes its own reasoned choices.

However, he has chosen an odd simile to communicate such a sentiment. Flowing oil is not self-propelled. It is moved by pouring and gravity. This suggests that Theodorus prefers smart, pliable pupils who can be set in constant motion toward goals that he sets for them.

Socrates reacts to Theodorus's report by exclaiming: "Good news!" The lad has most of the traits that Socrates has prescribed for the guardians of the just city and students of philosophy (*sôphrosynê*, moderation, has not been listed and this might prove significant; see Republic 375a– 376b, 535a–536a).[8] Socrates inquires "from which of the citizens" the boy comes. He wants to be sure that the lad is an Athenian. Theodorus cannot remember. He recalls only that the father died and that trustees squandered much of the boy's inheritance—but evidently not all of it, for the youth is wonderfully *eleutheri-otêta* (most liberal or generous) with the money that he has and he presumably pays tuition.—Theodorus seems to forget matters that are important to others and to retain only those things that affect his livelihood.—When the lad is pointed out in the center of a group of friends, Socrates recalls having seen him with his father, reports that the father had the same virtues as the son, asks the boy's name, is told that it is Theaetetus, and has him called over. It will be revealed soon that Socrates wants to examine Theaetetus's soul.

As with every interlocutor, Socrates will test Theaetetus by engaging him in a discussion of his opinions. Theaetetus is a *meirakion*, a "little lad." He is repeatedly addressed as *pai* in the dialogue, "child." He is said to be beardless and not fully grown. On the basis of these facts, we could guess that he is thirteen. However, he is handling his own money so he might be older. He could be as old as fifteen and still be small and beardless. Let us say that he is thirteen to fifteen, more likely fifteen. A youth of this age might be precocious and forming some views of his own. However, he is too young to have developed mature convictions independently. He undoubtedly has received many of his opinions from his teacher. Hence, to appreciate what Socrates will do with Theaetetus, one must start with a closer look at Theodorus.

Plato's portrait of Theodorus appears on the whole to render a negative judgment of him. Someone might object in advance that Plato could not have meant to create such an impression. There is an ancient tradition reported by Wilbur Knorr that Plato studied with Theodorus. Knorr even

---

8   Cf. Kenneth Dorter, *Form and Good in Plato's Eleatic Dialogues*, 69.

thinks that "Theodorus was the principal source for Plato's conception of geometry."[9] This would have made it unseemly for Plato to be critical of a master who had benefitted him greatly and whom he should have revered. By way of anticipating that objection, I answer that Plato was apt to assign both praise and blame where they were due. Further, if we stipulate for the sake of argument that Plato did study with Theodorus and acquired from him "his basic conception of the fields of mathematics . . . and a deep respect for matters of mathematical rigor,"[10] we can imagine that Plato also attempted to hold philosophic converse with Theodorus and received the kinds of rebuffs that he puts in the geometer's mouth in our dialogue.

Plato's sketch of Theodorus begins with the praise that is due. Socrates is made to affirm that young men are *justly* drawn to Theodorus on account of his geometry and for other reasons. In the play, Theodorus is portrayed as teaching geometric number theory. This is to say that he has transcended the gnomon arithmetic and geometry of the Pythagoreans and has instructively thought of numbers as geometric figures such as lines, squares, and cubes. Theodorus especially is depicted as applying this method to the study of incommensurable numbers and figures. Knorr credits Theodorus with a major role in the development of this field with rigorous proofs.[11] Plato also causes Socrates and Theaetetus to describe Theodorus as a teacher of astronomy, harmony, and calculation (or logistic, *logismos*). If this is a faithful picture, Theodorus probably preceded Archytas as a seminal contributor to these disciplines. Let us conclude that Theodorus's work in geometric number theory, incommensurability, astronomy, harmony, and *logismos* was excellent—but perhaps not wholly so. In Republic 527a–31d, Socrates criticizes geometers, astronomers, and investigators of harmony for turning the gazes of souls downward toward becoming rather than upward toward being. No scientists are exempted from this critique. If Theodorus taught Plato most of his geometry, he must have been one target of Socrates' criticism.

9   Wilbur Richard Knorr, *The Evolution of the Euclidean Elements: A Study of the Theory of Incommensurable Magnitudes and Its Significance for Early Greek Geometry*, 88.
10   Knorr, *Evolution*, 89.
11   Knorr, *Evolution*, 88–96.

We already have seen the first of Theodorus's negative features on display. The geometer is fearful and quick to suspect threats. He might like to dominate his students. He is opinionated about the criteria of beauty, which are either matters of taste or objective realities that lie outside his scientific competence. His overconfidence makes him tactless. That is, he is so certain of his non-mathematical judgments and probably so used to declaring his findings authoritatively that he is obtuse to human sensitivities. He also seems to be more interested in a boy's money than in his family or his potential role in the affairs of his city.

As Plato's sketch is developed, it also becomes apparent that Theodorus has intellectual limitations. Although he is a justly lauded scientist, Theodorus resists rising above his geometry. He dislikes philosophy, asserting that he turned away from its "bare words" to geometry early in life (165a2). Like some scientists of our era, he seems to regard discussions of the good, the just, the beautiful, and virtue as empty blather. He prefers to consider problems that he thinks can be handled with theorems that are the opposite of "bare" because they are proven. His opinion that his conclusions are not bare reflects an attitude described by Rebecca Goldstein as a belief in "the certainty of mathematics, the godlike infallibility it seems to bestow on its knowers."[12] Having shunned philosophy, Theodorus declines to participate in a search for higher truth, pleading that he is too old and unable to get used to such talk (146b). He also admits that he fears disgrace if he is refuted (165a–b). This means that he would rather preserve his image of infallibility than be freed of his errors. When Socrates shames him into the discussion against his will, he becomes angry and equates Socrates with Sciron and Antaeus, mythical marauding robbers and murderers who treated victims savagely (169a). He indirectly reveals that Socrates' probing of his views is unpleasant (177c). He cannot defend his opinions when Socrates challenges them. This does not inspire him to reform and become philosophic, as Polemarchus did. His views of the solidity and superiority of his science and his vexation with dialectic are clear symptoms of intellectual lotus-eating: complacency and irritable resistance to leaving for the

12 Rebecca Goldstein, *Incompleteness: The Proof and Paradox of Kurt Gödel,* 27.

philosopher's true home.[13] Plato-Socrates-Odysseus is in Lotus Land. As master of his school, Theodorus is the Lotus King.

At first glance, Theodorus also seems to be guilty of self-contradiction. Although he has scorned "bare words," he was a friend of Protagoras, a sophist who reveled in them (162a). (As a companion of Protagoras, he would have heard of the sophist's contretemps with Socrates. This would have inclined him to look askance on the philosopher. This is another reason to doubt that Theodorus and Socrates were friends prior to the latter's unexpected appearance in the geometry school.) Theodorus presumably has given Protagoras's book *Truth* to Theaetetus, who has read it often (152a). Although he has refused to participate in the conversation, he cannot refrain from barging into it when Socrates undertakes to criticize Protagoras (161a). He promptly backs out when Protagoras is attacked tellingly, declaring that he will not be party to the refutation of his friend (162a). He reenters it when Socrates scolds him for letting a child defend the sophist. He protests that Socrates runs his comrade down too much when Protagoras's teachings are about to be reduced to absurdity (171c). We wonder how a thinker who hates "bare speeches" could have befriended Protagoras, a windy intellectual, and how he could have mixed his geometry up with sophistry, passing that concoction on to his students. Perhaps there was something about *Truth* that struck Theodorus as scientific, thus acquitting him of inconsistency. We should look out for that. We also should observe that Theodorus's entrances and exits, his resentment of Socrates' attack on Protagoras, his anger at being opposed, and his classification of Socrates with criminal scourges like Sciron and Antaeus somewhat resemble the behavior of Anytus in Meno (89e–94e).

We may deduce the effects that Theodorus has had on Theaetetus. The

---

13 Goldstein writes: "Since the earliest days of the ancient Greeks, mathematical knowledge has seemed to be on the one hand the least problematic area of human knowledge, in fact the very model toward which all knowledge ought to aspire: certain and unassailable, in short, proved. . . . Yet, on the other hand, mathematical knowledge has seemed, to darker-souled epistemologists, highly problematic, its very certainty . . . making it suspect in warier eyes. How can any knowledge be certain and unassailable, in short: proved?" Although mathematics seems to be "perched on its topmost turret of *Reine Vernunft* [Pure Reason]," it has an Achilles heel, its intuition of its axioms, which can "insidiously lead us astray," 121, 123.

teacher doubtless has imparted to the student a wholesome love of scientific, mathematical inquiry and reasoning. All to the good. Simultaneously, Theodorus predictably has accustomed Theaetetus to looking downward at becoming rather than upward at being, leaving him unaware of the possibility and necessity of the latter. What is worse, this ruler of the Hellenic Lotus Land almost certainly has given the Socrates look-alike—seen as an allegorical comrade of Socrates-Odysseus—a taste of lotus and the boy will have developed an addiction to it, the lotus being the supposed certainty of mathematics, the respect that accrues to the status of a scientist, and Protagorean ideas. The task of making Theaetetus philosophic, or dragging him out of Lotus Land, will be difficult. It will require more than one talk to move a brilliant young geometer and an incipient Protagorean past complacency and attraction to the power of *Truth* to active philosophic seeking, so that Socrates cannot reasonably be blamed if he does not finish the job in a single sitting.

Socrates begins his examination of Theaetetus's soul in a way that eases him and us into an epistemological inquiry gradually. He tells Theaetetus that he wants to look at himself [as if in a mirror by looking at the boy] to see what sort of face he has, for Theodorus has said that they are look-alikes. Then he poses a hypothetical question. Suppose each of them owned a lyre. If Theodorus stated that the instruments were tuned alike, should they accept that or first consider whether Theodorus was skilled in music? The question is strange: it would seem that any non-musician with good hearing could tell whether two scales sounded alike. However, the nuances of sound might be such that musicians have superior ears for exact pitch. Perhaps assuming that, Theaetetus reveals that he defers to expertise by agreeing that the issue of Theodorus's musicality should be considered. Socrates transfers the problem to Theodorus's comparison of their faces. Should they consider whether Theodorus is good at drawing [before trusting his statement about their looks]? This query seems utterly preposterous: there are no human beings who doubt that they can tell whether people look alike or whether a pair of twins look identical. However, even here things might depend on the definition of "alike." If visually observable proportions must be minutely exact rather than merely close to meet the standard, it could also be necessary to submit Theodorus's judgment about the similarity of faces to the graphic artist. Perhaps thinking that, Theaetetus hesitantly agrees that Socrates' suggestion seems right. Socrates has alerted the boy to the problem of what constitutes expertise, implicitly accusing Theodorus of having rendered judgments about beauty without sufficient attention to criteria and prompting Theaetetus to reject Theodorus's authority to address matters outside his competence. A Theodorus who hates being disgraced must now be annoyed.

Socrates heads off an explosion of wrath by inducing Theaetetus to pronounce Theodorus skilled at geometry, astronomy, logistic, music, and many additional things bearing on education. Then he risks ire again. He suggests that it is not worthwhile to pay attention to Theodorus if he makes statements about similarities of bodies. He also inquires whether someone who heard the geometer praising a soul for virtue and wisdom should be eager to closely examine the one who is praised and whether the lauded person should eagerly display himself. Socrates thus declares that Theodorus has nothing valuable to say about bodies and further implies in a barely disguised way that Theodorus's appraisals of souls need verification. He is denying Theodorus's authority to judge either bodies or souls. The reason why Theodorus is rejected as an authority on souls is hinted at by Socrates' query. Socrates' indication that Theodorus has praised someone for virtue and wisdom (*aretên te kai sophian*) is false. Theodorus had celebrated Theaetetus for *eumathia*, courage, gentleness, and liberality but he had not mentioned *sophia*. Socrates has hinted that he is the rightful judge of souls rather than Theodorus, who misses the crucial criterion, capacity to progress toward the virtue for which philosophers yearn, wisdom. Theodorus now is fuming if he is listening carefully.

Theaetetus agrees that someone praised for virtue and wisdom should be examined and display himself. Socrates replies that Theaetetus is the individual in question, for Theodorus has praised many people to Socrates but never anyone so highly as Theaetetus. If Theodorus has, in fact, commended people to Socrates, this must have occurred during their occasional talks about who is doing what to advance science, for Theodorus never before has been asked by Socrates to recommend a student. Theaetetus tries to deflect Theodorus's compliment by suggesting that his master is joking. Socrates retorts that this is not Theodorus's way. (We now add humorlessness to Theodorus's negative traits.) Theaetetus must not say that Theodorus is jesting or the man will be forced to testify under oath, for no one would accuse him of perjury. This looks like Socratic banter until we remember that Socrates calls the grim charges of Meletus a joke in Apology

(27a) and that Meletus is required to testify under oath but is not charged with perjury. The humorless Theodorus is being assimilated to both of Socrates' prosecutors, Anytus and Meletus.

Socrates knows that wisdom, the highest virtue, is not part of Theaetetus's makeup. This does not imply that Theaetetus is corrupted. "Only god" is wise (Phaedrus 278d4). All human beings need to strive for wisdom. Socrates proposes to give Theaetetus the opportunity to begin that striving. One necessary step in that direction is the destruction of erroneous conceptions of wisdom that prevent people from starting the quest for it. To that end, Socrates asks Theaetetus if he learns geometry from Theodorus. The reply is yes. Astronomy, harmony, and logistic too? Yes. Then Socrates claims to be baffled about a little something that should be investigated with Theaetetus's help and with the aid of everyone present. He inquires whether learning is growing wiser about that which is learned. The boy responds: "How not?" So, if people are wise in that of which they have knowledge (*epistêmê*), are knowledge and wisdom (*epistêmê kai sophia*) the same? Theaetetus says yes. It is true that *epistêmê* and *sophia* are synonyms in Attic Greek, both words referring to "know-how," technical skill, in common parlance. On this level, Theaetetus's answer is correct. However, in Socrates' philosophy, *sophia* has long since become something more than knowing how to perform this or that technical task, such as making shoes or building ships or solving quadratic equations. The word has come to represent something that only gods have, something on the order of "knowing how to live rightly." In this light, Theaetetus's reply is wrong. Knowledge and wisdom should not be conflated. It is troubling that Theaetetus thinks that learning Theodorus's sciences is the acquisition of *sophia*. This impediment to his striving for it must be removed. Socrates gets to work. He asserts that something puzzles him: he does not know "just exactly what knowledge happens to be" (*epistêmê ho ti pote tugchanei on*). The bulk of the dialogue will investigate that issue. If Socrates can reduce Theaetetus to *aporia* about *epistêmê*, demonstrating that he has no solid grasp of what it is, this might persuade him that he does not understand wisdom either, thus initiating his search for it.

The epistemological study has begun in earnest. Regrettably, it has started in a way that renders it questionable and hard to understand. There are two difficulties. First, the query might be ill-conceived. Knowledge might be definable but it also might be something too elemental to define.

In that case, the quest would lead to blind alleys.[14] This would not automatically imply that Socrates (Plato) is grossly incompetent. It is possible that his purpose is precisely to prove that knowledge is undefinable, or at least that it is undefinable in ways that Theodorus and other geometers suppose. If that were his intention, his strategy could be to start with the hypothesis that knowledge is definable, at least in Theodorus's ways, and to prove the assumption untenable. Contrary to most modern interpretations of Theaetetus, then, what we would have in the dialogue would be not Plato's failed attempt to define knowledge but his limited survey and refutation of the Hellenic geometers' definitions of it, this as part of his analysis of the philosophic-scientific- political issues that concern him. Thus, doubts about the propriety of the inquiry do not suffice to dismiss it. We must follow it, provisionally assuming that knowledge is definable.

However, this brings up the other, more severe difficulty: Socrates' question is extremely vague. What does Socrates expect to learn by inquiring what *epistêmê* is? What does his "what" mean? Amirthanayagam David speculates that: "Perhaps Socrates is asking for an account that connects a name to a nature."[15] That might be so. But what could be envisaged as a "nature of knowledge?" Does Socrates want to be informed about a kind of material "stuff" out of which knowledge is made (for example, that it is "neural structures in brains"[16])? On the contrary, does he wish to be told about an immaterial "stuff" out of which *epistêmê* is made (for example, that it is a particular kind of the mind's or soul's consciousness, something along the lines of concepts we see in the simile of the divided line in Republic 509d–11d)? Or is he not thinking about a "stuff" of knowledge at all? Instead, does he want Theaetetus to identify an act or operation of the mind or soul that "knowing" is, such as "abstraction of essences" or "observation" or "logical inference" or "counting?" Or does he desire to establish which conditions of evidence and logic propositions must meet before they can be classified as *epistêmê*, the satisfied conditions being something like a formal cause that constitutes

---

14 I share this qualm with Bostock, *Plato's "Theaetetus,"* 36–37.

15 Amirthanayagam David, "Plato and the Measure of the Incommensurable," *The St. John's Review* 46:1 (2000), 5.

16 A definition of ideas in George Lakoff and Rafael E. Nuñez, *Where Mathematics Comes From: How the Embodied Mind Brings Mathematics into Being*, 33.

knowledge? Or does he not embrace any of these senses of "what" because he suspects that *epistêmê* is not something in itself but rather a catch-all name for different varieties of awareness? Neither Theaetetus nor Theodorus pushes Socrates to clarify his "what." When leading contemporary scholars come to 145e9–46a1, they generally are silent about the issue too.[17] Socrates, Theodorus, and Theaetetus never distinguish possible senses of a nature of knowledge: they indiscriminately lump several together. Modern analysts appear to assume a priori that Socrates is speaking about whichever sense of *epistêmê* interests them. So, I read the dialogue and the secondary literature with the disquieting feeling that I am not quite sure what is being sought or which kind of definition should be preferred. This is not necessarily a critique of Plato. Socrates might leave the meaning of his "what" open deliberately to see whether Theaetetus will respond with thoughtful puzzlement.

Having raised the question of what *epistêmê* is, Socrates inquires which of his auditors will speak up. He proposes a game calculated to animate children. Anyone who errs will have to sit down and be donkey and whoever solves the problem will be our king, with the right to order us to answer any question he pleases. Everyone present is stumped. Socrates asks why all are silent. He turns to Theodorus expressing concern, hoping that his keenness to make friends by conversing has not been rude. Although Socrates is being playful, he means what he says about friendship. Plato the playwright regards the conversion of young men to the good and the just as a means to bringing them ever into a state of friendship. He learned this from Socrates (Seventh Letter, 328de, 324e). Theodorus excuses Socrates from the charge of rudeness but he asks him to put his question to one of the boys, for he is not used to such talk and he is too old to become accustomed to it. He urges Socrates to improve Theaetetus by quizzing him. Theodorus is being evasive. It should not escape notice that he is no longer the king of his school. He is just another ass because he, like his students, has had to meet Socrates' question with silence. This cannot sit well with him. Plato's dramatized

---

17 See the writers referenced in note 4 above. Bostock, *Plato's "Theaetetus,"* 36, recognizes the question but he declares the idea of an essence of knowledge too vague for analysis and does not pursue the issue. Paul Stern speculates that Socrates has "inerrancy" and "right answers" in mind, *Knowledge and Politics*, 54. But are these not mere synonyms for knowledge?

confrontation between Socratic philosophy and Greek science has intensified with his portrayal of a leading scientist who cannot say what knowledge is.

When Socrates puts his question to Theaetetus and when the boy is coaxed to answer, he says that *epistêmê* is what Theodorus teaches: geometry, astronomy, harmony, and logistic, plus arts such as cobbling. This grouping of the mathematical sciences with productive *technai* is not surprising: Theaetetus is thinking of the normal Attic sense of *epistêmê* and giving examples of all the things that appear to him to represent "know-how." He probably also is exhibiting some complacency about his "perch on the topmost turret of *Reine Vernunft*"—showing symptoms of lotus-eating. With reference to my problem about the meaning of Socrates' question, Theaetetus apparently is assuming that "know-how" is an immaterial essence of knowledge and that he can satisfy Socrates by giving him a more or less exhaustive list of the kinds of "know-how." There are two things missing from his reply. First, his explicit inventory does not explain *epistêmê* as anything other than what the Hellenic concept means, "know-how." Failing that, it is an implicit circular statement that *epistêmê* is *epistêmê* and nothing has been gained. Second, while giving a list of types of *epistêmê*, it provides no criteria for membership in the set. This leaves open the possibility that *epistêmê* is a catch-all name for arts with no common essence. It is doubtful that Theaetetus believes that, for he does not argue that *epistêmê* is whatever anybody declares it is—at least not yet. He probably has criteria for determining what is or is not *epistêmê* that need to be articulated. Those standards would specify the nature of knowledge.

Socrates tries to ascertain whether Theaetetus does have criteria for defining knowledge by responding to him ironically. He praises the boy for his generosity in offering many, varied things when a single, simple one was desired. Theaetetus is mystified so Socrates explains. He points out that Theaetetus's answer lists types of *epistêmê* or arts and the objects that correspond to them. However, he was not asking for an inventory of the *technai* and their objects. What he wished was to discern "knowledge itself—whatever that is" (*epistêmên auto ho ti pot' estin*). For example, to specify what clay (or mud) is, it would not do to say potters' clay and oven-makers' clay and brick-makers' clay, as if we already knew what clay is. That would be ridiculous, right?

Theaetetus says "perhaps." He is not perfectly sure that his answer was laughable. There are modern commentators who doubt that too. To take one example, John McDowell maintains that "Socrates has not shown that a list of instances or kinds of knowledge cannot be of any use in answering the question 'What is knowledge?' . . . It cannot be assumed that in all cases there will be an answer to the question 'What do instances or kinds of X have in common?' which is more informative than, simply, 'They are all instances or kinds of X.' Where there is not, the question 'What is X?' cannot be answered by a single formula of the sort Socrates requires; and it would seem that an understanding of what X is should be approached (if at all) precisely via instances or kinds of X."[18] I would reply to McDowell that his possibly most informative answer is not informative. It does not tell us why anyone would decide that any given X is an instance of X and, thus, it leaves us with the conclusion that X is merely a name arbitrarily applied to things haphazardly.[19] This might be true of the concept knowledge but if it is, Socrates' inquiry would already be finished. Also, the more interesting case would be that Theaetetus does have grounds for selecting instances of *epistêmê* and that these criteria need to be articulated. As I have said, Socrates is trying to find out whether he does have standards.

Socrates encourages Theaetetus to specify his criteria for determining what *epistêmê* is by offering him an example: The simple thing to say about clay is that it is earth mixed with liquid. Socrates could be implying with his model that Theaetetus should define knowledge as a sort of material substance out of which it is made, driving us toward a conclusion such as "*epistêmê* is neural structures in brains." However, he might be speaking figuratively and have an immaterial "stuff of knowledge" in mind, a particular form of consciousness that could be defined in terms of a luminosity of some power of the mind or soul and its objects. Theaetetus thinks that he now understands Socrates. He supposes that Socrates is asking for something similar to a discovery that he and young Socrates, who is standing here, recently made. Socrates asks to be told about it. Theaetetus gives details. The boy's explanation eventually will move away from a material interpretation of Socrates' example and toward an immaterial one.

---

18   McDowell, *Plato: "Theaetetus,"* 114, 115. See also Bostock, *Plato's "Theaetetus,"* 32–36.

19   Bostock, who accuses Plato of error, *Plato's "Theaetetus,"* 34, merits the same reply.

Theaetetus's account rests on an epistemological assumption that does not appear to me to be generally noticed. Theaetetus begins by saying *"Peri dynameôn ti hêmin Theodôros hode egraphe tês te tripodos peri kai pentepodos apophainôn . . ."*[20] Sachs translates: "Theodoros here was diagraming something for us about potencies, demonstrating about the potential side of the three-foot square and about that of the five-foot square that . . ." For the moment, I want to focus on the phrase *"egraphe . . . apophainôn."* (Other terms in the statement will be clarified below.) The best philology regarding Theaetetus's locution renders it as "diagraming . . . demonstrating." I believe that it is a hard and fast rule among contemporary geometers that diagrams do not prove anything: demonstrations consist in logical deductions from axiomatic definitions while drawings merely facilitate understanding. This precept did not quite hold hard and fast among the ancient geometers. Wilbur Knorr, a formidable historian of Greek geometry, writes that: "From Aristotle we learn that the function of the diagram is to make the truth of a fact or a theorem obvious. . . . Thus, constructions were not mere accessories to mathematical arguments; their purpose was to make evident the truth of the theorem under investigation." Knorr supports this argument with a plethora of quotations from ancient commentators to the effect that "diagrams and theorems are the same" and he establishes that this was Plato's usage too by appealing to Meno.[21] Thus, what Theaetetus is declaring with his *"egraphe . . . apophainôn"* is that he and his friend were taught what Theodorus was trying to convey more or less immediately upon viewing his drawings. We all have had the same experience, or thought that we had it, in geometry classes when we looked at lines that intersect parallel lines. The congruence of the opposite angles seemed self-evident from the drawings. No further proof seemed necessary (even though a weak one was supplied).

I turn now to *dynameôn*, a plural form of *dynamis*. Liddell and Scott translate *dynamis* as "power," "strength," "might," and the like. Sachs makes *dynameôn* "potencies," observing that powers in this sense are what the Megarians denied. He adds that, in geometry, the term refers to the power of a line to generate a square. Knorr has a different view of the word. He

---

20 The Oxford edition deletes *apophainôn* for unexplained reasons. Knorr shows why it should be retained, *Evolution*, 70.

21 Knorr, *Evolution*, 72–73.

maintains that it does not primarily mean "surd" or "square root." Rather, "throughout Greek mathematical literature, the word *dynamis* signifies 'second power.'" Knorr also demonstrates that this usage of *dynamis* is "common in Plato's works." However, in Theaetetus's parlance, the word takes on a different coloration again. Originally, Theaetetus does intend it to signify "second power," as when he refers to *hê tripous dynamis*, "the power three feet in value." Eventually, he restricts the term to the second powers that are squares with sides incommensurable with the unit side. Then he uses *dynamis* as an abbreviation for the "line which is incommensurable with the unit length, but whose square is commensurable with the unit area," an "unfortunate" shorthand that gives the impression that *dynamis* means its opposite, "square root," "surd."[22] Myles Burnyeat agrees that *dynameis* (nominative plural) normally means squares constructed by multiplying line segments (numbers) by themselves.[23] The dictionary definitions of *dynamis*, Sachs' "potencies," "second powers," "squares," and Theaetetus's idiosyncratic transformation of the meaning of the word all must be kept in mind while interpreting his mathematical report. Eventually all come into play.

Theaetetus's first remark must be quoted in full. (I have altered the translation slightly.) It clearly does not pertain to the numbers four, nine, and sixteen:

> Theodorus here was diagraming something for us about powers [squares], demonstrating about the three foot and the five foot [power or square] that the side is not commensurable in length with that of the one foot and demonstrating in this way as he picked out each of them one by one up to the seventeen foot; at that one for some reason [or in a certain way, *pôs*] he got tangled up (*enescheto*).

Modern commentators generally err by failing to inquire into how Theodorus was doing his demonstrations. This information almost certainly is essential to an understanding of the first definition of knowledge that

22 Knorr, *Evolution*, 65–69.
23 Myles Burnyeat, "The Philosophical Sense of Theaetetus' Mathematics," *Isis*, 489–513.

Theaetetus will offer. To acquire it, we must consult the excellent works of Wilbur Knorr and Amirthanayagam David, who amends Knorr's reasoning in ways that are a little more closely attuned to nuances of the Greek.

Heeding Theaetetus's account, Knorr first derives conditions that any reconstruction of Theodorus's proofs must meet. In condensed, summary form, these conditions are as follows: (1) The proofs must be demonstrably valid. (2) The presentation of the proofs by special cases (some or all numbers three through seventeen) must be necessitated by the method employed. (3) Each demonstration must apply to an infinite number of cases. (4) The proofs may not rely anachronistically on Theaetetus's contributions to them or on his later discoveries but they must presuppose results of the earlier Pythagorean gnomon geometry. (5) The proofs must represent numbers as geometric magnitudes. (6) There must be a non-arbitrary mathematical reason why Theodorus got tangled in the case of seventeen so that he could not sustain a proof of it.[24]

Knorr painstakingly builds a foundation for Theodorus's proofs by demonstrating several elegant theorems about the properties of Pythagorean number triples with gnomon arithmetic and geometry. (Pythagorean triples are the numbers in the equation a2 + b2 = c2.) I cannot summarize the proofs in detail but I can list the theorems essential to Theodorus's work in algebraic form:

Theorem V.11 (chapter five, theorem eleven in Knorr's book): Let any odd number N be chosen. Then N, (N2 - 1)/2, (N2 + 1)/2 satisfy the Pythagorean condition.

Theorem V.12: Let any even number M be chosen. Then M, (M/2)2 - 1, (M/2)2 + 1 satisfy the Pythagorean condition.

Theorem V.13: Given the Pythagorean triple A, B, C, if two of the terms are even, the third is also even.

Theorem V. 13a: Given the Pythagorean triple A, B, C, if one of the terms is odd, then in fact two are odd and one is even.

Theorem V.14: If in a given Pythagorean triple the largest number C is even, then all three terms are even.

---

24 Knorr, *Evolution*, 96, 81–83. Knorr argues against a reading of Theaetetus's language that sees Theodorus as "stopping" before, at, or after seventeen capriciously. He persuades me.

Theorem V.14a: Given a Pythagorean triple A, B, C, if one of the terms is odd, then the largest term C is odd, and of the numbers A and B, one is odd and the other even.

Corollary: If the largest term C is divisible by four, then so are A and B.

Theorem V.15: Given the Pythagorean triple A, B, C, in which not all three terms are divisible by four, then either A or B must be divisible by four and it is the only such term. . . . Differences of odd squares in a triple are multiples of eight.[25]

Knorr shows that Theodorus could draw on these theorems and, in fact, that he had to do so as he moved to his own proofs. The next thing to observe, argued by David in another elegant reconstruction, is that Theodorus probably got his square numbers by considering right triangles formed by letting consecutive pairs of integers {b,c} = {1,2}, {2,3}, [3,4} . . . be the "b" leg and the hypotenuse of each. This produced triangles with sides {a} = J3, J5, J7, . . . J17, allowing for the construction of squares with values 3, 5, 7, . . . 17. David also reasons persuasively that Plato's language indicates that Theodorus used the three-foot square and the five-foot square as paradigm cases and that he probably restricted his proofs to the odd-numbered series of squares (some or all of 3, 5, 7, 9, 11, 13, 15, 17), omitting the proof for six that Knorr provides.[26]

I return to Knorr. He demonstrates with seven theorems that Theodorus's lesson cannot apply to isosceles triangles. Then he provides algorithms for the construction of right triangles of the sort arrived at by David. Next he argues that Theodorus used metric geometry and reductio ad absurdum theorems to prove the incommensurability of the sides of squares with values three and five with the unit side. The reductios commence by postulating that each of the sides "a" in question is commensurable with the unit side. Theorem VI.8 addresses the case of the square of value three. It posits a triangle of sides A, B, and 2B (whole multiples of a = J3, b = 1, c = 2). If A is commensurable with the unit, there must exist a ratio A:B such that the A and B are in the same ratio (not one to one, which would be

25 Knorr, *Evolution*, 155–59. The reader is strongly encouraged to study Knorr's proofs.

26 David, "Plato and the Measure," 10, 7–10.

the isosceles case). These sides may be taken in least terms. By theorem V. 14, the hypotenuse is even so all three sides are even. But choosing A and B in least terms means that at least one of these sides must be odd. Hence, that side is both even and odd. The absurdity proves that A cannot be commensurable with the unit. This proof does not work for the case of the square of value five. Knorr's theorem VI.10 treats that one. It posits the triangle of sides A, 2B, and 3B (whole multiples of a = J5, b = 2, c = 3), the sides in reduced terms. Again, there must exist a ratio A:B such that A and B are in the same ratio. Then, if B is even, the hypotenuse is also even and all three sides are even by theorem V.14. Then A:B is not in reduced terms so B is not even. But if B is odd, 2B is even and by theorem V.15 it is divisible by four, making it even. The absurdities demonstrate that A cannot be commensurable with the unit. Knorr provides further theorems demonstrating the generality of these results for numbers of the form 4N + 3 and 8N + 5, to which the methods for three and five respectively apply.[27]

David follows Knorr in his presentation of the three-foot case. He generalizes the result not by repeating Knorr's theorem V.9 about numbers of the form 4N + 3 but by noting that VI.8 must apply to all triangles with even hypotenuses. He deviates from Knorr in his presentation of the five-foot square. He observes that this case presents the only alternative paradigm produced by his numerical pairs (those with odd hypotenuses). The pairs available are {2,3}, {4,5}, {6,7} etc. yielding sides A = J5, J9, J13, etc. He posits a triangle of leg A, leg even number times B, hypotenuse odd number times B (essentially the same multiples of a = J5, b = 2, c = 3 envisaged by Knorr). Assuming that A is commensurable with the unit, least terms for the ratio A:B again are required and one or both of the numbers is odd. If B is even, the hypotenuse is even and A must be even (V. 14) so B must be odd, an absurdity. If A is odd, B2 equals a difference of odd squares (B2 = C2 - A2, by Knorr V.14a), which David says could only be true if it were a multiple of eight and sixteen (by Knorr V. 10, V. 15, V. 7), meaning that it would have a side that was a multiple of four. If C2 is odd, B must be an odd number and the B side is even times odd and is itself a multiple of four. So, the number pairs must be examined to see whether any of the even numbers satisfies that condition. If the condition is not

27   Knorr, *Evolution*, 174–87.

met, A can be neither even nor odd. The condition is met for {4,5} and A (3) is commensurable with the unit. The condition is not met for {2,3} or {6,7}. David observes that these examples establish the paradigmatic character of the five-foot case.[28] Together, the arguments of Knorr and David also prove that the method used by Theodorus necessitated his piecemeal presentation of the cases.

Now we come to the case of the seventeen-foot square in which Theodorus got tangled up. Knorr approaches the case by proving incommensurability theorems for the number six and for numbers of the form $2(2N + 1)$ and $S = 4N$ (of which some will have sides commensurable with the unit and some will not). He says that the only kind of numbers left to consider are those of the form $8N + 1$, of which seventeen is the paradigm instance. His task is to use Theodorus's method to prove that the side of the seventeen-foot square is incommensurable with the unit. He constructs a triangle of sides $a = \sqrt{17}$, $b = 8$, and $c = 9$ and a corresponding triangle of sides A, 8B, and 9B with sides in reduced terms. Hoping to do another reductio theorem, he assumes that A is commensurable with the unit. If B is odd, the hypotenuse is odd, 8B is even and divisible by four, and A would be odd. The Pythagorean condition is satisfied, so A could be commensurable with the unit. In fact, numbers of the form $8N + 1$ do produce several sides commensurable with the unit side. Theodorus's method fails.[29] David follows Knorr.[30] — All these proofs satisfy the conditions Knorr placed on any reconstruction of Theodorus's work. I therefore believe that we know what Theaetetus was being taught.

Theaetetus's account resumes. The boy reports that it occurred to him and his friend that the *dynameis* seemed to be unlimited in multitude. They decided to try to gather up these powers (squares) "into one" (*eis hen*), in which they could *prosagoreusomen* them all. Liddell and Scott translate *prosagoreuô* as "address, accost, call by name." Most translations of our dialogue have Theaetetus and young Socrates wishing to find "one name" or "term" by which to refer to all the *dynameis*. Professional classicists know Greek far better than I do so I suppose that this reading is correct. However, the boys

28 David, "Plato and the Measure," 11–13.
29 Knorr, *Evolution*, 191.
30 David, "Plato and the Measure," 14.

already had the name *dynameis* for all the *dynameis*. Why did they need another? And why did they wish to gather the *dynameis* "into one" when they were already "one" insofar as they were *dynameis*? I doubt that the boys went on a semantic or taxonomical quest. I suggest that they had a mathematical reason for their venture: They were interested only in those *dynameis* with sides incommensurable with the unit side. As mathematicians, they were dissatisfied with Theodorus's need to analyze these *dynameis* piecemeal with different methods. They hoped to *prosagoreuein* them all in the sense that they desired to "address" (or "approach?") them all under one mathematical rubric. They wanted to "gather them into one" in the sense that they desired to find a single way to prove the incommensurability of all their sides with the unit side, disposing of the whole infinite set in one fell swoop.[31]

Socrates asks Theaetetus if he and his friend found what they wanted. The boy thinks so. He says that they divided all numbers in two. One sort had "the potency to come into being as an equal times an equal by the shape of a square." They called this variety "square and equilateral." Socrates praises the result. The other type, found between the square numbers, were "three and five and every number without the potency to come into being as an equal times an equal, though it does come into being as a greater times a lesser or a lesser times a greater." They named this kind "oblong." So, every number was either a square or an oblong number. The boys called the sides of the squares (or square numbers) *mêkos* (lengths) and those of the rectangles (or oblong numbers) *dynameis*. (This is where the confounding of *dynamis* qua square with square root and surd comes in.) Socrates celebrates the result as "the best in human power" (*arista g' anthrôpôn*), leaving open the possibility that gods could do better. As a feat of taxonomy, the boys' move is not earth-shaking. However, as I argued above, they did not see the issue as taxonomic. Knorr nimbly proceeds to his theorem VII.6: "If a square contains an integral number of unit areas, and if that number is a square integer, then the side of the square will be commensurate with the unit line; but if that number is non-square, then the side will be incommensurable with the unit." He proves the theorem with dispatch, rigorously.[32] Sachs thinks that Socrates was pleased with the boys because he

31 McDowell suggests this interpretation with his translation of the passage.
32 Knorr, *Evolution*, 225, 228.

foresaw the easy demonstration.[33] Knorr and David develop the consequences of their definitions further at great length, mentioning numerous subsequent applications found in Euclid.[34] Plato's drama has attributed a significant geometric advance to the young Theaetetus.

Despite Socrates' praise, Theaetetus confesses that he cannot answer Socrates' question about knowledge in the same way as he handled *mêkos* and *dynamis*. In fact, it is necessary to bring up the issue of why Theaetetus thought in the first place that his work was relevant. That is, when Socrates suggested an explanation of *epistêmê* modeled on the definition of clay as earth mixed with liquid, why did Theaetetus think that Socrates might be looking for the sort of thing that he and young Socrates were discussing about Theodorus's proofs? What do all the theorems about incommensurability have to do with an essence of knowledge? Timothy Chappell cites a number of opinions about this question, ranging from David Bostock's view that the problem of defining knowledge "is not at all the same as the mathematical problem that Theaetetus and his friend young Socrates solved so successfully" to John McDowell's flat, unexplained claim that "the definition of powers arrived at by Theaetetus and the young Socrates is parallel to the sort of definition of knowledge that Socrates is asking for."[35] There is another problem: If Theaetetus's geometry actually was relevant, why did the boy doubt his ability to respond to Socrates' query?

I believe that these questions have related answers. Theaetetus first assumed that he had identified "oblongness" as the "essence" of an irrational *dynamis* so that his work was modeled on Socrates' picture of moist earth as the essence of clay. The obstreperous *dynamis* and clay are both depicted as being composed of a variety of substrate, oblongness, and wet earth respectively. (McDowell might have interpreted the argument in some such fashion.) This comparison of the substrates strikes me as problematic but it has a superficial formal appeal. However, Theaetetus promptly realized that he had not yet identified the substrate or "stuff" of knowledge that could be seen as analogous to oblongness and moist earth. He recognized

---

33 Sachs, note 5 to 148b.
34 Knorr, *Evolution*, chaps. vii–ix. David, "Plato and the Measure," 16–22.
35 Chappell, *Reading Plato's "Theaetetus,"* 40–41.

this as a profound problem with which he had struggled previously, when he heard tell of Socrates' habit of asking "what is" questions.

To understand Theaetetus's perplexity, we must realize that he still thinks that *epistêmê* is exemplified by all of Theodorus's sciences. This means that the reconstructions of Theodorus's demonstrations by Knorr and David are extremely important for our study. We may assume that the members of Plato's Academy were his primary audience. If it is true that he admitted no one to his school who had not learned geometry, his students would have had the Knorr-David proofs (or their equivalents) before their mind's eyes. Therefore, Plato could have let Theaetetus give an exceedingly terse account that would have made Academy personnel (but not us) fully aware of what was being discussed. To get some idea of Theaetetus's referents, modern readers really need to work through the Knorr-David proofs step by step. Doing so successfully, whether with much angst or as facilely as Theaetetus might have done, generates the following experience: the mind is compelled to assent to the proofs because they seem to be absolutely necessary, certain, and beautiful. One thinks one sees how irrational numbers must be and can only be understood and worked into an intelligible geometry (and perhaps, in the case of the crafts, one believes that one learns how things must be and can only be arranged if they are to function beautifully). This compulsion of the mind is accompanied by feelings of exhilaration, for it appears to offer a little portion of infallibility and unshakable reliability in this benighted and insecure existence of ours, a tiny share of what the gods have. The compulsion of the mind by sheer necessity, the certainty, the beauty, the joy, and the security had to be experienced across several sciences, as Theaetetus did, to be recognized as symptomatic. These experiences probably became the conclusive marks of *epistêmê* for Theaetetus, the criteria by which it is distinguished from ordinary awareness. But what *is* that possession that remains the same as one moves, perhaps, from geometry to harmony to astronomy to logistic to calculus to Einstein's equations to quantum mechanics? What is the common "stuff" of it or the mental operation by which it is acquired—if such a common feature exists? Theaetetus could suppose, whether rightly or wrongly, that such an essence or operation must exist as the cause of the recurrence of the same symptoms or signs. His aporia consisted in his inability to put his finger on it.

When Theaetetus confesses that he is at a loss to define knowledge in the same way that he defined irrational segments, and when Socrates encourages him to try nevertheless, indicating that the task really is not "small" but something for the ablest men, Theaetetus answers that he has heard of Socrates' questions previously and has struggled with them often, unsuccessfully. He cannot persuade himself that he has a satisfactory reply or that anyone else can give Socrates what he demands either. This worries him. His anxiety is both troublesome and promising. It is disturbing because it might show that Theaetetus thinks that everything should yield to geometric method and is frustrated by the problem's resistance to good science. It is encouraging because the lad is willing to admit failure and is bothered by his perplexity, which might mean that he can become philosophic.

Socrates answers Theaetetus's confession of aporia by informing him that he is pregnant. Theaetetus cannot comment on that: he can only say what he has experienced. We may take it that he has been reporting his experiences all along. Socrates begins an extensive explanation of his seemingly incomprehensible diagnosis. He says that as the son of a midwife he is a midwife too. He warns Theaetetus to keep mum about this. The admonishment must be playful: there are lots of little boys within earshot. Then, even more obscurely, Socrates implies that his maieutic activity accounts for the pregnant Theaetetus's bafflement. Theaetetus, simultaneously puzzled and intrigued, is eager to hear more. He will get a story that does not appear entirely coherent or logical on its face.

Socrates observes that only mothers who are now past bearing become midwives because the childless Artemis is the protectress of childbirth and this arrangement honors her. However, only women who have borne children may become midwives because Artemis judges that human beings cannot grasp *technai* that deal with matters outside their experience. Theaetetus, probably doubtfully, replies that this is "likely." Socrates' description of the qualifications of midwives is rather fancifully grounded in Homeric myths but that is not the main thing that raises eyebrows. His report rides roughshod over the fact that the experience of assisting births has nothing to do with that of giving birth. We also note that Artemis exempts herself from her own rule: although never a mother, she governs the midwife's art (and, in the myth, she helped her mother give birth to her brother Apollo painlessly, inspiring Greek women in labor to pray to her for similar luck).

Socrates goes further, declaring that midwives know better than anyone who is pregnant. He thus gives his own diagnosis of Theaetetus the stamp of authority. Midwives also can initiate labor pains by means of drugs and incantations—the opposite of what Artemis is asked to do but what Socrates implies he has done with Theaetetus—or they can make delivery easier or, if they so desire, they can cause miscarriages. What is not generally realized is that midwives are also the most skillful matchmakers because they know which unions will produce the best children. In this they resemble farmers who know which seeds should be planted where. However, they do not practice matchmaking because they fear being accused of bringing partners together unjustly and artlessly, as pimps do. Theaetetus might deduce that Socrates wants his maieutic *technê* kept secret because someone might charge him with causing his patients to associate with the wrong people— which has already happened in the case of Alcibiades.

Socrates keeps talking. He claims that the role played by female mid-wives is inferior to his. Women do not sometimes give birth to images rather than real children. His own maieutic art is similar to the female type but it differs in these ways: It is practiced on men, not women; it is prac-ticed on pregnant souls, not bodies, and it can test to determine whether a soul's offspring is an image (*eidôlon*) and a falsehood (*pseudos*) or a true (*alêthes*) one. Another difference is that Socrates is not only barren, like the older women practitioners, but sterile, having never brought forth anything in the way of wisdom. Thus, what people say about him is right, that he questions others but provides no answers of his own because he is not wise. We wonder whether Socrates has blasphemed by arrogating to himself a divine status: like Artemis, he can practice midwifery without having given birth. An alternative interpretation is that he can practice a maieutic *technê* devoted to males without being a "mother" because the masculine half of the art is ruled by a god rather than a goddess. In Apology, Socrates sug-gests that Artemis's brother Apollo governs his activity. Be that as it may, those whom the god permits make wonderful progress under Socrates, not because they have learned anything from him but because they have dis-covered fair things in themselves and brought them forth, the delivery being due to him and the deity. (The number of those thus favored by the god might be small. Only Plato and a few others come to mind.) Some of his patients—one thinks again of Alcibiades—have left him too soon and have aborted their true offspring owing to evil companionship. They have given birth to falsehoods and images that they valued more than truth. Some who have abandoned him have returned, begging to be taken back. He agrees if his daimon approves. Others who are not pregnant he sends to Prodicus and others who might do them some good. (Perhaps Prodicus is the least harmful sophist.)

Socrates wraps this eccentric discourse up by telling Theaetetus again that he is pregnant. He urges the boy to answer his questions. He will examine the answers and, if they prove to be images and untrue, he will quietly dispose of them. Theaetetus should not be angry if this occurs, as women are when their firstborn are taken away. Socrates reports that many have taken offense at him for throwing their infants away because they do not realize that he does it out of kindness—at the command of the god, as we remember, and no god is unkind (151d).

Plato has made Socrates go on about being a midwife at such great length that it is natural to wonder what was the point. Much of the commentary on this question has been a debate about Cornford's thesis that the midwife passages presuppose Plato's theory of *anamnesis* as awareness of Forms and that Plato intends Theaetetus as an indirect proof that knowledge cannot be defined without referring to the Forms. Cornford relies on plausible assumptions about the connections between Socratic *elegchus* and memory but he stretches exegetical ingenuity a long way and his once influential view now seems to have fallen out of favor.[36] More helpful is Burnyeat's remark that the passages are "an account of a method of education which is at the same time a method of doing philosophy."[37] Burnyeat does not elaborate. I would supplement his statement by arguing that the passages clearly presuppose a commitment to philosophic education as the reduction of souls to aporia. In chapter one, I have explained this pedagogical strategy as an attempt to purify souls, thus preparing them to receive the leaping flames of Plato's Seventh Letter. In this regard, I believe that Sayre has rightly seen a parallel between Socrates' courting of Theaetetus and the Seventh Letter's emphasis on *sunousia* (a keeping company with a teacher that more importantly is a keeping company with the subject matter that is necessary for

36 See Chappell, *Reading Plato's "Theaetetus,"* 46–47.
37 Burnyeat, *"The Theaetetus" of Plato*, 6–7.

illumination).[38] This leads to a frequently asked question: How could Socrates simultaneously claim to be competent to prepare souls for illumination and to lack wisdom himself? Wouldn't such a combination of competence with unwisdom be impossible? I think that the correct answer is foreshadowed by the absurdity of Socrates' argument that only women who have borne children can be midwives to women and by his exemption of himself from this rule in the analogous case of the "midwife" to male souls. Clearly, non-mothers can be midwives to women in labor. They need only to know how to get a baby out of the birth canal and examine it for defects that would lead to a decision for infanticide. Similarly, an unwise Socrates can be a midwife of souls. He needs only to know how to extract opinions from souls and inspect them for defects such as contradictions and nonsense that would justify rejecting them. After that he can ask whether anyone else has a promising suggestion, as he did after refuting Thrasymachus's argument that might is right at the end of Republic, Book I. These considerations prompt a final inference about the intention of the midwife passages. The midwife image indicates that Socrates now will do *nothing* but elicit and test Theaetetus's views to see whether they have fatal defects. Socrates can do this without affirming anything. The text effectively denies that Socrates will state or imply his own (or Plato's) positive doctrines.

For later reference in my discussions of Sophist and Statesman, it is interesting to observe that Socrates has explicitly grouped images (*eidôla*) with unrealities, impostures, and falsehoods and distinguished them from truth—at least four times.

Socrates has induced Theaetetus's labor. The lad offers his first thoughtful definition of knowledge: "[I]t seems (*phainetai*) to me that one who knows anything perceives (*aisthanesthai*) that which he knows, and as it appears (*phainetai*) to me now at least, knowledge is nothing other than perception (*aisthêsis*)." Theaetetus's statement has caused much consternation for modern scholars, who wonder whether it is seriously intended by Plato and what it means. For example, Bostock suggests that:

> [I]t must seem strange that Plato thought this claim even worth considering. Is it not *obvious* that we know a good deal about things

38   Sayre, *Plato's Literary Garden*, 17.

that we have not perceived, and indeed about things that could not in any ordinary sense be perceived? Moreover, the introduction to the dialogue seems designed to bring out just this point, for we are told that young Theaetetus is a mathematician, and has been engaged in the theory of *irrational* numbers. Surely he could not be supposing that he can *perceive* that certain ratios are irrational? Yet surely he would count this as something he knew?[39]

Bostock continues by saying: "There are various ways of understanding the thesis that knowledge is perception, and it will be useful to begin by making a few points about our ordinary use of the verbs 'know' and 'perceive.'" This leads him to the necessity of a distinction between knowing an object and knowing that something is the case and to an effort to assign one of these meanings to Theaetetus's remark.[40] McDowell followed the same path a decade earlier.[41] Burnyeat thinks that "'knowledge is perception' has a decidedly empiricist ring to it" and adds that "empiricism is the doctrine that all knowledge has its source in sense-perception."[42] Chappell comments that the boy's definition "is evidently meant as an identity statement." He surveys a number of efforts to establish the identity, starting with Liddell and Scott on *aisthêsis* (perception by the senses such as feeling, seeing, hearing, etc., also by the mind) and moving on to debates about whether Plato was referring to sense data or something else.[43]

How are we to solve the problem of what the definition means? I suggest that it is wrong to begin by considering "our ordinary use of the verbs 'know' and 'perceive'" or the "empiricist ring" that "perception" has for us. That is anachronistic. Neither is it useful in this case to look up *aisthanesthai* and *aisthêsis* in Liddell and Scott. The only justifiable approach is to consult the text to determine on the basis of Theaetetus's own words what it is that *he*—not someone else—could mean by his choice of terms. To do this, we must return to his statement that *epistêmê* was what Theodorus taught and

39   Bostock, *Plato's "Theaetetus,"* 30.
40   Bostock, *Plato's "Theaetetus,"* 41.
41   McDowell, *Plato: "Theaetetus,"* 118.
42   Burnyeat, *"The Theaetetus" of Plato*, 10.
43   Chappell, *Reading Plato's "Theaetetus,"* 53–55.

his report that the master was "drawing . . . demonstrating." In those remarks, Theaetetus points to pieces of knowledge that he acquired—let us
restrict our focus to Theodorus's theorems—and says how he got them—
they were demonstrated to him.

What happened here was complex. Theaetetus was shown diagrams.
He was led through the reasoning about the properties of Pythagorean
number triples and the absurd consequences of the postulates that the sides
of the three-, five-, seven-, eleven-, and thirteen-foot *dynameis* were commensurable with the unit side. He was shown the anomaly of the seventeen-foot square. He grasped the relationships of all the lines, triangles,
squares, and numbers in the graphics and the relationships of these things
established by the reasoning more or less immediately, perhaps in a manner
similar to that in which a Grand Master "sees" the next several score possible moves on a chess board all at once. He experienced the necessity, certainty, beauty, and security that I have noted. Thinking all this over, he
decided that Theodorus's theorems were what he knew, that he knew them
by virtue of instantly grasping the import of the diagrams and logic, that
"perceiving" was an apt name to give to that operation of his mind, that
"perception" was what he possessed as a result of his mental act, and, hence,
that *epistêmê* consists in *aisthêsis* (thus conceived).

Although *aisthanesthai* and *aisthêsis*, perceiving and perception, have
other connotations in Attic Greek and modern English, we are obliged to
understand Theaetetus's use of the words in the way that the text suggests
and to refrain from assigning to his concepts the other senses that people
attach to them. Therefore, contrary to Bostock's doubts, Theaetetus surely
did mean that he "perceived" that the oblong numbers were irrational. As
the boy named his mental act and its product "perceiving" and "perception,"
it did not occur to him to distinguish knowing an object from knowing that
something is the case because his perceiving did both at once. He knew
some objects (lines, triangles, squares, cubes) and he knew what was the
case about them (that certain lines were incommensurable with the unit
line, etc.) with the same movement of his intellect. Or so it seemed to him.

So, Theaetetus has defined *epistêmê* both in terms of an act of his mind
(perceiving, the more or less instantaneous grasping of something demonstrated) and in terms of an immaterial "stuff" that becomes the mind's possession (perception: awareness of numbers, figures, and their necessary

relationships). I assume that Socrates understands all this. Thus, he must know that Theaetetus's account is no straw man. However haltingly it was made, Theaetetus's attempt at a definition of knowledge has substance and is worth considering.

Socrates praises Theaetetus for speaking up and suggests an examination of his definition to see whether it is a wind-egg. Then he turns the boy's account around. Theaetetus had asserted that knowledge is perception but Socrates asks him if he thinks that perception is knowledge. It has been objected that the two formulas are not logically equivalent: *epistêmê* could be *aisthêsis* without all *aisthêsis* being *epistêmê*. However, Theaetetus goes along with the reversal. To him, "perception" and "knowledge" evidently are two names for the same reality, the former serving as a definition of the latter because it more effectively evokes a picture of the immediate grasp of objects and their relationships that he experienced. Socrates replies with a complicated argument over dozens of pages. He declares that Theaetetus's account is based on a saying of Protagoras. Then he grounds the Protagorean maxim on Heraclitus's core doctrine. He gets Theaetetus to assent to both moves. Then, shaming Theodorus into answering him, he demolishes Heraclitus and Protagoras in turn in order to refute Theaetetus. It is not obvious that Socrates' procedure is warranted. I have just explained Theaetetus's definition on the basis of his grasp of objective and apparently eternal geometric truths without having had to involve Protagoras and Heraclitus. So why does Socrates make Theaetetus's definition dependent on them?

The standard answer to this question has been proposed by Myles Burnyeat and Timothy Chappell. They maintain that there are two arguable interpretations of Socrates' behavior, one of which is probably the right understanding of "Plato's strategy." The first, which Burnyeat calls "Reading A," assumes that Plato regards the epistemology of Protagoras and the metaphysics of Heraclitus as true of sensible things, which are in perpetual flux. "Perception" is consciousness of this flux and the objects in it. It has no access to the Forms, the only things that are eternally stable. These always stable realities are the only things we can know, for the objects in the flux come and go in a twinkling, leaving nothing behind to know. This refutes Theaetetus's definition. The second interpretation, Burnyeat's "Reading B," holds that Plato entirely rejects the ideas of Protagoras and Heraclitus. He causes Theaetetus to accept their theories because an account of *epistêmê* as *aisthêsis* could be true only if those theories were true. When Theaetetus assents to the theories, his definition is exposed to a modus tollens refutation that controverts Heraclitus and Protagoras by subjecting each to a reductio ad absurdum. Chappell follows Burnyeat, calling Reading A the "Unitarian Reading" and Reading B the "Revisionist reading." Burnyeat opts for Reading B or, perhaps, for an unexplained "middle way" based on a "less restrictive definition of perception." Chappell prefers Reading A, the Unitarian reading, crucially changed to allow the objects in the flux to remain stable long enough to be known as participants in the Forms. There is much at stake in this disagreement. Chappell writes: "On the Revisionist reading, the strategy of the discussion of D1 [Theaetetus's definition] is to move us towards a one-world Platonism, a view which will imply that sensible phenomena have to fall under the same general metaphysical theory as intelligible phenomena." Reading B is "revisionist" because it has Plato changing his mind, repudiating the two-world ontology of Republic. Its rival, the Unitarian reading, upholds a two-world Platonism in which Forms are the true or fundamental realities—pending a perhaps absolutely new Platonism that will emerge in Sophist.[44] Although Burnyeat and Chappell are at loggerheads, they share the view that Plato brings Protagoras and Heraclitus into the discussion because he wants to tailor his epistemology to his current metaphysical doctrine. To that extent they agree with Cornford.

These suggestions about Socrates' conduct and Plato's strategy are erudite but they ignore three facts: First, Socrates announces in his "midwife" speech that he will examine and evaluate Theaetetus's views, promising nothing more. I have already noted that he could test the opinions for internal flaws without articulating or implying positive doctrines. Second, Socrates denies in his "midwife" discourse that he teaches anybody anything. He repeats this denial in his Apology. Third, Plato asserts in his Seventh Letter that there never has been and never will be a writing of his on the serious things. These facts militate against the assumption that Plato uses Theaetetus to bolster his metaphysics du jour. I also observe that Burnyeat and Chappell read their modern ideas of "perception" into Theaetetus's thought rather than trying to ascertain what he meant by

---

44 Burnyeat, "The Theaetetus" of Plato, 8–9; Chappell, Reading Plato's "Theaetetus," 48–52.

studying his experiences as a geometer. Therefore, I do not think that their accounts of Socrates' assimilation of Theaetetus to Protagoras and Heraclitus hit the mark. I shall attempt to elaborate a "Reading C" that explains Socrates' moves not as steps toward making "Platonism" coherent but as what they purport to be on their face, an effort to learn whether Theaetetus's definition of *epistêmê* can stand scrutiny on its own terms, which Socrates now is purporting to specify.

Of course, this brings me back to my original question: Theaetetus seems to have a solid foundation for his definition of *epistêmê* as perception in his experience of grasping Theodorus's theorems, so why does Socrates make his account rest on other bases supplied by Protagoras and Heraclitus? I surmise that he has three reasons for this:

First, Theaetetus's "perceiving" was, as I have said, a complex operation. It might admit of being broken down analytically into parts. Any one of those constituents could be viewed as basic and, thus, as something like the essence or efficient cause of the mathematical perceiving. Socrates needs to identify possible components and consider them to determine whether singly or in combination they afford a fuller understanding of Theaetetus's "perception." I believe that he will examine these elements seriatim throughout the remainder of the dialogue.

Second, if Plato can be trusted to report the teaching of Protagoras faithfully (and I know no reason to distrust him), Protagoras has a theory of the basic nature of perceiving, equating that essence with the analytically first element of Theaetetus's *aisthanesthai*, sense perception. The Protagorean thesis might well require or be strengthened by the support of Heraclitean teaching. If his quest for an account of *epistêmê* is to be thorough, Socrates must weigh Protagoras's theory and its possible Heraclitean foundation and either accept it or reject it to clear an avenue for an improved understanding of Theaetetus's "knowledge."

Third, we know from our drama that Theodorus was a comrade of Protagoras, that he has taught Theaetetus a mixture of geometry and Protagorean ideology, and that Theaetetus has read Protagoras's *Truth* often. In our play (and also in reality) Theodorus and Theaetetus might think that Protagoras has identified the essence or cause of the perceiving that Theaetetus has in mind. If they do, and if they are mistaken, two evils have arisen. Sophistry has corrupted mathematics. Having insinuated itself into mathematics, sophistry now can cloak its own "perceptions" in an aura of geometric certainty, distorting civic discourse. In tandem with his theoretical obligations, these evils would compel Socrates to assimilate Theaetetus to Protagoras (and then by theoretical association to Heraclitus) as a prelude to undoing the damage.

It is time to descend from generalities to details. We come now to the first of five critical junctures in Theaetetus. When Theaetetus asserts that *epistêmê* appears to be nothing other than *aisthêsis*, Socrates claims that Protagoras used to give the same account. If this is true—either literally or in a distorted way—we detect a powerful reason for the affinity between Theodorus, the father of Theaetetus's concepts, and Protagoras: they appeared to agree on the first premise of science. However, Socrates gives the definition a surprising twist. He says that Protagoras used to word it differently, declaring that: "*Pantôn chrêmatôn metron anthrôpon einai, tôn men ontôn, hôs esti, tôn de mê ontôn, hôs ouk estin*" (152a2–4).

This maxim is so grammatically ambiguous that it cannot be translated literally in a single way. Here are examples of valid alternatives: "Man is the measure of all things, of the things that are, that they are, of the things that are not, that they are not." "Man is the measure of all things, of the things that are, how they are, of the things that are not, how they are not." "A man is the measure of all things, of the things that are, that they are, of the things that are not, that they are not." "A man is the measure of all things, of the things that are, how they are, of the things that are not, how they are not." The saying is also substantively vague: What does it mean to be the measure of all things? Plato settles the translation issue and clarifies what being the measure of all things connotes by allowing Socrates to interpret Protagoras: "Then isn't this somehow what he means, that of whatever sort things appear (*phainetai*) to me each by each, that's the sort they are for me, and of whatever sort they appear to you, that in turn is the sort they are for you, and that you are a human being and so am I?" Thus, we are to understand Protagoras as referring not to mankind collectively but to each human being individually, as intending *hôs* to pertain to both the "that" and the "how" (the existence and every attribute) of everything, and as contending that the that and the how of every appearance are relative to each and every person, who therefore can pronounce on them infallibly. Theaetetus has read Protagoras often. He agrees that this is what Protagoras "says" or "means" (*legei*). I trust that Protagoras has been represented correctly.

This twist of the dialogue is critical to its drama because Socrates' midwifery depends on the accuracy of his diagnosis of the lad's initially celebrated pregnancy as a disappointing case of Protagorean wind. The turn also is critical to the validity of the dialogue's argument: If Socrates' imputation of Protagoreanism to Theaetetus is not both logically supportable and fair, our regard for Plato as a thinker will be diminished. In this respect, things do not look well. It is not clear how Theaetetus's definition of knowledge as the mathematical "perception" that he contemplates entails the notion that a man is the measure of all things or the relativistic "infallibleism"[45] that Socrates finds in Protagoras. Geometers are not measures: they are ruled by the truths they seek. Far from trafficking in appearances that might vary for everyone, they demonstrate theorems that are the same for everyone. Scholars who interpret Theaetetus's *aisthêsis* not in his mathematical manner but in their own modern English ways cannot find any logical relationships between the types of perception they envisage and the Protagorean ideas either.[46] Hence, there is widespread suspicion that Plato either incompetently or dishonestly has devised a transparently flimsy excuse to attack Protagoras and Heraclitus, thus embarrassing himself and his readers.[47]

It seems to me that Plato can be saved from this ignominy by a fuller explanation of what I have presumed to be his reasons for bringing Protagoras and Heraclitus to bear. Let us return to the fact that Theaetetus's *aisthanesthai* and *aisthêsis* are complex. They probably are amenable to being divided analytically into parts or steps or events. The first of these components would be sense perception. Theaetetus would begin to learn Theodorus's theorems by seeing the teacher's diagrams with his eyes and hearing his reasoning with his ears. This suffices to oblige Socrates (Plato) to consider the theoretical possibility that seeing and hearing are the essential operations in Theaetetus's mathematical perceiving, that what is

45 I have taken this term from Gail Fine, *Plato on Knowledge and Forms*, 184–90.
46 For example, Sayre, *Plato's Analytic Method*, 61.
47 Adequately summarized and reported by Chappell, *Reading Plato's "Theaetetus,"* 58–59.

seen and heard is the whole content of his perception, and therefore that there is no real distinction between the boy's geometric perception and sense perception. Socrates will assume for the sake of argument that this is what Theaetetus has proposed whether he believes that the boy meant to do so or not because he needs to test the sense perception theory, weighing all its presuppositions and implications. A further justification for this move is that Protagoras (presumably) intends the reduction of mathematical perception to sense perception, this being the point of his stress on "appearing," and "it's likely that a wise man is not talking nonsense." Socrates is being ironic but Protagoras's position will not seem wild if we observe that, in our time, "cognitive scientists" seriously argue a variant of it. They say that: "For the most part, human beings conceptualize abstract concepts in concrete terms, using ideas and modes of reasoning grounded in the sensory motor system." The consequence is that: "The only mathematics that human beings know or can know is, therefore, a *mind-based mathematics*" and, accordingly, that "human beings can have no access to a transcendent Platonic mathematics, if it exists."[48] If we lack access to a transcendent Platonic mathematics, geometers are not ruled by the truths they seek: they or their sensory motor systems are the sources and measures of their theorems. In the absence of proof that sensory motor systems all function identically, there are no guarantees that appearances might not vary for every individual. We are back to Protagoras. Socrates has an obligation to take an important thinker's views into account. A final justification for Socrates' move is that a Theaetetus taught by Theodorus might take the Protagorean position for granted without having given it much thought. Thus, Socrates does not exceed his warrant if he assumes that he needs to make Theaetetus confront the Protagorean doctrine as if it were his.

Socrates effects his reduction of Theaetetus's geometric perception to sense perception by appealing abruptly to the relativity of feelings. There are times when the same wind makes one person shiver with cold but not another. Socrates asks Theaetetus whether we should say that the "wind itself in itself" is cold or that the wind is cold for one individual but not for the other. The boy chooses the relativistic option. This exchange is curious. One wonders why Theaetetus did not reply to Socrates' query by correcting it.

48   Lakoff and Nuñez, *Where Mathematics Comes From*, 5, 4.

Theaetetus should have said: "Socrates, to inquire whether something is cold or hot or heavy or light or hard or soft in itself is to ask a meaningless question. Such adjectives are inherently relative to ranges of comparison and perspectives." (I do not think that this objection is contradicted by Socrates' discussion of participation in Forms as causes in Phaedo 100C–101D.) These insights could not have been beyond the reach of Hellenic science so we have to explain why Theaetetus failed to invoke them. I suspect that the concept of *epistêmê* being foisted upon him, that it is *aisthêsis* qua sense perception, stood in his way. If sense perception actually were the sum and substance of knowledge, it would be doubtful that we could get access to the wind itself in itself or to anything else itself in itself. It would follow that there could be no guarantee of the commonality of perceptions of anything. It also would follow from this, in the formula of A. E. Taylor, that "Reality itself is individual in the sense that I live in private world known only to me, you in another private world known only to you."[49] Chappell contends that Taylor errs by saying this because "there seems to be a bit of a gap between talking about our perceptions in a relativistic way, and admitting the existence of a plurality of private worlds."[50] This would be a valid criticism if we were only observing that the wind chills me but not you. However, when we add that we have no basis for claiming access to anything "in itself" Taylor is vindicated. It is not that we can affirm that multiple worlds objectively exist. Rather, it is that they exist for us *in effect* because, for all we know, we are isolated inside our individual perceptions. Plato's Protagoras has arrived at the same impasse as our modern science. Arnold Brecht, the author of a celebrated treatise on scientific method, confesses that we must stipulate that the same object can generate different perceptions, or that there is only one world that we all inhabit, and that there is "consubjectivity." He admits that, with this premise, "Scientific Method makes its first and greatest concession to common sense. For Scientific Method is unable by the formal steps of its own procedure to prove that consubjectivity exists." He wants consubjectivity because he believes that there could be no "intersubjectively transmissible" science without it.[51]

---

49 A. E. Taylor, *Plato: The Man and His Work*, as quoted by Chappell, *Reading Plato's "Theaetetus,"* 60.
50 Chappell, *Reading Plato's "Theaetetus,"* 60.
51 Brecht, *Political Theory*, 33.

Protagoras could claim to be a braver thinker than Brecht. He does not take Brecht's leap of faith to save science.

One wonders how the scientist friends of Protagoras could have adhered to his position if science requires consubjectivity. Protagoras does not appear to have worried about this issue. It will become clear later that he saw a way around it or, to be more exact, that Socrates can suggest an argument that Protagoras might have used to try to get around it.

Socrates has just posited three interpretive equivalences: (1) "knowledge is perception" = "man is the measure etc.," (2) "man is the measure etc." = "of whatever sort things appear to me each by each, that's the sort they are for me, and of whatever sort they appear to you, that in turn is the sort they are for you," and (3) perception = sense perception. Next he posits what he seems to portray as some implications of those equivalences: (4) appearance = sense perception and (5) sense perception = appearance, (6) appearance of X = sense perception of X = consciousness of being of X [that is, of as much being of X as could be accessible to us] and (7) appearance of X = sense perception of X = knowledge of X without falsity [as much knowledge of X as will ever be accessible to us] for each person. Equivalences (6) and (7) are my interpretations of the claim: "Therefore perception is always of what is, and, being knowledge, is without falsity." Some may suspect that Socrates' inferences from the first three equivalences are logically dubious.[52] That objection to Plato would be moot if Socrates has represented the historical Protagoras's teaching fairly. It already is dramatically moot because the guileless Theaetetus accepts the implications as genuinely Protagorean. This completes Socrates' summary of Protagorean epistemology.

A difficulty for Protagoras is that, while observations of the relativity of perceptions raise the question of whether we can get access to things themselves in themselves, they neither prove that we cannot do so nor explain why we could not. Socrates offers Protagoras an argument that, if true, supplies both deficiencies. Swearing by the Graces—goddesses of splendor, mirth, and good cheer who entertain the gods—he asks whether the "all wise" Protagoras taught relativism to the many while communicating

---

52 See McDowell, *Plato: "Theaetetus,"* 120–21. McDowell is so bothered by one of the inferences that he translates a phrase of the text with his own interpolation to smooth out the logic.

another, secret doctrine to his disciples, namely, Heraclitus's notion that all things are always changing, such that nothing ever is, everything always becomes, and it is a mistake to use the verb "be." Universal flux would make for infinite numbers of new transients perceiving infinite numbers of new realities with every instant, with no hope of getting to being or essence.— Socrates' grounding of Protagorean epistemology on Heraclitean flux is a subject of ongoing dispute between Chappell's Unitarians and Revisionists.[53] I disagree with the premise of their quarrel, that Plato's ontology is at issue. I do think that, if Socrates is serious about basing Protagorean relativism on Heraclitean flux (a big if) it is because the former would have the best (but not the only) chance of being true if the latter obtained.

The ironic fuss that Socrates makes about Protagoras's concealment of his dependence on Heraclitus tells us that the sophist never published any notice of his belief in the flux. The oath by the Graces also reveals that a divinely funny joke is in the works. The only thing not clear to me is where the prank begins. Does Socrates not really think that Theaetetus's definition entails Protagorean doctrine? Is it the attribution of esotericism to Protagoras that triggers the first belly laugh? Does Socrates not actually suppose that Protagoras needs Heraclitus? What is plain is that the coming "proofs" of the veracity of Heraclitean teaching are ridiculous, this being a point that works against the claim that Socrates (Plato) subscribes to the flux metaphysics. My guess is that the humor starts with the oath and that Heraclitean flux is brought in facetiously as the best—but not the only— possible foundation of Protagoreanism.

The laughable arguments adduced in favor of Heraclitean flux are as follows: All of the wise except Parmenides, especially Protagoras, Heraclitus, and Empedocles, teach it. So do the greatest poets, Epicharmus and Homer. Homer's complicity is proved by Hera's remarks in *Iliad* xiv (201, 302) that the Titan Ocean (who represents flow) was the origin of the gods and that his Titaness wife Tethys (who represents motion) was their mother. This, Socrates contends, shows that Homer meant that all things are the offspring of flow and motion. Further, motion (*kinêsis*) produces becoming, which is mistaken for being, while stillness (*hêsuchia*) produces nonbeing and dying. Motion produces fire and the generation of animals. The *hexis*

---

53 Chappell, *Reading Plato's "Theaetetus,"* 62–64.

(translated by Sachs as "the condition that holds" and by others as "habit") of bodies is preserved by exercise, which is motion, and the *hexis* of souls is preserved by learning, which also is motion. Thus the good (*to agathon*) for both body and soul is motion. Still winds becalm ships but motion of the wind moves them. Finally, the myth of the golden chain (*Iliad* viii, 18–27) implies that as long as the sun is in motion all things are saved whereas, if this motion ceased, all would be destroyed.

Socrates' citations of "the wise" and the poets are ridiculous because they are arguments from authority that prove nothing, because the ironic Socrates regards neither "the wise" nor the poets as wise, and because his theological inferences do not follow from the texts adduced. The comments of Hera quoted to celebrate flow and motion are parts of a lie that she tells Zeus. The interpretation of the golden chain is especially ludicrous. In the story, Zeus calls an assembly of the gods. He warns them not to interfere in the Trojan war and he threatens dire consequences if they disobey. He boasts that if they made a golden chain with which to drag him out of heaven and if they all pulled, he would easily pull them, earth, and sea up to the peak of Olympus, wrap the chain around the peak, and leave them all hanging there. The tale suggests permanence rather than change at the apex of being. Further, the fact that becoming, fire, the generation of animals, and physical and psychic well-being involve (different sorts of) motion does not demonstrate that motion is their source and salvation or that motion is their (sole) good. Finally, nothing said by Socrates could serve to establish the universality of flux and the absence of being. Socrates has staged a parody of Heraclitean reasoning. By making Theaetetus agree to all the propositions, Plato either has forced him into a straight-man's role or has commented on the boy's theological naivete and severely impaired non-mathematical logical ability. He also has made the lad equate the good with survival, a contradiction in terms if nothing survives the passing instant.

Having given his parodic proofs of the truth of Heraclitean flux theory, Socrates moves to a new description of *aisthêsis* qua sense perception that incorporates the flux. Theaetetus must conceive of perception this way: With regard to vision, we must not say that what we call white exists either in something outside the eye or in the eye, for this would assume its being. Nothing can be said to be something in itself. We are to suppose that transients out there and the eye are always changing. Therefore, the perception of white is the in-between product of a momentary meeting of a motion from without and a motion that is eye. This occurs privately for each (so we do clearly live in effectively separate worlds). Or does Theaetetus think that a color appears to a dog or any other animal as it appears to him? Theaetetus swears by Zeus that he does not. So, Socrates continues, does Theaetetus believe that anything appears the same to any man as it does to him? Or is he not much more convinced that nothing ever appears the same even to himself because he is always changing too? The boy replies that this is his conviction. His definition of knowledge has led to the replacement of his being by a constant becoming in which he is always something new. It is unclear that he or we could now speak intelligibly of him as a being with a persistent identity. He does not seem to be aware of this difficulty. Socrates postpones calling it to his attention.

What Socrates does next has puzzled most of Plato's readers, exciting perhaps as many comments as there are scholars. The analyses disagree so much that I shall simply ignore them and offer my own surmise. I think that Socrates moves to preempt a mathematical objection that could and should be brought against Protagorean-Heraclitean theory. In reply to the claims that nothing can be said to be something in itself and that nothing remains itself, why should we not expect a brilliant young mathematician like Theaetetus to exclaim: "Wait! What about numbers, squares, triangles, circles, and the incommensurability of the sides of oblong *dynameis* with the unit side? Aren't those things perceivable as eternally stable natures?"

Socrates needs to head off that sort of rebellion before it can arise by casting doubt on the immutability and permanence of numbers and figures. He begins this project by recurring to his sophisms about adjectives that are inherently relative to ranges of comparison and perspectives. He proposes what he and Theaetetus have just agreed would be a counterfactual. Suppose that there were something that was white or large or hot [in itself, in an abiding way]. Assume also that it were compared with something [that was, let us say, whiter or larger or hotter]. The first object, Socrates maintains, "becomes different" [in my example, less white or smaller or cooler] from what it was. Socrates says that this [relational change] could not have occurred if the first object had not changed [absolutely, in itself]. He states further that the second object [which, in my illustration, initially was white or large or hot by itself and now has become whiter or larger or hotter] could not have escaped change [in itself] either.

Having advanced these claims gratuitously, Socrates next suggests that Protagoras would agree that we are compelled to utter amazing, laughable statements. Theaetetus is perplexed. He asks Socrates what he is talking about. This gives Socrates his chance to quash the mathematical objection to the Protagorean-Heraclitean doctrine that he foresees. Socrates instructs Theaetetus to consider six dice. If you compare them with four, they are "more." If you compare them with twelve, they are "less." Is this true or false? Theaetetus gives the only possible reply. Of course the calculations are true. Well, Socrates continues, can something become greater without being increased? Now Theaetetus is paralyzed. He wants to say "no," the thing must have increased, but his previous answer requires him to reply "yes," the six have remained six while becoming more [than the four]. He has been stymied by a sophism that plays on senses of "becoming."

Socrates is delighted. He swears by Hera (the liar) that Theaetetus's answer is good and divine. He comments that if they were clever and wise he and Theaetetus now could clash like sophists about the paradox. However, they need to calmly re-evaluate their reasoning. Retracing their steps, they agree that nothing could become more or less in number or size while remaining equal to itself, that something to which nothing is added or sub-tracted remains equal to itself, and that something that once was not could not now be without having become. Socrates also asserts that Theaetetus, who is smaller than Socrates, will grow and become larger than Socrates and that Socrates will have become smaller than Theaetetus without having shrunk. Socrates speculates that Theaetetus understands, for he is not new to such matters. The boy swears that he is lost in wonder about them. Num-bers and magnitudes have been set adrift in his mind. Socrates states that this proves that Theaetetus is philosophic, for wonder is the only beginning of philosophy, as is shown by Hesiod's report that the god Thaumas (Won-der) is the father of Iris, the messenger of the gods. (Philosophy must be divine inspiration.)

Socrates' praise probably is both sincere and ironic. Socrates believes that he is making progress with his boy. However, Theaetetus's amazement shows that he is still philosophically naive. Francis M. Cornford states an obvious objection to Socrates' dice and size paradoxes that Theaetetus should have thought to make: "Plato interpolates some alleged puzzles about what we call 'relations' of size and number, whose relevance to their context is by no means obvious. Nor is it easy to understand why anyone should be perplexed by them."[54] The paradoxes appear to be artifacts of blatant sophistry. One could solve them easily by observing that "six" has remained itself while always having had its relationships with other numbers. Socrates has even hinted to Theaetetus that this is so by choosing the numbers four, six, and twelve, which form an enduring harmonic mean with which the lad surely is familiar. The three numbers must remain what they are in themselves, even when brought into comparison with one another, for the harmonic mean to persist. But Theaetetus fails to come up with this objection because he is still overwhelmed by Socrates' sophistical reasoning about the adjectives white, large, and hot. This raises a question for us: How could Theaetetus fail to see through Socrates' sophisms?[55]

To explain this in a manner that avoids the inference that Theaetetus is simply stupid, we need to find something in the previous arguments that would dispose him to be impressed by the contradictory propositions that things remain what they are when considered alone but change in themselves when they are compared with other things. I think that what we are looking for is the proposition that sense perception is the sum and substance of knowledge. Let us take vision as our example. What does the operation of the eye obtain for us? The answer must be "images." Images are composites of shapes, colors, and motions. The eye does not differentiate them into Aristotelian categories such as substance, quality, quantity, and relation. The images are compact masses. Any changes in what we regard as substance, quality, quantity and relation make a mass appear as something totally different from what was seen before. Six dice acquiring relations to four and twelve dice, or the naked number six acquiring relations

---

54 Francis MacDonald Cornford, *Plato's Theory of Knowledge: "The Theaetetus and Sophist,"* translated with a running commentary, 41.

55 Amirthanayagam David provides an answer to this question that differs from mine, one concerning harmonic, arithmetic, and geometric means, in "Plato and the Measure," 20ff. I will address his reply in a subsequent chapter.

to the numbers four and twelve, cannot be perceived as the same six dice or the same number six because they are buried in the two compact composites. The contradictions in Socrates's paradoxes dissolve: six is both equal to itself when perceived by itself and different from itself when perceived in relation to four and twelve. It is in this perspective that Cornford's objection to Plato becomes misconceived and the problems of relation that Socrates has adduced become both relevant and perplexing. Theaetetus has been prevented by the restriction of knowledge to sense perception from insisting on what all mathematicians, I think, would hold true.

Socrates inquires whether Theaetetus now understands how Protagoras would solve these puzzles. The answer is no. Therefore, Socrates inquires whether Theaetetus would be grateful if he helped him learn the secrets of famous men. He would. Socrates ironically urges Theaetetus to make sure that none of the uninitiated are listening, for he will disclose mysteries (the capital offense that Alcibiades committed). The uninitiated think that tangible objects are the sum total of reality and deny the existence of actions (*praxeis*) or generations/becomings (*geneseis*) and all of the invisible (*kai pan to aoraton*). Commentators wonder about the identity of the non-elect. I suspect Socrates of sadness. If the uninitiated are those who know nothing of the highest stratum of reality, the invisible Forms about which Socrates is silent in this drama, and if the actions and generation (becoming) that they deny are the process by means of which the Good beyond being emanates existence and being (Republic 509a–c), the uninitiated are everyone present, including Theodorus and Theaetetus. Socrates would love to be talking about these mysteries. However, I digress. It is the secret of famous sophists that Socrates will reveal. The intangibles that he will posit on behalf of Protagoras are not Forms but substrate motions. The uninitiated are those who do not know that everything visible and tangible is made of invisible, intangible motions.

The mystery that Socrates reveals is an expansion of the Protagorean-Heraclitean flux-perception theory. There is nothing in the universe but motion.[56] There are two kinds of motion, one active and one passive. From the collisions of these two there always arise twin realities, the sensations

---

56   If for Hegel being is thought that thinks, for Protagoras being is now motion that moves.

and the senses. So, perception and perceiving are forever joined. Above the level of the substrate motions, nothing exists in itself. Rather, everything arises at the junctures at which the motions meet. Now, some of the substrate motions are fast, some slow. The fast approach the slow and the slow generate. The things generated are faster, being borne away. (Evidently this is to say that perceptions and, therefore, what we take to be things, are fleeting.) Therefore, for example, the color white could not exist in itself but arises only at the juncture of the motion that is eye and a motion that is commensurate with eye, whereupon white is generated, not (the Form) whiteness. This process holds for all things. Active and passive do not even exist until they encounter each other. Accordingly, we must do away with the concept of "being," applying the terminology of "becoming" to every object and *eidos* (form) that we believe to be something standing still as itself. —Contemporary scholars like to ask whether this flux-perception doctrine is in harmony with the teaching of Timaeus. If such an identity were shown to either exist or not exist, nothing about the uniformity or development of "Platonism" would be proved. This would demonstrate only that Plato had dramatized the ideas of two thinkers, one of whom is said to be Protagoras and the other of whom cannot be declared a spokesman for Plato a priori.

Socrates inquires whether Theaetetus likes their results. The boy is unsure and wonders whether Socrates is stating his own views. Socrates tells him for the second time that he knows nothing. He is merely practicing his maieutic *technê* to deliver Theaetetus's opinions. He asks again: Does Theaetetus accept what has been said? Theaetetus calls the analysis wonderful.

Socrates proceeds to bolster Theaetetus's confidence in his opinion, raising an objection to the Protagorean-Heraclitean world view and then disposing of it. The objection brings up the possibility of false perceptions (*pseudeis aisthêseis*) for the first time. It seems formidable: How can we maintain that the things that appear to us *are* to us if we are subject to dreams, diseases, and insanity, in which nothing is as it appears? Theaetetus admits that those who insanely think that they are gods or dream that they are flying are "opining falsely" (or "judging falsely," *pseudê doxazousin*). The question and the reply contradict the dictum to which they had agreed earlier: "Therefore perception is always of what is, and, being knowledge, is without falsity." It appears that the Protagorean-Heraclitean flux-perception doctrine has collapsed.

We must pay close attention to what Socrates has just done surreptitiously. According to my assumption, Theaetetus defined *epistêmê* as *aisthêsis* on the basis of his quick understanding of Theodorus's theorems. Socrates then reduced Theaetetus's perception to sense perception in order to arrive at the flux-perception theory. The idea was that the man in the wind felt cold, the moving eye that collided with a motion from without saw white, Theaetetus grasped the truth of Theodorus's theorems with his eyes and ears, and that was that. If we were to continue regarding sense perception as the only element of knowledge, we would still be obliged to argue that there could be no falsity in perception: the man in the wind really does feel cold, the eye actually does see white, Theaetetus (perhaps) really does gather on the basis of his vision and hearing that sides of oblong *dynameis* are incommensurable with unit sides, the insane individual really does sense godhood in his being, and the dreamer actually does experience himself flying. In short, people really have the sensations that they have. But a little reflection suggests that sense perception is not the only element of Theaetetus's understanding of Theodorus's theorems. Socrates' question about delusions comes close to moving the discussion past sense perception alone and appealing to a second part of the act of knowing without announcing that it has done so. The new element would be a judgment that images that one senses reflect what exists independently of sensation, that the wind really has a very low mean temperature that would chill most healthy people so that the shivering is not a sign of fever; that what the eye sees actually is light with photons vibrating in a given energy spectrum so that color blindness is not the issue; that the opposite angles in the diagram that look congruent actually are congruent so that we are not deceived by skewed vision, and that irrational numbers really are incommensurable with whole numbers such that there have been no flaws in the proofs. That is, Socrates' question comes close to presupposing that we can check images of sense perception against things sensed themselves in themselves, getting access to realities behind the sensations. This suffices to make Theaetetus worry about false opinion or false judgment, the possibility of which has just occurred to him. He does not catch the trick that Socrates has played on him by hinting at an element of knowledge beyond sense perception.

Socrates temporarily rescues the doctrine with a long argument that relies on deductions already accepted. Dreaming, sickness, madness, and other deluded states are cases of universal flux in which different individuals are perceiving. Socrates dreaming, ill, and insane are not the same person as Socrates waking, healthy, and sane, so each "Socrates" can be right about what he senses. For the moment, this keeps the discussion at the level of reporting sense perception, thus avoiding the need to ask whether images correspond to the realities of things sensed. Theaetetus does not notice that a serious problem is being skirted. He agrees that the theory has been saved and gladly proclaims it his firstborn. He and Theodorus must be elated that his performance has gone so well. Socrates chooses this moment to lower the boom.

Socrates abruptly declares that the newborn babe must be tested to determine whether it should be kept or exposed. Such pleasure as Theodorus has had in the discussion has been short-lived. He is gravely alarmed and intervenes. He demands to know whether Socrates thinks that Theaetetus's definition of *epistêmê*, with its foundations in the relativism of Protagoras and the flux of Heraclitus, is wrong. Socrates is compelled to emphasize for the third time that none of the arguments come from him. He knows only enough to extract a *logos* from a wise person and treat it in a measured way.

Making another abrupt move while he has Theodorus in his sights, Socrates informs the geometer that even though he likes "the other things" Protagoras has said, particularly that what appears to each *is* that to each, he is amazed that Protagoras announced at the beginning of *Truth* that "man is the measure." The first part of this statement encourages those who argue that Plato accepted Protagorean relativism, Heraclitean flux doctrine, and the associated flux-perception theory insofar as those teachings pertained not to Forms but to objects of the senses. I would say that Socrates' remark commits him only to the observation that people can report infallibly that they are having the sensations that they are having, and not at all to the metaphysical implications of its Heraclitean extension. Further, it is possible that Socrates is being ironic about his liking for Protagoras's "other things." "What appears to each is that to each" originally was said to be what the "man is the measure" doctrine meant. Socrates now is starting to challenge "man is the measure." He will demolish that maxim soon (171a–c). Socrates' acceptance of "what appears to each is that to each" could not be reconciled with his refutation of "man is the measure" if he were serious about his interpretation of the famous dictum. Further, Socrates appears to revise, if not retract, his acceptance of "what appears to each is that to each" with his following comments and questions.

What happens next is that the Socrates who professed himself "measured" in argument a moment ago now proceeds comically to unfair reasoning. He declares that he is astonished that Protagoras did not contend that the pig or the baboon or the little round frog is the measure, for those animals are sentient. He also asks how Protagoras could claim expertise if what appears to each is that for each:

> For if whatever he might hold as an opinion [or judgment] by perceiving will be true for each person, and no one else will discern another person's experience any better than he, nor will anyone be more authoritative in examining the opinion [or judgment] than anyone else, as correct or false, but as has been said many times, each person himself will form his opinions alone about his own experience, and these are all correct and true, how in the world, companion, was Protagoras wise, so as to consider himself worthy of being a teacher of others, justly charging high fees, while we were more lacking in understanding and had to go to school to him, though each one himself is the measure of his own wisdom?

For that matter, Socrates continues, why are his own midwifery, examinations of the appearances (*phantasias*) and opinions [or judgments] of others, refutations, and dialectic not folly if it is true that all are right about their own? Theodorus is in a quandary. He wants neither to endorse the refutation of his friend nor to give up scientific claims to expertise. He escapes this dilemma by beating a hasty retreat, urging Socrates to return to his questioning of Theaetetus.

Socrates' sudden attack on Protagoras is unfair for three reasons, the third of which I shall let Socrates himself mention later. The first is that dragging pigs, baboons, and tadpoles into the picture is a sophistical appeal to emotion. Chappell points to the second. He asserts that as long as our discussion is restricted to sense perception, Protagoras cannot be assailed on the grounds that Socrates has chosen. If animals could report their sensations, their statements would be just as true as those of any human being. Chappell rightly says that "the objection would work much better if it were rephrased as an objection about *judgments about perceptions*." Then he notices that, in fact, the objection *has* been phrased as an objection about judgments of perceptions.[57] In the passage reproduced above, Socrates has referred four times to opinions or judgments about *aisthêsis*, *pathos*, and *phantasia*. This is the first time that he has used such language. Chappell remarks that "this might seem like a change of subject." Chappell does not go far enough. This is a change of subject. Socrates has played unfairly by surreptitiously changing the premise of the inquiry, decisively moving the conversation past mere sense perception to judgments or opinions about what the senses perceive. Now the possibility of getting behind sense perception to things themselves in themselves is on the table even though Theaetetus and Theodorus do not recognize that yet. Socrates is attempting to push Theaetetus to the realization that, while honest reports of sense perception are infallible, "Protagoras' further claim that judgment about sensory awareness is infallible"[58] is untenable. It will be a while before the boy begins to think in these terms. Socrates attempts to goad Theodorus into the conversation. He asks Theodorus whether he could expect to be excused from stripping naked in a wrestling school in Sparta when others had to expose their embarrassing physiques. The geometer hopes that he can convince Socrates to excuse him on the grounds of his age. Socrates accedes to his request. He asks Theaetetus if he is surprised to be proclaimed as wise as a god, for Protagoras's argument must apply to both gods and men. Socrates has veered from beast to god to man in his examples of beings for whom the now expanded principle of Protagoras would have to hold. Theaetetus answers that he has totally abandoned the theory. Then Socrates shows Theaetetus what fair play is really like. He tells the lad that he is young and easily victimized by demagoguery. Protagoras would reply that he excluded gods from scientific discussion and that com-

---

57   Chappell, *Reading Plato's "Theaetetus,"* 90–91.
58   Chappell, *Reading Plato's "Theaetetus,"* 91.

paring human beings with beasts was an appeal to *hoi polloi* based on like-lihood rather than proof. The exclusion of gods is sophistical: Protagoras is trying to forbid a valid question. However, his charge that Socrates has appealed to likelihood rather than proof reveals the third reason why Socrates has been unfair. Geometry has rigorous standards of proof that demand the logical compulsion of minds. Socrates admits dragging in pigs and baboons does not meet them. Theaetetus agrees that such tactics are unjust so Socrates will have to supply a proof that is mathematically rig-orous later. This makes twice that Socrates has repudiated one of his own refutations of Protagoras. He will do it twice more. Important parts of his work are to teach Theaetetus the tricks that sophists play and what fairness to an argument is. He also needs to get Theaetetus out of the lotus-eating habit of deciding that inquiries are finished with a few moves, devious or sound, and into the habit of testing his own reasoning thor-oughly.

However, Socrates is not quite finished with his cheating. He begins a new refutation of Protagoras that cites difficulties of a sense perception definition of knowledge. What about this: We hear an unfamiliar foreign language spoken. Should we say that we do not hear it or that we both hear and know what was said? Or suppose we see an alien alphabet. Do we say that we do not see the letters or that we see and know them? Theaetetus replies that we know exactly what we have heard and seen, the sounds and shapes, but not what was meant. Socrates is not satisfied with the answer: Theaetetus still has not fully realized that knowledge requires judgments about what the senses have perceived. Socrates raises yet an-other objection. Seeing is perceiving and, thus, to see is to know. Well, as-sume that someone sees something, remembers it, but shuts his eyes so that he no longer sees it. If to see is to know, not to see is to not know, so that the person recalls what he saw but does not know it. Is that right? Theaetetus thinks it monstrous to argue that one does not know what one remembers but he cannot see through the fog. He concedes that *aisthêsis* and *epistêmê* must be different. Socrates repudiates his own refutation of Protagoras for the third time. He denounces himself as a worthless game-cock who crows about a victory when that he has merely played sophisti-cally with words. He means that he has appealed to two senses of "know," using them to manufacture a contradiction. His self-criticism is fair but it masks a truth: unless remembering somehow is perceiving, *epistêmê* cannot be sense perception alone.

Before proceeding, Socrates baits Theodorus again. It is important for Socrates to goad Theodorus into the discussion so that when Protagoras is decisively undone no one will be able to contend that a child's inexperience accounts for the result. So, he says that Protagoras could defend his "myths" if he were alive but now that the tales are orphans, not even the guardians (or trustees) whom he left behind, among whom Theodorus is one, will come to their aid. This is a stinging rebuke in the presence of Theaetetus, whose guardians betrayed him. Socrates remarks that he and Theaetetus evidently will have to secure justice for Protagoras. Theodorus begs off again, claiming that not he, but Callias, is the trustee and citing his dislike of bare speeches, from which he turned to geometry. He implores Socrates to defend Protagoras and to use Theaetetus as interlocutor. He adds that he fears possible disgrace if he replaces the boy.

Socrates lets Theodorus off the hook again with ironic language that seems to mean: "All right! If that is what you want, watch this!" He then attacks Protagoras with his most sophistical criticism yet. Still presupposing the sense perception account of knowledge, he asks Theaetetus whether it is possible to know and not know something at the same time. The lad replies that this is impossible. Then he inquires whether a person who has one eye open and one eye shut, such that he both perceives and does not perceive, simultaneously knows and does not know. Socrates is enjoying himself. Theaetetus crumbles under the onslaught. Socrates observes that a host of similar difficulties could be adduced. Then he takes on the persona of Protagoras and addresses himself to further shame Theodorus. As Protagoras, he scolds Socrates for scaring a child with fake contradictions. He maintains that it is not he, Protagoras, but the boy, who is refuted by the tricks. The contradictions were phony because they supposed that same person was perceiving and remembering, that a memory is the same thing as an original perception, that someone who has become unlike is the same as before he became unlike (implying that someone who closes an eye becomes a different person), and that someone is one person at all, not infinitely many people in succession. Protagoras urges Socrates to attack his real doctrines, proving that perceptions are not private (or that consubjectivity exists, which Brecht declared impossible). Further, the talk about pigs and baboons was vulgar. Protagoras demands fairer treatment.[59] Then he undertakes a positive restatement of his doctrine.

We come to the second critical point in the dialogue. Protagoras (acted by Socrates) and perhaps even his friend Theodorus realize that there was a serious, potentially fatal objection to the relativistic, Heraclitean man-is-the-measure doctrine lurking in Socrates' sophisms: If there is no consubjectivity and no stable being, a science of reality is impossible and it is foolish to pay an instructor when everyone is already "wise." Socrates-Protagoras must qualify his argument to neutralize the difficulties arising from his denial of consubjectivity and his embrace of perpetual flux. However, he reaffirms his relativism and Heraclitean flux. This compels him to confess that no one has ever made someone who judged falsely judge truly. People cannot judge what is not (namely, falsehoods). They can judge only what they experience and experiences are always true (the experiences evidently now including both sense perceptions and judgments about them). So, it is given that there is neither intersubjectively transmissible science nor any knowledge of natures, which do not exist. Protagoras is extremely serious about denying Socrates any ability to know things themselves in themselves. In that way, he is a thoroughly modern man by our own lights. Still, by attempting to maintain a consistent argument, he has made it exceedingly hard to argue that he is a wise man who should be consulted and paid.

To vindicate his wisdom and science, Protagoras says that in the world of universal flux there are *technai* of producing appearances of goods and eliminating appearances of evils for the always isolated and ever fluid people who experience these perceptions. If bad things appear and are to one of us, the wise person is he or she who can cause good things to appear and be to that individual instead. Protagoras gives an example: food that seems bitter to the sick can be caused to taste sweet by medical therapy. (An interesting point about the wise doctor's treatment is that his administration of a drug alters the patient's condition not in a manner that restores a nature

59 For an inventory of difficulties in Protagoras's apology, see Chappell, *Reading Plato's "Theaetetus,"* 105–07. I think that Protagoras could answer most of the objections to his defense easily so I pass over them in favor of the most important, which I take up next.

to health, enabling it to perceive the food's "real" taste, which is impossible if natures do not exist, but rather in a way that changes the patient's perceptions so that he has a "better"—presumably more pleasurable—opinion of his condition, 167a. Actually, I should be more radical and say that the therapy produces a totally new person who enjoys his self-perceptions more.) Therefore, Socrates-Protagoras now defines wisdom as the ability to substitute some relative perceptions for others that will be liked better by those who undergo the substitutions. "Goods" and "evils" must be whatever always-changing people like and dislike from instant to instant. So, his reformulated position is that there is an *epistêmê* that requires neither consubjectivity nor a reality because its object is not changeless truth but the generation of perceptions of pains and pleasures. Scientists who possess this art are objectively wiser than others and it is rational to pay for their services because, we infer, they and not the many are the measures of means to pleasure. We may call the first, unqualified version of Protagorean relativism, in which every individual is the measure of *everything* that is and is not, its strong form and the revision that exempts the scientist's wisdom from relativism by making him alone the measure of means to pleasure its weak form.

Socrates-Protagoras's weak-form relativism amounts to a claim to know how to manage the flow of eternal flux in realms that appear both external and internal to each person. If I may be permitted an anachronism, we could call his vision totalitarian. Wise physicians can aspire to an absolute command of bodies that repeatedly reconfigures them to feel pleasure. Teachers and sophists can do with speeches what doctors do with drugs, configuring minds to take pleasure in their sensations. Wise farmers, oddly, can "induce in plants, in place of burdensome perceptions, whenever any of them are sickly, serviceable and healthy perceptions and truths." This language seems to contradict what has just been said but I think that Protagoras means all of his adjectives and his noun "truths" in relativistic ways. His point is that what we take for things of nature have "perceptions" in some intelligible sense and accordingly are subject to the absolute control of the scientist who can manipulate perceptions, perhaps in ways that are "serviceable" and "healthy" less to the things than to us. Further, Protagoras's good orators can make whole cities perceive differences between utilities and inutilities and cause them to see the former as just (166d–67c).

(Now it is clear that Protagoras defines perception as sensation plus judgment about sensation.) It follows that his rhetoricians would have a comprehensive *epistêmê* that usefully governs every other science and art as well as all polities, with the goal of producing universal euphoria. Under the direction of the rhetoricians, all the sciences could cooperate to achieve the felicitous result. Such appraisals of science might have been what drew Theodorus to Protagoras and moved him to couple his geometry with sophistry, for it enables every scientist to expect elite status, a right to power, and a reputation for philanthropy besides. Thus, in the person of Protagoras, Socrates has explained the merger of Hellenic mathematics and natural science with Protagorean political science, showing their agreement on the doctrine that *epistêmê* is *aisthêsis*, their strong and weak commitments to relativism and Heraclitean flux, and their joint despotic but benevolent intent.

The establishment of the alliance of Hellenic science with Protagorean political activism has been a necessary preparation for achieving the dramatic-analytic purpose of Theaetetus. Now Plato can make Socrates-Protagoras identify the political aspect of the united Greek sciences that will play a key role in the death of Socrates. The mimed Protagoras states that whatever appears just and noble (*kala*) to a *polis* is so for as long as the city thinks it is so (167c–d). By insisting on the relativity of all things, including justice, Hellenic science allied with sophistry convicts and condemns Socrates by undermining his ability to defend himself with appeals to an eternal reality of justice that a jury would feel obliged to weigh. When elites and majorities of others have been convinced by a society's intellectual leaders that their perceptions of justice are always right, an accused person is at the mercy of the transitory whims of the public. The guilt of Greek science for the murder of Socrates, indirect and unintended as it may be, is great.

Protagoras, as impersonated by Socrates, completes the restatement of his teaching with another demand for fair treatment from Socrates. He appeals to Socrates' notion of fairness. He insists that a dialectician should avoid trying to score debating points and instead should present his opponent's views in the best possible light and argue at the level of principle. He should not make slippery uses of words. This will attract the young to philosophy instead of driving them away. I think it unlikely that the historical Protagoras would have said this. Socrates is using his platform to teach Theaetetus the difference between philosophy and sophistry again.

Theodorus applauds Socrates' defense of Protagoras, demonstrating that he likes its weak epistemological and ontological relativism and its social and political aspects. Socrates responds by shaming him for letting a boy serve as Protagoras's guardian. He exhorts him to enter the lists on behalf of his friend at least long enough to learn whether he is superior to all men in diagrams and astronomy or whether all are their own measures of what is and is not in these sciences. This question should be a danger signal for Theodorus. It ought to occur to him that the Pythagorean theorem and his own results are always true for everybody despite all claims about Heraclitean flux. Perhaps he senses that this problem is looming for he resists Socrates' cajoling stubbornly, maintaining that Theaetetus would still serve perfectly well as interlocutor. However, he cannot hold out forever against Socrates' shaming. At last he submits, accusing Socrates of resembling Sciron and Antaeus and resigning himself to an exceedingly unpleasant time, on condition that he will participate no longer than Socrates has said. In the context of his behavior hitherto, his reply does not look like banter. He is angry. He probably expects an embarrassing proof that scientific truths are not relative, thus preserving his own expertise at the expense of his friend.

Socrates surprises us. He does not explore Theodorus's expertise. Instead, he attacks the strong form of Protagoras's relativism. He postpones a critique of the weak form because he has put that iteration in Protagoras's mouth himself. He wants to argue fairly by quoting Protagoras directly and the sophist's claim was "what seems so to each human being also is that way for the one to whom it seems that way." Theodorus agrees that Protagoras said that. I imagine that the quotation is a literal transcription of a sentence in Protagoras's *Truth*.

Socrates launches his assault, saying: "Well, then, Protagoras, we're also stating opinions of a human being, or rather of all human beings, and claiming that no one at all does not consider himself wiser than others in some respects and other people wiser than himself in other respects." He points out that all who are in great danger, for example those fighting wars or traveling at sea, look for saviors, experts who know how to pass safely through the trials. They do not admit that every opinion in such situations is true. Rather, they consider wisdom true thinking and lack of understanding false opinion. Theodorus agrees: it would not be credible to deny that this is how people behave. Then Socrates asks about Theodorus's own experience. If Theodorus declares an opinion, Protagoras asserts that it is true for him, but may not the rest of us judge his judgment? Do we always say that what Theodorus has said is true? Theodorus swears by Zeus that myriads oppose him, causing all the troubles that he has with human beings. Socrates inquires whether it is the case, then, that Theodorus's opinion is true for him but false for those who oppose him. It is, Theodorus says, according to Protagoras. Well, then, if no one, not even Protagoras, believed that a human being is a measure would not his maxim be the truth for no one? But if he himself did believe it but no one else did, would it not be so that his opinion was false by however many more thought it false? Theodorus agrees that it would. Then Socrates administers the coup:

> This next point is the most exquisite subtlety it has in it: he goes along with the belief about his own belief of those who hold the opposite opinion, by which they consider him to be saying something false, since presumably he agrees that the things all people hold as opinions are true. . . . Then he'd be going along with calling his own belief false, if he's agreeing that the belief is true of those who consider him to be saying something false? . . . But the others do not go along with saying that their own opinions are false? . . . And he agrees that even that opinion is true from what he has written. . . . Then since it is disputed by everyone, the *Truth* of Protagoras will be true for no one, not for anyone else and not even for him himself.

Plato (not Socrates) has earned a great deal of modern criticism for making this argument. Some are uncomfortable because Plato has imputed to Protagoras a method of deciding truth by counting votes. I am not concerned about that because I think that Socrates is teasing. The move that inspires the serious objections is that Plato has slipped or cheated by omitting the words "for him" and "for them" in his attack on Protagoras's theory. Thus, for example, Bostock:

"However it is clear that Protagoras has a perfectly good reply. The theory is that whatever a man believes is true *for him*. So it must be admitted that the theory actually is *false for others*, and since Protagoras recognizes this it must also be *true for Protagoras that it is false for others*. But it does not follow that it is *false for Protagoras*. This conclusion only seems to follow if we carelessly omit the qualifications 'true *for so and so*' which the theory does insist on, and Socrates does omit these qualifications when stating this 'very subtle' argument. But Protagoras has been careful to retain them. . . . Socrates is pressing the argument too hard when he goes on to claim that Protagoras will have to admit that the doctrine has turned out to be false for Protagoras himself."[60]

Lovers of Plato must be crestfallen to see the philosopher making such an egregious error. Some have tried to rescue him by interpreting his argument in ways that rationalize his omission of the words "for him" and "for them." Chappell puts paid to these efforts.[61] However, it seems to me that McDowell provides an excellent starting point for a right reading that does justify the omission. With reference to Protagoras's "man is the measure" doctrine and its interpretation as epistemological relativism, McDowell says: "If all that Protagoras can say to us is '(P) is true *for me*, it may or may not be true *for you*,' we are justified in wondering why we should find what he says interesting." With McDowell, I think that Protagoras must intend his maxim to be the one proposition that is true for everybody, *simpliciter*, and that Protagoras's opponents would claim that it is "false simpliciter."[62] Plato surely sees the situation this way. Now, if Protagoras does believe that "man is the measure" is true for everybody, *simpliciter*, Socrates is within his rights to insist that the

60 Bostock, Plato's "Theaetetus," 89–90. See also Burnyeat, "The Theaetetus" of Plato, 29; McDowell, Plato: "Theaetetus," 171; Sayre, Plato's Analytic Method, 87–90 ("This argument is surely unsound, as Plato himself seems to recognize."); Chappell, Reading Plato's "Theaetetus," 113.
61 Chappell, Reading Plato's "Theaetetus," 113–17.
62 McDowell, Plato: "Theaetetus," 171.

doctrine and its epistemological corollary must submit to the test of being self-referential. This sets up the following (adequately indicated) refutation of Protagoras:

(1) Let p = "It is true for everybody, *simpliciter*, that man is the measure, such that what seems so to each human being also is that way for the one to whom it seems that way."
(2) Assume the validity of p.
(3) For Protagoras, p seems and therefore is true for everybody, *simpliciter*.
(4) For Socrates, p seems and therefore is false for everybody, *simpliciter*. (For Socrates this already suffices to refute p but the next step finishes the argument.)
(5) It is absurd to maintain (3) and (4) simultaneously. P cannot be both true and false for everybody *simpliciter*. Therefore, the assumption of (2) is invalidated.

In other words, Socrates has given Theodorus a reductio demonstration similar in form to the geometer's proof that the side J3 is incommensurable with the unit side because assuming its commensurability makes side "a" both even and odd. Protagoras's assumption that "man is the measure" is true for everybody, which is unstated but implied, results in the impossibility that it is both true and false for everybody simply. As such, Socrates' refutation of Protagoras is valid. It can be declared invalid if one denies that Protagoras meant his maxim to be true for everyone, *simpliciter*, which would render the doctrine otiose, or if one were willing to allow him to utter nonsense.[63] Socrates' refutation also is the geometrically rigorous demonstration that he implied was coming when he declaimed as Protagoras, denouncing his proofs that appealed to likelihood. This might be why Theodorus accepts it without lodging the protests of Bostock *et al.* Instead of objecting to the logic, Theodorus grumbles testily that Socrates is running his comrade down too much. Socrates retorts that they are not clearly outrunning what is right.

Socrates mollifies Theodorus by confessing that Protagoras was wiser than both himself and Theodorus. His gracious self-abnegation is comic

---

63 Which Chappell, in *Reading Plato's "Theaetetus,"* 115, seems ready to let him do.

because it contradicts Protagoras's strong-form relativism. Socrates soothes Theodorus some more, musing that if Protagoras were to pop up from the earth at their feet, even if only as far as the neck, he undoubtedly would demonstrate that they were behaving foolishly by judging his teaching false. Then he would vanish (like one of Heraclitus's transients). This is funny too, for it would be impossible for Protagoras to prove anything of the sort if his doctrine were true. Socrates declares that he and Theodorus now must think for themselves in Protagoras's absence. Next he appeals to Theodorus's vanity by asking whether we must say that some people are wiser and some less so than others. Strong relativism should incline Theodorus to reject this proposition. However, pride in his scientific superiority induces him to affirm this, thus finishing off the strong form of Protagoras's relativism for good.

Next Socrates lets Theodorus think that there is hope for the weak form. He asks whether he himself gave Protagoras's teaching its firmest footing in his defense of it. Theodorus says yes. Socrates sums up this *apologia* with statements that were not made earlier but which surely were implied. First he recalls an example of the weak principle: Physical sensations such as hot, dry, and sweet are to all people as they seem to them. However, "cures" of illness depend on superior insight. Theodorus agrees. Then Socrates asserts that, "therefore" (*oukoun*, 172a1), with respect to political affairs, the noble and disgraceful, just and unjust, and pious and impious *are* to each *polis* whatever it supposes and legislates them to be, no city or citizen being wiser than another. The just and unjust and the pious and impious lack natures so "common opinion" (*koinê doxan*) about them becomes true and remains true as long as it is believed. However, the polities that are the measures of justice need expert advice concerning the advantageous and the disadvantageous. No one thinks that just any course of action will prove expedient so, here, one counselor excels another. Theodorus is silent, signaling assent. We recall that Protagoras advised Pericles.

The consequences of the Protagorean weak-form relativism for Socrates in our dialogue may now be restated. The explicit deduction, "If Protagorean science, then Protagorean political doctrine," reconfirms the unity of Hellenic science and ethical relativism. The "*oukoun*" might not be logically justified but all that matters in our tale is that Greek intellectuals suppose that it is, as Theodorus does. Protagoras's denial that justice and piety have natures, such that they *are* whatever cities declare they are, compounds the destruction of Socrates' ability to defend himself in court by appealing to an eternal justice. Jurors selected from a pool educated by Protagoreans will not listen to arguments that in the divine or natural order of being, Socratic philosophy saves young Athenians from the city's corruption or that its positing of realities higher than the gods of Athens is not impiety. In a city in which citizens have been taught that their *aisthêsis* is *epistêmê*, so that they see no reason to test their perceptions (sense data plus judgments of same), Socrates cannot even hope to persuade his jurors that he is not an atheist. Thus, he has made it clear that the science of his day is one of the cultural features of Athens responsible for his condemnation.

We have arrived at the third critical stage of Theaetetus, a long speech by Socrates placed at the center of the dialogue in which he abandons question-and-answer dialectic, remarks on the vicissitudes faced by the devotees of philosophy in law courts, and extends that comment into a lecture on legal rhetoricians, philosophers, and godly and ungodly patterns of life. Socrates calls his discourse a *parerga* (177b8). This word is always translated as "digression." The etymology of the term is *para-* (alongside, beside) plus *ergon* (work). I wonder whether we should translate the word as "digression" or more literally as "alongside work." Of course, the former alternative is absolutely correct and the latter would be outrageous in the light of all Greek usage. However, Socrates' speech occupies the center of the dialogue. Plato habitually places the most important parts of his plays in their middles. This suggests the possibility that Socrates' characterization of his speech as a *parerga* in the sense of "digression" is ironic and that Plato is indicating that the lecture is an "alongside work" as crucial to Theaetetus as the sun, line, and cave are to Republic. Which translation to choose? Perhaps it would be best for now to leave the word untranslated.

There are three sorts of modern scholarly reactions to the *parerga*. Bostock ignores it, as if it were not there. Gilbert Ryle declares it "philosophically quite pointless." McDowell asserts that, "on its face, it is quite irrelevant to the dialogue," although it could be a sort of "footnote" to other Platonic works. Sayre calls it "an interlude in which Socrates with characteristic eloquence pleads the virtues of philosophy over mere rhetoric," saying not another word about it.[64] I judge this dismissive type of response inadequate because it neglects to inquire into the significance of Plato's placement of the material in the center of the dialogue, declines to study the *parerga*, and thereby presumes to know better than Plato what is and is not philosophically relevant. Burnyeat remarks that, with the *parerga*, Plato "interrupts the argument and launches into rhetoric." (I do not think that the argument is being interrupted but Socrates' speech is, indeed, rhetorical.) He does not infer from this that the *parerga* is a philosophic nullity. Rather, he says that it is either a discourse on justice and prudence that contrasts the life of the philosopher who seeks happiness in justice with that of the unscrupulous man, or an allusion to Republic and its doctrine of Forms, it being his reader's task to decide. Dorter notes that the beginning of the *parerga* coincides with "the point where values are ascribed to convention rather than nature." This astute observation is followed by an analysis of the *parerga* as a reflection on "the difference between a life devoted to corporeal, mortal values, and one devoted to intelligible, divine values." Chappell thinks that the *parerga* "paints a picture of what it is like to *live* in accordance with the two different accounts of knowledge, the Protagorean and the Platonist, that Plato is comparing." Thus, it shows "what is ethically at stake in the often abstruse debates found elsewhere in the Theaetetus." Disagreeing with the ordinary characterization of the *parerga* as a digression, Ronald Polansky argues that it can be understood to "fit perfectly not only into its immediate context, but also that of the whole dialogue." This is because its advice to become just, holy, and wise is itself wisdom and virtue, thus revealing what knowledge is and answering the central question of the entire dialogue.[65] I appreciate this second kind of reaction for its efforts to get at theoretical substance but I think it errs by misconstruing the origin and meaning of the *parerga's* account of philosophy. I shall say what I mean by this in a few moments.

64 Bostock, *Plato's "Theaetetus,"* all; Gilbert Ryle, *Plato's Progress*, 158 (and as quoted by other authors); McDowell, *Plato: "Theaetetus,"* 174; Sayre, *Plato's Analytic Method*, 90.

65 Burnyeat, *"The Theaetetus" of Plato*, 31–37; Dorter, *Form and Good*, 86–89; Chappell, *Reading Plato's "Theaetetus,"* 126–27; Ronald Polansky, *Philosophy and Knowledge: A Commentary on Plato's "Theaetetus,"* 134, 142. Polansky has a good summary of criticisms of the *parerga*, 134n.

KNOWLEDGE, SOPHISTRY, & SCIENTIFIC POLITICS

To the best of my knowledge, the third type of response to the *parerga* is represented by a single author, Paul Stern, whose work on the passages in question is superior. Stern regards the *parerga* as an analysis of three kinds of characters, the orator-politician, "the Philosopher" who is not a Socratic/Platonic thinker but, rather, a person who shares the dreams of Theodorus, and theocratic philosopher.[66] It will be seen that I agree with Stern about quite a lot. However, I part company from him on one or two important points that will be taken up in due course.

Following Polansky, my present task is to learn whether the *parerga* does fit perfectly not only into its immediate context but also that of the whole dialogue. It does not appear to do so at first glance. The *parerga* has three sections that seem unrelated to the play and incompatible with Socrates' character and philosophy. In the first, Socrates introduces the subject of philosophers' troubles at law as if it were a stray thought. It goes without saying that this vexes all the readers who think that Plato's duty is to invent epistemology. It creates problems for me too. Socrates does not give any new explanations of the links between Protagorean science and philosophers' ordeals. Instead, he argues that the longtime legal orators become slavish and vicious, ultimately belittling them for not knowing how to drape their cloaks like freemen (172d–75e). My analysis of Theaetetus as a drama about the relationships between Greek geometric physics and Socrates' doom has not foreseen a spate of invective that deviates from this theme. Neither has it predicted Socrates' apparent effort to spite his killers with a churlish bit of snobbery about men's fashion. Like the first part, the second and third present nothing about the role of mathematical science in Socrates' death. The second compares philosophers favorably with habitués of the courts. Some commentators see this as Socrates' proclamation of his superiority to the fools who are about to condemn him, a venting of spleen pertinent to no previous argument. Oddly, Socrates' picture of philosophers and their habits describes neither himself nor his pursuits faithfully. The third part states opinions on godliness and ungodliness that Socrates might really hold but it presents them as assertions stripped of mythological settings and philosophic reservations. Thus, it exhibits a dogmatism that is unlike Socrates and unbecoming to him. All this would seem

66   Stern, *Knowledge and Politics*, 162–82.

to speak poorly for Plato's intellectual rigor and to controvert my interpretation of Theaetetus.

Reflection suggests responding to these worries by heeding Plato's dramatic guidelines. Socrates has stressed three times at great length that his reasoning comes not from him but from his interlocutors. When he finishes presenting Protagoras's weak relativism, which Theodorus likes very much, he asserts that a *greater logos* arising out of a lesser (172c1) is overtaking them. (To me, this seems to be Plato's indication that it is the *parerga* that is the most important part of Theaetetus rather than the epistemology so widely regarded as the only philosophically relevant material in the play.) We who have been told three times whence the arguments in the dialogue originate should understand that *the new one comes not from Socrates but from Theodorus*. This inference is supported by a later development. After concluding the critique of the legal orators, Socrates asks Theodorus whether they should contrast the members of "our chorus" with them. He thus includes himself and the geometer in the same class, a fact that appears to contradict my distinction between the two as sources of the new logos. However, after discussing the "chorus heads," the philosophers, Socrates completes his sketch of "our chorus" by telling Theodorus that such is the man "whom *you* call a philosopher" (my italics, 175e1). *The philosopher portrayed in Socrates' speech is the person whom Theodorus defines as a philosopher, not the person whom Socrates views as a philosopher.* It is a "philosopher" who is responsible for Socrates' discourse in the *parerga* and the "philosopher" whom Socrates causes to speak is Theodorus, not Socrates. All commentaries that interpret the *parerga* as an expression of Socrates' opinions are mistaken. Socrates' inclusion of himself and Theodorus in the same set was a courtesy. It probably made Theodorus think that Socrates was trying to ingratiate himself with a real scientist. Theodorus is unlikely to have regarded Socrates as a thinker on his own plane.

We need to study the *parerga* thoroughly. The first matter to consider is how it happens to come up. The last substantive remark in the summary of the weak Protagorean relativism was that the just, unjust, pious, and impious have no natural being, thus allowing "common opinion" about them to become truth. The next thing that Socrates says is that the *greater logos* is arising. Then, agreeing with Theodorus that they apparently have leisure for the new argument, he claims that this reminds him of philosophers' problems at law. Without warning the *parerga* has already bloomed in full flower. Socrates does not immediately tell Theodorus what the new argument is, or why it is approaching, or why the word "leisure" brings the philosophers' troubles in court to mind. We must ponder these questions even if we suppose that we already know that the idea of leisure makes Socrates think of the court because he will be soon be in the dock, where he will have no leisure.

So, what is the *greater logos*? Why is it coming? I see one argument that "perfectly fits its context and the dialogue as a whole." The *parerga* clearly is triggered by the proposition that because the just, unjust, pious, and impious have no natural being, common opinion determines them. (This is why Dorter's observation, quoted above, is so astute.) This claim raises a serious practical difficulty for Protagorean relativism: What about the case in which an individual citizen perceives the just and the pious as "A" while the *koinê doxan* of the city is that they are "B?" Is "A" true only for the man whose view is outweighed? Is "B" valid only for the majority? Or is "B" also "true" for the proponent of "A" in the sense that the *polis* will put him on trial and kill him for his opinion? This problem is no hypothetical conundrum. For Socrates it is personal and fatal. I infer that Socrates spots an argument about the conflict between individual and common perceptions approaching. His current trouble suggests an explanation of why he does so but this is just a misleading coincidence. We must remain hermeneutically consistent and remember that the *logos* comes from Theodorus. It is Theodorus, not Socrates, who endorses Protagorean weak-form relativism, who contends that the just, unjust, pious, and impious have no natural existence, leaving them to be fixed by common opinion, and who implies that the *koinê doxan* of the *polis* will win every dispute with every dissenter. Therefore, it is the inexorable logic of Theodorus's position and no random thought that conjures up the argument. The issue at stake is obvious to the proponent of "A": Does he really want to continue endorsing Protagorean relativism when it has this horrific consequence for himself? It is pertinent to add that this is no more an abstract theoretical problem for Theodorus than it is for Socrates. One of the charges that Aristophanes stirred up against Socrates was that he investigated things beneath the earth and in the heavens. This accusation applies in spades to Theodorus. This probably explains why Theodorus has had troubles with "myriads" of human beings who disagree with his opinions. As an astronomer he is walking a tightrope. If he is not careful about what he says to whom, he could find himself in the same predicament as Socrates, under indictment for denying and blaspheming gods.

Per Burnyeat, the first section of the *parerga* is rhetorical, not logically analytic, because Socrates is attempting to make Theodorus's flesh creep by suggesting a relationship between his Protagorean opinions and a fate that could be awaiting him. I do not regard this as a philosophic sin. If philosophy is primarily about ways of life, not analytic logic, rhetorically emphasizing the possible existential consequences of theoretical commitments is philosophically legitimate, even necessary. It will not take much for Socrates to accomplish his philosophic-rhetorical purpose. He will adopt the tactic of making Theodorus experience the issue vicariously by looking at the plight of a "philosopher" in court through his own eyes. The accused whom Theodorus will see there is himself. Incidentally, Socrates' ploy will teach us more about Theodorus's personality and attitudes.

Socrates begins by observing that students of "philosophies" appear ridiculous in court. (This unique pluralization of "philosophy" warns us that a name can conceal great differences.) This startles Theodorus. He asks Socrates what he is talking about. Socrates responds that the life-long habitués of courts stand to philosophers as slaves stand to freemen. Socrates is referring to slaves and freemen in Hellas, not to the psychic types delineated in Republic, about whom the geometer is not likely to know. Theodorus apparently is contemptuous of slaves and proud of his freedom. Socrates' gambit is calculated to dismay him. What if a "philosopher" should fall prey to the perceptions of those litigious slavish types in a world in which all perceptions are true for those who have them? Socrates continues. Philosophers flit from argument to argument at their leisure, as they like. They do not care how long they speak provided that they hit upon what is. (Socrates obviously is trying to revivify Theodorus's sense of geometry's eternal truths. Under Protagoras's doctrine, nothing "is.") In court, the litigants are always hurried by the water clock and they must stick to previously filed briefs. This is calculated to frighten Theodorus again. He knows himself to be a man who moves from one geometric and astronomical problem to another, leaving each unfinished until he can get a grip on it. He realizes that leisure to pursue problems at length is essential to the discovery of valid solutions. Socrates has increased his foreboding by suggesting that the truth about his case, such as it might be when all perceptions are true for the slavish characters who have them, would be unlikely to surface in a tightly timed trial.

Socrates plows ahead mercilessly. He drives home the scariest point, that the courtroom game is often played for the defendant's life. This idea occasions an assessment of the quality of the opposition. Socrates declares that the legal rhetoricians grow tense, shrewd, crooked, petty, unjust, and completely devoid of anything healthy or true in their souls over the years. They also become good at fawning on their masters (the juries), like lifelong slaves who have learned how to wheedle their despots and thus think themselves clever and wise. This is calculated to make Theodorus despair of his chances of winning a game played for his life. Theodorus will realize that he is not practiced or cunning in the ways that the rhetoricians are. He certainly would lose to his servile but canny prosecutors. Socrates again is forcing him to face the possibility that his granting of the right to define justice and piety to common opinion could land him on death row. So, this part of the *parerga* clearly departs from epistemology and analytic logic but it arises as a natural consequence of the epistemological reasoning so far. Therefore, it does fit its immediate context. It also fits what I have taken to be the larger design of Theaetetus as an analysis of the relationship between Hellenic science and Socrates' fate. After all, Socrates will be condemned by jurors who are educated by Protagoreans and who respond to slavish prosecutors.

Now Socrates asks Theodorus whether the members of "our chorus" should be described. Theodorus favors this because he likes Socrates' statement that the philosophic choristers are not servants of their arguments. The *logoi* are their servants and must wait to be finished at his and Socrates' pleasure. Further, he and Socrates are beholden to no judge or spectator who can give them orders. Socrates did not exactly say this. He did speak about having leisure to move freely from one *logos* to another but not about master-slave relationships with arguments. Theodorus has betrayed a strange desire to dominate not only his students but his arguments too. His good seems to be closely associated with his libido dominandi.[67]

Socrates proceeds to describe the "chorus heads." From the time of his youth, a leading philosopher has no idea where the agora, the court, the council house, and other common places of the city are. He is ignorant of the laws and policy debates. He avoids office-seeking, political clubs, and drinking parties with flute girls. He knows nothing of noble or low births, nothing of hereditary curses. He does not even know that he does not know these things. It is only his body that is at home in the *polis*. His mind roams below the earth and above the sky, "geometrizing" (*geômetrousa*), "astronomizing" (*astronomousa*), and studying the nature of every whole without ever stooping to consider what is near. He is like Thales, who tumbled down a well because he was gazing into the sky and missed what was at his feet, for which he was mocked by a Thracian servant girl. (Note well: ridiculed by a slave girl, an outrage for a freeman like Theodorus even if she was a beauty.) The chorus head also is totally unaware of the people around him. Instead, he asks abstractly what man is and what is proper for such a being to do and undergo.

This much being set forth, Socrates reverts to dialectic for a moment. He asks Theodorus if he understands. Theodorus answers that Socrates is telling the truth. This does not mean that he inexplicably has been converted to Socratic philosophy in an instant. He likes what he hears because not Socrates but he himself is its origin and subject. As Harry Berger Jr. was one of the first to notice, and as practically everybody else has observed since, none of Socrates' statements applies to himself.[68] Socrates spends all his days in the agora. He will walk to court soon without having to ask his way. Although he has never sought office or joined political factions, he took his turn as a councilor and a *prytanis*. As a *prytanis*, he was acquainted with the law well enough to hand down a correct ruling regarding the trial of the generals who won a great naval battle but had to flee without their dead (Apology 32b). As a socialite, he went to

---

67   Cf. Stern, *Knowledge and Politics*, 165.

68   Harry Berger, Jr., "Plato's Flying Philosopher," *The Philosophical Forum* xiii:4 (Summer 1982), 385–407.

Agathon's symposium, which dispensed with flute girls only temporarily, and drank everyone under the table, as was his wont. Although he is indifferent to inherited honors, he is aware of family lineage, as witness his information about the father of Theaetetus. We know from Phaedrus that his mind is as much at home in the city as his body: he normally refuses to leave the city because he can learn only from his fellow citizens (230d). In his Apology, he vigorously denies that he explores things above the sky and beneath the earth; the comic Aristophanes brought this charge against him years ago and many believe it but he challenges all and sundry to testify that they ever heard him discuss such matters (19b–d). He does not devote himself to geometry and astronomy. These disciplines are mere preparations for philosophy, to which he is dedicated completely. Far from being oblivious to the things and people at hand, he was a good soldier and he goes about testing acclaimed men and promising lads, as he is doing with Theaetetus now. He does inquire abstractly what human beings are but he knows concrete individuals too and attempts to lead them to virtue along paths tailored to their particular characters. Above all, he knows what he does not know. Scholars find it difficult to explain how Socrates could make such remarks about philosophers when the record of his life contradicts every one of them. Even the most careful and insightful must guess wildly, as when Dorter speculates that Socrates is speaking as a transformed philosopher lately returned from the Blessed Isles.[69] That is not the case. It is Theodorus who is describing the philosophic chorus head. Socrates is only his mouthpiece. Theodorus is the one who has kept to his schools all his life, "geometrizing," "astronomizing," and teaching his sciences to the exclusion of all other activities. *He* is the ascetic, itinerant professor who is at home in no city, cannot find the market or the political quarter of any town, knows nothing of policies and laws, and forgets the names of his students' parents but not the state of their finances. We have not heard yet what he thinks man is. It would be rash to assume that he will give the same answer as Socrates merely because Socrates explores the same topic.

Having delineated Theodorus's philosopher, giving the geometer a snapshot of himself, Socrates turns to the theme of this person's troubles

69   Dorter, *Form and Good*, 89.

not only in lawsuits but in society at large. When this "philosopher" speaks privately or in court or in public about worldly matters, of which he knows nothing, he is perplexed and awkward and is laughed at by "the mob" (*tô allô ochlô*). He also is ridiculed for knowing no malicious gossip. However, when he hears others applauded for their ancestry or wealth, he openly laughs at them. Then he is criticized for being disdainful. When tyrants and kings are envied for their felicity, he thinks that he is listening to celebrations of herdsmen who milk their beasts profitably but who have to tend peevish, treacherous animals. People scoff at him for this too. Again, little of this is true of Socrates. To be sure, Aristophanes lampooned Socrates. However, he did not ridicule him for being unaware of common things. He solemnly charged him with atheism, sophistry, and witchcraft (Athenians were concerned about the black arts when they accused people of meddling beneath the earth and above the sky) and he added crude jokes about asceticism, poverty, imprudence, thievishness, conceit, homosexuality, and absurd research. Further, Socrates was well acquainted with mundane things (we recall the types of clay). He was accused of scorning his interlocutors but this was because he embarrassed them, not because he laughed at them. He taught that despots were unhappy and that the many qua many would never be educated to philosophy and virtue en masse. Still, he claimed to love the Athenian people when he first addressed Theodorus (143d4–5). He will suggest in Euthyphro that he loves human beings generally (3d7). Earlier he had told Glaucon not to be too hard on the many despite their shortcomings (Republic 498d), perhaps because he thought that every person *could* be turned toward the light of the Good (Republic 518c). Thus, his understanding of human nature was not misanthropic on principle. Socrates has not described his own social situation or attitudes. However, Theodorus answers that things happen just as Socrates has said. I infer that Theodorus is recognizing his own mortifying experiences of social ineptitude and his contempt for various classes, which he cannot refrain from announcing. He also is endorsing the view of human beings as temperamental, treacherous herd animals. He probably thinks that it is proper for the human beasts to be milked, distrusted, and harshly managed in the previously discussed scientific manner for the sake of their own happiness—and for his own safety.

Socrates concludes this part of the *parerga* by observing that when the philosopher draws the small-souled man away from talk about mutual injuries and up to examinations of the natures of justice, injustice, kingship, happiness, and unhappiness, the tables are turned. Then this man is the one who becomes ridiculous, not in the eyes of servant girls and uneducated people but in the eyes of those who have been brought up free and not slave. (Theodorus probably never got into conversations about justice, etc. and never turned the tables on people in the way described but he probably saw his friend Protagoras do it. The "philosopher's" doctrines about these topics that he likes probably are those of Protagoras.) Such, Socrates says, is the character of each type, the man "whom you call a philosopher" and the other man who knows how to make a bed but not how to drape his cloak like a free man, talk harmoniously, and rightly hymn the true life of gods and happy men. Theodorus answers with one of the most astonishing statements in the Platonic dialogues: If Socrates could persuade all men of the truths he has just pronounced, there would be more peace and less evil on earth.

This comment amazes because there is nothing in Socrates' speech that seems conducive to the elimination of strife and evil. This can be seen by boiling the harangue down to its basic propositions: (1) Philosophers appear foolish and their lives are endangered in court because they are confronted by slavelike, dishonest, degenerate orators who do not allow them to bring out the truth scientifically and who inveigle gullible jurors. (2) Philosophers are ignorant of everything political, at home in no *polis*, ascetic, and antisocial. (3) Philosophers descend beneath the earth and soar high above the skies in their studies, geometrizing and astronomizing. Therefore they are unfamiliar with worldly things and socially inept, which exposes them to mockery by slaves and "the mob." (4) Philosophers are aggressively contemptuous of blue-bloods and the rich and their sneers are reciprocated. They equate kings and tyrants with herdsmen who rule treacherous beasts. (5) Philosophers can confuse their small-minded critics with talk of justice and injustice, kingship, and the nature of happiness. (6) These are the differences between philosophers who are free men and characters who, as lifelong slavish types, do not know how to dress, speak well, and rightly praise the gods and happy men.—Far from conducing to peace on earth, this diatribe seems much better calculated to stir up murderous rage against "philosophers" on the part of the rulers, aristocrats, and common people being derided, a group that includes nearly everybody.

It seems to me that only one explanation of Theodorus's astonishing remark makes sense. It is not that he has been won over to Socratic philosophy by mysterious means and therefore is overflowing with enthusiastic joy. We passed over a previous lament by Theodorus too quickly. When asked by Socrates if people contradict him, he swore by Zeus and answered that "myriads" oppose him, giving him all trouble. We failed to appreciate then how isolated and threatened he feels. Socrates has helped us see that Theodorus has inspired attacks on himself by flying below and above the earth, parading as a philosophic freeman, and scorning others as slavish members of "the mob." Theodorus is delighted by Socrates' diatribe because he thinks that it commands respect for his person. He imagines that Socrates has argued that everyone should acknowledge his superiority and leave him alone. If this were to occur, there would be "more peace and less evil" in the world in the sense that myriads would no longer menace, mock, and humiliate him.

This second part of the *parerga* "perfectly fits" its immediate context insofar as Socrates has been preparing Theodorus psychologically to renounce the claim that justice and piety must be defined by myriads who trouble him. It also advances Plato's overarching aim of portraying Greek science as a cause of Socrates' murder in two ways. It suggests that the geometrizing and astronomizing of indiscreet people like Theodorus lent credence to popular fear that philosophers prowled above the skies and below the earth like witches. It also suggests that the scientists gave philosophers a bad name for being cityless, arrogant, and contemptuous of Athenian citizens.

Socrates responds to Theodorus's strange statement by telling him that "it's not possible for evils to be done away with . . . since it's necessary that there always be something contrary to what's good." Stern believes that this "expresses one of the most far-reaching statements in the Platonic corpus about the nature of humanity and the world we inhabit." If Socrates teaches that evils "cannot perish because there must always be something contrary to the good," then

the existence of that which is good in itself must be dubious. Rather, that which is good is so only in relation to something else, specifically in relation to evil. Without evil, good does not exist. With this claim, in the central portion of the dialogue, Socrates conjoins the apparently disjointed strands of the dialogue: the "epistemological" and the political-ethical. For he makes it clear that the abstract question of wholes . . . which engenders the problem of knowledge, is most salient with respect to our good. The desire to see only wholes, wholes of perfect uniformity, evident in mathematicians and the Philosopher, derives from the desire to accept only an unadulterated good, a good that is so in its parts and as a whole.[70]

It is here that I must part company from Stern—depending on what he means. He seems to say that Plato is teaching the non-existence of the good in itself, simply. On the other hand, I might be misunderstanding Stern: he might mean that the non-existence of the good in itself is a Platonic doctrine not about reality as a whole, but about "this world" as opposed to the realm of the Forms, or that it is not Socrates' concept but that of the Protagoreans or of the mathematician "Philosophers." I would disagree with the former reading of Theaetetus but agree with either or both of the latter two. A Socrates who posited the Form of the Good beyond being in Republic and of "Beauty itself in itself" in Symposium would not teach the impossibility of "the good in itself" simply. Further, a Socrates who proposed that "without evil, good does not exist" would be contradicting himself with his very next proposition, "nor is it possible for evils to be situated among the gods." The "Socrates" who is speaking explicitly adds that the evils "make the rounds of the mortal nature and of this place here." Socrates might well believe that goods cannot exist without evils in the world that we inhabit, this because the most we are ontologically capable of doing is participating in the Good without being the Good. Then again, if Socrates subscribed to this view, he would have to face the Augustinian question of whether evils actually exist even in this world. Evils might not exist at all insofar as they are defects of being.

70 Stern, *Knowledge and Politics*, 171.

There also is the matter of hermeneutic discipline to consider. We must recall again that it is Socrates/Theodorus, not Socrates as himself, who is speaking. In this regard, I suggest that "the impossibility of the good in itself" is understood better as a result of Protagorean relativism and of Heraclitean flux than of "Platonism" (if the latter exists). For the Protagoras sketched by Plato there is nothing "in itself." Further, for Protagoras goods and evils are relative to pleasures and pains. Hedonism knows of no pleasures that are not escapes from pains. Hence, for it, there could be no goods without evils. (Socrates, on the contrary, is aware of pleasures of philosophy that are not cessations of pain, Republic 583e–585a.) In the hedonist's world, pain is the prelude to pleasure. Therefore, Theodorus will agree with Socrates' next remark, that the inevitability of evil in this world makes it desirable to escape to that of the gods quickly and that fleeing there is to become "like a god as far as is in one's power." Theodorus primarily conceives of deities as beings not subject to evils (pains) so he very much would like to become like a god. (Socrates, to be sure, personally recommends going to the next life as quickly as possible in Phaedo 61b. His reasons differ from that of Theodorus. He says that, if our myths are true, he expects to rise to an abode in which he is purified, 114b–c, there to meet poets and heroes and philosophize, Apology 41a–b, which would be the greatest blessing. He differs from Theodorus by expressing doubt that the myths are exactly true, Phaedo 114b–c. Socrates/Theodorus has no such reservations. This passage in Theaetetus is one of the places in which Socrates is acting out of character—on the mistaken assumption that he is speaking with such certainty in his own name).

Socrates further advises Theodorus to become like god ethically. This involves becoming just, holy, and wise (possessed of *phronêsis*), for the true cleverness of a person lies in becoming as just as possible. Knowing this is wisdom and virtue. These opinions look genuinely Socratic. Polansky argues that Socrates' assertion of them reveals what knowledge is, thus answering the central question of the entire dialogue.[71] Of course, he is right—in a way. Socrates attempts to formulate verbal images of his serious insights with such language. However, Socrates' remarks here once again

---

71 Polansky, *Philosophy and Knowledge*, 142.

lack their normal mythical settings and reservations. In fact, Socrates claims
to "know" what he just said about ways of life (177b1) even though he has
proved nothing, which is suspiciously unlike him. There is the additional
point that Plato has denied that serious insights can be communicated verbally. Words are too weak to do that. Indeed, Socrates' words are so weak
that Theodorus might agree with them while understanding them to mean
something much different from what Socrates speaking in his own person
would intend.

Let us consider this a little. We may assume that when Socrates declares that there must be evils, Theodorus nods glumly. Myriads of people give him trouble. But what is an evil? For example, is a free man's
contempt for slaves and *hoi polloi* evil? Or is a common man's anger at
pretentious, snobby foreigners and aristocrats who insult him evil? Is
the killing of an individual citizen for opposing the opinion of the majority right or wrong? Is a great king's treatment of his subjects like herd
animals that deserve to be exploited an evil or a good? Looking farther
afield, is the resistance of Melos to Athens evil or is the Athenian punitive annihilation of the Melians wicked? Obviously, the fact that Socrates
and Theodorus both use the word "evil" answers no substantive question.
Socrates counsels all to become godlike. We know that Theodorus nods
again, for in Sophist he contends that philosophers are divine (216b9–
c1), perhaps indicating that he believes that he already is becoming like
god. But what are gods like? Do they correspond to the picture that
Socrates draws of them in Republic or to the Homeric image that Euthyphro has of them? Does one "rightly hymn the true life of gods and
happy men" in Homer's or Socrates' manner? What is the justice of the
gods? Are they kind and merciful like the God of Jesus or do they bully
and crush objects of their wrath, like Zeus, showing that their justice is
the interest of the stronger? Do they detest hubris and exalt the humble,
arranging for the last to be first, or do they love powerful, haughty intellectuals and hate people of low status and modest intelligence? What
is the virtue that Theodorus envisages? Is it the courage, self-control,
justice, and wisdom that Socrates advocates or something along the lines
of what Thrasymachus would preach? What is wisdom? Is it the insight
of geometric scientists, the shrewdness of a Pericles, the proclaimed ignorance of a Socrates? Given Theodorus's friendship with Protagoras,

the advice to become as godlike as possible probably will move him to aspire to something entirely different from what Socrates speaking in his own person would have in mind, even though the same words are being used by both.

So, if questions like the ones I have raised remain open between Socrates and Theodorus—and we have no evidence that they are settled between the two—has Socrates' speech really taught Theodorus or us readers what knowledge is? I doubt that Socrates would think so. Even if he and Theodorus shared a single understanding of the words, would Plato believe that causing his characters to mouth them would establish their truth and convey their experiential substance to us? The Seventh Letter's author could scarcely imagine that. I suppose that, far from trying to impose his philosophy on Theodorus and us by dogmatic preaching, Socrates has spoken with the geometer's faux certainty about becoming like god for a strategic purpose.

Socrates' aim becomes clear as he continues the third part of the *parerga*. When Socrates tells Theodorus that to become godlike is to become righteous, holy, and wise, that cleverness is to become just, and that awareness of this is wisdom and virtue, he adds that failure to perceive this is worthlessness, cowardice, ignorance, and evil. It is in this connection that he will say in a few moments that there are two paradigms of living set up in being, the divine and the atheistic, without inquiring into the substantive content of each—a surprising, ironic omission given that he presently stands accused of atheism. Instead of taking up the philosophic investigation that would be needed to make his words meaningful, Socrates argues that conformity to each pattern is its own reward and then turns to a harangue against the unjust. He is playing on Theodorus's sensibilities again, for the geometer will view himself as the just, holy, wise person and identify the worthless, cowardly, ignorant, evil, godless men with the slavish enemies whom he holds in contempt. Socrates says that the wisdom of godliness makes all other kinds of cleverness seem banausic, whether in politics or the arts, thereby invoking Theodorus's prejudice against what we might call blue-collar workers. Then he reaches the deduction at which he has been driving: We must refuse to grant to the unjust that they are clever. This would let them believe that they are not useless burdens on the earth but men who can stay safe in a city. We must tell them the truth, that they are what they are, which is both a terrible penalty in itself and a barrier to their reception in blessedness after death. This rhetoric will precipitate Theodorus into high dudgeon against the unjust, who happen to be the myriads who oppose him. He will completely cease to be disposed to let the content of justice be defined by "those people" who represent the *koinê doxan*.

Accordingly, Socrates' purpose in this and the other two parts of the *parerga* has been to bring Theodorus's opinions about the disparity between himself and his opponents to light and, hence, to get him emotionally ready to reject the proposition that justice and piety are determined by the *koinê doxan*. Now, far from being willing to let aristocrats and inferior vulgarians dictate norms of goodness to him, Theodorus is ready to proclaim his superiority and their worthlessness to them (as he has always been itching to do) and to order them to shut up lest they display their uselessness to the *polis* that lets them live on sufferance and be sent straight to hell. Again, this makes the *parerga* relevant to its immediate context. The third part of the *parerga* contributes to Plato's larger project as well by showing what happens when science abdicates responsibility for considering the questions of what godliness, justice, holiness, piety, and wisdom are. The issues remain shrouded in a vagueness that no inquiry tries to dispel, leaving them to the prejudices of various social castes and finally permitting power to define them, with deplorable results. Elite opinion and the *koinê doxan* might be decent occasionally but, unexamined as they usually are, they tend to be atrocious as often as not.

The *parerga* also constitutes an event in the meditative-mythical voyage of Plato's *psyche* along the course of Socrates' mortal *Untergang* and spiritual ascent. It refigures the main trope in the story of Odysseus's visit to the land of the lotus-eaters. The portrait of Theodorus displays a victim of the form of lotus-eating that is practiced in Hellenic intellectual life. Theodorus feeds daily on the lotus of belief that being a mathematical scientist is the ultimate human perfection. Philosophically, he is a wreck. He pursues his geometry (his lotus) energetically but, otherwise, he is so lethargic that he cannot work up the energy to reason. He thinks that merely to utter his opinions is to finish all necessary work and broadcast wisdom. He does not notice and cannot bring himself to ask great questions when they are dancing before his mind's eye begging to be investigated. He irritably resists Socrates' efforts to rouse him, proving that he never will leave for his soul's true home voluntarily. Further, his complacency about his knowledge and virtue is so gratifying to him that he turns nasty when contradicted. Plato-Socrates-Odysseus knows that he must escape from the lotus land of Athenian science, trying to take his comrades with him.

One question about this part of Theaetetus remains to be considered. Why does Socrates call it a *parerga*? He probably does so because he ultimately is planning on an analytic refutation of Protagorean weak-form relativism. He knows an elementary logical rule: To demonstrate that the existential consequences of a doctrine are unacceptable does not disprove it. Statements can be true whether we like what follows from them or not. Socrates has been showing implications of Protagorean teaching that are obnoxious to Theodorus, so he has to allow that it is a departure from the main logical argument. However, Socrates is not dealing with a logic machine sealed in a vacuum; he has a whole person before him. When trying to show that a proposition is wrong, it is important not only to get the reasoning right but to break passionate attachments that audiences have to the falsehood. Otherwise they will hold fast to it stubbornly, defying all logic. The tasks of refuting the logic and silencing the reason-resistant passions must be accomplished together. The former is the primary job. I now am prepared to call the latter not so much a digression as an "alongside work." This necessary double task can be represented best dramatically, which would be one reason why Plato wrote dialogues.

Socrates has finished the psychologically requisite *parerga*. He announces that it is time to return to the main *logos*. Theodorus regrets this. He says that conversations like the one now completed are "not more unpleasant" than the principal argument because they are much easier to follow. His use of litotes must be translated literally here. Theodorus is not saying that he just had a wonderful time. His ease in keeping up with the *parerga* does not occasion surprise. The "alongside work" was a recitation of his prejudices. His brain did not need to work to follow it. He is unhappy to return to the unpleasant labor of thinking.

Our study of Theaetetus now has carried us a little past the middle of the dialogue. This is a good place to pause and take stock of what has been accomplished and what still needs to be done.

Inside the drama, Socrates has begun his descent into death, having run afoul of his legal prosecutors and the scientific culture that is partially responsible for having bred them. He has reacted by trying to recruit Theaetetus to philosophy. He has taken the first step in this campaign by delivering the boy and Theodorus of their opinions that *epistêmê* is *aisthêsis* and vice versa; that sensing and sense objects are mutually relative because all things are in flux; that *aisthêsis* is an as yet inadequately differentiated blend of sense perception and judgment about things that the senses perceive, such that arguments can be clinched by appealing to sense perception strictly or to judgment about perception, whichever works; that the one exception to the rule of relativity is that scientific insight into the means to pleasure is superior to ordinary thought; that Protagorean strong-form relativism refutes itself; and that justice, piety, and holiness are defined by arbitrary, variable common opinion codified in law. Socrates has also disposed Theodorus psychologically to repudiate Protagorean weak-form relativism. Standing outside the dialogue as its author, Plato has contrived its plot and argument to prove that the Protagorean relativism of Greek science was one of the remote, primary causes of the murder of Socrates. In his meditative-mythical voyage, Odysseus-Socrates-Plato has visited the lotus-eaters, seen how ingesting lotus reduces souls to a spiritually enervating, trance-like lethargy, and resolved to escape with his comrades.

Back inside the drama, Socrates now must undermine Protagorean weak-form relativism and Theodorus's and Theaetetus's intellectual attachment to it. (One could suppose that to refute the strong form was to destroy the weak form too. However, a somewhat different theory might require another sort of disproof.) Then he must show that there is no non-Protagorean basis for arguing that *epistêmê* is *aisthêsis* and no other geometric foundation for defining knowledge, thus aiding Theaetetus's philosophic growth by reducing him to *aporia*. In his meditative-mythical travel, Odysseus-Socrates-Plato has to effect his escape from the lotus land, taking his comrades with him. These tasks will necessitate a lot of epistemological discussion. However, as I argued above, Plato's aim will not be to elaborate a positive theory of knowledge. His epistemological purpose will be negative, to prove that Greek science was unable to say what knowledge is and hence, that it had no scientifically authoritative warrant for abetting Socrates' murder.

Socrates picks up the main argument where the *parerga* diverged from it, summarizing it as follows: Relativists still contend that being carried along is what is, that whatever appears to a man *is* for him, and that whatever a *polis* proclaims just is just for it as long as the city thinks so. However, no one maintains that whatever a *polis* deems advantageous is always so. Theodorus confirms all this. Socrates then points out that all discussions of advantage pertain to the future. He asks Protagoras whether every man could be the measure of what will be. Or do we expect experts to be better measures of the future than laymen? Physicians should be the best judges of who will become ill. Farmers are apt to be the best judges of which wines will be sweet and dry. Musicians probably have superior insight into notes that will make good melodies. Chefs know which dishes will please banquet guests. Protagoras himself claimed to be the supreme judge of arguments that would be persuasive in court. If he had not promised that, no student would have paid his high fees. In these ways, some people are wiser than others. They, not the non-experts, are the measures. (It should not be inferred that Plato has just said that the wise are the measures of all things. "Wisdom" about sickness, grapes, harmony, culinary tastes, and rhetoric that sways assemblies is not wisdom simply. Neither is it philosophic wisdom. The Athenian stranger later will say that god is the measure, abjuring pretensions of the humanly wise. Socrates has merely expanded upon his summary of the claims of elite scientists who argue for the weak relativism.) Socrates, therefore, is not obliged to be a measure. Theodorus agrees again that experts are wiser than laymen in their fields. He also reaffirms the conclusion that strong-form relativism refutes itself. He has abandoned the strong-form relativism forever in favor of the weak and the weak is on its last legs. Indeed, many think that the objection about the future has been decisive.

Contrary to the satisfied scholars, Socrates advises that his objection about the future has not yet been decisive. This is because he views Heraclitus as a more formidable adversary than Protagoras. So, he comments that although not everyone's opinion about matters of the kind just discussed can be true, Theaetetus's fundamental definition of *epistêmê* as *aisthêsis* might still be right. We must look some more at the premise that underpins the definition, testing "this carried along being" (*pheromenên tautên ousian*) to see whether it rings true or not. A war is raging over it, with many combatants. This sets Theodorus to ranting against Heraclitus and his followers. He fumes that it is impossible to get the Ephesians to hold still for a rational conversation: they seem to be always in motion, refusing to allow anything to be stable. They do not reason calmly even with each other. They have no students whom they teach peaceably, for they all spring up independently. The Heraclitean position must be treated like a [geometry] problem. Theodorus did not raise such objections when he thought that Protagoras was coming off well. One wonders what has motivated this outburst. Perhaps the *parerga* has taken its toll on him. Having begun to fear the potential consequences of the weak-form relativism for himself, he is ready to jettison it and all its supports.

Socrates responds that Theodorus has spoken in a "measured" way. This looks like a pun on geometry as earth measurement (the literal meaning of geometry). Socrates then repeats that the Heraclitean theory goes back to the ancients (especially Homer), who concealed it in their poetry, and adds that contemporaries teach it openly to win honor. This is the second time that Socrates has mentioned esotericism. Stern speculates that this is a signal that Socrates makes a judicious use of esotericism too, on the grounds that people are unequal and most are not able to bear all truths. He expects Socrates' coming reference to Parmenides to be esoteric.[72] Whether Socrates is esoteric or not, a matter that is as may be, I do not believe that these texts suggest the inference. Socrates' first reference to esotericism, with its bombastic oath by the Graces, was a heavily ironic joke. It *asked* whether the practice should be attributed to Protagoras, who was not an ancient. Socrates also knew perfectly well that Protagoras was a self-proclaimed sophist who boasted that he rejected esotericism as ineffective (Protagoras 316c–17c). Therefore, the first reference to esotericism in Theaetetus was horseplay from which anything can be concluded. It was followed by Socrates' first citation of Homer's alleged doctrines about Oceanus and Tethys. In its initial appearance, this

---

72   Cf. Stern, *Knowledge and Politics*, 194–96.

teaching was not portrayed as esoteric but, rather, as a poetic stanza with a straightforward interpretation. Socrates' reading of it seemed ironic inasmuch as the line was packaged in Hera's lie. Socrates contradicts himself by reclassifying the doctrine as esoteric. This ironic confusion would be compounded again if Socrates actually were creating the comic spectacle of the ancients and Protagoras taking enormous pains to hide a teaching that is about to be proved wrong. If we couple this oddity with the circumstance that esotericism has ostensibly been attributed to a sophist of whom Socrates disapproves on ethical grounds, it is hard to draw the conclusion that he has hinted at an esotericism of his own. The idea that Socrates (Plato) was an esotericist, which may or may not be correct, must find evidence other than these texts.

Socrates temporarily postpones his treatment of the Heracliteans by abruptly changing the subject. Continuing in an ironic vein, he claims unbelievably that he almost forgot that some teach the opposite of Heraclitus's doctrine. He affects to quote Parmenides as follows: "Since it is wholly motionless, being is the name for the all."[73] There are commentators who believe that Socrates has cobbled this line together out of the end of one sentence in Parmenides and the start of another, changing Parmenides' sense in the process. Stern offers an excellent analysis of the ways in which this trimming would make problems in Parmenides' views less evident. He holds that Socrates is being esoteric about Parmenides in order to "subject his predecessor to scrutiny without wholly subverting that which makes him so venerable" and also to protect those who do not "set the motionless things in motion."[74] Again, I am not so sure about the esotericism. As I shall argue in a few moments, Socrates' proclamation of Parmenides' venerableness is probably ironic. Further, the proposition that *some* realities are motionless is not necessarily subverted by a refutation of the theory that *all* are one and motionless: Socrates does not need esotericism to shield those who do not set truly motionless things in motion. If Socrates does purposely distort Parmenides (we cannot be certain of this because Socrates might be quoting a lost fragment), he might do so as a way of

---

73 Sachs translation of 180e1. Stern omits "the" in *Knowledge and Politics*, 196. Fowler in Loeb has "So that it is motionless, the name of which is the All."

74 Stern, *Knowledge and Politics*, 195–97.

disposing of Parmenides with a joke. This would be a comic refutation that did not require a full-scale treatment of Parmenides. Whatever the case, Socrates notes the essential fact: Melissus and Parmenides declare that everything is one and motionless. Socrates inquires what he and Theodorus should do about that. He says that they have fallen between two parties, indicating that he belongs to neither—hardly a concealment of the fact that he has some criticisms of Parmenides. He suggests that they should examine each in turn, siding with the one whose argument seems sound. He adds that if neither party is found reasonable, he doubts that he and Theodorus could say anything valuable after having trashed the teachings of such wholly ancient and all-wise men. The sarcasm in this description of Heraclitus, Parmenides, and their friends as partisans who are "all-wise" is unmistakable. Socrates asks Theodorus whether they should go forward into the great danger of taking on such luminaries. Theodorus answers that it would be intolerable not to investigate both doctrines thoroughly.

Socrates then tackles the Heraclitean problem that Theodorus envisages and makes short work of it. He secures Theodorus's agreement that there are two kinds of motion (if not more). The two are change of place and alteration. Heraclitus would have to concede that both sorts of motion always occur. Nothing could ever stay put or remain the same in itself. This implies that there could be no lasting qualities, substances, or other objects of cognition, no stable senses to perceive things, no stable people who perceive, nothing static to which speech could apply, and, hence, no *epistêmê*. Thus, the Heraclitean basis of the claim that *epistêmê* is *aisthêsis* is refuted. Note well that Socrates has not disproved Heraclitus's thesis that all things are in flux. He has demonstrated only that if Heraclitus is right, language is meaningless because nothing lasts long enough to be captured by a word, thereby making knowledge impossible. Chappell argues that if a sensation endures long enough for me to call its object, say, white, then language is not absurd. He thinks that Socrates' argument can be saved by viewing it as an effort to distinguish a realm of unstable and moving things from a realm of stable meanings.[75] I am not sure that Heraclitus believed that objects of sensation remained stable long enough to

---

75 Chappell, *Reading Plato's "Theaetetus,"* 138–40.

be described or even that there are moving objects with transitory qualities. Socrates interpreted him as maintaining that there are no such things as natures, all perceptions being nothing but the sparks generated by collisions of substrate motions. If there is no real object that could be white and no nature of whiteness, the idea "white thing" is absurd. Chappell might answer that the concept is significant not as regards an object and a quality but as the symbol of a sensation that lasts long enough to be named. That reply founders on another Protagorean or Heraclitean premise, that we cannot know whether all people have the same sensations. Perceptions that elicit the word "white" from various observers might differ. This goes for the successive selves that I mistakenly interpret as myself: what I call white at instant "t" might not be the same as what the new I calls white at "t + 1," let alone what anybody else "sees" at either time. Convention has no assured intersubjective ground. Hence, I think that Socrates has carried the day. To the extent that any reality is in perpetual flux, no word could be trusted to describe it and no perception of it could count as knowledge of it.

Theodorus concedes these points meekly. Then he retires from the discussion, pleading that he had contracted to answer Socrates only as long as Protagoras could be helped. This is the fourth critical moment of the play. Despite his call for an examination of Parmenides, Theodorus has just demonstrated that he has not suddenly begun to love philosophic discourse. As a leopard who has not changed that spot, he may be presumed to have kept his other features as well. We may infer that he feels disgraced and is enraged on behalf of his comrade. This gives us cause to regret Eucleides' decision to change the mode of Theaetetus. If Socrates' exact words had been recorded, we might have heard something about Theodorus's reaction. Just as Socrates described Thrasymachus blushing in Republic, he might have told us that: "Having spoken thus, Theodorus drew his robes around him and sat, seething." That aside, it is fair to conclude that the geometer has become a scientific Anytus.

Theaetetus wants to postpone the resumption of his role as interlocutor until Socrates and Theodorus have analyzed Parmenides. However, Socrates reneges on that promise. He wishes to avoid treating the Eleatics generally and Parmenides particularly. He explains that Parmenides "appears" to him, in Homer's words, "venerable" and "terrible." As a youth he met Parmenides, when that philosopher was old. Parmenides "appeared" to him to have an entirely noble depth. Socrates fears that they would not understand the great man's words or what he meant by them. Besides, treating Parmenides would introduce hordes of arguments that would swamp the present project, so it would be better to continue to inquire what knowledge is (183d–e).

Socrates' refusal to consider the Eleatics and especially Parmenides seems ironic, for two reasons. First, although Socrates ostensibly excuses the Eleatics from consideration, he smuggles them back in quickly, invoking Parmenides indirectly and imitating Zeno to befuddle Theaetetus. In doing so, he implicitly criticizes them. Second, Socrates' emphasis on "appearing" occasions doubt that he really looks up to Parmenides. In this respect, one should note that when the words venerable and terrible are combined in the Homeric texts, someone is always being overrated or misrepresented. In *Iliad* iii, 172, Helen submissively tells Priam that he is venerable and terrible to her. Priam is a weak, irresolute, imprudent king, very much to blame for the destruction of his city. Also, at the moment, he is sitting on the walls of Troy gazing at Agamemnon on the plains and appraising him as "kingly," unaware of his serious faults. In *Odyssey* viii, 22, Athena makes Odysseus look more formidable than he is to inspire the Phaeacians to revere and dread him. In *Odyssey* xiv, 234, Odysseus is disguised as a vagrant. He says that he was venerable and terrible in the course of spinning a whopping lie about having been a Cretan pirate. The appearances do not match the realities in any of the cases. Socrates probably thinks that Parmenides is overrated and fears hosts of new arguments if he takes him up because the argument that being is one and motionless has as many difficulties as Heraclitus's being as motion. Chief among them are the problems of how things could appear to be in motion when they are not, how being, appearance, the whole, the all, and the one could be merely one, and how the existence of these names would not itself refute the proposition that there is no multiplicity.

Things seem settled. We expect Socrates to move to a consideration of new accounts of knowledge. However, it turns out that we are not quite finished with Theaetetus's definition of *epistêmê* as *aisthêsis*. Socrates undertakes what must be understood as yet another refutation of that account, as if he were not satisfied with the ones already offered. However, it is not that he considers the conclusions just reached inadequate. Although we are given another refutation of the definition, that is incidental to Socrates' new purpose. What he actually wants to do now is address the hitherto unchallenged confusion of sense perception with judgment of what is sensed. Theaetetus must be cured of his tendency to confound these two acts so that he can conceive of another definition of knowledge.

To accomplish this aim, Socrates once again restricts "perception" to what is registered by the senses. Now, apologizing for splitting a hair, he asks Theaetetus whether our eyes are that *with* which we see or *through* which we see, and whether our ears are that *with* which we hear or *through* which we hear. The boy answers that we sense *through* our eyes and ears. Socrates likes this answer: he declares that it would be queer if we had many *aisthêseis* sitting inside us as if we were wooden horses, without them being united in some *idean* (look or form or idea). What he means is that we must account for the facts that we understand that we have five senses and that we can relate diverse sense perceptions to the same object. There must be something in us that unifies the senses in these manners. Socrates suggests that we call it *psychê* or whatever else we choose. This causes some commentators to become exercised and accuse Socrates of religious dogmatism. These scholars should rest assured that Socrates has not just attempted to sneak in a demonstration of an immaterial, immortal soul that goes to the Blessed Isles or Hades after we die. All that we know about this faculty so far is that it performs the unifying function. Socrates has not even insisted on the name "soul." The statements made by Socrates and Theaetetus about this something seem unexceptionable.

Next Socrates asks Theaetetus whether the five senses have bodily seats. Of course they do. Then he inquires whether any of the sense organs can do the work of another, for example, whether eyes can hear. They cannot. Is it possible to say that sight and hearing are the same as themselves and different from each other? Yes. By which organ do we think this? Socrates cuts off a reply to this query by posing another. By what do we notice what things have in common? Theaetetus understands what all things have in common to be being and nonbeing, likeness and unlikeness, the same and the other, one and the rest of number, and the odd and the even. (This inventory, or parts of it, will appear again in *Sophist*.)

He sees no way that one of the five bodily organs already cited could perceive these things. He decides now that the soul seems to him to view (*episkopein*) the common things directly. Socrates enthusiastically advises Theaetetus that he is beautiful, not ugly as Theodorus had reported, for whoever speaks beautifully is beautiful and good. (Theodorus cannot be happy about this betrayal of a confidence. Theaetetus might be annoyed with Theodorus too.) Socrates had hoped that Theaetetus would say that and is pleased to be spared a long argument. Socrates' stance again elicits modern charges that he is dogmatic. I repeat that Socrates has not just attempted a sneaky proof of an immaterial, immortal soul. He has only pointed out correctly that the five senses are not faculties that perceive what all things have in common and therefore that something else must do the work.

Now Socrates asks whether Theaetetus also places the beautiful, the ugly, the good, and the bad in the category of things grasped directly by the *psychê*. Yes. Socrates inquires whether one can arrive at truth without having ascertained being. No. Then, given that the soul discerns being, Socrates sums up the consequences: knowledge is not in the five physical senses. It arises from the soul's *syllogismôs* (a gathering up or reckoning) of what things have in common. Thus, *epistêmê* is not *aisthêsis* understood as sense perception, not even in some non-Protagorean way. Theaetetus agrees. I should observe that sense perception has not been dismissed as irrelevant to knowledge in this development. The knowing soul is applying its *episkopeia* and *syllogismôs* to the common elements of the things of the narrowly understood *aisthêsis*. Socrates is making the distinction that he wants Theaetetus to see and hinting that knowledge is located not in *aisthêsis* qua sense perception but in the *episkopeia* and *syllogismôs*.

Socrates encourages Theaetetus to essay another definition of knowledge that locates it in the soul. Theaetetus guesses that to know is *doxazein*. This word can be translated either as "to opine" or "to judge." For reasons that may have to do with my idiosyncratic sense of the terms, I prefer to report that Theaetetus has said that to know is to judge. Socrates encourages him in this new supposition. Theaetetus adds that not all judgment is correct so he concludes that to know is to possess true judgment. Note well that Theaetetus is convinced that there is false judgment.

It is interesting to ask where Theaetetus got this definition. The obvious answer is that he followed the lead that Socrates just gave him. However, there is more to it than that. Theaetetus is still thinking as a geometer and amending his original account of *epistêmê* accordingly. If we imagine him looking at a line that intersects parallel lines or at Theodorus's diagrams, he now is asserting not that he perceives but that he judges truly that the opposite angles are congruent and that the theorems are valid. If we put Socrates' comments together with Theaetetus's suggestion, knowing has become a mental act that moves through three distinct steps, the first two occurring more or less simultaneously and the third of which follows directly: *aisthêsis* of phenomena by means of the senses; psychic *episkopeia* (viewing or inspection) of what the appearances have in common, which marks being, identity, similarity, difference, beauty, ugliness, good, evil, and the like in the objects that give rise to the appearances; and *syllogismôs*, which gathers the results of the inspections. (A geometric example: sensory *aisthêsis* of lines, curves, and angles; the soul's *episkopeia* of these objects, their being, identities, similarities and differences, etc., *syllogismô*s in theorems. We are still very much in the territory of geometric understandings of knowledge.) *Epistêmê* as true *doxa* is the sum or product of these operations. Socrates praises Theaetetus for having spoken up. They can examine his new definition and either find what they are seeking or discover that they still do not know it, which would be no mean reward in itself.

Socrates is always full of surprises. He does not promptly take up the new definition as we expect. Instead he greets it with a difficulty, saying that he cannot tell what the experience of having false judgment is or how it comes about. This reminds us of the words that Socrates put in the mouth of Protagoras earlier: "One does not, however, make someone who's been having false judgment (*pseudê doxazonta*) judge truly (*alethê doxazein*) for there is no power to judge (*doxasai*) either the things that are not (*ta mê onta*) or other things besides those one experiences, and the latter are always true" (167a6–8). Protagoras denies that there is false judgment. Acting as midwife, Socrates feigns to think this might be right, probably because Theaetetus's new idea makes one genuinely curious. If one can, say, look at a diagram and judge by means of *aisthêsis*, *episkopeia*, and *syllogismôs* that the opposite angles formed by intersections of lines with parallel lines are congruent or that irrational segments are incommensurable with unit lines, where does the possibility of falsehood come in? Why would one not always perceive, examine, and gather what is? (Another question, not ever taken up, is how do *aisthêsis*, *episkopeia*, and *syllogismôs* hit upon correct judgments? What is it in these operations that makes for accuracy?)

Socrates complicates his investigation of false judgment by asking Theaetetus whether he holds that there are only two possibilities, to know something or not to know it. Theaetetus does maintain that. This indicates that Theaetetus has hardly changed his definition of knowledge at all. He is still thinking of it as a kind of immediate apprehension, as if *aisthêsis*, *episkopeia*, and *syllogismôs* working together added up to a psychic equivalent of sense perception. For the sake of convenience, let us call this product of *aisthêsis*, *episkopeia*, and *syllogismôs*, as understood by Theaetetus, a psychic perception. As with *aisthêsis* qua sense perception, one could only have a psychic perception or not have it. In the former case, it might seem that the psychic perception would be infallible. In the latter, there would be nothing in the soul that could be or explain the existence of false judgments that Theaetetus envisages. The assumption that *epistêmê* is psychic perception is the new epistemological ground of the argument that "One does not make someone who's been having false judgment judge truly, for there is no power to judge either the things that are not or other things besides those one experiences, and the latter are always true."

Socrates now embarks upon five considerations of the possibility of false judgment. My treatment of these reflections will be entirely unorthodox—if orthodoxy is defined by modern scholarly consensus. Contemporary commentators almost universally see the five considerations as Plato's serious efforts to develop models of *epistêmê* that would explain how false judgment could come to be. In the works of the analytic philosophers, there is a great deal of wonderment about what Plato could have meant by various flawed assertions and, frankly, how he could have been so far wrong as to utter them. These assessments depend on the wholly a priori assumption that Socrates' function is to work up Plato's theories, a supposition that totally ignores Socrates' triple warning that *all* of his *logoi* come from his interlocutors, thus causing complete failures to understand what Plato actually is doing. Chappell is the only scholar who escapes this error by attributing the faulty models to Socrates' empiricist opponents.[76] Other than Chappell, virtually no one realizes that Plato makes Socrates let the coming arguments be ruled by the Protagorean belief that "there is no power to judge either the things that are not or other things besides those one experiences, and the latter are always true" and by Theaetetus's corollary that knowing or not knowing something are the only possibilities (or that knowledge is a psychic equivalent of sense perception that one can only have or not have), all this to achieve a negative purpose.

What Plato actually does in the five considerations is to depict Socrates giving Theaetetus reductio refutations of his new definition of knowledge. Plato does not tell readers of our era that this is what he is doing because he is addressing audiences of his own time, who would recognize his strategy without having to be reminded of what was going on in Theaetetus's education. The reductios will have the same form as Theodorus's theorems: "Suppose that such and such is true and watch the absurdities mount up." The assumed truths, all of which originate with Protagoras or Theaetetus, have been posited above: (1) There is no power to judge either the things that are not or other things besides those one experiences, and the latter are always true. (2) *Epistêmê* is a psychic equivalent of sense perception. (3) Nevertheless there are false judgments. (Incidentally, Protagoras's denial of the possibility of false judgment produces a humorous paradox: It is a false judgment to say that there are false judgments.) These three propositions cannot stand together. Something has to give.

First Reductio

Socrates declares that if the only possibilities are to know or not know something, such that *epistêmê* is (what I have called) psychic perception with regard to all things, it follows that learning and memory play no roles in knowledge and need not be discussed. Theaetetus agrees for reasons that are not clear. Perhaps his idea of his knowledge of

76   Chappell, *Reading Plato's "Theaetetus,"* 150–96 in various places.

geometric figures and proofs as things immediately apprehended makes learning and memory seem dispensable at first glance. In keeping with the stated assumption, Socrates observes that someone who judges does so either about something that he knows or something that he does not know. Again by assumption, if the person knows it, he cannot not know it. If he does not know it, it is impossible for him to know it. Then does a person who judges falsely suppose that the things he knows are not those things but other things that he knows, such that knowing both he is ignorant of both? Theaetetus replies that this is impossible. Then does the individual think that things that he does not know are other things that he does not know? Theaetetus does not see how this could be. Then does the person hold that things he knows are things that he does not know? Theaetetus views this as monstrous. Socrates answers that they have exhausted the possibilities of false judgment, meaning that false judgment has been proved impossible. (Socrates has omitted the case in which someone thinks that things that he does not know are things that he knows, which is common but also impossible in his scenario.) Socrates will not be so tedious as to cross t's and dot i's, informing Theaetetus that he has just been shown a reductio. A Theaetetus schooled by Theodorus certainly will grasp that he must surrender either his new description of knowledge or his opinion that there are false judgments. To give up the latter would be an incredible denial of experience.

Scholars generally complain that "Plato" has unduly restricted the numerous senses of the word knowledge in this first study of the possibility of false opinion. However, Plato was not so incompetent as to have been unaware of this. The defect lay not with him but with Theaetetus's epistemological premises that he was dramatizing. Some scholars also object that Socrates has restricted this discussion of *epistêmê* to identity statements. I am not convinced that this is so. It seems to me that he and Theaetetus could be contemplating any form of *epistêmê* that arrives via psychic perception and find themselves forced into the dichotomy of knowing/not knowing that leads to the absurdity. Socrates does refer to identity statements but this is only by way of giving the easiest examples.

Second Reductio

Socrates suggests putting Theaetetus's assumption that knowledge is psychic perception on a different basis. Instead of concentrating on knowing and not knowing, perhaps they should look at being and not being. They could say that false judgment is a matter of judging the things that are not (*ta mê onta*). Theaetetus likes that. However, Socrates resurrects Protagoras's claim that it is impossible to judge the thing that is not (*to mê on*). The boy thinks that this is possible but Socrates, trusting that people will remember the source of what he is about to say, reiterates Protagoras's argument that people can judge only things that they experience and that no one can experience what is not. To see is to see something that is. To hear is to hear something that is. To touch is to touch something that is. Hence, to judge is to judge something that is. To judge what is not is to judge nothing, or not to judge. Thus, to judge falsely cannot be to judge what is not. False judgment has been proved impossible again by Theaetetus's assumptions but for him (as for us) this remains absurd. The inference, which does not need to be spoken, once again is that Theaetetus's revised concept of knowledge cannot be right. Theaetetus will see this.

Modern commentators allege that "Plato's" second disproof of false judgment is both a sophism and a stupidity that confuses senses of "is." They are right, except that the sophism and the folly are not Plato's. They are the errors of a youth educated by a Protagorean teacher.

This might be a good place to pause and observe that Socrates has smuggled the Eleatics back into the drama again. He has fabricated epistemological equivalents of Zeno's paradoxes, which have features in common with reductio refutations.[77] The construction of such paradoxes is easy. One lays down a major premise by definition, for example, that space and time consist in infinite numbers of continuous points. The premise is alien to reality: somehow

---

77 I had thought that I was the first to notice this. However, I eventually discovered that Paul Stern saw it before I did, *Knowledge and Politics*, 224–25. Perhaps others whom I have not had the chance to read discovered it before he did too. It is hard to be first.

the continuum envisaged by Zeno misrepresents spacetime. Neglecting the disconnection between premise and reality, one applies the former to the latter and proceeds to conclusions that contradict empirical evidence, for example, that motion is impossible and illusory.[78] There is no escaping the results if one accepts the starting points. Theaetetus's premises lead inexorably to the impossibility of falsehood. This implies a critique of Zeno, whose assumptions led to absurdities, and perhaps of Parmenides, who taught Zeno and whose "being is one" position produces absurd contradictions.

Third Reductio

Socrates suggests another way of rescuing Theaetetus's argument. Perhaps falsehood is engaging in "other judging" (*allodoxian*): We might speculate that a person wrongly thinks that an existing thing is another existing thing, thus without declaring that he thinks what is not. The Eleatic stranger gives an example of this in Sophist: seeing a wolf, someone might suppose that it is a dog. In a later context, Theaetetus will present an example of this too: Seeing at a distance someone whom he does not know, he might conclude that he sees Socrates, whom he does know. At the moment, however, he appears to be smarting from Theodorus's insult so he can only come up with this example: to judge ugly beautiful or beautiful ugly is to make a truly false judgment.

Socrates replies by contentiously ridiculing Theaetetus's expression "truly false." Then, waiving this critique grandiosely, he continues to play the sophist, dismissing cases of mistaken identity and misappraisal as impossible absurdities. He prepares this new mischief by warning that he does not know what he is about to say. Given that his general plea of ignorance usually suffices for his modesty, this particular reminder is an extraordinary disavowal of what follows. Theaetetus will quickly agree with what he says, so we know that Socrates is still up to his usual trick of bringing his interlocutor's opinions to light for the purpose of testing them. Channeling Theaetetus, Socrates proceeds to define thinking

---

78 I do not wish to go deeply into arguments about Zeno's paradoxes, which would be to become trapped in a quagmire. For essays on this extremely complex matter, see Wesley C. Salmon (ed.), *Zeno's Paradoxes*.

(*dianoeisthai*) as mental discourse in which the *psychê* interrogates and answers itself, affirming or denying judgments. When the soul decides, it has *doxa*, which is still the concept of knowledge on the table. The new idea is that thinking is affirmation or denial of the judgment "I am having a psychic perception of X." (Socrates himself does not teach that all thought is affirmation and denial of such judgments. In Republic he gives a much more complex analysis of mental operations. In Phaedrus he speaks of wordless visions of realities beyond the heavens.) Having established this definition of thought, Socrates inquires sarcastically when anyone ever attempted to persuade himself that beauty is ugliness, that just is unjust, that odd is even, that a cow is a horse, or that two is one? He thus succeeds in reducing obvious examples of false opinion, misidentification and misappraisal to the previously analyzed case of knowing something and not knowing it, which by prior assumption is impossible. For the third time, false judgment has been shown to be impossible, thus implying that Theaetetus's new understanding of knowledge is wrong. The reasoning has been unsatisfactory but it had to go as it did, based as it was on Theaetetus's premises. (*Allodoxian* will be rehabilitated as the essence of error by the Eleatic stranger in Sophist, where the argument is not governed by Theaetetus's assumptions. The apparently widespread belief that Plato himself was actually stumped for any length of time by the problem of accounting for false judgment is simply incredible.)

Contemporary scholars appear to see some potential analytic merit in "Plato's" *allodoxian* suggestion. However, they also join McDowell in suspecting that Plato is not entirely clear about the points he is making. Chappell disagrees, stressing that Socrates is attacking empiricists.[79]

Fourth Reductio

Socrates ostentatiously worries that rejecting the picture of falsehood as "other judging" (which he now calls *heterodoxein*) will lead to absurdities. He pledges to try to avoid exposure of himself and Theaetetus to ridicule.

79 McDowell, *Plato: "Theaetetus,"* 205; Chappell, *Reading Plato's "Theaetetus,"* 168–71.

He will go so far as to contradict his previous denial that it is possible for people to judge that things that they know are other things that they do not know. Theaetetus remarks that back then he suspected (but did not say) that it was possible for someone who knows Socrates to see another person and mistake him for Socrates. For his new analysis, Socrates brings learning and memory back into play. This makes more sense than the previous assumption that learning and memory are irrelevant even when Theaetetus's genius is taken into account: Theaetetus must realize that he had to learn and remember Theodorus's demonstrations. However, in the new model of knowledge, learning will still look like immediate apprehension. Establishing that learning occurs, Socrates asks Theaetetus to suppose that we possess blocks of wax in our souls. The wax varies in quality from one *psychê* to another, being larger or smaller, pure or impure, hard or inflexible, and sometimes "measured" (just right). The wax is the gift of Mnemosyne (Memory), the mother of the Muses. When we wish to remember whatever we have seen, heard, or thought [that is, our sense and psychic perceptions], we stamp our perceptions and thoughts (*aisthêsesi kai ennoias*) on our memory wax, making impressions in it [learning things], much as we use seal rings to make impressions in wax. Whatever is imprinted we remember and know (*epistasthai*) as long as the impressions last, their duration depending on the nature of our wax. Theaetetus's account of *epistêmê* as true judgment (psychic perception) has been preserved in this image in a new form. Knowledge is now true judgment subsisting as memory.

Promising to demonstrate that one can err by mistaking something known for something unknown, Socrates first lists fourteen cases in which no one could identify "A" with "B." These objects are Theodorus and Theaetetus in Socrates' later examples, so this time we apparently are talking chiefly about identity statements. In compiling his survey, Socrates presents one of the densest inventories of possible alternatives in the history of philosophy. An effort to summarize this catalogue with words inevitably would end in a hardly understandable verbatim repetition of Socrates' statement or something similar. People therefore resort to different expedients to avoid the awkward result, such as translating the compact page into symbolic logic. I see no choice but to do something like that too. I shall offer matrices, with heartfelt apologies for the necessity of paying close attention to marks in boxes. I shall say that Socrates posits six categories into which

"A" and "B" could fall: known (remembered), not known (not remembered), perceived now, not perceived now, perceived as remembered, perceived not as remembered. The symbols of these classes in the matrices will be defined as follows:

A: First Object, for example, Theodorus
B: Second Object, for example, Theaetetus (or, I should like to add, Protagoras)
K: Known (Remembered)
NK: Not Known (Not Remembered)
P: Perceived (Now)
NP: Not Perceived (Now)
P = M: Present Perception and Memory Correspond
P * M: Present Perception and Memory Do Not Correspond.

CASES OF IMPOSSIBILITY OF ERRING
BY IDENTIFYING A WITH B

CASE 1

Epistemological Status	Of A	Of B
K	X	X
NK		
P		
NP	X	X
P = M		
P * M		

CASE 2

Epistemological Status	Of A	Of B
K	X	
NK		X
P		
NP	(X)	(X)
P = M		
P * M		

(X) = Mentioned not initially but in Socrates' later summary

CASE 3

Epistemological Status	Of A	Of B
K		
NK	X	X
P		
NP	(X)	(X)
P = M		
P * M		

(X) = Mentioned not initially but in Socrates' later summary

CASE 4

Epistemological Status	Of A	Of B
K		X
NK	X	
P		
NP		
P = M		
P * M		

CASE 5

Epistemological Status	Of A	Of B
K		
NK		
P	X	X
NP		
P = M		
P * M		

CASE 6

Epistemological Status	Of A	Of B
K		
NK		
P	X	
NP		X
P = M		
P * M		

CASE 7

Epistemological Status	Of A	Of B
K		
NK		
P		
NP	X	X
P = M		
P * M		

CASE 8

Epistemological Status	Of A	Of B
K		
NK		
P		X
NP	X	
P = M		
P * M		

CASE 9

Epistemological Status	Of A	Of B
K	X	X
NK		
P	X	X
NP		
P = M	X	X
P * M		

CASE 10

Epistemological Status	Of A	Of B
K	X	X
NK		
P	X	
NP		
P = M	X	
P * M		

CASE 11

Epistemological Status	Of A	Of B
K	X	
NK		
P	X	X
NP		
P = M	X	
P * M		

CASE 12

Epistemological Status	Of A	Of B
K		
NK	X	X
P		
NP	X	X
P = M		
P * M		

CASE 13

Epistemological Status	Of A	Of B
K		
NK	X	X
P		
NP	X	
P = M		
P * M		

CASE 14

Epistemological Status	Of A	Of B
K		
NK	X	
P		
NP	X	X
P = M		
P * M		

Having listed his fourteen cases in which it is impossible to err by identifying "A" with "B," Socrates details three cases in which such falsehood could arise, as follows:

CASES OF POSSIBILITY OF ERRING BY IDENTIFYING A WITH B

CASE 15

Epistemological Status	Of A	Of B
K		
NK	X	
P		
NP	X →	← X
P = M		
P * M		

(X) = Mentioned not initially but in Socrates' later summary
X with Arrows = Interchanged memories, like shoes on wrong feet

CASE 16

Epistemological Status	Of A	Of B
K	X	X
NK		
P		X
NP		
P = M		
P * M	(X)	

(X) = Mentioned not initially but in Socrates' later summary

CASE 17

Epistemological Status	Of A	Of B
K	X	X
NK		
P	X	X
NP		
P = M		
P * M	(X)	(X)

(X) = Mentioned not initially but in Socrates' later summary

Having finished itemizing these cases and having heard Theaetetus's confession that he is hopelessly lost, Socrates goes back over six of them, adding things that he had not stated initially. He reviews the first three cases of impossibility of falsehood in more understandable terms: Case 1: If Socrates is acquainted with Theodorus and Theaetetus but does not perceive them, he could not judge that one is the other. Case 2: If Socrates knows either Theodorus or Theaetetus but not both and does not perceive either, he could never judge that one is the other. Case 3: If Socrates knows neither and perceives neither, he could not think that one is the other. Theaetetus agrees with all these analyses. Socrates tells him to figure out the remaining eleven cases himself. Then he does his review of the cases of possibility of error. Case 15: If Socrates knows both Theodorus and Theaetetus and sees both at a distance but indistinctly, and if he remembers both properly, he might assign the imprints of each in his memory wax to the other, as if he were putting shoes on the wrong feet. Case 16: If Socrates knows both Theodorus and Theaetetus but perceives only Theaetetus, and does not remember Theodorus properly, he might assign the imprint of one in his memory wax to the other. Case 17: If Socrates knows and sees both Theodorus and Theaetetus but remembers neither properly, he might assign the imprints of each in his memory wax to the other. Theaetetus now understands perfectly, thinks that Socrates' descriptions are wonderfully divine, and decides that false judgment has been vindicated. However, there are problems.

Now that Socrates' seventeen cases have been presented in tabular form and explained, one perceives immediately that his analysis is flawed. The three accounts of error are reasonable but the possibilities of falsehood are understated. For one thing, Socrates himself has admitted that distance is a variable that affects outcomes. Every matrix in his list should contain at least two more rows: PD = Perceived Distantly and PC = Perceived Closely. Further, Socrates has left several cells in his matrices blank. Marking them would have produced more chances of error. For example, what if there were Cases 2a and 4a in which "B" (in 2a) and "A" (in 4a) were PD, with the P = M and P * M cells still unmarked? Could the unknown persons not be mistaken for the known ones? What if there were a Case 5a with "A" and "B" marked PD and P * M? Could Theodorus and Theaetetus standing in a later police lineup not be mixed up by a witness? What if there were a

Case 6a in which "B" was known and the sighting of "A" was from afar? Could not the known Theodorus be mistaken for the known but unperceived Theaetetus? What if there were a Case 8a that was the mirror image of 6a? What if there were a Case 7a in which "A" and "B" were not perceived and unknown in the sense of met once long ago and badly remembered? Could not Theodorus and Theaetetus be confused in thought? How about a Case 10a with "A" perceived from afar? Could Theodorus not be taken for Theaetetus? How about a Case 11a with "A" and "B" marked PD? Could there be confusion? What if there were a Case 13a with either "A" or "B" perceived for the first time in Theodorus's school? Could no one have heard tell of Theodorus and Protagoras and, without knowing either, seen one and supposed that he was the other? This makes for at least nine missed possibilities of error and twenty-three total cases and I have been restraining my imagination to avoid boring the reader. (One could think of additional variables.)

Ronald Polansky argues that Socrates has mimicked Theodorus's mathematics by seeking potentials for falsehood in seventeen cases, dismissing fourteen of them and affirming three, just as Theodorus sought numbers with rational square roots among the first seventeen numbers but discovered fourteen irrational square roots and only three rational ones above the unit.[80] This is interesting but questionable. The Greeks did not consider one a number. Theodorus did not do seventeen cases. He omitted one and two because they were already known, leaving a possible total of only fifteen, and he may have looked at fewer than that, dealing only with odd numbers. I suppose that Plato actually is signaling the reader that just as Theodorus could have proceeded beyond his perhaps fifteen cases with increasingly complex diagrams, finding additional rational square roots as long as he lived, one could complicate Socrates' matrices greatly with ever more variables that affect outcomes and find infinite possibilities of error.

We soon shall lose incentive to compare Theodorus's and Socrates' different caseloads, with Socrates' fourteen negatives and three positives, for Socrates will declare his three positives unimportant. Suddenly he expresses dismay. Theaetetus asks what is wrong. Socrates observes that they have asserted that false judgment inheres not in perception and not in thought

---

80   Polansky, *Philosophy and Knowledge*, 189.

but in the connection of perception with thinking. That is true. He then inquires whether a person who is perceiving neither a man nor a horse would suppose that a man is a horse. Of course not, replies the boy. Well, Socrates points out, we do not perceive abstract numbers, we merely think them. Could anyone who only envisages twelve and eleven in the abstract believe that twelve is eleven? No, says Theaetetus. If not, how does a person who sums five and seven get eleven? Did we not say that twelve and eleven are imprinted in our wax? Thus, are we not claiming that arithmetical mistakes amount to the taking of one thing that we know for another thing that we know and that this occurs in thought that does not involve perception? Did we not declare that impossible (for example, just now, when we said that no one would think that a man is a horse)? If there is false judgment in the matching of perception with thought (which Socrates actually denies was granted with the three positives), that is trivial. The important thing is that by Theaetetus's fundamental assumptions we have proved that there cannot be false judgment in thought (thus implying that we do not make the kinds of errors in arithmetic that were just illustrated). Theaetetus will grasp that the denial of such mistakes is absurd. Again, his premises must be rejected or the absurdity must be accepted. Socrates explicitly adds that we must prove that false judgment is something other than the interchange of perception with thought. It must be found in thought itself.

Modern commentators devote much thought to the question of what "Plato's" wax tablet implies for his theory of Forms. I do not think it necessary to engage in that exercise. The wax block is a reductio refutation of Theaetetus's idea of *epistêmê*, not Plato's ontology or incipient epistemology.

Fifth Reductio

Socrates takes up the task of proving that there can be false judgment in thought. This is, of course, yet another (faux) move to rescue Theaetetus's second concept of knowledge together with the possibility of false judgment. Socrates suggests a "shameless" deed, to say what it is to know. This act would be shameless because it would be to give an arbitrary, unreasoned answer to the question that they have been pursuing. In a way, they have been presuming upon the right answer all along, for they have been saying that they know or do not know things as if they knew what knowledge is. Theaetetus wonders how they could have refrained from speaking that way. He encourages Socrates to proceed with his shameless deed.

Socrates proceeds. He now distinguishes between "having knowledge" (*epistêmês hexin*) and "possessing knowledge" (*epistêmês ktêsin*). He gives an example of the distinction: If a man bought a cloak and left it in his closet we could say that he "possessed" it but not that he "had" it. This sets the stage for Socrates' creation of his "aviary" image. A man might catch birds and put them in an aviary. Upon doing so, he would possess the birds but not have them. We could say that each human soul contains an aviary. This aviary is empty at birth but it is gradually filled as we learn. The birds are pieces of knowledge. Learning is still a kind of immediate apprehension in this image, with the pieces of knowledge being things that we either possess or do not possess. Theaetetus's second definition of *epistêmê* remains intact, with the aviary taking the place of wax tablet memory and the insertion of birds into the aviary replacing the stamping of the wax. Once the birds of knowledge have been released into our aviaries, we possess them but we do not have them. To possess them is to know them [in a first sense of the word]. To try to get hold of them again while they are flying around in the aviary is to seek them as if we did not know [in another sense of the word] what we knew. To catch them again is to come to re-know (relearn) what we already know from ourselves [in the two senses of the word]. Socrates presents the example that a mathematician "knows all number" and says that counting accordingly is to consider what one knows as if one did not know it. Theaetetus is shocked by this use of words. However, Socrates suggests that we always possess what we possess, so that we cannot possibly know and not know the things we know [in the first sense]. Further, we conceive false judgments by looking for one bird in our aviaries and catching another and we form true judgments when we recapture the bird we seek. Theaetetus is mollified and agrees. He is easily persuaded by images.

Socrates promptly kills the boy's hopes. Abandoning the double senses of "know" that he used to construct the aviary picture, he reverts to a single sense and claims that it is absurd for someone who has knowledge of something to be ignorant of it, not by means of ignorance but by means of this very knowledge. It is equally absurd to say that the soul's knowledge is ignorance. Theaetetus attempts to save the image by suggesting that we also insert pieces of ignorance into our aviaries. To catch a bit of ignorance is to have false opinion. This does not work. Socrates construes the suggestion to mean that a person who knows both knowledge and ignorance fancies that the one is the other. The individual thus thinks that one thing he knows is another thing he knows, a possibility that was just rejected in the wax block metaphor. Theaetetus's assumptions have closed off all of his escape routes. He cannot simultaneously have his *epistêmê* as true *doxa* (qua psychic *aisthêsis*) and false judgment.

Socrates abruptly calls a halt to the effort to explain false judgment, leaving the problem hanging. This does not signal a failure on Plato's part, for he never meant to elaborate a theory that succeeded. He has stopped the project because he has shown Theaetetus reductio refutations of his second definition of knowledge from every possible viewpoint. Enough is enough.

In a last effort to save his definition of *epistêmê* as true judgment, Theaetetus reaffirms it, arguing that it at least is safe from error. Socrates makes short work of it. He objects that, in law courts, jurors sometimes reach true judgments without having been eyewitnesses to the events in question and without having been sufficiently taught in the short time periods in which the cases have been presented, so that they have persuasion without knowledge. (He evidently thinks that having been an eyewitness and having been adequately taught are two valid paths to knowledge, either or both of which might do depending on the nature of the thing the jury needs to know. I note that juries do not seek knowledge of Forms. Plato apparently admits of senses or extensions of the word knowledge that apply beyond Forms to this-worldly things. This is a common-sense position. Not every Socratic epistemological thought has implications for Platonic metaphysics.) Theaetetus yields. Knowledge is not true judgment, at least not true judgment simply.

It may be no accident that Socrates chose the example of the jury for his final refutation of the second definition. The idea that there could be psychic perceptions of just and unjust (or of guilt and innocence?) was another instance of the scientists' legal endangerment of Socrates.

Theaetetus suddenly recalls that he heard someone say that knowledge is true judgment with a *logos*. The term *logos* has numerous English equivalents so any translation chosen will be disputable. I shall take "with a *logos*" to mean "with a rational account" or "with an argument" or even Fowler's "with reason." "Definition" seems out of place here. Definitions may or may not be trustworthy. Theaetetus continues his report. The person whom he heard speaking added that a true judgment that was *alogon* (without a *logos*) was *ektos epistêmês* (beyond knowledge) and that *alogon* things are *ouk epistêta* (unknowable or, per Sachs, unintelligible). Socrates asks how *epistêta* and *ouk epistêta* were distinguished. This apparently is to inquire what lends itself to a *logos*. Theaetetus cannot explain it but he thinks that he could follow someone else's effort. Socrates answers that he will tell Theaetetus a dream in return for a dream.

It is necessary to raise four questions about this exchange. First, what are Theaetetus and Socrates talking about as they study the proposition that *epistêmê* is true judgment with a *logos*? What is this *logos*? Second, why does Socrates declare that his summary of the new theory will be a dream? Third, in a drama in which Socrates and Theaetetus have had no trouble identifying the authors of other doctrines, why have their memories suddenly gone blank with respect to the identity of the teacher of the "dream theory?" Fourth, who is this unnamed sage?

To facilitate consideration of the first question, I need to bring a number of assumptions to bear. One is that Theaetetus probably conceives of the *logos* that he has suddenly remembered as something that will supply the defect of the jury's true judgment, that is, as something that can be added to the true judgment to turn it into knowledge. Thus, it probably is something that will consist in pertinent teaching (which might need to be supplemented by empirical evidence). We still must ask what such instruction could be and how it could be decisive. Because Theaetetus is ever the geometer, it seems likely that he thinks of the *logos* as a rational proof. For example, he can see a line intersecting another line, truly judge the congruence of the opposite angles, and add a demonstration to clinch the judgment. However, this reply only pushes the query back. What makes for a successful proof? The emergence of this issue might explain Socrates' resolution to tell Theaetetus a dream in exchange for a dream. As Chappell notes, Socrates himself inquires in Symposium (202a5–9): "Don't you know that to have correct beliefs while lacking the ability to give an account (*logon dounai*) is not to have knowledge? For how could anything be knowledge that was without an account (*alogon*)?"[81] Socrates probably views knowledge,

---

81 Chappell's translation in *Reading Plato's "Theaetetus,"* 199.

or one variety of it, as true judgment plus a *logos* but he must have his own
idea of what a sufficient *logos* would be. In a circumstance in which all the
arguments Socrates adduces come from his interlocutors, he probably will
tell Theaetetus a dream insofar as he will feed the boy his own inadequate
views of a proper *logos*. Theaetetus will have received these concepts from
Theodorus. This probably is why the author of the dream theory remains
unidentified. The unnamed source is sitting next to Theaetetus and Socrates
already fuming, thus creating a delicate situation. (Another possibility is
that a sophist grammarian obscurely mentioned at 202e—perhaps Protagoras again?—had the dream and that Theodorus adopted it because he liked
its relevance to geometry.) Theaetetus and Socrates probably feel obliged
to develop uncharacteristic amnesia to avoid pushing Theodorus into a tow-
ering rage.

Relating his dream, Socrates reports that he seemed to hear people
claim that the primary elements (*prôta stoicheia*) out of which we and
everything else are composed have no *logos*. It is possible to perceive and
name them but not to describe them, not even with words such as "is,"
"this," and "that." Therefore they are unknowable. Compounds of these
elements do have *logoi*, for they have names and *logoi* are names strung
together. Thus, the compounds are knowable. A person who has true
judgment but no *logos* of something has truth in his mind but no knowledge. If he obtains a *logos*, he acquires knowledge too. Theaetetus agrees
that this is what he heard. I think he heard it from Theodorus because
the dream reminds one of the things that are discussed in geometric
proofs. The elements of geometry are points, which lack *logoi* (positive
accounts). We can "perceive" their presence to the mind and observe
their representations as dots on paper but we cannot endow them with
attributes, perhaps not even that of existence, for geometers deny them
mass and dimension. Figures are compounds of points. For example,
lines are the shortest distances between two points and are made up of
points. Circles are all the points in a plane the length of a radius (a line
between two points) from a point. Curves are all the points in planes at
various distances from points. Geometric science consists in perception
of points, perception of the compounded points that are figures, and
logoi (proofs) about the compounds. Thus, Socrates seems to be alluding
to a geometer's definition of *epistêmê*, extended beyond mathematics to

all things.[82] This presumably is why Theaetetus calls the dream theory beautiful.

Contemporary scholars engage in complex debates about the content of the dream theory. Their issue is whether Plato envisages propositional or objectual knowledge or a logical atomism that transcends such distinctions.[83] I doubt that Theaetetus would grasp why the writers have this problem. He seems to think that one perceives and names the elements of which compounds are made and then furnishes a *logos* by linking the names of these objects, such that his knowledge is simultaneously objectual, propositional, atomistic, and whatever else it happens to be depending on the case. Theaetetus assumes that his new definition encompasses every kind of knowledge and that it applies to knowledge of everything, just as Socrates said. If this overlooks difficulties, we must keep in mind that we are dealing with a youth's groping efforts, not with sophisticated theories that Plato is constructing in his own name.

Socrates replies that the dream theory probably is beautiful, for what could *epistêmê* be in addition to right judgment and *logos*? What indeed? We recall that Plato, in the Seventh Letter, laments the weakness of *logoi* while envisaging a perfect fifth-level knowledge over and above every fourth-level science consisting in name, image, and *logos*. Be it never so well founded, the *epistêmê* that Plato makes Socrates discuss here and in the lines from Symposium cited above is built on name, image, and *logos* and must be inadequate, falling short of the higher knowledge to which Plato aspires. The dialogue Theaetetus has been rigorously limited to the epistemology of fourth-level science. I think that Socrates' question—What more could knowledge be than true judgment plus *logos*?—is intended to stimulate

---

82 Chappell doubts that the dream refers to geometric demonstrations, *Reading Plato's "Theaetetus,"* 198. However, the focus of his objection is another scholar's mistaken argument that Socrates has the formal steps of a proof in mind when Socrates actually talks about elements of things being discussed. Chappell's objection is inapposite to my reading. It is Socrates' citation of the elements of the things that makes the case for reading the dream as an extrapolation of the geometric demonstrations, which for Theodorus evidently are strings of the names of the things compounded in figures.

83 Nicely summarized by Chappell, *Reading Plato's "Theaetetus,"* 205–12. Chappell's discussions of the secondary literature are extremely valuable.

wonder, not to end the search for an account of knowledge within the confines of "true judgment plus logos." Socrates describes much more that knowledge could be in Republic, Symposium, and Phaedrus.

Having inquired what more knowledge could be, Socrates objects to the dream theory at what he calls its most elegant point, the claim that elements are unknowable but compounds are knowable. The originator of the theory offered the letters of the alphabet and syllables of words as examples of what he meant. The letters, he said, have no *logoi* but the syllables do have them (so the former are unknowable and the latter are knowable). Socrates tests this by referring to the first syllable of his name. He induces Theaetetus to say that the syllable "*Sô*" has a *logos*, that it is sigma and omega, but that these letters have no *logoi* because they only represent sounds. This sets up a refutation of the new definition that will come presently.

Before getting to that, I should note that Theaetetus explains the sounds of the letters with lucid precision at length. This reminds us of Wittgenstein's precept, "whereof one cannot speak, thereof one must be silent," and of Russell's retort that Wittgenstein spoke quite a lot about that whereof one cannot speak. One wonders why Theaetetus does not think that he is giving *logoi* of sigma and omega as he tells their sounds.[84] This must be a function of what he wants a *logos* to do. He is defining the letters by identifying the classes of sounds for which they stand, proving that elements actually do have descriptions that go well beyond the words "is," "this," and "that." Such definitions would count as *logoi* in ordinary Greek parlance but they are not demonstrations that confirm truths so they probably do not do what Theaetetus expects *logoi* to do. This brings back the question of whether we ourselves should accept definitions as parts of knowledge. We can consider the examples implicitly and explicitly suggested by the text. Geometers assume a true judgment that there are points. It is not clear that this judgment is true. The judgment plus the explanation that points are invisible objects in unique locations possessing neither mass nor dimension show that even the points can have informative (negative) descriptions. However, the definition would appear to establish knowledge only if the existence of points were empirically confirmed. Grammarians

---

84   Cf. Chappell, *Reading Plato's "Theaetetus,"* 218.

assume a true judgment that there is a conventional letter sigma, saying that it represents a hissing sound. Something in us makes us want to consider this judgment plus the definition to be knowledge. However, it may be that we have this reaction only because the existence of the conventional sigma and its representation of hissing sounds can be empirically confirmed. Thus, one can see why Theaetetus might be reluctant to accept true judgments plus *logoi* qua definitions as knowledge. On the other hand, this points up a fundamental flaw in the new definition of *epistêmê*. As channeled by Socrates, Theaetetus has not understood that there are *logoi* of elements that sometimes may not and sometimes can be parts of knowledge. Neither has he made it clear that it is not the addition of a mere "string of names" *logos* that turns a true judgment into knowledge but the addition of a *logos* that either verifies itself or has an empirical verification. Further, the epistemological status of the *logos* will depend on its verifiability and not on whether it refers to elements or compounds. Theaetetus's ambiguity about these matters will give Socrates plenty of play to make trouble for his latest definition. Perhaps Plato intended to suggest all this by letting Theaetetus give his definitive account of letters and sounds.

Socrates refutes the dream theory by offering Theaetetus an impossible choice. The first option: Professing ignorance of sigma and omega, the elements of *Sô*, we claim knowledge of the compound. Theaetetus thinks that terrible and *alogon*. The second option: Perhaps the syllable is no longer the sum of its letters but a new form that has emerged from their union. What then? Theaetetus likes the new suggestion. However, Socrates then claims that the new whole cannot have parts. If a whole has parts, it is necessary for it to be all its parts. Theaetetus believes that the whole can be different from all its parts. Socrates talks him out of this conviction by citing the example of numbers. Six is formed by adding or multiplying its constituent numbers and no matter which way we present them, six is undeniably the sum or product of those numbers, right? Theaetetus is beaten down, whereupon he accepts two more examples in which the whole must be the sum of its parts: the numbers of the plethron and the stade are the same as the plethron and the stade, right? The number of the army is the same as the army, right? The boy meekly agrees. If *Sô* is a new whole different from its parts, the compound is a simple and, by prior assumption, it must be unknowable. The dream theory is undone.

Many scholars are exercised by perceived fallacies in Socrates' response to Theaetetus, some of which are real atrocities and others of which can be explained away.[85] There especially is a lot of discussion about Socrates' unsound denial of the existence of emergent wholes that are more than and different from the sums of their parts. Two commentators argue extensively that Socrates' silliness is pedagogically strategic rather than serious.[86] I agree with them for reasons of my own. In my opinion, Socrates' answers are governed again by Theaetetus's assumptions and Socrates once more is subjecting Theaetetus to reductio refutations. Plato has already caused Theaetetus to show that elements are knowable in some sense or other. However, if elements are unknowable and if there are no emergent wholes, it follows that ignorance of elements must also be ignorance of their compounds. Socrates' fallacious denial of emergent wholes is based on an interesting trick. Socrates argues that the *numbers* of the plethron and the stade and the *numbers* of the army are the same as the plethron, the stade, and the army. This is true if the numbers of things are the same as what they are, which the young mathematician seems to believe, but it is not the case that the numbers of things are their essences. Socrates is pushing Theaetetus to see that he either must give up the idea that the numbers of elements in a compound are that thing or accept the absurdities that there is no knowledge of elements, that there are no emergent wholes, and that knowledge of objects is impossible. The boy does move grudgingly toward surrendering his mathematical dream. Socrates must do more to bring him fully around.

Socrates administers the coup de grace to the dream theory easily, by observing that one learns spelling by going in the direction opposite to that suggested by it. One learns letters first and only then proceeds to the formation of words. (Of course, one learns to speak words before learning to spell them but that is a different matter.) Now Theaetetus is convinced.

85   See Chappell, *Reading Plato's "Theaetetus,"* 210–222. Chappell successfully defends Socrates against many of the charges.
86   See Rosemary Desjardins, *The Rational Enterprise: Logos in Plato's "Theaetetus,"* all index entries under "emergent generation" and "emergent whole" as well as her long and earnest analyses of Platonic *kompsoteros* theory. See also Stern, *Knowledge and Politics*, 266ff, with his particularly good argument about the difference between an aggregate of men and an army.

Socrates affects to make one last effort to save the third definition of knowledge, saying that he and Theaetetus never examined the meaning of *logos* in the phrase "true judgment with a *logos*." This highly inadequate discussion also will be ruled by one of Theaetetus's assumptions, that a *logos* is a string of names. This issue already was implicit in the oddity that Theaetetus did not consider his definitions of letters and their sounds *logoi* and now it becomes explicit.

Socrates offers three possible definitions of *logos* (qua strings of names). The first is that giving a *logos* is to explain the meaning of what one has said. This idea lacks merit. All people, says Socrates, can clarify their statements (with the silent implication that not all know what they are talking about.)

The second is that a *logos* is a complete enumeration of a thing's elements. For example, a wagon is known if one can enumerate its one hundred parts. Theaetetus likes that. However, Socrates observes that it is possible to list an element without understanding it, as in the case in which someone correctly spells "Theaetetus" with a theta and an epsilon but then wrongly spells "Theodorus" with a tau and an epsilon. A *logos* that turns true judgment into knowledge must do something more than enumerate elements because that could happen by accident.

The third possibility is that knowledge is an ability to point out a characteristic of a thing that distinguishes it from other things. For example, the sun could be called the brightest object in the sky. This suggestion serves as a start toward Aristotle's concept of the specific difference but it will not do. Socrates says that if the *logos* refers to difference, the original judgment must have neglected difference. Thus, for example, the first judgment of Theaetetus would not have distinguished him from others and could hardly have been a true judgment about him. Not only that. A *logos* of difference presupposes knowledge of that difference. (I would add that defining *episteme* as true judgment plus a *logos* presupposes that the *logos* is knowledge of whatever turns the true judgment into knowledge.) Hence, Theaetetus's third definition is circular: It translates to the proposition that knowledge is true judgment plus knowledge. This unavoidable inference is fatal.

Sayre maintains that "there is a quite common use of the term *logos* which Plato does not permit himself to consider in the Theaetetus. This is the use according to which *logos* means "ground." Promising further meanings of "ground" would be "principle," "explanation," "cause," and "reason." Sayre contends that if these meanings had been considered "the dialogue could not have ended on the entirely negative note for which it has been famous." Thus, he asserts that the third definition of *epistêmê* has been rejected "quite prematurely." It has never been "subjected to any analysis which would put its sufficiency to the test." Plato must have more to say about the third hypothesis in a better context, such as Sophist.[87] I agree with Sayre up to a point. Just as I argued that Theaetetus's *logos* would have to contain or point to its own verification to turn a true judgment into knowledge, I accept the possibility that appeals to principle, etc., could serve as the needed verifications. I would like to reformulate this last statement. Let us say that a true judgment needs a verification (which might appeal to principle, etc.) to be turned into "a piece of knowledge." Well and good. However, I am not satisfied that this tells us what knowledge *is*. I do not see how Sayre escapes the charge of circularity that Socrates has leveled against the third definition. Sayre's favored definition apparently would reduce to "knowledge is true judgment plus knowledge of principle or explanation or cause or reason." In later applications that interest Sayre as an analytic philosopher, his better definition might reduce to "knowledge is an account of all the necessary and sufficient conditions for something to be F," which would be to say that "knowledge is knowledge of the necessary and sufficient conditions." That looks circular to me.

This difficulty returns me to my original problem with the epistemological content of the dialogue Theaetetus: I do not understand Socrates' question "what is knowledge?" What does he want to learn by posing that question? What does his "what" mean? Socrates evidently wishes to get deeper into the nature of *epistêmê* than the tautology "knowledge is knowledge." But what could be meant by "the nature of knowledge?" Does the phrase refer to a material or immaterial stuff out of which knowledge is made? Or to an act or operation of the mind? Or to a condition of the soul that is awareness of the evidence and good logic necessary to the possession of truth, as Sayre seems to assume? The dialogue has touched on all these possibilities unsuccessfully. I therefore see no reason to prefer any of the

---

87   Sayre, *Plato's Analytic Method*, 136–37.

choices, let alone that which Sayre makes a priori. In saying this, I do not mean to accuse Plato of being muddled. There is an excellent reason why he might have left his inquiry in such an indeterminate state deliberately, namely, that all he wanted to do was to demonstrate that the scientists who helped to condemn Socrates were the ones who were muddled. Had Theodorus known what he was about, he would have demanded clarification of Socrates' question at the beginning of the investigation.

Theaetetus abandons his last definition. He confesses that his offspring have been wind eggs. Socrates tells him that this is good, for he has acquired the wisdom to avoid thinking that he knows what he does not know. He is thrilled to have found a potential philosopher. This is the last critical moment of the dialogue. Socrates informs the group that he now must go to answer the indictment that Meletus has filed against him. This comes as a surprise to readers who thought they were studying a dialogue primarily about epistemology: "Why would Plato end his groundbreaking inquiry with an irrelevant point like that?" As I have maintained throughout, the answer is that the dramatic point is relevant. Theaetetus has not been primarily about epistemology but, rather, about the relationship of Greek science to the trial and death of Socrates.

In my opinion, my analysis of Theaetetus has verified the hypothesis about the drama set forth in chapter two. With regard to epistemology, the play is deliberately aporetic. It shows that adopting Protagorean/Heraclitean/geometric premises leads to bafflement about knowledge. To maintain that Theaetetus represents Plato's floundering struggles to understand knowledge, or his partially successful effort to lay a foundation for a sound epistemology that will be worked out in Sophist and Statesman, as many do, is to misconstrue the text. My interpretation of the plot and reasoning of the play as a portrayal of the remote scientific cause of Socrates' condemnation has been borne out by exegetical proof that these two elements work together to achieve that result. This cooperation is epitomized by Socrates' demonstration that Protagorean/Heraclitean theory leads to an ethical relativism that makes justice depend on the *koinê doxan*.

Socrates requests another meeting at dawn tomorrow. He clearly wants to keep working with Theaetetus. He has begun the project of rescuing his comrade but he still has a long way to go before he can consider it well started. (Unfortunately, he will lose his young friend soon, just as Odysseus lost all his comrades.) An agreement to meet again is reached off-stage. We must ask what else occurs there. I believe I have shown that Theodorus is no friend of Socrates. He is a mathematical Anytus. He supposes that he needs to save his boy from corruption by the sophist who has embarrassed him and torn down Protagoras. He lays a plan to do that by bringing along the Eleatic stranger on the coming dawn.

4
SOPHIST: CASTS OF THE NET

In Phaedrus, Socrates indicates that he is particularly enamored of the philosophic method of division and collection. He also mentions the importance of this procedure in Philebus. In the dialogue that I shall study next, Sophist, the Eleatic stranger, a new protagonist, relies heavily on division and collection (to which I shall often refer simply as *diaeresis*, division, letting the word stand for both aspects of the method). This has given rise to a presumption among many scholars of different stripes that the stranger is either a friend of Socrates who develops his philosophy by putting *diaeresis* to use in new contexts or a successor of Socrates who employs *diaeresis* to arrive at fresh Platonic insights that supersede Socratic teachings that have been found inadequate. Although Eva Brann and her translation partners, Peter Kalkavage and Eric Salem, doubt that the Eleatic stranger's dialectic is exactly the same as that of Socrates, they still seem to view the stranger as a friend of Socrates who applies his philosophy to new topics. They write that the stranger speaks truth, apparently with the approval of a silent Socrates, who, "we may imagine, stands by smiling" at the stranger's often deliberately comical discourse.[1]

Stanley Rosen and other students of Leo Strauss maintain that Plato is an esoteric writer. Regarding the text that we are about to examine, Rosen cryptically declares that: "There is then a close connection between philosophical rhetoric and diaeresis, or the division and collection in accordance with kinds . . . Philosophical rhetoric, as rooted in a knowledge of kinds or forms, speaks the truth, if in an accommodated sense."[2] The

---

1   Eva Brann, Peter Kalkavage, Eric Salem (trans. and ed.), *Plato's "Sophist": The Professor of Wisdom*, 6.
2   Stanley Rosen, *Plato's "Sophist": The Drama of Original and Image*, 2.

argument is that Plato makes the stranger use *diaeresis* to adjust truths to the capacities of the many and simultaneously to indicate what the undoctored verities are to the few who can think. I cannot claim to know the unaccommodated Platonic truth, although I suppose that it has to do with the opinions of Rosen and Seth Benardete that Socrates is guilty of the philosophic crimes that the stranger implicitly imputes to him, which will be discussed later.[3]

Professors of analytic philosophy generally maintain that Plato's Sophist and Statesman constitute a new departure in his thought. Transcending Theaetetus, which was his first, failed, but still constructive effort to devise a theory of *epistêmê* that abandoned the Forms of his middle period, Plato uses Sophist to solve the *aporiae* of Theaetetus, develop an adequate epistemology, and lay the foundations for an ontology that comes to happy fruition in Statesman and Philebus. I hope to be permitted to choose Kenneth Sayre as the spokesman for this argument. Regarding Sophist, Sayre tells us that the dialogue discloses Plato's "mature method of philosophic analysis, illustrating in its structure the very procedures of collection and division" that the Eleatic stranger defines as philosophy, the "free man's knowledge." It "chides" Socrates for practicing the art of refutation without the new method, thus always producing "disappointingly inconclusive" results. This truly philosophic method "exhibits and describes what was kept beyond our reach at the end of Theaetetus, the sense in which knowledge can be conceived as true judgment accompanied by an account." It thereby realizes "the Platonic goal of achieving knowledge in the form of proper definitions," which present all "the necessary and sufficient conditions for the truth of particular propositions." In addition to successfully explaining the nature of knowledge, Sophist improves Plato's earlier metaphysics by affirming what was previously denied, that the Forms can undergo a kind of change by combining with one another. So, "Sophist appears to be Plato's manifesto of independence" both from Socrates and from his other revered precursor, Parmenides.[4]

Sayre's thesis powerfully flies in the face of Francis M. Cornford's argument that Plato wrote Theaetetus to prove that knowledge could not be

---

3   Rosen, *Plato's "Sophist,"* 24; Seth Benardete, *The Being of the Beautiful*, II-99.
4   Sayre, *Plato's Analytic Method*, x, 152, 229, 165–66 n25.

understood without the "middle period" Forms.[5] Thus, his position has been countered by scholars who stand, to some extent at least, in Cornford's tradition. I shall select Kenneth Dorter as their spokesman. He rejects "the strongly revisionist view that the Eleatic dialogues are a retreat from some of the more distinctive features of the theory of forms." He also rejects the opposite opinion that these works contain objections to the theory of Forms that are not Plato's own. Dorter regards the Eleatic dialogues as thought experiments in which Plato outlines the epistemological problems of the Forms in Parmenides; tries but fails to explain knowledge without the Forms in Theaetetus; brings some of them back in Sophist to solve the epistemological puzzles of Theaetetus, failing to illuminate the nature of the sophist because he prescinds from the Form of the Good; and finally, in Statesman, relates the transcendent Good to politics through "the mean," a "just right" that is found between extremes, thus formulating a satisfactory higher hypothesis about politics while tacitly acknowledging that the Forms have explanatory limits.[6]

These allusions could not possibly extend or do justice to all the analyses of Sophist that stand on library shelves, not even if they were expanded to hundreds of pages. However, they do suffice to indicate the varieties of interpretations of the dialogue with which I wish to contrast my own. In my first two chapters, I have noted Plato's warning that he never put his serious insights into words, inferring that his works are aporetic on principle. They intend to drive readers into a perplexity that frees them to see higher realities for themselves. Every dialogue purposely pushes acclaimed hypotheses to their breaking points. I also have argued that the logic in Plato's plays must be understood in the light of their stories and vice-versa. In this respect, I have suggested that the Theaetetus/Sophist/Statesman trilogy belongs to a set of seven dialogues centered on the judicial murder of Socrates; that these plays study the remote cultural reasons why Socrates was condemned; that their dramas and arguments represent intellectual indictments and prosecutions of Socrates that parallel Socrates' legal ordeal; that the Eleatic stranger is Socrates' prosecutor in Sophist and Statesman; that the trilogy also reflects a meditative-mythical voyage of Plato's soul

---

5   Francis M. Cornford, *Plato's Theory of Knowledge*.

6   Kenneth Dorter, *Form and Good in Plato's Eleatic Dialogues*, 12 and throughout.

that has become Socrates-Odysseus as Plato wrestles with philosophic temptations symbolized by the trials of Odysseus; and that, in Sophist, Plato-Socrates-Odysseus has found himself in the country of the Cyclops facing Polyphemus in the person of the Eleatic stranger. I suppose that my treatment of Theaetetus has lent credence to my suggestions that this dialogue is meant to test Protagorean-Heracleitean-geometric premises about *epistêmê*; that it achieves its aim by refuting and reducing those premises to absurdity, thus opening the souls of those who continue to think on their own to higher knowledge; that Theodorus is the Lotus King and Anytus in that play, and that Plato-Socrates-Odysseus effects his escape from the Lotus Land (the temptation of geometric certainty). Regarding Sophist and Statesman, my hypotheses remain to be verified.

I know that I am incurring considerable risk by disagreeing with thinkers as accomplished as Eva Brann, Stanley Rosen, Seth Benardete, Kenneth Sayre, and Kenneth Dorter. I also know that I am indebted to all of them. Differences of opinion do not suggest that I have not learned more from them than I dispute. Respect for their erudition and good will requires that I briefly indicate my reasons for diverging from their analyses.

I cannot follow the excellent Eva Brann and her partners because I think that the Eleatic stranger demonstrably does not always speak truth. I also doubt that Socrates would be amused by the stranger's thinly veiled accusations that he is a sophist. Aristophanes' similar accusations did not delight Socrates, who did not see friendly humor in the indictment that led to his death.

Rosen and Benardete are full of brilliant particular insights of which I shall avail myself. (I must confess that I do not always understand Benardete's arguments.) I doubt their conviction that Plato esoterically indicates serious propositional truths because I think that such verities are essentially ineffable. I also disagree with their opinion that Socrates is guilty of the charges that the Eleatic stranger levels against him, he being the individual whom Plato calls the most just of his time.

In the case of Sayre, Plato's comments in the Seventh Letter about the weakness of *logoi* cause me to doubt that the goal of Platonic thought is achieving knowledge in the form of proper definitions. Plato says that such *logoi* cannot penetrate to essence. They are imperfect science. Socrates also called Sayre's favored idea of knowledge circular. I believe that Sayre is wrong to forsake his original argument that Plato's works should not be read as compendia of philosophic doctrines: I do not believe that Sayre ever succeeds in squaring his reversal with Plato's warning that his serious insights never have been and never will be committed to words, especially not to written words. Neither am I convinced that Plato's aporetic results are disappointing; I think that they are his intended guides to philosophic truth. I suspect that defining philosophy as collection and division that enable us to arrive at necessary and sufficient conditions for propositional truths sells philosophy short; philosophy is rather the undefinable ascent to the vision of the Good. I do agree that the Eleatic stranger's uses of collection and division are quite different from what we see in other dialogues but I do not favor a priori choices to view them as developments of Plato's ideas or support the opinion that we find the same practices in Philebus. These usages could be regarded as well or (as I think) better as Plato's tests of a conception of philosophy that Catherine Zuckert has described as antagonistic to that of Socrates.[7] This philosophy could be opposed to Plato's too, a possibility that Sayre never considers. If my identification of the Eleatic stranger as Polyphemus is correct, this would tip the balance against Sayre's interpretation. This brings up my last objection to Sayre, that he largely ignores the dramatic aspects of Sophist, except for one remark that the Eleatic stranger might deserve to be called a god because he is unusually astute. Letting speculation about the order of composition of Plato's dialogues and the development of his thought replace attention to his dramatic clues neglects to give due regard to his chosen form of writing.

Dorter's analysis is superior in its recognition of the Eleatic trilogy as a series of thought experiments and in its identification of one point at which Sophist cracks, its failure to analyze the sophist correctly owing to its suppression of the Good. With regard to these matters I shall follow Dorter closely. What I am unable to affirm is that Plato maintained a theory of Forms that was set aside in Theaetetus to see whether knowledge could be explained without them, partially reinstated in Sophist, and restored as qualified in Statesman, ending in a satisfactory analysis of the *politikos*. Theaetetus was, indeed, an experiment. However, it aimed not to determine what would happen to epistemology without the Forms but to see whether Protagorean, Heracleitean, and geometric arguments could account for

---

7   Catherine Zuckert, *Plato's Philosophers*, 706.

epistêmê. I do not doubt that Plato envisaged Forms about which he was never sure. However, I do not think that he ever gave a sufficiently detailed definition of these Forms that could serve as a baseline against which to measure alterations of a continuously developed theory of them. The Forms were too serious for definite *logoi.* I believe further that Socrates and the Eleatic stranger attribute such diverse ranks or natures to the Forms that the argument that in Statesman the Good is related to politics by virtue of adherence to "the mean" becomes debatable. This raises the possibility that the stranger's analysis of the *politikos* ultimately subverts itself. I expect to find that Statesman is fully as aporetic as Sophist.

So much for prolegomena about secondary literature. It is time to attempt an analysis that integrates the drama and reasoning of Sophist.

As I have recounted in my earlier analysis of the dramatic setting, Socrates is waiting at the geometry school at dawn when Theodorus, Theaetetus, young Socrates, and an unidentified man approach him. Theodorus says: "According to yesterday's agreement, Socrates, we have come ourselves *kosmiôs* (orderly), and we bring also this stranger, by origin [birth] from Elea, a comrade of those around Parmenides and Zeno, very much a philosophic man" (216a1–4). I have already observed that this seems to be a formulaic, legalistic oration that initiates the intellectual prosecution of Socrates. There is more to be said about Theodorus's statement.

In its dramatic context, Theodorus's speech generates suspicion that he is hiding what he knows about the newcomer. Theodorus seems to be trying to create the impression that this man just happened to drop into Athens within hours of Socrates' effort to co-opt Theaetetus; meet a famous geometer whom he did not know; neglect to tell his name; impress the mathematician as a philosopher (presumably on the basis of "bare speeches" offered to a scientist who hates them), and agree to attend a dawn meeting with a local personage under indictment for capital offenses, which any shrewd alien might have judged hazardous to his health. This picture beggars belief prima facie. It also is belied by the fact that Theodorus had to know the man well if he could say that his *tropos* (way, habit, character) is more moderate than the natures of people who embroil themselves in eristic (216b). Unless Plato is an incompetent playwright who creates incredible scenarios, he wants us to think about the true relationship between Theodorus and his "stranger."

There are additional reasons for hesitating to take Theodorus's speech at face value. We have become acquainted with his un-Socratic idea of a philosopher. It would be naive to regard his testimony that the stranger is a philosopher as evidence that Plato thinks so. All we know is that Theodorus thinks that he is a philosopher. Also, the expression "a comrade of those around Parmenides and Zeno" is odd. While implying that the stranger is an Eleatic thinker, a student of Parmenides and Zeno, all it actually says is that he associated with their disciples. Stanley Rosen remarks that the stranger's doctrines do not seem to be attributable to any known Eleatic school.[8]

Dramatic imagination suggests a notion of what Theodorus might be hiding: He and the stranger probably have been living as metic neighbors and friends in the Piraeus, enabling him to contact the stranger overnight, ask him for a favor, brief him, and bring him to the meeting. The stranger has been earning a living by teaching his methods of analysis and has built a reputation in the Piraeus as a formidable wordsmith. Theodorus wants to pit him against Socrates because he thinks that he is capable of combating the crafty sophist who has embarrassed him. He hopes that the stranger's work will convict Socrates of sophistry and reclaim Theaetetus for geometry and its Protagorean applications. He knows the man's name. He conceals it because he wants to catch Socrates off-guard. If Socrates heard the name, he might be forewarned.

Does Plato, as playwright, have a different reason for withholding the name? I know that many scholars believe that the stranger is Plato himself: Plato is using this character as his avatar because he wants to soften the shock of his turn against Socrates. In light of Plato's description of Socrates as the most just man of his era, Plato's love of Socrates as a friend, and the stranger's role as the prosecutor of Socrates on charges of sophistry, I doubt that. I believe, rather, that the man's name is irrelevant. It is enough to know that he is Socrates' prosecutor. Another point to observe is that Theodorus's concealment assimilates Socrates' fictitious intellectual prosecutor to his real one. Meletus was an *agnôs*, generally unknown in Athens proper (Euthyphro 2b8).

Socrates is not caught off-guard. He knows perfectly well that Theodorus has brought the stranger along to refute him. He urbanely hints

---

8   Stanley Rosen, Plato's *"Sophist": The Drama of Original and Image*, 67.

that he has caught on, suggesting that Theodorus has unwittingly brought "some god," for Homer says that the god of strangers accompanies the reverent and just beholding the hybristic and righteous deeds of mankind. Perhaps the person is one of the higher powers come "to refute us who are worthless in *logos*, a kind of refuting god." Theodorus denies that the stranger is contentious but asserts that he considers the man divine, for he says that of all philosophers. Socrates answers that it is not easier to recognize philosophers than gods, for real philosophers, not the fakes, *phantazomenoi dia tên allôn agnoian epistrôphôsi poleâs* (per Cornford: "appear, owing to the world's blindness, to wear all sorts of shapes"). The shapes are those of unsavory politicians, sophists, and madmen. I have previously suggested that Socrates' subtle transfer of authority for the remark about real and pretended philosophers from Homer to himself indicates that he is warning the stranger against an act of hubris and that he is Odysseus confronting Polyphemus in the country of the Cyclops. There is more to be said about this. Theodorus has introduced the stranger as a philosopher. Socrates has ironically replied that he might be a god. Countering that, Theodorus has answered that the stranger is divine insofar as he is a philosopher. Socrates has retorted that real philosophers, as opposed to fakes, are hard to recognize because they are seen as sophists, politicians, and madmen. Thus, having twice heard the stranger proclaimed a philosopher, Socrates has quickly responded with a warning about the difficulty of distinguishing sham philosophers from real ones. It is hard not to construe this as a hint that he suspects the stranger of being a fake philosopher. At the very least, his remark alerts us to the possibility that somebody in the play is a real philosopher, that somebody else is a sham, and that Plato wants us to think about which is which. This contingency is often missed by those who ignore Plato's drama. Of course, the scholars who are impressed by the stranger's reasoning infer that Socrates is the one who does not measure up and that the stranger is the god.

Socrates inquires whether the stranger would be agreeable to saying what his countrymen thought about sophist, *politikos*, and philosopher, whether they considered them as one, two, or, as the number of names suggests, three *genê* (kinds). His question refers back to the tendency of the ignorant to project the appearances of sophists and *politikoi* onto real philosophers, omitting the category of madmen. Socrates foresees which directions his prosecution will take. Asked by Theodorus, the stranger says that he has no objection to discussing the topic and that the names represent three distinct but difficult to define types. If the stranger were really an Eleatic in the mold of Parmenides, he might have viewed all three as one. If he were inspired by Socrates' call for a philosopher king, he would have equated *politikos* with "statesman" and said two. He does interpret *politikos* as "statesman" but he has said three. Theodorus reports that, "by chance," he and his party were discussing similar questions before arriving. One wonders why this comment is not superfluous. The answer, I think, is that Plato desires us to think more about what is going on in the drama. Theodorus has been deceptive about the stranger's identity and presence on the scene and he probably is prevaricating again. I doubt that his group was talking about Socrates' question by chance. Theodorus probably had been seeking a preview of the prosecution's case. The stranger had put him off, probably not wanting to perform twice. Theodorus states that the stranger did admit that he had heard the topic analyzed thoroughly and that he had not forgotten what he had heard. This is another peculiar statement. Why does Plato insert it? Is it because he intends us to wonder about the stranger? The remark raises the question of whether the stranger is a real philosopher—an insightful thinker who pretends to repeat the arguments of others for some as yet undisclosed pedagogical reason—or a lesser intellect.

Continuing to act the suppliant, Socrates begs the stranger not to refuse to grant the first favor he has requested. (This is another indication that Socrates is Odysseus and the stranger is Polyphemus.) Then he asks the stranger whether he prefers to proceed by giving a long speech by himself or by questioning. Once, when he was a young man and Parmenides was old, he was present when Parmenides used questions to good effect. The stranger replies that dialogue with another is easier if the interlocutor causes no pain and is obedient to the rein; otherwise he opts for speaking by himself. Unlike Socrates, he is unwilling to allow the interlocutor's caprices to guide the conversation. Socrates recommends Theaetetus as interlocutor. The stranger answers that he feels ashamed not to converse with brief exchanges of word for word instead of giving a long account even while speaking with another. However, this topic demands the long account. He will accept Theaetetus as interlocutor on the basis of his earlier talk with him. He must have found the boy tractable. His desire to keep a tight rein on his interlocutor and his warning about the long account suggest that he will conduct a dialogue that actually is a monologue. This is a sufficient summary and expansion of my previously stated understanding of the dramatic setting of Sophist. It remains to check this analysis against the dialogue's argument.

Theaetetus inquires whether everyone will be pleased if he is chosen as interlocutor. The stranger replies that the issue is settled. If Theaetetus gets too tired, Theodorus and Socrates will be to blame. Theaetetus doubts that he will tire but says that young Socrates can replace him if that occurs. The stranger replies in effect "that is your affair." The identities of his interlocutors are all the same to him. His indifference indicates that he does not tailor his presentations to the differing characters of his students.

The stranger advises Theaetetus that they must search for and make plain what the sophist is by means of *logoi*. Just now they share only the name and they might have different ideas of what it means so they must come to agreement about the thing itself by *logos*. Socrates (Plato) could approve of this beginning, for it is necessary to pass up and down among the four properly, acquiring the best possible verbal understanding of a subject, to clear a path to enlightenment at the level of perfect knowledge of the fifth.

The stranger suggests a preliminary exercise. The tribe (*phulon*) of the sophist is not easy to comprehend. Investigations of great things (*tôn megalôn*) should be practiced on small ones before the greatest (*tois megistois*) are addressed. The sense in which the stranger classifies the sophist as one of the greatest things is not made clear. In this context, he probably means that the subject is most important. The stranger adds that they should practice the method of hunting on something easy, taking a lesser thing as a paradigm (*paradeigma*) of the greater. He thus initially employs the method of paradigms that he will introduce formally in Statesman. He suggests that they take as an example something small and unimportant but well known, the angler. He hopes that the angler offers a method and a *logos* not unsuited to their purpose. There is an ambiguity here. Is what the stranger will present a paradigm of the method of investigation or a paradigm of the sophist? His "method and *logos* not unsuited to the purpose" language makes it look as if the answer is "both." If so, we might be justified in supposing that the stranger will construct a template of what he thinks he knows about the sophist rather than search for what he believes he does not know. It is hard to see how he could provide a paradigm of the *logos* of the sophist if he did not assume that he knew what a sophist is.

The stranger begins by inquiring whether the angler is a *technitên* (a person with an art) or *atechnon* (artless), possessing some other power (*dynamin*). Theaetetus answers "least of all" *atechnon*. Appearing to agree, the stranger says that of all the arts there are roughly two forms (*eidê*). One, exemplified by a collection consisting in agriculture, care of mortal bodies, things synthesized and molded that are called equipment, and the art of imitation, all bringing into being objects that did not previously exist, is most justly named the art of production (*poiêtikên*). The other class (*eidos*), exemplified by a collection consisting in learning, getting knowledge, money-making making, competing (*agônistikon*) and hunting (*thêreutikon*), all of which are engaged in *xeiroutai* (forcefully handling, conquering, coercing, subduing, or taking by deed or word or preventing the same) might appropriately be named the art of acquisition (*ktêtikê*). Given that production and acquisition are all of the arts (*xumpasôn ousôn tôn technôn*), the stranger asks in which of these the angling art belongs. Theaetetus replies that it clearly is an acquisitive art. The stranger then inquires whether there are not two forms (*eidê*) of acquiring, one being exchange (*metablêtikon*) between willing persons by means of gifts, wages, and purchases and the other being *cheirôtikon* (handling, conquering, coercing, subduing, taking possession of, violently), all of its parts taken together. Next *cheirôtikon* is divided in two. The open part is competing (*agônistikon*) and the hidden or secret part is called hunting (*thêreutikon*). The stranger asserts that it would be *alogon* (unreasonable) not to divide hunting in two, the hunting of the not ensouled (or lifeless) and the ensouled (or living). Theaetetus wonders whether both kinds of hunting exist and is asked "how not?" Hunting of the not ensouled is exemplified by diving and dismissed as trifling. Hunting of the ensouled is renamed animal hunting. This has a double class (*eidos*), the parts being hunting of the footed kind (*genos*) and that of the swimming animal, respectively called footed [animal] hunting and water [animal] hunting. The swimmers are divided into the winged and those living in water. Hunting of the former is called birding (fowling); hunting of the latter is called fishing. The hunt for water denizens has two greatest parts, fishing with enclosures such as baskets, nets, seines and snares and fishing by striking with tridents and hooks. Striking that occurs at night is called fire hunting. That which takes place during the day with tridents and hooks is called barb hunting. Striking downward with tridents is called tridentry. Striking upward not at any chance part of the body of the fish but only around the head and mouth is, Theaetetus infers, angling.

FIGURE 1: ANGLING

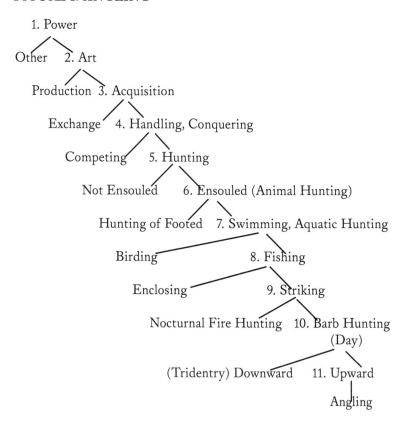

TABLE 1: ANGLING (GREEK)

1. *Dynamis –> Allên Dynamin, Technê*
2. *Technê –> Poiêtikên, Ktêtikês*
3. *Ktêtikês –> Metablêtikon, Cheirôtikon*

4. *Cheirôtikon –> Agônistikon, Thêreutikon*
5. *Thêreutikon –> Apsychon, Empsychon (Zôothêrikên)*
6. *Zôothêrikên –> Pezothêrikon, Neustikou, Enugrothêrikon*
7. *Enugrothêrikon –> Ornitheutikê, Halieutikê*
8. *Halieutikê –> Herkothêrikon, Plêktikên*
9. *Plêktikên –> Pureutikên, Agkistreutikon*
10. *Agkistreutikon –> Triodontia or Eis to Katô, Anô*
11. *Anô = Aspalieutikê*

Summary: *Technê, Ktêtikon, Cheirôtikon, Thêreutikon, Zôothêreutikon, Enugrothêrikon, Halieutikon, Plêktikon, Agkistreutikon, Anô, Aspalieutikê*

The stranger summarizes or collects the results of his operations that pertain to angling. He declares that, considering art as a whole, half was acquisition. The relevant halves of the next divisions were handling (conquering), hunting, animal hunting, aquatic [animal] hunting, fishing, striking, barb hunting, and striking from below (angling), respectively. He uses the same Greek terms in the summary as he used in the original presentation. The summary is partially accurate. The stranger has not repeated his remarks that animal hunting is hunting for ensouled creatures, that barb hunting occurs during the daytime, and that the upward striking aims not at any chance part of the body of the fish but exclusively at the head or mouth.

Now that the angler paradigm is on the table, we may inquire what we have before us. It is plain that we have a paradigm of the collection and division method of hunting and a *logos*, in the sense of definition, of the angler. Sayre states that the definition is "untroublesome, and the first among three successful divisions accomplished in the dialogue." It is successful in that "it captures both necessary and sufficient conditions for angling within the same chain of division." Each characterization in the chain "is *necessary* to angling, on the one hand, in that no activity which cannot be characterized in each of these ways could properly be called angling." All of the characterizations taken together "in themselves are sufficient for being an angler," for any person engaged in all of them is an angler "by virtue of being correctly describable in this fashion."[9]

9   Sayre, *Plato's Analytic Method*, 141, 142, 143.

Sorry to say, it seems to me that Sayre's assessment of the paradigm and its definition of the angler is rather too sanguine. Several of its aspects strike me as problematic. I shall list the troublesome items approximately in the order in which they appeared.

Collecting his examples of production, the stranger remarked that all of them are cases of bringing into being things that did not previously exist. Agriculture and the care of mortal bodies might be more suitably described as the nurture and tending of already existing things, seeds and bodies, aimed at helping these things realize their inherent potentials to become what they are not yet, such as mature plants and better conditioned bodies. Perhaps this is a nitpick. However, as examples of making, agriculture and the care of mortal bodies do not belong in the same category as synthesis and imitation except by virtue of an unacknowledged reliance on multiple senses of "making" and "bringing into existence." Equivocations are unacceptable in strict logic.

Giving his examples of acquisition, namely, learning, getting knowledge, money-making, competing and hunting, the stranger asserted that they were all instances of *cheirôtikon*, a word that simultaneously connotes handling, conquering, coercing, subduing, and taking possession of by manipulative violence or force. Again, the several activities offered as examples of getting do not belong in the same category except by virtue of an unavowed multiplication of senses of the term *cheirôtikon*. Geometry, astronomy, and philosophy are not "conquered" or "possessed" in the same sense that a fish is captured and killed by violence. Equivocations are unacceptable in strict logic. Further, if every manner of acquisition is *cheirôtikon*, the exchange between willing persons that is a subdivision of acquisition in the movement from steps three to four would have to involve both conquering and being coerced—a contradiction in terms—and the *cheirôtikon* that appears at step four in the chain must be a subdivision of the *cheirôtikon* that is synonymous with all acquisition in step three, thus a subdivision of itself.

Having made his first division of art (*technê*) into two parts, production and acquisition, the stranger proceeded to say that the identified categories "are all of the arts" (*xumpasôn ousôn tôn technôn*). This pronouncement is misleading. It gives the impression that *technê* is divided into just these halves either by nature or by logical necessity, which the stranger does not really believe is the case. Early in Statesman, the stranger does another division of *technê*. He starts by asking young Socrates whether the sciences (*epistêmas*) should be divided in the same manner as when they were considering the sophist. His question equates this dialogue's *epistême* with the earlier dialogue's *technê*. The stranger answers his own question with a "no." He informs young Socrates that instead of employing the previous division, they have to "make our souls conceive all the sciences" as splitting into the classes *praktikên* and *gnôstikên* (258c7, for now "practical" and "intellectual" will do). This makes it evident that the stranger divides and redivides classes according to varying criteria, casting them in different lights that suit changing purposes. Thus, his cuts are guided not by essences or logical necessity but by rhetorical intention. His ostensible practice of dividing forms into halves also is a rhetorical device. Later in Sophist it will turn out that *technê*, which explicitly was declared to have been divided "as a whole" into the "halves" of production and acquisition (221b3), has a third half, separating.[10] Divisions by two are jettisoned or revised when it becomes expedient to look at something from another perspective.

The next problem concerns divisions six and seven. The stranger undertakes to divide the species of hunted animals according to their means of locomotion. Honoring his rule of division by two, he initially splits these species up into those that go on feet and those that swim, omitting those that fly. He should have heeded natural kinds and abandoned division by two, resorting to division by three. Plato knows this well. At Laws 823b, his Athenian stranger correctly divides hunting into the pursuit of water animals, fowl, and land animals. The Eleatic stranger moves to remedy his gaffe by dividing aquatic hunting into fowling and fishing. This misses the hunting of birds that are not waterfowl. Much of winged motion has been left out of account.

It also transpires that Sayre is mistaken in arguing that the definition of the angler offered by the paradigm as a whole precisely delineates the necessary and sufficient conditions for being an angler. I take the necessary and sufficient conditions of angling to be "*attempting* to catch fish by using hook, line, and bait." Under this rubric, it is not necessary for angling to be a *technê*, or expertise. I have often observed the following situation: Two people are standing side by side on a boat or a bank. One knows the art of using the

---

10 Thus Eva Brann and her colleagues rightly show "expertise" divided into the three parts of "getting," "separating," and "making" in their chart titled "The Sophist's Thicket," *Plato's "Sophist,"* 5.

tackle and catches fish. The other is holding the tackle but is *atechnos*, clueless, and catches nothing. They are both angling. A game warden will arrest the dilettante if he or she is found to be bumbling without a license. In ancient Greece, the owner of a pond or a waterfront will also consider the *atechnos* individual who is fishing without permission an angling poacher. Acquiring fish is not necessary to being an angler either. I have frequently observed the following circumstance: a fisherman who is a consummate artist catches nothing because the fish are not biting. Hunting is not always necessary to angling either. Good anglers often know where the fish are without being able to see them. The problem is not to find the fish but to succeed in luring them. Sayre or the stranger might answer that these critiques are petty. They could maintain after the manner of Thrasymachus that the paradigm and its *logos* are salvageable if we restrict the concept angler to "the true angler" who does know how to use the equipment, does "hunt" fish in a broad sense, and does manage to catch them. Well and good. I yield. But the true angler could not forget bait or think that angling can occur only in daylight.

Bait is necessary to angling. Daylight is not.[11] Sayre attempts to finesse these issues by arguing that Plato is contemplating catching fish that must be seen by daylight to enable snagging them only around the head or mouth.[12] The idea of trying to steer a bare hook under the head or mouth of a fish visible in a wine-dark sea, river, or lake in order to hook it exclusively there must occasion mirth in experienced fishermen. This might be why the stranger neglects to repeat his strictures about daylight and fish body parts when he summarizes his paradigm.

One thing can be conceded to Sayre. The stranger surely does intend his paradigm to be viewed as a definition of angling that captures its necessary and sufficient conditions. However, the logic of his paradigm is on various occasions inexact, deceptive, garbled, plainly wrong, and patently ridiculous. My scholarly duty requires me to notice these flaws, report them, and inquire why they are present, especially if they persist, not to avert my eyes from them as admirers of the stranger do. These errors aside, it remains to be seen whether the angler *diaeresis* actually is an adequate paradigm of the sophist, even in the stranger's own final judgment.

11   I have caught fish by hook and line at night myself, with bait, by moonlight.
12   Sayre, *Plato's Analytic Method*, 143.

Despite all its mistakes, let us accept the angler paradigm for the sake of argument. The stranger recommends that they try to find the sophist *kata touto to paradeigma*, according to this paradigm. He asserts that their first query about the angler was whether he was *idiôtên* (a person who is "private" insofar as he lacks a professional *technê*) or an individual possessing a *technê*. In like fashion, they have to inquire whether the sophist is *idiôtên* or truly *sophistên* (possessed of wisdom). The stranger thereby equates wisdom with having a *technê*. Theaetetus originally did the same thing in the previous dialogue, in keeping with Athenian common parlance. He seems not to have learned better, for he now replies that the sophist is far from wise and he is surprised when the stranger asserts that they still must assume that the sophist has some sort of *technê*. He wonders what that expertise could be. The search for it commences. The reasoning apparently will not be informed by awareness of the contrast between a wisdom that is technical know-how and Socrates' higher wisdom that is (incomplete) insight into how to live rightly.

Before joining the stranger's quest, we should recall that Socrates characterizes sophistry and sophists in a number of dialogues. In Gorgias, he remarks that sophistry, like rhetoric, is one of four branches of flattery, an *epitêdeuma* (pursuit, practice) that strives to produce gratification. As such, it is not a *technê* but a kind of *empeiria* (experience of or acquaintance with something, 462c–463d). In Protagoras, Socrates warns Hippocrates, son of Apollodorus, that a sophist is an *emporos* (traveling merchant) or a *kapêlos* (domestic retailer) who markets provender for souls, *mathêmasi* (teachings), and that he should be wary of what his soul ingests (313c). In Phaedrus, he indicates that sophists have souls grievously disordered by failures to catch any glimpse of the essence really being during their primordial flights in the ether. Therefore, they are human types that rank only above tyrants (247b–48e). Of these passages, the Gorgias texts are immediately relevant to the present context.

The Gorgias passages are interesting here because Socrates disagrees with the stranger's statement that sophistry is a *technê*. Instead, he calls it an *empeiria*. One wonders what he thinks is the difference between these two forms. I shall venture a guess. He probably regards a *technê* as a knowledge of the nature of a thing that allows caring for or working with it in manners ruled by its essential structure and limits, such that a good for the thing or for a human being usually is achieved. The practice of the art does not inevitably have a felicitous result because natures are subject to contingencies. An *empeiria* probably is an experiential acquaintance with cause and effect or stimulus and response that neglects natures. It is an observation of the regularity that a particular treatment of something normally moves it toward certain outcomes, no matter what the nature (if any) of whatever is being acted upon. We saw an extreme example of such an *empeiria* in Theaetetus, where Protagoras denied the existence of natures but still proclaimed his science of producing perceptions of appearances. The stranger might eventually define sophistry as that very *technê* (or, as Socrates would have it, *empeiria*). If he does so, the fact that his divisions are determined by rhetorical intentions rather than by natural kinds and logical necessities indicates that he seems to be describing the character of his own *technê* or *empeiria* as well.

Replying to Theaetetus's question about the identity of the sophist's *technê*, the stranger pretends to have been surprised by an insight. He says that the sophist is akin to the angler. Both are hunters (*thêreuta*). Thus, it is clear that the stranger intended his angler analysis not only as a paradigm of his analytic method. He also envisaged his *logos* of the angler as a paradigm of the *logos* of the sophist. He will execute a number of *diaereseis* (divisions) that start from categories in the angler paradigm and result in five definitions of the sophist. He will add another *diaeresis* that begins with his "third half" of *technê*, separating, and terminates with his sixth definition of the sophist.

The first *diaeresis* that leads to the sophist begins with the angler paradigm's category of acquisition (*ktêtikês*) and summarily descends to the steps of handling/conquering (*cheirôtikon*), hunting (*thêreutikon*), and animal hunting (*zôothêrikon*). Then, the stranger says, the angler and the sophist diverge. He and Theaetetus previously divided hunting as a whole in two, the target animals being swimming (*neustikou*) and footed (*pezou*). They did not divide the footed. Now, where the angler turns to the sea and rivers and lakes, the sophist turns to the land and especially toward its "rivers of wealth and youth," intending *cheirôsomenos* (forcible handling, conquering, coercing, subduing, taking possession) of the nurslings there. Theaetetus asks what the stranger means. The stranger's reply is that there are two greatest parts of hunting of the footed, hunting of the tame (*hêmerôn*) and the wild (*agriôn*). Theaetetus wonders whether there is hunting of the tame. The stranger answers aggressively, telling the boy that there is hunting of the tame if man is tame but that he may assume whatever he likes, that there is no tame animal, that man is wild and some other animal is tame, or that man is tame but there is no hunting of man. Every Greek knows that there are tame animals and that men are hunted. Theaetetus has been given only one real choice. He says that man is tame and that there is hunting of the tame. The stranger collects the *technai* of piracy, kidnaping, tyranny, and war as examples of hunting of the tame by force or violence and divides them off from another collection of the arts of litigating, demagoguery, and conversing which he calls the art of producing persuasion (*pithanourgikên*). This art is divided in two. One part takes place in public, the other in private (*idia*). Hunting in private is divided into a part that bears gifts and a part that earns pay (*mistharnêtikon*). Theaetetus does not understand the gift-bearing part. The stranger tells him that he is ignorant of the hunting of lovers, who give presents to their quarry. This is admitted. The ugly Theaetetus has had no suitors. Next, one part of the paid kind of persuasion hooks by giving pleasure and demands sustenance as its wages. It is called the art of flattery (*kolakikên*) or the art of pleasuring (*hêduntikên*). It is divided from the persuasion that is undertaken for the sake of virtue (*hôs aretês heneka*) and demands to be paid in cash (*nomisma*). The practitioner of the latter type of persuasion is the sophist.

FIGURE 2: HUNTING (SOPHIST I)

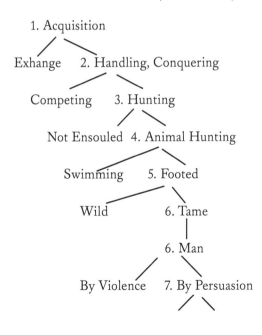

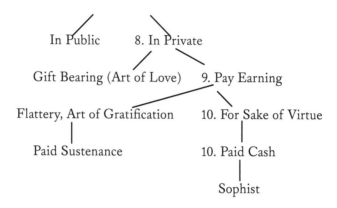

TABLE 2: HUNTING (GREEK): SOPHIST I

1. *Ktêtikês –> Metablêtikon, Cheirôtikon*
2. *Cheirôtikon –> Agônistikon, Thêreutikon*
3. *Thêreutikon –> Apsychon, Zôothêrikon*
4. *Zôothêrikon –> Neustikou, Pezou*
5. *Pezou –> Agrôn, Hêmerôn (Anthrôpôn)*
6. *Hêmerôn (Anthrôpôn) –> Biaion, Pithanourgikên*
7. *Pithanourgikên –> Dêmosia, Idia*
8. *Idia –> Dôrophorikon (Erôtikês Technês), Mistharnêtikon*
9. *Mistharnêtikon –> Kolakikên (Hêduntikên) (Trophên), Hôs Aretês Heneka (Nomisma)*
10. *Hôs Aretês Heneka (Nomisma) = Sophistên*

Summary: *Oikeiôtikês,* Cheirôtikês.* Thêreutikês, Zôothêrikias, Chersaias, Hêmerothêrikês, Anthrôpothêrias, Idiothêrias, Mistharnêtikês, Nomismatopô-likês, Doxopaideutikês, Neôn Plousiôn kai Endoxôn . . . Thêra, Sophistikê.* (*Manuscripts vary. See discussion below.)

The stranger sums up or collects the results of this *diaeresis* that pertain to the sophist. He says that what belongs to the arts of appropriating (*hê technês oikeiôtikês*), handling/conquering, hunting, animal hunting, hunting on land (*chersaias*), hunting of the tame, man hunting, private hunting, pay earning, being paid in cash, pretending to educate (*doxopaideutikês*), all this being a hunt for wealthy and reputable youths, is sophistry. This summary would be correct if the terms that the stranger substitutes for originals were taken for synonyms. However, they are not exactly synonyms. It is worth noticing the changes that the stranger has made between the *diaeresis* and the summary. He has converted *ktêtikês* to *oikeiôtikês*, shifting from a word that simply means acquisition to another with a meaning that in some contexts has a slight flavor of appropriating articles for the household. (*Ktêtikês* reappears in some manuscripts.) He has changed the class of hunting footed animals into land hunting. He has turned persuading for the sake of virtue into persuading as pretending to educate. He has changed rivers of wealth and youth to wealthy and reputable youths, moving the altered phrase from the first to the last step.

In this *diaeresis*, the stranger has given full sway to his penchant for making his rhetorical intentions the principles of his divisions. He has done so by depicting sophists in ways that will inflame Athenians already hostile to them, like Theaetetus. His descriptions are debatable. To see this, let us consider the sophist's alleged traits from a neutral standpoint, from the stranger's viewpoint, and from the perspective of the self-admitted sophist Protagoras. Neutral: the sophist seeks tuition-paying students. Stranger: the sophist hunts wealthy youths in the same sense that an angler hunts fish. This is to say that he is a predator intending harm to rich young innocents. Protagoras: the sophist justifiably searches for students willing and able to support his livelihood in return for instruction (just as American college professors have always done, if not personally then through the agencies of admissions office representatives). Neutral: the sophist enters into contractual relationships with students. Stranger: the sophist acquires students in the same sense that the angler acquires fish, or perhaps even in the same sense that a master acquires slaves for a household. These students are pathetic victims. Protagoras: the contracting parties enter into the normal relationship of teacher and student for their mutual benefit. Neutral: the sophist provides the instruction for which the students pay. Stranger: acting like the angler, the sophist conquers, coerces, subdues, takes possession of the student. Thus, he does grave harm to the youth in ways analogous to the angler's killing of the fish. Protagoras: the sophist earns his pay by conveying valuable information to the student. Neutral: the sophist teaches what he and his customer both regard as worth knowing. Stranger: the sophist ostensibly persuades for the sake of excellence or virtue (understood by Athenians not as an ethical disposition but as the possession of all qualities necessary for success in the city) but he really only pretends to educate. Protagoras: the sophist teaches excellence as understood by the Athenians. His students fare well. These comparisons demonstrate that the stranger meant to bias Theaetetus against perceived sophists by his choices of terms, making Theaetetus conceive of them as dangerous to any boy like himself. Otherwise, he could have chosen the neutral or Protagorean phrases to describe the same phenomena.

It will be objected that Plato's readers already have been shown the sophist's depravity in his other works, that neutral descriptions of sophistry are inadequate to its evil nature as defined by Plato, and that the hunter *diaeresis* reflects his earlier view of sophists. Therefore, I ought not to maintain that the stranger has described sophistry with prejudicial language without adequate warrant. I have two replies. First, it is true that Plato's other dramas have identified sophistry's evil nature and that Socrates undoubtedly would sympathize with the stranger's bias. However, the stranger's description of the sophist lacks the foundation that would justify it, his own prior analysis of the evil of sophistry's nature. The fundamental ontological and ethical dimension is missing. It has been replaced by an account of phenomenal behaviors. Second, I would contend that the stranger's description is unfairly prejudicial even if he had justified it ontologically and ethically. I say this because its target does not appear to be sophists in general. Neither does it seem to be Protagoras in particular, for Protagoras was Theodorus's friend. The stranger appears to be subtly trying to make Theaetetus suspicious of Socrates. He has made the sophist a hunter. Theaetetus will remember that Socrates came to the geometry school yesterday hunting for a new student. The stranger has portrayed the sophist as a person who purports to teach for the sake of virtue but who only pretends to educate. Socrates approaches boys as someone interested in their virtue. The stranger has stressed that clients of the sophist are rich, reputable youths who suffer gruesome injuries, the natures of which are left to the imagination. Theaetetus knows himself as such a promising boy and as a victim whose wealth has been looted by betrayers of his trust. It is not necessarily clear to Theaetetus that Socrates the hunter is not a pretender with intentions like those of his previous exploiters. Thus, the stranger has painted the sophist with a face that could be that of Socrates. We know that this portrait has missed Socrates badly, that Socrates hunts for students with the intention of doing them good and that he does not merely pretend to educate but tries to lead boys to a higher virtue. We also know that he does not demand cash for his services. These facts do not matter. Theaetetus does not know Socrates' intentions. He may not be aware that Socrates does not request pay. Even if he knew that, he could suspect that a man indicted for capital crimes now urgently needs money for bribes. He also could doubt that Socrates' methods really produce virtue. Without being direct, the stranger has planted seeds of distrust of Socrates.

Some additional, random comments about the hunting *diaeresis* are in order. The stranger could let Theaetetus choose between man as wild and man as tame because he planned to make man the example of the hunted prey whatever the boy said. It is noteworthy that the stranger has moved in his dividing straight from the hunting of footed, tame animals to the hunting of man, on his own motion. In Statesman he will scold young Socrates for jumping straight from the art of tending herds to a distinction between tending beasts and men (262a–b). He will also interject a number of cuts between herding walking animals and tending man ((264e–66e). This all seems to depend on what he wants to emphasize. The stranger also has left readers to wonder whether he thinks that man really is tame or wild. Next, if the sophist acquires his prey by practicing the art of producing persuasion (*pithanourgikên*), his acquiring literally has become identical with a kind of production. Next, the stranger has distinguished the *technê* of flattery (*kolakikên*) from sophistry, whereas Socrates had defined sophistry precisely as a division of that *epitêdeuma*.

Another necessary random observation concerns a technical point of philology. Stanley Rosen notes that our Greek manuscripts differ in their presentations of the stranger's summary of the hunting *diaeresis*. The manuscripts that he trusts include *ktêtikês* right after *oikeiôtikês* and omit *cheirôtikês*.[13] Others omit *ktêtikês* and insert *cheirôtikês*. Others skip both and go straight to *thêreutikês* (hunting). Being unqualified to resolve differences in manuscripts, I have used the Loeb text with an eye on the differing Oxford edition, trying to keep all major possibilities open. The initial *diaeresis* is as I have reported it. Therefore, the discrepancies in the manuscripts of

13   Rosen, *Plato's "Sophist,"* 105.

the summary will not affect my analysis unless I discover that they mean something.

Now the stranger suggests looking at sophistry in a different way, for it is a many-sided art and it appears to belong to a class different from the one just stated. He says that acquisition (*ktêtikês*) was previously split into hunting (*thêreutikon*) and exchange (*allaktikon*). Theaetetus agrees. Exchange is either by giving (*dôrêtikon*) or *agorastikon* (variously translated as selling, marketing). *Agorastikon* divides into the marketing of one's own products (*autopôlikên*) and the selling of the works of others, which the stranger chooses to call exchange (*metablêtikon*). Then the half of this sort of exchange that is carried on in the city is classified as retailing (*kapêlikê*) and that which transfers goods from one city to another is called *emporikê* (standard translations of this term vary widely; let us say commerce). *Emporikê* separates into the sale for cash of things that nourish the body and selling of things for the soul. Theaetetus does not understand the latter. The stranger says that he is talking about all kinds of music (the Hellenic term for the things of the Muses, which include poetry, painting, music, dance, and, surprisingly in the stranger's list, conjuring [*thaumatopoiikên*]). Some of these types of music are sold for amusement, others for serious purposes. Apparently lumping both varieties together, the stranger calls trading in them soul commerce (*psychemporikês*). He divides this into an art of display (*epideiktikê*) and another no less ridiculous form that also deals with knowledge and needs a name related to its business, which becomes selling of knowledge (*mathê-matopôlikês*). He surprisingly splits the latter into the sale of knowledge of all the arts except one, named *technê* selling, and that which deals with knowledge of virtue, sophistry. (I say surprisingly because this last move is counterintuitive. He seems to have claimed that the sale of all the arts except one is just as ridiculous as sophistry, the *technê* under review. One wonders why the marketing of all the other arts is laughable.)

Summarizing his *diaeresis*, or collecting the halves of its kinds that pertain to the sophist, the stranger says that sophistry has appeared for a second time as a part of the acquisitive *technê* that involves exchange (*metablêtikon*), marketing (or selling), commerce, soul commerce, selling of *logoi* and *mathêmata* (words or arguments plus bits of knowledge or doctrines) that have to do with *aretê* (excellence or virtue). It is necessary to observe that the stranger has introduced some ambiguity into both his exchange *diaeresis* and its summary. In the *diaeresis*, his first remark that acquisition previously divided into hunting and exchange is wrong on two counts. Acquisition previously divided into exchange (*metablêtikon*) and handling/conquering (*cheirôtikon*), not into exchange (*allaktikon*) and hunting. Step one of this *diaeresis* has inaccurately inserted *allaktikon* in place of *metablêtikon*, which might be an insignificant substitution of a synonym, and surely has garbled step one of the angling and hunting *diaereseis* by dropping *cheirôtikon* and inserting hunting in its place. Theaetetus proves that his memory is weak by agreeing with this distortion of the previous steps one. In the summary, the stranger has switched the word for the exchange that results from the division of acquisition from *allaktikon* back to *metablêtikon* and has omitted the movement from steps three to four by dropping the distinction between selling the works of others (*metablêtikon*) and selling one's own products. He also has added the selling of *logoi* to the marketing of *mathêmata*. Theaetetus does not catch these changes either.

FIGURE 3: EXCHANGE (SOPHIST II)

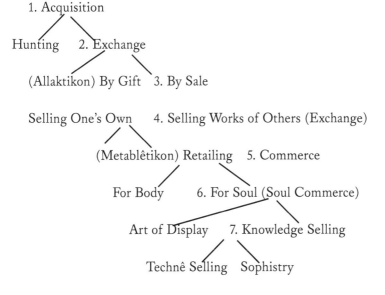

1. Acquisition

Hunting   2. Exchange

(Allaktikon) By Gift   3. By Sale

Selling One's Own   4. Selling Works of Others (Exchange)

(Metablêtikon) Retailing   5. Commerce

For Body   6. For Soul (Soul Commerce)

Art of Display   7. Knowledge Selling

Technê Selling   Sophistry

TABLE 3: EXCHANGE (GREEK) SOPHIST II

1. *Ktêtikês –> Thêreutikon, Allaktikon*
2. *Allaktikon –> Dôrêtikon, Agoristikon*
3. *Agoristikon –> Autopôlikên, Metablêtikon*
4. *Metablêtikon –> Kapêlikê, Emporikê*
5. *Emporikê –> Sôma, Psychê (Psychemporikês)*
6. *Psychemporikês –> Epideiktikês, Mathêmatopôlikês*
7. *Mathematopôlikês –> Technopôlikon, Sophistikon*

Summary: *Ktêtikês, Metablêtikês, Agorastikês, Emporikês, Psychemporikês, Peri Logous kai Mathemata, Aretês Pôlêtikon, Sophistikê*

It is unclear whether what follows next is two more very short *diaereseis* of acquisition or two variations on the exchange *diaeresis*. The stranger states that there is a third case and raises a question: If someone settled in a city and sold the same kinds of *mathêmata*, [buying some and?] making some himself, would not Theaetetus give him any other name than the one he just used? He would. The stranger summarizes (collects) the result, arriving at perhaps two more accounts of the sophist. He says that acquisition (*ktêtikês*), exchange (*metablêtikon*), marketing or selling (*agorastikon*), *kapêlikon* (which in the original exchange *diaeresis* was a half of *metablêtikon* and defined as selling of the works of others) or the selling of one's own products (*autopôlikon*), both ways, as long as they belong to the category of knowledge selling (*mathêmatopôlikon*), is what Theaetetus will call sophistic. The boy agrees. Inasmuch as Sophist II was depicted as a person who sells the work of others while engaged in intercity commerce, Sophist III can be defined as someone who sells the products of others in the single city in which he lives, and Sophist IV can be understood as a person who markets his own works in that city, all three purveying "the same kinds" of teachings, which must be doctrines for the soul that purport to concern virtue.

We are obliged to observe that the stranger has introduced additional ambiguity into his divisions. In the original exchange *diaeresis*, *metablêtikon* was split into *kapêlikê* and *emporikê*. Now *agorastikon* has divided into *kapêlikon* and *autopôlikon*. The pairs are garbled. To arrive at "the same kinds" of *mathêmata*, *psychemporikês* also must be changed to *psychkapêlikes* and something like *psychautopolikês*, at least implicitly, and it must be assumed that both categories then are tacitly divided by following steps six and seven of the first exchange *diaeresis*.

With the stranger's three exchange *diaereseis* or his trio of variations on the same division having been presented, some additional comments will be appropriate.

First, the stranger once again has defined the sophist by alluding to phenomenal traits of people whom Athenians call sophists while omitting foundational ontological-ethical comment. This has led to some embarrassing modern consequences. As I intimated with regard to the case of the hunter *diaeresis*, American college professors are troubled by being called sophists because they hunt for students who will pay tuition in return for teaching calculated either to make them good or to equip them for social success. Having been a professor myself, I deny that hoping to acquire students was enough to make me a sophist and I think that my colleagues would join me. The same denial applies to the present three cases. Voluntarily exchanging instruction in return for compensation, the things taught being *mathêmata* produced either by oneself or by others and the venues being either several cities or just one, does not suffice to make a person a sophist. We professors should breathe easily as long as we are not convicted of the ethical transgressions that Socrates ascribes to sophists.

Second, the stranger still appears to be trying to make Theaetetus suspicious of Socrates, who could be thought to be a man with whom students engage in voluntary exchanges and who purveys his own doctrines about virtue in one city. We have observed that Theaetetus might be unaware that Socrates does not demand pay. Thus, he could think that the *diaeresis* that leads to sophist IV is a picture of Socrates even though the portrait misses its mark (both phenomenally and ethically).

Third, the three definitions of a sophist that result from the exchange exercise(s) are very close to Socrates' account of the sophist in Protagoras as either an *emporos* (traveling merchant) or a *kapêlos* (domestic retailer) who sells provender for souls, *mathêmasi* (teachings). There is one major difference between the stranger's and Socrates' views. The stranger does not include the warning that the student should beware of what his soul ingests. This has to do with the fact that the stranger has been concentrating on phenomenal behaviors of sophists and ignoring their ethical characteristics.

FIGURE 4: SECOND TYPE OF EXCHANGE (SOPHIST III)

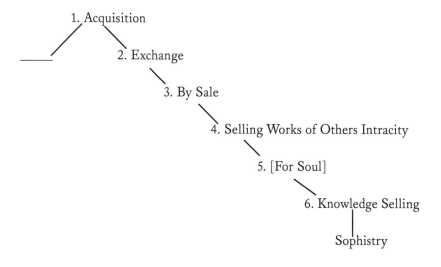

FIGURE 5: THIRD TYPE OF EXCHANGE (SOPHIST IV)

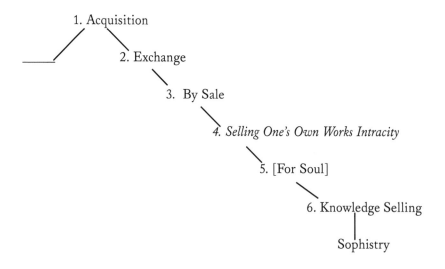

*COMBINED TABLES 4 AND 5: ADDITIONAL TYPES OF
EXCHANGE (GREEK) SOPHISTS III AND IV*

1. *Ktêtikês* –> *Metablêtikon*
2. *Metablêtikon* –> *Agoristikon*
3. *Agoristikon* –> *Either Kapêlikon or Autopôlikon*
4. *Either Kapêlikon or Autopôlikon* –> *Mathêmatopôlikon*
5. *Silently Assumed*
6. *Mathêmatopôlikon* = *Sophistik*

Summaries: Same as Combined Tables

Fourth, in view of the possibility that the stranger omits *cheirôtikês* or *cheirôtikon* in his summary of the hunter *diaeresis* (depending on whether the Loeb or Oxford manuscript is right), considering the fact that he replaces it with *thêreutikês* in the first exchange *diaeresis*, and given his garbling of *allaktikon, agoristikon, autopôlikên, metablêtikon* and *kapêlikê* in the exercise(s) leading to sophists III and IV, even the most ardent admirers of the stranger would have to admit in all honesty that his *diaereseis* and summaries have become something of a mess. The logic of the *diaereseis* has deteriorated rather than improving. It is beginning to look as if we eventually shall be obliged to inquire why these errors are in the manuscript.

Now the stranger returns to step four of the angling *diaeresis*, pointing out that *agônistikê* (competing, contending) was a part of *ktêtikês* (acquisition). In fact, it was part of *cheirôtikon*, which continues to be suppressed. Theaetetus does not recall this. The stranger suggests that it would be fitting to divide *agônistikê*. One part of it is *hamillêtikon* (another word for competing or contending) and the other is *machêtikon* (variously rendered as pugnacious, battling, fighting). The part of battling that pits bodies against bodies is doing violence (*biastikon*). The other half, which pits words against one another, is controversy (*amphisbêtêtikon*). Controversy that takes the form of long speeches about justice and injustice in public is forensic or judicial (*dikanikon*). That which occurs in private and consists in speeches chopped up into questions and answers is argumentation or disputation (*antilogikon*). Part of the latter disintegrates into numerous kinds of artless debates about business contracts and suchlike; it will go nameless. The half that is artful and discusses justice itself and injustice is eristic (*eristikon*), a kind of wrangling. The etymology of this word might involve Eris, the goddess of strife. It seems to me that it often has a pejorative connotation in Plato. Eristic has a part that wastes money (*chrêmatophthorikon*) and another that earns it (*chrêmatistikon*). The former is prating (*adoleschikou*). With the latter we encounter the sophist (*sophisten*). Note that nothing is said about this word warrior discussing virtue.

The stranger summarizes or collects the results of his *diaeresis* that pertain to the sophist. He repeats all of the terms that appeared in the *diaeresis* except that he presents them in reverse order. This might anticipate his myth of the oscillating cosmos in Statesman. The summary is accurate, except that the stranger jumps from *agônistikê* to *ktêtikês*, once again suppressing the *cheirôtikon* that he included in the original angler paradigm and the hunter *diaeresis*.

FIGURE 6: COMPETING (SOPHIST V)

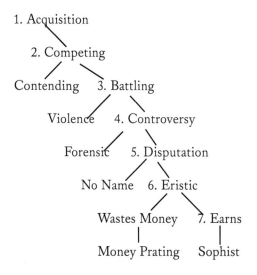

1. Acquisition
2. Competing
Contending   3. Battling
    Violence   4. Controversy
        Forensic   5. Disputation
            No Name   6. Eristic
                Wastes Money   7. Earns
                Money Prating   Sophist

TABLE 6: COMPETING (GREEK) SOPHIST V

1. *Ktêtikês –> Agonistikê*
2. *Agonistikê –> Hamillêtikon, Machêtikon*
3. *Machêtikon –> Biastikon, Amphisbêtêtikon*
4. *Amphisbêtêtikon –> Dikanikon, Antilogikon*
5. *Antilogikon –> ?, Eristikon*
6. *Eristic –> Chrêmatophthorikon, Chrêmatistikon*
7. *Chrêmatistikon = Sophistên*

Summary: *Sophistên, Chrêmatistikon, Eristikon, Antilogikon, Amphis-bêtêtikon, Machêtikon, Agonistikê, Ktêtikês*

The competing *diaeresis* has retained a trace of the kinds of logical confusion that plagued its predecessors with its omissions of *cheirôtikon*. It also has perpetuated the previous practice of citing phenomenal characteristics of those whom Athenians call sophists, neglecting any mention of their ethical characteristics. Although this might raise doubt about its adequacy as a definition of sophistry, we must notice its chief rhetorical effects. The description of the sophist as a battler with words who is doubly disputatious (*amphisbêtêtikon, antilogikon*) and practices an irritating eristic that chops conversation up into small bits of questions and answers matches the popular view of Socrates. The fact that Protagoras and the stranger prefer long speeches and the account of the sophist as someone who insists on short ones exempt Protagoras and the stranger from the charge of sophistry and transfer the onus to Socrates. As I have said before, the fact that Socrates does not charge for his teaching might not be part of the Athenian understanding of him. Thus, Theaetetus now could fear that Socrates is a hunter who acquires victims by pretending to teach virtue, a retailer who sells doctrines about virtue, and a pest who goes about contradicting people without really caring about virtue. That is what the stranger seems to want.

Ostensibly frustrated by the many-sidedness of the sophist, the stranger asks Theaetetus whether he now sees that the beast cannot be caught with one hand. The boy answers that then they must use both. Some commentators have taken this to imply that the sophist must be found on both sides of the stranger's divisions. I agree that this must be the stranger's intention.

Now the stranger inquires whether there are some terms connected with domestic chores in common use. Theaetetus is puzzled by the unexpected question. He replies that, yes, there are many. He asks which ones are meant. The stranger lists straining, sifting, winnowing, separating (*diakrinein*), carding, and others, all of which seem to have to do with wool-working. Theaetetus inquires why they are mentioned. The stranger responds by declaring that all the terms envisage *diakritikên*, dividing or separating. He collects his examples under that name and declares that *diakritikên* is a *technê* (226c6). Dividing and separating are neither acquisition nor production so *diakritikên* has to be a "third half" of *technê*. The stranger suggests dividing *diakritikên* in two. Taking up his own proposal, the stranger maintains that there is separation of worse from better (*cheiron apo beltionos*), which is called purification (*katharmos*), and the division of like from like (*homoion aph homoiou*), which has no name. Worse and better are not defined. I should observe that the separation of like from like is what the stranger practices. His refusal to assign a name to his activity probably is ironic. His art can be called *diaeresis*. He will use it to examine its co-quotient in the *diaeresis* of *diakritikên*, that is, *katharmos*, separation of worse from better. He will do this in order to elaborate a second paradigm (same method, new *logos*) of the sophist.

FIGURE 7: DIVIDING OR SEPARATING
LEFT SIDE: DIAERESIS OF PURIFICATION OF BODIES

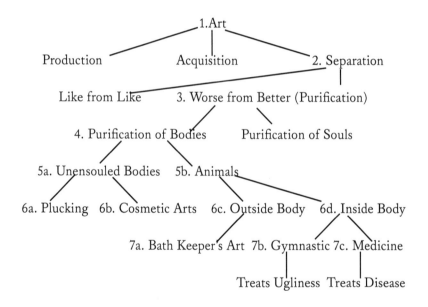

TABLE 7: DIVIDING OR SEPARATING (GREEK) LEFT SIDE: DIAERESIS OF PURIFICATION OF BODIES

1. *Technê –> [Poiêtikên], [Ktêtikês], Diakritikên*
2. *Diakritikên –> Homoion aph Homoiou, Cheiron apo Beltimos (Katharmos)*
3. *Katharmos –> Peri to Sôma, Peri tên Psychên*

4. *Peri to Sôma –> Tôn Apsychôn Sômatôn, Zôôn*
5a. *Tôn Apsychôn Sômatôn –> Gnapheutikê, Kosmêtikê*
5b. *Zôôn –> Peri Taktos (Peri ta Ektos), Entos Sômatôn*
6c. *Peri Taktos –> Balaneutikê*
6d. *Entos Sômatôn –> Gymnastikês, Iatrikês*
7b. *Gymnastikês –> treats Aischos (from 228a)*
7c. *Iatrikês –> treats Noson en Sômati (from 228a)*

No Summary

The new paradigm begins by mentioning purification of the body (*peri to sôma*). It takes this *diaeresis* quite a while to finish with the body and declare that the other half is purification of the soul (*peri tên psychên*). We thus are offered an unusual division of the "left" side of the cut and a corresponding postponement of division of the "right" side. Perhaps the stranger is acting on Theaetetus's discovery that both hands are needed.

Having arrived at *katharmos* of bodies, the stranger cuts that into cleansing of unensouled (inanimate) bodies and the cleansing of animals. The purification of the former splits into the art of plucking or brushing (translated in the Loeb edition as the fuller's art) and the whole cosmetic *technê*. The purification of animals divides into the cleaning of what is outside and that which is inside the body. The cleansing of the outside is trivial to mention and is represented by the art of the bath keeper. The purification of the inside is handled by gymnastic, which treats deformity or ugliness (*aischos*, imported from 228a), and medicine, which treats disease (*noson*, also imported from 228a).

With the basic steps of the *diaeresis* of the purification of bodies established, the stranger allows himself some *obiter dicta*. He says that the cleansing of unensouled bodies has ridiculous names. However, his method does not concern itself any more with taking medicine than it cares about sponging, no matter whether one benefits us greatly and the other little. When finding out what is akin in the arts, generalship and louse-catching are equally honored. He further declares himself indifferent to what name is given to the purification of bodies (figure 7, step 4) as long as we understand that it is to be kept separate from the cleansing of souls. The stranger apparently has declared that his method is value-free in every possible sense.

One wonders whether the stranger actually learns what is related in the arts. The kinship to which he points seems to be purely semantic. Here he traffics in equivocations on *katharmos*. "Purification" means different things in the cases of bathing and destroying germs or cancer cells.

Theaetetus agrees that purification of bodies differs from purification of souls. Now the stranger can divide the "right" side of "worse from better," *katharmos* of souls. He asks whether we say that wickedness or villainy (*ponêrian*) and virtue or excellence (*aretês*) are distinct in the soul. Yes. We also stated that purification was throwing out the bad, mean, or base (*phlauron*)? Yes. Then any removal of the bad or evil (*kakias*) from the soul is *katharmos*? Yes. *Ponêrian*, *phlauron*, and *kakias* appear here to be synonyms for the stranger, words usable interchangeably. When he decides next to divide *kakias* in the soul, one assumes that he is splitting *ponêrian* and *phlauron* in the same breath. Now he remarks that one type of *kakias* in the soul is comparable to a disease in the body (*noson en sômati*) and the other is comparable to an ugliness or deformity (*aischos*) in the body. Theaetetus does not understand. The stranger explains that *noson* (illness, disease) is the same as *stasin* (discord), a disagreement of the naturally related, while *aischos* is *ametrias* (disproportion). We observe that in the souls of the *phlauros* opinions (*doxas*) disagree with desires (*epithymias*), *thymos* (spiritedness, the spirited element of the soul) with pleasures (*hedonais*), and reason (*logos*) with pains (*lupais*). On the other hand, if things that partake of motion (*kinêseôs*) always miss the mark at which they aim, the cause is disproportion (*ametrias*) of each to the other (*pros allêla*). Every soul is ignorant unwillingly. Ignorance (*agnoousan*) is a motion of the soul that aims at truth and misses. So, a soul without reason (*anoêton*) is deformed or ugly (*aischos*) and disproportionate or lacking in measure (*ametron*). What it means to declare that the soul is in motion when it aims at truth is unclear. Similarly, the sense in which a soul is disproportionate when it misses truth is not evident. Is the *ametrias* intrinsic to the soul, taking the form of an asymmetry of its parts that renders it incapable of seeing truth, or does it consist in some lack of fit between the soul and truth, as indicated by the *pros allêla*, or both? (Note well that *ponêrian* and *aretê* finally have entered the stranger's calculations but not in relation to the sophist. Rather, they pertain to other people. They probably have conventional meanings.)

Next the stranger says that, therefore, there are two kinds of evils (*kakôn*) in the soul, one of which is called *ponêria* (translated above as wickedness or villainy), a disease, and the other of which is called ignorance (*agnoian*), which is an evil (*kakian*) although people do not recognize it as such in the soul. Now it is not clear whether *kakia* and *ponêria* are still synonyms or *ponêria* has become a subdivision of *kakia* qua disease and *agnoian* is a type of *kakia* that needs its own name that sets it off from *ponêria*, or whether *kakia* has become half of itself as the co-quotient of *ponêria*. Whatever the case, Theaetetus admits what he says he just disputed, that there are two sorts of *kakias* in the soul, with cowardice, intemperance, and injustice being disease (*noson*) and the manifold condition of ignorance being ugliness or deformity (*aischos*). The stranger proceeds to draw comparisons between arts that treat the body and arts that treat the soul. For *aischos* in the body we have gymnastic, for *noson* we have *iatrikê* (medicine). For hubris and injustice and cowardice in the soul we have *kolastikê*, the art of punishment, which has to be the analogue of *iatrikê*. For ignorance there is teaching or instruction, *didaskalikês*, which must be the analogue of gymnastic. Ignorance can be split in two "in the middle." One part is just as weighty as all the other parts put together. (This is an interesting idea of "middle." It raises the question of how all the other divisions into halves have been calculated. I think it fair to say that generally the cuts have been determined by semantic opposition and that a new criterion for dividing has just been introduced, weight, so that we now have equivocations on "halves.") The weighty ignorance is thinking that one knows what one does not know. It is called *amathia*, variously rendered as lack of learning or stupidity. Urged by the stranger, Theaetetus says that *amathia* is cured by *paideia*, education, and that the other parts are treated by *dêmiourgikas didaskalias* (vocational training). The combination of all the other kinds of ignorance receives no name.

FIGURE 8: DIVIDING OR SEPARATING (SOPHIST VI) RIGHT SIDE: DIAERESIS OF PURIFICATION OF SOULS

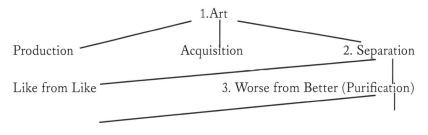

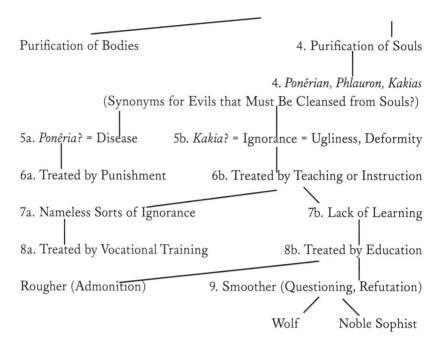

TABLE 8: DIVIDING OR SEPARATING (GREEK) SOPHIST VI
RIGHT SIDE: DIAERESIS OF PURIFICATION OF SOULS

1. *Technê –> [Poiêtikên], [Ktêtikês], Diakritikên*
2. *Diakritikên –> Homoion aph Homoiou, Cheiron apo Beltimos (Katharmos)*
3. *Katharmos –> Peri to Sôma, Peri tên Psychên*
4. *Ponêrian, Phlauron, Kakias* (in soul) *–> Noson = Stasin, Agnoousan =*
    Aischos = Ametrias
5a. *Noson –>* treated by 6a. *Kolastikê*
5b. *Aischos –>* treated by 6b. *Didaskalikês*
6b. *Didaskalikês* directed to 7a. Nameless, 7b. *Amathia*
7a. Nameless *–>* treated by 8a. *Dêmiourgikas Didaskalias*
7b. *Amathia –> treated by* 8b. *Paideia*
8b. *Paideia –> Nouthetêtikên, Elegchos*
9. *Elegchon –> Lykos, Gennaia Sophistikê* (from summary)

Summary: *Diakritikês, Kathartikê, Peri Psychên, Didaskalikês, Paideutikê,*
Elegchos, Gennaia Sophistikê

It is necessary, says the stranger, to see whether *paideia* can be divided. He thinks that he sees a way to do so. One type of instruction in argument or words (*en tois logois didaskalikês*) is rough, the other smooth. Our fathers employed apparently rough admonition on their progeny, sometimes exhibiting anger at their errors and at other times gently exhorting them. Others have concluded that *amathia* is involuntary. (The stranger must be one of those. He just said at 228c that every soul is ignorant unwillingly.) Therefore, they think that those who believe themselves wise are unwilling to learn what they suppose they already know, so that admonition is a waste of time. Accordingly, they try to counteract *amathia* in another way. They question the person who imagines that he is saying something, proving that his opinions contradict themselves about the same things in the same respect. Those who grasp this grow harsh toward themselves and tame toward others, losing their high and mighty opinions of themselves. This process affords great pleasure to listeners and takes a firm hold of the person who has been subjected to it. For just as doctors who care for the body think that it cannot benefit from any food until it has been purged of its impediments, so someone who thinks that he knows cannot benefit from any *mathêmatôn* (teachings) that he has been offered until his soul has been purged by *elegchon* (questioning or refutation) of the opinions that obstruct the doctrines. *Elegchon* is the greatest and most lordly (*kuriôtatê*) sort of purification. So, who bestows this superlative benefit? The stranger is loath to say that it is the sophists. This would confer too great an honor on them. Theaetetus remarks that the description just given is like someone of that sort. He probably is thinking of his recent experience with Socrates. The stranger reacts by issuing a warning. A wolf is much like a dog, the wildest animal very like the tamest. One must beware of similarities. Nevertheless, we will say that the helpful refuters are sophists and be on guard against the wolves who look like them.

As usual, the stranger summarizes (collects) the products of his divisions that pertain to sophistry. He declares that purification is part of the separating *technê* and that it divides into the cleansing of the soul, teaching, education, *elegchos* of empty *doxosophian* (opinion of wisdom), and sophistry. The summary is correct except that it omits the *aischos* (ugliness, deformity) that needs to be purged from souls and changes *amathia* to the empty *doxosophian*. These relatively minor alterations are accompanied by the vagueness concerning *ponêrian*, *phlauron*, and *kakias* in the original *diaeresis*. There is also a deeper confusion at work in the *diaeresis*. When he states that teachers try to purge the soul of *amathia* with *elegchos* just as physicians attempt to purge the body with medicine, the stranger forgets that he had made medicine analogous to punishment and teaching equivalent to gymnastic. His lines are crossed.

Philosophically, the *diakritikên diaeresis* is the most substantive of the divisions that we have examined so far. This necessitates some additional comments.

First, in the *diaeresis* of the kinds of ignorance, the stranger's substitution of weight for semantic opposition as the criterion that determines the halves of a class brings back the question of what he is doing with his dividing. I suggested earlier that he is making his cuts represent his rhetorical intentions rather than the essences or natures of the things being analyzed. His change of principles for identifying categories here seems to confirm this. His casual nonchalance about consistency in rules of method suggests a plan to look at things in ways that are expedient at the moment and a studied indifference to what things are in themselves. The stranger's declaration of value freedom also indicates a rejection of the hypothesis that the participation of something in an order of excellence or goodness is crucial to its being. In that view, for example, generalship and louse catching could not be considered related. Neither could sponging and medicating. A philosophic case could be made for the stranger's attitude. If essences or natures do not exist, as Protagoras maintained in Theaetetus, the stranger's policy would be a useful tool of control in a fundamentally unknowable world and, hence, sensible. However, it would not be Socratic.

Second, the stranger's analysis of disease in the soul seems to reflect Socrates' theory of the order of the soul in Republic, at least at first glance. (Republic 611a–d makes it plain that this account is not proposed as serious knowledge. However, we may take it as an approximation of what Socrates views as the truth of the matter as far as we can understand the soul in our present natural condition.) Socrates posits three parts of the soul, the rational (calculating, *logistikon*), the spirited (*thymos*), and desire (*epithymia*). The soul is well ordered when the calculating part governs the others and the spirited is its ally (441e), such that the soul has the cardinal virtues of courage, moderation, justice, and wisdom. Socrates' putative equation of virtue with knowledge, discussed in dialogues such as Protagoras and Meno, finds its expression here in a description of courage as the preservation of an educated, lawful opinion about what is terrible (429b–d) and a definition of temperance or moderation as a mastery of oneself in which pleasures governed by calculation, intelligence, and right opinion are preferred to the exclusion of others (431a–c). The corollary of the proposition that virtue is knowledge is the notion that vice is ignorance. Socrates implies this with his remark that *amathia* holds sway in the unjust soul (444a). The rational part acquires *phronêsis* (prudence, wisdom) only when it has been dragged out of the cave and beheld the Good (517b–c). Thus, the right order of the soul depends on its attunement to the Good.

The stranger seems Socratic when he says that the soul is ignorant unwillingly. Socrates makes statements like this at Republic 413a and 589c. The stranger also seems Socratic when he argues that, in the souls of the base, opinions (*doxas*) disagree with desires (*epithymias*), *thymos* with pleasures (*hedonais*), and reason (*logos*) with pains (*lupais*). It looks as if he is saying that the right order of the soul is the rule of true opinion over desire, *thymos* over desire for pleasure, and reason over fear of pain. However, this is not what the stranger has said. He has demanded *accord* between opinion and desire, spiritedness and pleasure, and reason and pain. This is not necessarily the rule of true opinion, spiritedness, and reason over desire, pleasure, and pain. If there is discord between the opinion-*thymos*-reason faction and the desire-pleasure-pain faction, this problem can be handled in either of two ways. Desire, pleasure, and pain can be brought into accord with opinion, *thymos*, and reason. Opinion, *thymos*, and reason also can be brought into line with desire, pleasure, and pain. For example, opinion, spiritedness, and reason can persuade a thief to give up the stealing that appeases his desires, affords him pleasure, and spares him pain but desires, pleasures, and pains could convince his opinion, *thymos*, and reason that he deserves his take. Opinion, *thymos*, and reason could persuade an adulterer to leave off the philandering that gratifies his desires, affords him pleasure, and soothes his sexual ache but desires, pleasures, and pains could convince his opinion, *thymos*, and reason to "get in touch with his feelings" and repress his guilt. Each resolution of these cases would eliminate the *stasis*. The stranger's view of the healthy soul could be thought Socratic only if reason were explicitly declared the ruler of *thymos* and desire, and only if reason's supremacy were explained by its attunement to the Good. These elements are missing from the stranger's argument. Therefore, all he has actually argued explicitly is that the well-ordered soul is internally harmonious or "well-adjusted."

Third, for cowardice, intemperance, and injustice in the soul Socrates both recommends and practices education, with mild punishment as a supplementary tool and severe punishment as a last resort for incurable cases. That is why Republic is primarily a *Bildungsroman*. In Laws the Athenian stranger advocates the same policies. Both Socrates and the Athenian expect *paideia* to combat *noson* (the "disease" of vice) and therewith *amathia* (ignorance) in the soul. This means that they see *noson* as an important (but possibly not the only) cause of *amathia*. By designating punishment as the cure of the disease of vice and reserving *paideia* for the treatment of *amathia*, the Eleatic stranger breaks the causal link between vice and ignorance that is posited not only by Socrates and the Athenian stranger but by Plato himself, in his own name, in the Seventh Letter. Thus, the *diakritikên diaeresis* might be not only un-Socratic but un-Platonic.

One dramatic feature of the *diakritikên diaeresis* also calls for an additional comment. It seems that nearly everyone who has written about Sophist maintains that the portrait of the noble sophist unmistakably refers to Socrates. Kenneth Sayre even remarks that it appears likely that Plato meant to make the identification of Socrates with the good sophist "irresistible."[14] Perhaps at great risk to scholarly opinions of my judgment, I disagree. Three conditions for the equation of Socrates with the noble sophist must be satisfied: (1) Socrates must employ *elegchos* to purify souls. (2) Socrates' proofs that his interlocutors are contradicting themselves with respect to the same things in the same regard must cause the ones who grasp what he has done to become harsh toward themselves and tame toward others, losing their high and mighty opinions of themselves. Socrates' ministrations to his patients must afford pleasure to bystanders. The first of these conditions is always met. The second is met too, but only rarely. In Meno, the general confesses that Socrates has reduced him to *aporia* but reacts by stating that people rightly describe Socrates as a wizard and a torpedo fish whose sting numbs the brain (80a). After Meno has been calmed by the exhibition with the slave boy, Anytus happens by and is shown that

14   Sayre, *Plato's Analytic Method*, 151.

he contradicts himself. He becomes angry and gives Socrates a thinly veiled death threat (94e). In Theaetetus, which we have considered at great length, Theodorus responds to the Socratic treatment of his student not with pleasure but with alarm. When he is subjected to inexorable *elegchos* himself, he complains angrily that Socrates is running his friend Protagoras down too much. In Apology, Socrates says that when he showed a *politikos* who thought himself wise that he was not wise, he incurred the man's hatred. This also occurred when he went to many other Athenians (see the repetitions of variations on the verb *apechthainomai* at 21d1, 21e3, 23a1). So, the vast majority of Socrates' interlocutors react to his teaching with outrage, remaining gentle with themselves and becoming harsh toward Socrates, and only a few such as Plato become harsh toward themselves and tame toward others. As for the third condition, Socrates' bystanders also were mostly annoyed by the effects that he had on young men and his refutation of Meletus evidently undermined him with his jury. Hence, what I see the stranger doing with his picture of the noble sophist is not equating that figure with Socrates but proving that Socrates goes about *elegchos* the wrong way, producing the wrong outcomes, such that he could *not* be the noble sophist. Who is this noble sophist then? My guess is that he is the stranger himself or any one of his friends such as Protagoras. Who or what is Socrates then? The answer seems clear to me. Socrates is the wolf who only looks like the noble sophist, the beast against whom we must stand on guard, meaning that the whole point of the *diakritikên diaeresis* seems to have been to negate the malignant effect that Socrates had on Theaetetus yesterday. (Wolves strike their victims dumb; in effect Socrates did that to the boy.) The stranger has given Theaetetus cause to wonder whether Socrates is the wolf, not the genuine noble sophist who is a friendly dog but the dangerous lookalike.

Theaetetus agrees to the stranger's summary of the *diakritikên diaeresis* but he is worried. The sophist has appeared to be so many things that he cannot tell what he really is. The stranger replies that it is the sophist who must be worried that he cannot escape all of our wrestler's grips. We must pursue him vigorously. Before doing that, however, we should summarize our results. First, the sophist appeared as a paid *thêreutês* (hunter) of the young and wealthy. Second, he was an *emporos* (a merchant engaged in intercity commerce) selling *mathêmata* (doctrines, teachings, articles of knowledge) for the soul. Third, he was a *kapêlos* (one who sold the works of others in one city) peddling the same *mathêmata*. Theaetetus chimes in that fourth he was an *autopôlês* (a person who sells *mathêmata* that are his own productions in one city). The stranger replies that Theaetetus has a good memory. In the original presentations it was unclear whether this was the fourth definition or a member of a set of three variations on one that followed the hunter account. This settles on the former alternative. That is fine, although Theaetetus might have demonstrated his good memory better by recalling the confusion. Fifth, resumes the stranger, the sophist was an athlete of *agonistikês* (competing) in words who practiced the *technê* of eristic. The sixth case was debatable but we agreed to make him someone who purifies souls of opinions that obstruct learning. All this seems to me to be approximately correct if the stranger's intent was to provide a capsule account, omitting details and the wolf. It would have been historically accurate to add that the sophist could exhibit any or all of these phenomenal behaviors from time to time.

Instead of making some such observation, the stranger asks the boy whether he sees that there is something wrong with the appearance when we attribute knowledge of many things to a person who practices one *technê*. We have failed to see what all the definitions have in common. It is time to begin our search anew.

Before following the stranger into his new quest, we can assess the results of his efforts so far, with attention first to method and then to substance. My evaluations will pertain only to what we have seen up to here, not to what might follow subsequently.

With regard to method, we have seen that the stranger's *diaereseis* have been pervaded by terminological sloppiness, equivocations, principles for dividing that are unexplained as well as inconsistent, and other sorts of logical confusion. All of the *diaereseis* have been shown to have one or more of these flaws. Thus, we have incurred an obligation to ask why Plato has made his character, the stranger, speak this way. The following reasons suggest themselves:

(1) Plato is incompetent. I reject this explanation out of hand.
(2) As Eva Brann and others have held, Plato is writing comedy, causing the stranger to clown around with his *diaereseis*. I doubt this because I

cannot detect the point of the supposed humor. It might be that the witticisms fly over my prosaic head. Against this view is the further problem that I do not see how or why Socrates would be amused by jokes that culminated in the barely veiled accusation that he is a sophist.

(3) Plato wants us to judge that the stranger is incompetent. I regard this explanation as a leading candidate for selection as the true one, particularly because a capable philosopher could not regard Socrates as a sophist, "noble" or otherwise. I hesitate to settle on this account because the stranger strikes me as shrewd. His mistakes might be deliberate.

(4) If the stranger has erred purposely, this could be for a rhetorical reason. The stranger knows that he is dealing with a bright young geometer but a philosophic neophyte in Theaetetus. He might be taking advantage of that circumstance with a view toward befuddling the boy, using rhetorical tricks to conceal difficulties in his argument. This account is another leading candidate for selection as the right one.

(5) If the stranger's gaffes are deliberate, this also could have pedagogical reasons. Plato could be in the process of showing that *diaeresis* is a method that inevitably starts with confusion in a complex world and that necessarily rises to truth by lifting itself up by its own bootstraps in ever better stages of itself. Alternatively, the stranger could be teaching Theaetetus that *diaeresis* is a mode of investigation that must proceed by empirical trial and error, correcting itself at every turn. If either of these explanations is the correct one, we must expect to see improved reasoning and more persuasive results as we go along. I am happy to wait and see, but I note that I cannot understand how the logical slovenliness of the stranger's divisions fits this picture.

Still with respect to method, the stranger's divisions clearly have not been founded on the natures or essences of the things being discussed, if there actually are such things as natures and essences. One possible explanation of this that I have suggested above is that his cuts have been founded on his rhetorical intentions. Another is that the stranger simply does not understand the essence of sophistry, which probably has to do with the ethical-ontological elements of the issue that he has overlooked. Indeed, both explanations could be true.

With regard to substance, the stranger by his own admission has taught us how sophists can be looked at (this thanks to observation of the phenomenal characteristics of people whom the Athenians call sophists) but not what a sophist is. However, if his arguments have proved philosophically inadequate, there is a sense in which they have been a rhetorical success. Acting as Socrates' prosecutor, the stranger has raised the suspicion that Socrates fits all the definitions of the loathsome sophist offered above (hunter of rich youths, one or another kind of peddler of teachings about virtue who only pretends to educate, athlete of eristic, wolf). He is a philosophic Meletus. He also is much like Polyphemus. Later, we shall see that he hopes to catch the sophist in a net of word devices, the sophist being Socrates-Odysseus. All of his casts of his word net so far have missed Socrates, just as the blind Cyclops groped in vain for Odysseus.

Other items of philosophic import have been mentioned in passing but left undeveloped. The stranger clearly has taken some positions that are un-Socratic. He differs from Socrates on the following points: (1) Whether sophistry is a *technê* (art) or a division of flattery; (2) Whether warnings about the dangers of sophistry should focus on threats to souls or to the financial and social kinds of well-being of its victims; (3) Whether accounts of sophistry require discussion of the relationship of reason to the Good, or whether philosophy is properly value-free; (4) Whether *technê* is guided by knowledge of essences or observation of regularities of cause and effect; (5) Whether wisdom is knowledge of a right way of life or technical know-how; (6) Whether there is a causal link between vice and *amathia*. We do not know yet whether the stranger will treat these issues more thoroughly and adequately.

Let us join the stranger in his renewed quest.

5

SOPHIST: ANOTHER MISS

The subtitle of Sophist, which was supplied either by Plato or a later editor, and which is accepted by the publishers of the Loeb Classical Library but not by those of the Oxford Classical Texts, is *Peri tou Ontos: Logikos* (*On Being: Logical*). The name could be an affirmation of the dialogue's logical ontology. However, it also could be merely a signal that a logical metaphysics will be on offer. This interpretation would allow for the possibility that, far from unquestionably being "Plato's late ontology," the dialogue contains a thought experiment in which Plato causes a character to conduct a logical study of being on the basis of certain assumptions to see whether it works. Logic and the chosen premises may or may not illuminate being. In either case, we are about to examine the part of Sophist that inspires the subtitle. The choice between the possible meanings of the name will have to be based on both the drama and arguments of the document.

We resume analysis of the dialogue where we left off. Having used *diaeresis* to compile six accounts of the sophist, the stranger worries that something has gone wrong. When a person seems to know many things but is called by the name of one art, we are failing to notice what all our studies have in common. I have suggested that the stranger has missed an ethical essence of sophistry but he might disagree, siding with Protagoras in the controversy about whether natures or essences exist. He might intend now to identify something else, a phenomenal element that all his concepts of the sophist share, one that ties them together. In a world devoid of natures, this would be the only possible handle on the appearances that Athenians call sophistry.

As a first step toward learning what is common to his several definitions of sophistry, the stranger selects one of them and says that it describes the sophist best: he is a disputer or debater (*antilogikon*; see Table 6, step 4). Then he asks: "Did we not also say the sophist taught this art to others?"

Theaetetus replies: "Certainly." However, this is the first mention of the teaching of the *technê* of disputing. The stranger has stimulated a false memory in the boy. Someone might object that the teaching of techniques of eristic was implicit in the observation that the disputer was a money-maker, but that is not certain and money-making does not reappear in this renewal of the *antilogikon* account.

Natural curiosity prompts questions: Why does the stranger cite the disputer definition as most revelatory of the sophist? Why does he implant the false memory in Theaetetus? It seems to me that the answer to both questions is the same. The opinion that the sophist is primarily an *antilogikon* and that he teaches his art to others fits not only the principal Athenian conception of a sophist but also the principal Athenian view of Socrates, which is exemplified by Aristophanes' charge that Socrates "is making the weaker argument the stronger and teaching these same things to others" (Apology 19b5–7). This accusation has been heard in Athens so often that Theaetetus readily can imagine that he recalls having heard the stranger say something like it about sophistry generally—and immediately think of Socrates.

Moving along, the stranger suggests that they enumerate the things about which sophists purport to teach others to dispute. There are five such topics: (1) Divine things that are invisible to the many; (2) Visible things of heaven and earth; (3) In private discussions, the generation and being of all things. If the first two subjects embrace the traits, qualities, and behavior of gods and the visible objects of heaven and earth, the third might differ from them by treating the manners in which these things become and their modes of existence as well as generation qua generation and being qua being; (4) Disputation about everything concerning laws and political affairs. The stranger inquires rhetorically whether sophists teach this. Theaetetus replies that no one would speak with them if they did not; (5) The expert knowledge of every art, which the sophists have set forth in treatises. Theaetetus recalls that Protagoras wrote about wrestling and other *technai*. The stranger caps this inventory by asking whether the *antilogikon technê* seems to be a power to contend about everything and whether this is possible. Swearing by the gods, he demands to be told further whether any person could know all things. Theaetetus answers that mankind would be blessed if this were possible. Well, the stranger continues, can someone who is ignorant say anything sound in debate with one who knows? "In no way," replies Theaetetus. Expanding his point, the stranger inquires what the magic power (*dynameôs thauma*) of the sophistical art could be then. Theaetetus asks what he is talking about. The stranger answers that sophistical power is magical insofar as young men see sophists seeming to argue correctly about everything—which is impossible—and infer that sophists are therefore wisest in all things.

We have here, at least provisionally, a new definition of the sophist: He is a disputer who pretends to know all things and has a magic power of appearing to young men to demonstrate in debates that he actually is omniscient. We recall that the stranger's initial view of the sophist as a man who practices a *technê* differed from that of Socrates, who held that the sophist pursued an *empeiria*, a practical reliance on observations of behavioral regularities that guided flattery rather than a *technê*. We wonder now whether the stranger approaches Socrates' or reflects Plato's late, improved account. The query justifies a brief excursus into other Platonic portraits of sophists.

In Gorgias, Socrates urges Gorgias to disclose the subject of the rhetoric that he teaches. Gorgias answers that the topic is the best of human affairs and the greatest good. Socrates asks what that is. Gorgias answers:

> I call it the ability to persuade with speeches either judges in the law courts or statesmen in the council chamber or the commons in the Assembly or an audience at any other meeting that may be held on public affairs. And I tell you that by virtue of this power you will have the doctor as your slave, and the trainer as your slave; your money-maker will turn out to be making money not for himself but for another—in fact for you, who are able to speak and persuade the multitude (452e, Loeb translation).[1]

Socrates persists. He asks whether people who know their subjects can persuade others. Gorgias affirms that they can. Then, Socrates asks, is

---

1   Although Gorgias describes himself as a rhetorician, not a sophist, I think that his replies about the Good, his purposes, and his association with Polus suffice to establish his sophistry.

there a difference between having learned and having believed? Yes. Thus, is there false belief and true belief? Yes (454d). Therefore are there two kinds of persuasion, one producing belief without knowledge and the other producing knowledge? Yes. Which sort of persuasion does the rhetorician inculcate? Gorgias admits that he produces belief without knowledge. Then he goes on to claim that this does not matter. He is not a doctor but he can persuade patients to submit to their treatments when physicians cannot do so. He could persuade an assembly to appoint him as a doctor, defeating the real physician who was vying for the position in debate. He could speak more persuasively than any *dêmiourgos* (let us say "professional") in such a contest (456a–c). Well, inquires Socrates, could the rhetorician persuade a physician who knows medicine or can he convince only the ignorant many? Only the ignorant many, replies Gorgias (459a). All this seems tantamount to a cheerful admission by the sophist that he does not know everything and that he appears wisest about all things not to people who know but only to the ignorant many. Accordingly, if the Gorgias portrait is indicative, the stranger would have to amend his new definition of the sophist to align it with that of Socrates. He would have to argue not that the sophist pretends to know all things and has a magic power of appearing to his students to know, but that the sophist persuades the ignorant many that he knows everything and appears to his followers to have a clever knack of pulling this deception off. This is to realize that the sophist's students are not taken in but laugh up their sleeves along with him. Although the difference between the two definitions is slight, it is important. In Plato's Gorgias exchange, there is nothing magical about the sophist's power. The sophist simply has a capacity to outwit the ignorant, which is straightforward and not in the least arcane. If Plato himself now advocates the stranger's definition, he has revised the opinion implicit in this Gorgias portrait.

In the dialogue that bears his name, Protagoras is pressed to say what subjects he teaches. He denies having anything to do with most *technai*, boasting that he does not force students into logistic, astronomy, geometry, and music. He prepares his followers to exercise good judgment in their own affairs. Socrates inquires whether this means that he teaches *tên politikên technên*, the political art, and that he aims to make men good citizens. Protagoras says yes (318e–19a). Although this is a daunting project,

Protagoras has not thereby claimed to know everything and has advised a prospective student (Hippocrates) that he will not teach him all things.

In a dialogue named after him, Hippias is reported to have bragged that he has mastered more arts than anyone and has never met anyone who excelled him in anything (Lesser Hippias 364a–68e). This is prodigious chutzpah but it falls well short of a claim to know everything. I pass over the ridiculous sophist brothers in Euthydemus, who "prove" that they know everything by arguing, in effect, "I know everything that I know and 'I know everything' is part of this true statement, therefore I know everything" (293e–96c). Their performance is burlesque.

Our little survey of Platonic portraits of sophists seems to show that the Eleatic stranger's definition of the sophist as a "disputer who pretends to know all things and has a magic power of seeming to his students to do so" is unrepresentative of the pictures of the formidable sophists in Plato's other plays. However, to be fair to the stranger, we have seen that Gorgias has lodged a claim to be able to speak convincingly about everything before ignorant crowds, persuading them that he knows all things. I would add one comment. If we go back over the inventory of things about which sophists allegedly teach others to dispute, a list that led to the charge that they feign to know everything, we can see that the catalogue implicates Socrates. (1) Divine things that are invisible to the many. It probably is well-known in Athens that Socrates did an extensive critique of Homeric theology. This resulted in the accusation that he denied the city's gods. (2) Visible things of heaven and earth. Athenians thought that Socrates treated heavenly things, calling the sun a stone and the moon earth rather than revering them as gods (Apology 26d). He frequently discussed visible earthly things ranging from mud to political regimes. (3) In private discussions, the generation and being of all things. When he was young, Socrates openly sought the wisdom called "learning about nature" (*physeôs* historian). He tried to find the causes of things—why they come into being, exist, and perish (Phaedo 96a–b). For all Theaetetus knows, Socrates still could be conducting such research privately. He would have to do it secretly because his studies were heterodox. (4) Disputation about everything concerning laws and political affairs. Socrates often criticizes Athenian politics and law. (5) The expert knowledge of every art. Socrates has interrogated every master of every *technê* whom he has encountered. He could have struck these hapless characters as a busybody who pretended to know their *technai*. So, every element of the growing definition of the sophist—that he is a disputer, that he feigns to know and talks about everything, that he magically persuades his followers that he knows all, and that he is a fraud, can be construed as a trait of Socrates, although only the first touches his teaching even slightly.

Theaetetus accepts the stranger's argument that the sophist has a magic power that makes him seem all-wise to his students even though he deals in mere opinion. Having persuaded the boy about this, the stranger orders him to pay close attention. He must regard his next move as extremely important. He begins: If someone claims not that he can assert or dispute but that he has a *technê* of making all things—but here Theaetetus cuts him off, inquiring what "all things" and "making" mean. The stranger answers that someone might claim to make people, animals, trees, the sea, earth, heaven, and gods, offering to sell them cheaply. Theaetetus suspects a joke. The stranger retorts that pretending to know and teach all things for a small price is a joke. He explains that he is referring to *mimêtikon*, the art of imitation. So, for example, the painter can create imitations with the same names as the real beings that they imitate and he can trick duller children by showing them pictures at distances, making them suppose that he can do whatever he wants. Evidently the children are amazingly dense and think that they are looking at real things. We gather that the stranger is about to define the sophist as an imitator who is analogous to the painter. We should notice that no important sophist in Plato's dramas explicitly claims either to know or to make all things. However, in Theaetetus's mind it has been established that sophists pretend to know all things and the stranger now has equated that behavior with a claim to be able to make them all (by imitating them).

Before continuing with the stranger's new tack, we must observe that his sarcastic speech about imitators such as painters is virtually identical with Socrates' fulminations against them in Republic. Socrates remarks that a certain manual artisan "makes everything that grows naturally from the earth, and he produces all animals . . . and in addition to that, produces earth and heaven and gods and everything in heaven and everything in Hades under the earth." Glaucon answers: "That's quite a wonderful sophist you speak of." Socrates and Glaucon add that someone who paints a couch not only does not construct the Form of a couch, which is a god's work, but also fails to build the carpenter's material couch. The painter only makes what looks like a material couch, which lacks being insofar as it is at a third remove from the real couch, the Form (596a– 97a, Bloom translations). So, the Eleatic stranger is attacking sophists as imitators and Socrates is attacking imitators as sophists. Their propositions seem equivalent. We may suppose that the surprising agreement between the stranger and Socrates reflects Socrates' real antipathy toward imitators—unless Socrates is merely acting as a midwife to Glaucon's views, a possibility that cannot be explored here. (Several commentators mark the irony that Plato uses Socrates to attack imitators and poets despite the fact that as a playwright he is an imitator and poet himself.)

The stranger proceeds with his analogy. He asks whether we may not expect that there is another *technê* that employs speech to produce verbal images (*eidôla*) of everything, bewitching (*goêteunein*) the young who stand so far from the truth of things that they imagine that they are hearing real truths. He clearly has switched his original *paradeigma* of the sophist, which led to analyses defining sophistry as acquisition, the opposite of this deceptive production. Presumably this is another example of grasping the savage beast with both hands and not a repudiation of the acquisition models, which have implicitly attributed the phenomenal characteristics of sophists to Socrates. Again, I am obliged to mention that the stranger's analogy between a painter's images and "spoken images" (*eidôla legomena*) that fool callow youths parallels an analogy that Socrates draws between a painter who "will make what seems to be a shoemaker to those who understand as little about shoemaking as he understands" (Bloom translation) and the poets, Homer first of all. The poets are "imitators of images of virtue" (*mimêtas eidôlôn aretês*), fail to lay hold of the truth, and appear to the ignorant who observe only speeches to speak well (Republic 600e– 01a). The analogy inspires me to enter a protest, perhaps against the stranger alone and perhaps against Socrates and even Plato himself. In my opinion, the reasoning that establishes the equivalence of "verbal images" with visual images does not quite work. In the first place, I doubt that any child could be dull enough to mistake a painting, say, of a person, for a person. A portrait captures the look of a person but it does not look like a person. It looks like what it is, a painting of a person. If distance causes an optical illusion that, say, a cardboard cutout picture is a person, the illusion is dispelled by a few moments' continuous observation that detects absence of life. In the second place, the devious painter's image of a cobbler does not "look like" a cobbler in the same sense that Vermeer's portrait of the girl with a pearl earring looks like the girl. This painter has created an image of someone other than a cobbler. Then he has told an ignoramus that the picture looks like a cobbler. The dolt is deceived by the lie, not by the image. Similarly, the stranger's verbal definitions of a sophist do not "look like" Socrates. Rather, the stranger has described types that are not Socrates' type—predatory hunter who pretends to educate, salesman of doctrines about excellence, disputer who uses eristic to earn money, wolf who resembles a purifier of souls. He has subtly let his listeners infer that those accounts rightly interpret Socrates' behavior. A person ignorant of Socrates will be deceived not by the descriptions but by applications of those slurs to him that misconstrue evidence. In the third place, to be precise, words are not images. They are sounds that signify realities such as things, actions, and relations. If they mislead, this happens not because they make things "look like" what they are not but because they signify that realities are other than they are, tricking people who do not know better. Socrates is on somewhat firmer ground when he argues that poets "imitate," if by this he means "portray by making characters act and speak thus and so." However, when such "images" deceive, they do so by falsely signifying who it is that behaves that way. In sum, metaphors are shaky foundations for logical reasoning.

I reported above that the stranger has stated that the sophist possesses a *technê* that uses speech to produce verbal images of everything, bewitching (*goêteunein*) the young. With this, he has recurred to the sophist's *dynameôs thauma*, upping the ante with regard to the magic power. Earlier, I argued that Socrates' definition of the sophist envisages not magic but a straightforward ability to fool ignoramuses. Someone might have objected that I was stressing the issue of magic too much in a passage in which the stranger was only speaking extravagantly. I answer that *goês*, with all the grammatical variations on its root, is an interesting word. Liddell and Scott render it primarily as "one who howls out enchantments, a wizard, a sorcerer," and secondly as "a juggler, cheat." Some translators prefer "juggler." However, the stranger's use of *goêteunein* here clearly means bewitching. The stranger will deploy variations of the term often as the drama continues. In fact, insisting that he wants to move Theaetetus closer to truth, the next thing that the stranger does is indicate for the second time that the sophist is a *goês* and an imitator of beings (235a1–2). He urges Theaetetus to agree with this assessment. Theaetetus does so. Evidently nervous about the boy's commitment, the stranger immediately presses him again to affirm that the sophist is a *goês* and an imitator (235a8). He gets a third confirmation. Then he informs Theaetetus that the sophist is nearly encircled in the net of devices used in speeches or arguments about such things. We must not let the beast escape the conclusion that he belongs to the class of wonder workers or conjurers (*thaumatopoiôn*, 235b5). This rapid-fire, quadruple insistence on *goêteunein*, *goês*, and *dynameôs thauma* indicates that the stranger is extremely serious about convincing Theaetetus to believe in the magic power, whatever he thinks about it himself. He seems to be slyly alluding to Aristophanes' well-publicized charge that Socrates "investigates the things beneath the earth and in the heavens" and hence, by Athenian standards, practices witchcraft. To convict Socrates of sophistry, he wants to associate witchcraft with sophistry in Theaetetus's mind. However, he has merely asserted emphatically, not proved, that magic is involved.

Having secured Theaetetus's agreement that the sophist is a *goês*, an imitator of beings, and a *thaumatopoiêtês*, the stranger suggests a return to *diaeresis*, which has not been used to get the latest results. He calls for a division of *tên eidôlopoiikên technên*, the image-making art. He and Theaetetus will pursue the sophist by order of "*logos* (reason) the king," either capturing him immediately or hounding him relentlessly through all the divisions into which he flees until he is caught, whereupon he will be delivered to the king and displayed.

The stranger posits two classes of *mimêsis*. One is *eikastikên* (the likeness-making art), in which the maker produces his imitation by following the proportions of the original in length, breadth, and depth, adding appropriate colors. The other is *phantastikên* (the phantasm-making art) which constructs gigantic objects. It distorts the proportions of originals so that viewers at ground level will have the illusion of seeing properly formed figures. The stranger worries that he cannot tell to which class the sophist belongs: this *thaumatos anêr* (magical or wonderful man) has withdrawn into a category where he is hard to track. Theaetetus replies that this seems likely. The stranger asks him whether he has said this just because he has become accustomed to going along or because he understands. Theaetetus has no idea what he means. The stranger explains that they are about to enter upon a very difficult inquiry involving appearing and seeming but not being (*to gar phainesthai kai to dokein, einai de mê*) and asserting things but not true ones. For it is difficult to say or opine that falsehoods really exist without getting involved in contradictions. If we maintain that falsehoods exist we must assume that nonbeing (*to mê on*) exists. Although the stranger has claimed to be uncertain about the class of *mimêsis* in which the sophist belongs, it is plain from this that he is leaning toward locating him in *phantastikên*, which "abandons the truth," giving imitations not the proportions of their originals but only those that seem beautiful (236a). Later, after having explained the impossibility of speaking consistently about nonbeing, the stranger will declare that the sophist villainously (*panourgôs*) has hidden himself behind that problem (239c), implying or asserting that images (239d) and falsehoods (241a) do not exist.

To return to an issue that I raised above, this characterization of the sophist as a man who denies the existence of falsehoods clearly does not tally with other Platonic pictures of sophists. We recall that we were just looking at an exchange between Socrates and Gorgias. "Gorgias, is there false belief and true belief?" (*Ar esti tis, Ô Gorgia, pistis pseudês kai alêthês;*) "Yes" (*Nai*) (454d5–6). If Gorgias holds that there is false belief he thinks that there is falsehood. He firmly declares that he opposes spreading false opinion (468b). In Lesser Hippias, Socrates and Hippias discuss false men at length. Hippias says that false men have power and that they are "wise and powerful in uttering falsehoods" (*sophoi te kai dynatoi pseudesthai*, 366b4–5). Protagoras would seem to present a hazier case because he contends that all perceptions are true for those who have them. However, one meaning of this is that statements perceived as false are false for those who perceive them as false. Further, he does not conclude from his relativism that people cannot lie. At Protagoras 358c, he affirms with an entire company of sophists that ignorance is false opinion. At Republic 337a, Thrasymachus accuses Socrates of irony, which is a sort of dissembling. So, the stranger's account of the sophist as a man who denies the existence of falsehood is unique in Plato. It probably contradicts Plato's unchanging opinion too. Plato could not have repudiated his earlier portraits of sophists credibly. Sophists did typically catch others in self-contradictions, thus convicting them of false belief, which is belief in falsehoods.

If Plato never had drawn his earlier dramatic sketches of sophists, the stranger's argument that sophists deny that there are falsehoods would still be startling because it contradicts his own previous accounts of sophists. Let us revisit his *diaeresis* of separating, which culminated in his definition of the noble sophist. In that exercise, we saw that ignorance is one of two disorders of the soul, in which reason aims at the truth and misses it because of some disproportion or lack of measure (228c–d). The cure for ignorance is *elegchos* (230d), a word often correctly translated as "refutation" (per Liddell and Scott). *Elegchos* sets a person's opinions side by side, showing that they contradict each other about the same things with regard to the same points in the same ways. This is to say that the noble sophist, whom the stranger invented, goes about proving that at least one statement in every self-contradictory set is false. It also appears that the present *diaeresis* that the stranger is conducting, which begins with his account of the sophist as a disputer, necessarily assumes that the ordinary sophist affirms the existence of falsehood. The point of disputation is to convict people of false belief and exhibit the truth.

The disparity between Plato's usual portraits of sophists and the stranger's argument that sophists deny the existence of falsehood generally escapes the notice of Plato scholars. So does the stranger's self-contradiction in maintaining his thesis. This is unacceptable. Plato, I believe, wants us to notice and account for every twist and turn in his dialogues. Therefore, we must ask why he writes the observed discrepancy and contradiction into Sophist. I can see one dramatic reason. I know of only one speaker in Plato who calls the possibility of falsehood into question. Socrates, in Theaetetus, raises difficulties for the idea that there are falsehoods in order to reduce the young geometer's epistemological premises to absurdity. Theaetetus, Theodorus, and young Socrates repeatedly forget that Socrates acts as a midwife. Thus, for them, defining the sophist as a person who proclaims the non-existence of falsehood pins a badge of sophistry squarely on Socrates—and on him alone. If this is the stranger's conscious intention, he dares to contradict himself because he is sure that he will get away with his contradiction (he has been doing so for centuries) and because he wants to further his prosecution of Socrates.

So, our dramatic situation seems to be that the stranger defines the sophist as a scoundrel who denies the existence of falsehoods as a means of snaring Socrates. His critique of the claim that one cannot logically affirm the existence of falsehoods will be a refutation of Socrates. That analysis

also will be a new departure into the material that analytic philosophers regard as Plato's mature metaphysics. Therefore, this will be a good place to
pause and summarize the stranger's theoretical work up to here. So far, his
arguments have been devoted to defining the sophist. He began with an
angler paradigm meant both as a model of the method of hunting the
sophist and as a guide to the substance of sophistry. He followed that with
a number of *diaereseis* that led to six accounts of the sophist. The angler
paradigm and the subsequent *diaereseis* were sometimes logically defective
and frequently internally garbled. Further, the divisions of his *diaereseis*
seem to have been dictated more by his rhetorical purposes than by real
essences or logical necessities. The resulting definitions pointed to phenomenal characteristics of people called sophists. They were pronounced
inadequate by the stranger himself because they marked no element common to all of them. Since that juncture, the stranger has been developing
a new definition of the sophist. The sophist has become (1) primarily an
antilogikon (disputer), (2) who teaches others the art of disputation, (3) who
pretends to know all things, (4) who not only has a magic power of seeming
to his students to know all things but who is a *goês*, a wizard who howls enchantments, (5) who claims to be able to make all things, (6) who tries to
back that claim up by creating word images that "imitate" their originals
and deceive youths who stand far from the truth, (7) who fabricates his
word images by practicing *phantastikên*, the *technê* of distorting the proportions of the originals, forsaking the truth in order to make copies that only
seem beautiful, and (8) who defends himself against the charge that he is
an image maker by denying the existence of images and falsehoods. Socrates
and Plato might accept (1) and (2) as descriptions of behavior typical of
most sophists. They would correct (3) by adding "before the ignorant only."
They would not recognize (4) and (5) as traits of any sophists they have
known. They might weigh (6) and (7). They would reject (8) on the grounds
that no one has ever encountered a sophist who denied the existence of images and falsehoods and that sophists practice refutation, implying that
people are sunk in falsehood. I have noted that the stranger has contradicted
his own views of the noble sophist as a purifier and the ordinary sophist as
a disputer by maintaining (8). I also have objected to (6) and (7), even if
they should turn out to be Platonic doctrine, because they are metaphors
that I think misrepresent what occurs in lying. Falsehoods neither imitate

nor distort proportions, creating illusions. They signify untruthfully, as do deceptive dramatic portraits. It matters that words are auditory signs, not visual images. Metaphors can only be stretched so far.

In response to the need to explain why Plato makes the stranger derive his first accounts of the sophist from exercises that involve apparently arbitrary methods and too frequently garbled logic, I have proposed alternative reasons in the previous chapter. Decisive evidence for picking the right one has not emerged yet. However, I now am leaning toward the explanations that the stranger is either incompetent or shrewd. In the latter case, he would be erring or, as we have just seen, also misrepresenting facts, purposely, this with a view toward either befuddling Theaetetus with rhetorical flimflam or teaching him that *diaeresis* must wade through all kinds of mistakes, correcting itself as it rises toward truth. A substantial objection to the pedagogical explanation is that Theaetetus might begin to suspect the stranger of lying as soon as he realized that no sophists (other than Socrates?) denied the existence of falsehoods.

Standing outside Sophist as a reader of the dialogue, I have conceived another objection too. What are we to make of a metaphysics that will be constructed as an answer to a supposedly sophistical thesis that no sophist has ever uttered, or as the solution of a conundrum arising out of assumptions that Socrates wanted to reduce to absurdity? What should we think of an ontology motivated by an assertion about sophists that contradicts the premise of the analysis it is meant to advance? Could Plato intend that metaphysics as sound philosophy? Or is he signaling that the logic that we will see next is as suspect as its inspiration?

With questions like these in the background, we examine from the beginning the material usually interpreted as Plato's late metaphysics (or as the first expression of that ontology). The stranger tells Theaetetus that they are about to undertake a very difficult inquiry. "For appearing and seeming, but not being (*to gar phainesthai touto kai to dokein, einai de mê*) and saying things but not true ones (*kai to legein men atta, alêthê de mê*) are always matters full of perplexity now and in the past." It is hard to understand how one can say or think that falsehoods genuinely exist (*pseudê legein kai doxazein ontôs einai*) without becoming involved in contradiction because this sentence "has dared to suppose that nonbeing is (*to mê on einai*). For otherwise falsehood would not come to be what it is" (*pseudos gar ouk an allôs egigneto on*) (quotes and paraphrases follow Eva Brann translations).

The stranger does not immediately explain what he means by these statements. Neither does he say why or in what senses he thinks them true. We must sort out possibilities ourselves.

Let us start with "appearing and seeming but not being." The phrase is vague because it has no subjects and predicates. Does it mean that "X appears and seems but is not in being?" If so, the phrase might refer to a hallucination or a mental aberration: "Caesar's ghost appeared and seemed to menace me but no ghost was there." "John appeared and seemed to me to be present but he was absent." On the other hand, do the words mean "X appears and seems to be Y but is not Y?" If so, the phrase could pertain to different sorts of misidentifications: "The man wearing a uniform appeared and seemed to be a policeman but he was an impostor." "The cutout picture momentarily appeared and seemed to me to be the movie star but it was not a real person." "The man I picked out of the lineup appeared and seemed to be the robber but upon closer inspection I see that it was not he." The words also could refer to misjudgments: "The proposition appeared and seemed to me to be true but it was false." Conceived in such ways, the phrase is intelligible. But what is meant by saying that the falsehood of the statements "It was Caesar's ghost," "John was there," "He was a policeman," "It was the star," "He was the robber," and "The proposition is true" entails proclamations of the being of nonbeing? Why does the stranger maintain that? Certainly labeling the propositions untrue entails no affirmation of the being of nonbeing simply (which Stanley Rosen calls "the *nihil absolutum*"). Caesar's ghost did not exist but a delusional image was in my mind and that was something. John was not there but a misplaced image was in my mind and that was something. My examples all reduce to instances of "It was not this being but the existence of that different thing or case." Probably the stranger would have spoken more accurately by calling the judgments of falsehood not claims that nonbeing exists, but negations of the presence of one being in favor of the presence of another. We do not ordinarily regard such negations as affirmations of a being of nonbeing. To mark an absence is not to posit a presence (Hegel and Heidegger notwithstanding). Absences are not present, despite the grammatical form assumed by "it *is* absent." Perhaps the stranger was speaking loosely and he meant that exposing falsehoods involves "not this but that" negations. We shall have to wait to find out.

Next, what does the stranger intend by intimating that falsehoods genuinely exist (*pseudê . . . ontôs einai*, 236e4)? Further, what does he mean a bit later when he accepts the proposition that an icon (*eikona*), with qualifications that will be taken up in due course, really is (*estin ontôs*, 240b11–12)?[2] correctly observes that (in Republic, at least) Plato associates terms such as *ontôs einai* and *ontôs on* with Forms, thus prompting us to distinguish between the *being* that the Forms possess and the *existence* of spatio-temporal instances. Plato's Socrates probably would not have posited Forms of falsehood and image. If he did, he still would not have called falsehoods and images *ontôs einai* and *ontôs on*, thus abolishing his analysis of the gradations of being. As Rosen concludes, "The application of terms like *ontôs on* . . . in our passage thus seem to carry senses differing from those invoked in passages in Republic X."[3] The stranger appears to be on the way to fabricating an ontology in which Socrates' gradations of being are abolished. For him, all things, Forms, material objects, and images, seem to share the same level of being.

Having asserted without explanation that saying or thinking that falsehood exists assumes the being of nonbeing, the stranger immediately recalls that "Parmenides the Great" always used to issue a warning: "This [he says] should not ever prevail in your thought: that the things that *are not, are*; Rather do you keep your mind well shut off from just this way of searching" (Eva Brann translation). The stranger's move raises two new questions: What did Parmenides mean? What does the stranger take him to mean? The first query probably is unanswerable because we only have fragments of Parmenides' work. However, a few guesses are possible. Parmenides could have meant that we should not suppose that the *nihil absolutum* or anything attributed to it exists. That would make sense. He also could have meant that we should not believe in figments of the imagination, such as unicorns. That would make sense too. More controversially, he might have been arguing that we should not credit statements positing the real existence of things

2 The stranger seems to be mixing up his own terms again. Icons replicate the proportions of originals. Shouldn't he be talking about phantasms in connection with falsehoods?
3 Stanley Rosen, *Plato's "Sophist,"* 194–95. Here, see Rosen's critique of Vlastos.

apart from the One. On the other hand, I doubt that he could have meant that we should avoid "not this but that" negations. Anyone who gives his work a cursory glance will notice that *ouk* (not) and *mê* (not) appear in it, so he would have been violating his own precept had he forbidden negations.

The stranger solicits Theaetetus's agreement to consider Parmenides' warning first. The boy somewhat disappointingly replies that he will agree to anything the stranger suggests and he urges the stranger to take him along wherever he goes. He is too tractable. So, the stranger asks whether we dare speak about "the in no way whatsoever being" (*to mêdamôs on*). It is not quite clear what this implies. Does the stranger suppose that Parmenides was speaking about the *nihil absolutum*? Is he himself saying that affirming the existence of falsehood entails proclamations of the existence of the *nihil absolutum*? Or is he merely bringing this topic up first in order to get it out of the way? Whatever the case, Theaetetus replies: "For how not?" We do talk about "the in no way whatsoever being." We are referring to our imagination of the total absence of being that we extrapolate from the absences of particular things, in Hegel's fashion.

Next the stranger requests serious consideration of a problem: to what would a student of Parmenides be able to apply the concept "nonbeing" (*to mê on*, still understood as *to mêdamôs on*)? Theaetetus cannot say. There follows an especially lucid explanation by the stranger of the logical difficulty of using the term. Nonbeing cannot be applied to any beings. Neither could it be attached to the word *tis* (some, something), for that would be to apply it to a being implicitly. It cannot be modified with phrases denoting singular, dual, or plural number, for there is nothing there to count. It would seem that a person who talks about nonbeing (still *to mêdamôs on*) says nothing and therefore does not speak at all. (This seems to me to be wrong. The individual does speak meaningfully, referring to a total absence of being. Again, to denote an absence by saying "is absent" is not to utter nonsense. Human grammar intends being, such that we cannot avoid "is absent," but we all understand what we mean.) Theaetetus thinks that they have reached the limits of paradox. Nevertheless the stranger presses on, observing that nothing can be attributed to nonbeing (still *to mêdamôs on*). He repeats that we cannot attach number to it. We contradict ourselves when we say "things that are not" or "a thing which is not." We slip up again when we refer to nonbeing as "that" or "it." It is impossible to utter or conceive nonbeing *auto kath' auto* (itself by itself). It is unspeakable and irrational. All very true, with the exception about absence that I have noted. Incidentally, it should be observed that this entire passage is implicitly a use of *elegchos*, a setting of statements side-by-side to demonstrate that they contradict each other about the same things in the same respects and showing that the whole series of these statements cannot stand. The stranger can intelligently employ methods that are common to Socrates and sophists, particularly the method that he himself attributes to the noble sophist, when he wishes.

So, speaking about nonbeing (still *to mêdamôs on*) is impossible. The stranger says that this means that someone who attempts to refute nonbeing finds himself in *aporia*. He cannot do so without using the terms just forbidden, thus contradicting himself. The stranger claims to be defeated and turns on Theaetetus, urging him to say something about nonbeing without ascribing being or unity or plurality to it. Theaetetus begs off. The stranger concludes that the sophist has villainously hidden himself where he cannot be tracked. Therefore, if we argue that he practices *phantastikên technên*, the art of making phantasms or appearances, and if we assert that he is an *eidôlopoion*, an image-maker, he will counterattack by asking what we mean by *eidôlon* (image), forcing us into the contradictions we just encountered because speech about images presupposes the existence of nonbeing. We must admit either that there are no images or that nonbeing exists.

Stanley Rosen apparently accepts this reasoning. Explaining why the stranger makes the sophist pose the image question, he writes: "This, of course, is because an image contains non-being, or rather, because we cannot explain what we mean by 'image' without explaining what we mean by 'non-being.'"[4] I disagree. I do not see where nonbeing comes into play. I think of an image as "a form or shape imparted to a medium, which form or shape resembles the look of a being other than the informed medium." There are only beings in this definition. Rosen arrives at his position by divorcing the image from its medium: "The way of imaging is not reducible to the 'matter' in which the image is realized." From this, he infers that: "An (accurate) image of a given original 'is and is not' the original, and *in the same respect*, not in two different respects. An accurate copy of a certain look is the same look."[5]

---

4   Rosen, *Plato's "Sophist,"* 185.
5   Rosen, *Plato's "Sophist,"* 191.

I believe that this is a mistake. An image has its own look that is constituted by its medium. That is how we recognize it as an image. No matter how true the copy, the looks of original and image differ in this crucial respect. However, I understand that there is an implicit "not this being but that being" negation in my account of an image. The image is not the thing imaged. If such negation is behind the stranger's and Rosen's arguments, they seem to be on the verge of equating negation with invocation of nonbeing. As I said above, this is an odd way of speaking. It also is misleading, given that the stranger caused *to mêdamôs on* (the *nihil absolutum*) to determine the understanding of nonbeing at the beginning of these passages.

Ever true to his habit, Theaetetus replies to the question about the meaning of "image" by giving examples. He asserts that the word refers to what we see in water, mirrors, paintings, and sculptures. The stranger objects. He speculates that Theaetetus has never seen a sophist. If he had seen one, he would know that the sophist will seem to have his eyes shut or to be blind. He will pretend that he knows nothing of images in paintings, etc. He will demand that Theaetetus use words alone to explain the one thing ("image") referenced by his illustrations. This is not the same objection that Socrates raised to Theaetetus's first definition of knowledge. True, Socrates asked what common essence was shared by the pursuits called *epistêmê* but he did not question the existence of knowledge. The sophist not only will expect Theaetetus to say what makes what is seen in mirrors, etc. "images" but also to demonstrate with logic that the named nature exists. The stranger requires Theaetetus to accept the sophist's challenge. This stipulation negates the definition of "image" that I just offered as well as Theaetetus's illustrations. Material "forms," "shapes" and "media," are invisible to a man who has shut his eyes.

At this juncture, I am forced to raise a question. Is the stranger's demand legitimate? It seems to me that words must refer to human experiences. If a person lacks ability to experience X, a word that denotes X can never be explained to him. Someone blind from birth can never be made to understand "blue." So, on what reasonable basis does the stranger require Theaetetus to accept the condition that he explain image without appealing to the experience of seeing images? Why let the sophist get away with denying the existence of some visible X and refusing to accept visual proofs or a definition that refers to seen things by closing his eyes? Shouldn't Theaetetus respond by challenging such an arbitrary stipulation?

The disappointing Theaetetus crumbles. Attempting to comply with the stranger's order, he gives the ingenious reply that an image is *to pros talêthinon aphômoiômenon heteron toiouton*. Stanley Rosen translates this with "another such thing that is made like the true thing." All other translators give similar renditions. Their readings are absolutely correct. However, I should like to alter them in two ways to clarify an important point. First, I would write "another such [thing] that is made like the true [thing]." This change would indicate that no independent noun "thing" (such as *pragma*) appears in the Greek. *Talêthinon* (the true) and *heteron toiouton* (another such) are adjectival forms that function here as nouns and "thing" is properly understood as the implied substantive referent in both cases. Second, I would reduce the phrase to "another such made like the true." This version would be literal, representing Theaetetus's actual words. The answer is ingenious because it goes as far as Greek grammar allows toward avoiding references to visible things. Consider: concepts anything like material "form," "shape," and "medium," my preferred terms, are omitted. Perhaps in deference to the sophist who might claim not to understand what a "thing" is, even that concept is muted.

As usual, our task now is to learn what Theaetetus's definition means. Unfortunately, the phrase is self-contradictory. Calling an image "another such" means that it is of the same kind as something else (namely, "the true"). Rosen points out that this reading requires a Form of Image standing above both original and copy, with an infinite regress of Image Forms looming.[6] If the original and the copy share one nature we also lose what is needed to distinguish between them (the different embodiments). To counter these problems, "made like" implies that the image is not of the same nature as "the true" but only similar (the likeness inhering in the looks?). Thus, the definition is opaque. This will cause difficulties.

To perceive the potential for trouble, we must examine Theaetetus's words a little more closely. As Rosen observes, the term for the image, "another such" could have only one referent in the definition, "the true." "The true" is clearly the original. But what is meant by calling the original "the true?" Is "true" merely a synonym for "original?" Or does the word imply that the original truly exists? If so, does the "another such" not really exist,

6   Rosen, *Plato's "Sophist*," 190.

simply? Or does it not truly exist qua original? If the latter, how does it fail to really exist qua original if it is "another such," being of the same kind? Meanwhile, is the referent of "the true" some unspecified [thing]? Or is its referent "the other of the another such?" If so, the account is a self-referential closed circle. It would escape the empirical and logical control that references to visible original objects, shapes, and media would afford. Again, if the "another such" is "made like the true," does that mean that it is "not true?" Then how could it be "another such?" If it is "true," why is it only "made like" and not "the same as" the "true?" These questions become especially salient when we shift from the stranger's talk of paintings to his language of "proportions." Rosen correctly argues that two ratios are either identical or different.[7] The word "similar" is inapposite. How could an "image" of words be "like the true" if it is a different ratio and optical illusions are not at work? I cannot answer such queries. The potential for difficulties lies in this ambiguity. Theaetetus's definition of image will become the basis of the stranger's argument that an image simultaneously contains being and nonbeing. We must wonder whether an account that has been produced in compliance with arbitrary empirical and logical strictures, with the consequence that it is self-contradictory and otherwise extremely vague, is an adequate basis for such a radical metaphysical leap. Plato seems to be causing the stranger to undermine the foundations of his own reasoning.

The stranger plays on the ambiguities just noted. He inquires whether Theaetetus means "another such true [thing]" (*heteron . . . toiouton alêthinon*): In what sense is he utilizing "such?" The boy replies: "In no way true but like." The stranger asks: "But by true you mean 'really is' (*ontôs on*)?" Yes. "The not true is the opposite of the true?" Yes. Then the like (*eoikos*) "really is not" (*ouk ontôs on*)? Theaetetus protests that it somehow is. The stranger answers "but not truly" (*oukous alêthôs*). The boy admits that but still wants to say that it really is an icon (*eikon*). The stranger accepts both the admission and the caveat: "Then what we call a likeness genuinely is in not *genuinely* being" (*ouk on ara ontôs estin ontôs ên legomen eikona*). We must conclude that "nonbeing somehow is" (*to mê on . . . einai pôs*, Eva Brann translations). Theaetetus agrees. He definitely has been led into a confusion of "not being that" with "not being." Meanwhile, if the stranger is serious about his

7   Rosen, *Plato's "Sophist,"* 192.

terminology, it seems that *eikastikên* and *phantastikên* have both been classified as arts of falsehood. If philosophy corresponds to the former and sophistry to the latter, philosophy's truth must be somehow untruthful.

Attention now is switched back to the phantasm (*to phantasma*). If, the stranger inquires, we say that the sophist practices an art of deception, shall we say that our soul is induced to opine falsely? Yes. Does false opinion think the things that are not (*ta mê onta*)? Yes. Does it think that things that are in no way whatsoever somehow are (*pôs einai ta mêdamos onta*) and also that things that are entirely are in no way whatsoever (*mêdamôs einai ta pantôs onta*)? Yes. Thus, for the moment at least, it seems clear that the stranger induces Theaetetus to believe that falsehood does involve the *nihil absolutum*. Declaring statements untrue goes beyond invoking negations of the type "not this being but that being," which merely point from one being to another.

Theaetetus now is in a quandary. He understands that the sophist has entangled him and the stranger in a contradiction, for they have said that being cannot be attributed to nonbeing and that being must be attributed to nonbeing in the cases of phantasms and falsehoods. The stranger says that something must be done about the sophist, who has backed us into this corner because we have classified him among the falsehood-workers and wizards who howl enchantments (*tôn pseudourgôn kai goêtôn*). He asks if Theaetetus will pardon him if he withdraws a bit from the sophist's strong argument. He further requests Theaetetus not to regard him as a parricide, for he will have to put the *logos* of his father Parmenides to the test (or the torture) and argue forcibly that nonbeing (*to mê on*) in some way is and that being (*to on*) in some way is not. Theaetetus thinks it clear that some such venture is necessary. The stranger responds that this must be plain even to the blind. He might mean that he has made his point obvious to his self-blinded person. He adds that because he cares for Theaetetus, he will undertake the refutation of Parmenides for the boy's sake, thus risking the judgment that he is mad because he is about to reverse himself.

The stranger proposes to begin by examining what now seems evident. This will not be a review of material already covered. Rather, it will be a study of Parmenides and all others who ever marked off "the how many and what sort of beings" (Eva Brann translation). It will also be a discussion of "being" (*to on*). This combination of subjects will produce enormous confusion because it will treat two questions as if they were one: (1) Which entities count as eminently real, either because (a) they are the first things, (b) they outrank lesser things on a scale of fullness of being, or (c) they are the only things that are? (2) What is being? What is its nature or essence? When the stranger considers Parmenides and the others who have marked off "the how many and what sort of beings," he alludes to thinkers who wrote about the number of fundamental realities and how they formed the being that we know. Then he conflates their musings with definitions of being qua being that can be subjected to criticism.

Before delving into the stranger's substantive analyses, I need to raise a methodological issue. When the stranger first mentions the people who marked off "the how many and what sort of beings," he charges that they were careless. All of them told us myths as if we were children. Now, at Phaedrus 229b, Phaedrus asks Socrates whether he believes the tale about Boreas having kidnaped Oreithyia. Socrates replies that if he disbelieved, as the *sophoi* (wise men or sophists) do, he could *sophizomenos* (play the wise man or the sophist) by explaining that the north wind blew the girl off rocks flanking the river Ilissus. However, he regards such efforts as inventions of a clever but unenviable man. He has no leisure for this sort of rationalizing when he has not yet managed to know himself [in keeping with the oracle's commandment]. One conclusion that can be drawn from this passage is that Socrates thinks it inappropriate to read myths, with their analogical symbolizations of insights into divine reality, as if they were prettified poetic accounts of physical facts that can be restated in prose. The stranger might be preparing to do that to the works of Parmenides and the others, treating them as if they were meant literally as propositional metaphysics.[8] (Lesley Brown, for one, suspects that "it is highly likely that most of the theorists whom Plato takes to task did not in fact conceive of themselves as giving any sort of account of being."[9]) Without access to all the texts, we cannot certainly decide whether the stranger will be interpreting his predecessors as they wanted to be

---

8 For example, compare the stranger's analysis of Parmenides at 244b–45e with that of Eric Voegelin in *Order and History*, vol. 2, *The World of the Polis*, chap. 8. For one treatment by Voegelin of the reification of symbols into doctrine, see "Immortality: Experience and Symbol," in *The Collected Works of Eric Voegelin*, vol. 12, *Published Essays 1966–1985*, 52–54.

9 Lesley Brown, "Innovation and Continuity: The Battle of Gods and Giants, *Sophist* 245–49," in Jyl Gentzler (ed.), *Method in Ancient Philosophy*, 204.

understood or missing their meanings. All we can say is that his procedure might be un-Socratic. Having mentioned that, we must follow him into the field of ontology as he conceives it, or even as he invents it.

Substantively, the stranger complains that one of his predecessors tells us that the beings (*ta onta*) are three, that they went to war, and that they then became friends and married and had children. Another states that the beings are two, wet and dry or hot and cold, and were married. The Eleatics insist that all things are one. The Ionians and Sicilians thought that being (*to on*) is many and one, held together by enmity and friendship, now at war with itself and then residing in peace. Notice that the reporting has moved unobtrusively from *ta onta* to *on*. Notice too what Lesley Brown observes, I think rightly: "It is clear that the arguments do not represent a serious attempt to understand what the theories in question were driving at."[10] The stranger says he will not presume to decide whether these famous men of old spoke truly or falsely. However, he will go so far as to say that their utterances are impossible to understand. He used to suppose that he knew what was meant by "nonbeing" (*to mê on*) but now he is in perplexity about it. Perhaps our minds are in the same condition with regard to being (*to on*). The movement from the *ta onta* of the ancestors to *to on* is already complete. The stranger asserts that we need to investigate being (*to on*), to which he refers without supporting argument as *tou megistou te kai archêgou prôtou* (243d1–2).

Received translations of the Greek phrase are disparate. Eva Brann gives us "greatest and first originator." Fowler (Loeb edition) has "the greatest and foremost chief." Catherine Zuckert offers "the greatest and first principle." Cornford has "chief and most important [thing]." Jowett contributes "the chief captain and leader." White (Cooper edition) opts for "the most important and most fundamental expression." A teacher of ancient Greek whom I consulted privately likes "the greatest and originating first thing" because this best renders *megistou archêgou prôtou*. I shall choose the translation of my Greek professor, which closely resembles that of Eva Brann. However, in light of the issue to which I proceed next, it might not matter much which version is selected. At Republic 504d2–3, Socrates declares that a guardian must arrive at "the greatest and most fitting study" (*tou megistou te kai malista prosêkontos mathêmatos*). He is asked

10 Brown, "Innovation and Continuity," 185.

what that is. He replies that it is "the idea of the Good" (*tou agathou idea*, 505a2). He argues that the idea of the Good is the cause of the knowability and truth of things. In a famously mystical passage, he adds:

> Therefore, say that not only being known is present in the things known as a consequence of the good, but also existence (*to einai*) and being (*tên ousian*) are in them besides as a result of it, although the good isn't being but is still beyond being, exceeding it in dignity and power (*kai tois gignômenois toinun monon to gignôskesthai phanai hupo tou agathou pareinai, all' kai to einai te kai tên ousian hup' eikeinou autois proseinai, ouk ousias ontos tou agathou, all' eti epekeina tês ousias presbeia kai dynamei huperechontos* (509b6–10, Bloom translations).

Now, whichever translations of the terms are most suitable, it cannot be simultaneously correct that being is *archêgou prôtou* and the idea of the Good is *epekeina tês ousias presbeia kai dynamei huperechontos*. Neither can it be that being is *archêgou prôtou* when we are told of the idea of the Good *kai tois gignômenois toinun monon to gignôskesthai phanai hupo tou agathou pareinai, all' kai to einai te kai tên ousian hup' eikeinou autois proseinai*. Looking to the English equivalents upon which I have settled, it cannot be simultaneously true that being is "the greatest and originating first thing" and that the idea of the Good is responsible for the truth, knowability, being and existence of things and "beyond *ousias* (being or existence), exceeding it in dignity and power." It is clear that the Eleatic stranger is proposing a metaphysics that contradicts Socrates' teaching in Republic. He attributes to being the place and function that Socrates reserves for the idea of the Good. In fact, he silently drops the idea of the Good out of account. The phrase "idea of the Good" appears nowhere in Sophist. As far as I can ascertain, the adjective "good" occurs only three times in the dialogue, in 251b–c, in the context of references to how people speak. In the stranger's own thought, the very word "good" is suppressed, at least in this play. His account of being as *tou megistou te kai archêgou prôtou* is the decisive indicator that he presents an un-Socratic doctrine here.

Getting down to cases, the stranger interrogates his perceived predecessors as if they were present, with Theaetetus replying for them. He inquires what some of them mean by maintaining that all things are two, such as hot and cold. What are they saying of the two when they declare them to be? Are they pointing to being as a third, making "the all" three ? If they try to escape their dilemma by saying that the two together are "being," they have the same problem in reverse: now "being" is one. The stranger asks whether Theaetetus thinks these questions improper. He does not. However, Theaetetus should object that the stranger has turned an account of primary beings into a definition of being qua being that can be dismissed as untenable.

The Eleatics, particularly Parmenides, now come up for criticism. They say that "the all" is one but they also speak of "being" (*to on*). What do they intend? Are they giving "the all" two [additional] names ("one" and "being")? If so, it is ridiculous to hold that two names exist when they insist that nothing is but "the one." In fact, it makes no sense to accept the statement that a name has any existence whatsoever. Even one name would be one too many, for it would be an existing thing in addition to "the one." Clearly, these thinkers contradict themselves by making being qua "one" plural. The same objection can be brought against their practice of calling "the whole" the "one." That adds up to two [or three counting "being"]. As for Parmenides himself, we know that he describes his whole as "Like to the mass of a sphere nicely rounded from every direction, Out from the center well-matched in all ways. For no greater Nor any smaller it needs must turn out, both on this and on that side" (Eva Brann translation). This saying attributes parts to being. The truly one could not have parts. Further, if a being of parts is one by virtue of being unified by the one, it will differ from the one. If it is a whole without having been unified by the one, being lacks itself. Again, if the whole is not, being could not come to be, for what becomes must do so as a whole. Parmenides' thought is riddled with absurdities.

On the assumption that the stranger has understood these ancestors aright, his criticisms could be considered cogent. They are legitimate deductions from the normal meanings of words as they appear in Athenian common parlance. However, the authors probably intended the terms analogically or symbolically and Parmenides and the other ancestors have been treated as if they were theorizing literally.[11]

---

11 Among other things, the stranger misses what Aristotle sees. Parmenides distinguishes between a being that is ungenerated, imperishable, whole, unique,

This much suffices, the stranger says, for those who have "spoken precisely" about being and nonbeing (*to on tou mê ontos*). He means that those people spoke precisely insofar as they counted the components of being. Now he turns to ancestors "speaking otherwise," who do not count. They are locked in a conflict that resembles the battle of the giants and gods (*Iliad* 5.385– 90; *Odyssey* 11.305–20), some playing the role of the giants who assaulted Olympus and others playing the part of those who defended the heavens. They disagree with each other about *ousias* (existence?).[12] While considering the stranger's analysis of the embattled parties, we need to be on the lookout for something observed by Kenneth Sayre. He remarks that whereas the precise predecessors "had attempted (fruitlessly) to provide an exact *logos*, or definition, of the Real by attributing to it properties (unity, plurality) . . . the Gods and the Giants attempt to explicate (but not to define) the Real with single terms whose referents are claimed to be coextensive with it."[13]

The giants drag down to earth everything from heaven and the invisible. That is, they say that only that exists which is tangible. They are what we call materialists. According to Sayre, it is not that they define being as matter. Rather, they contend that "the Real is the *same thing* as body, or what can be touched. Body, or tangibility, is the property which all real things possess, and which moreover is not possessed by anything

unmoved, and perfect and the phenomenal objects that are subject to genesis and perishing. This distinction moves Aristotle to all Parmenides' being an *archê* (principle) and to surmise that this *archê* is "one in *logos* but many in sensation" (*Physics* 1.3, *Metaphysics* 986b30–35), evidently meaning that "being" qua "the one" is the essence of all existing things and that the existing things are all manifestations of that "one." The stranger's critique glosses over and distorts this. I do not believe that any of our modern scholars would let me get away with such an indiscriminate review of the great poet. See also *Metaphysics* 1089a1–30 and note 8 on Voegelin above. Further, see Brown, "Innovation and Continuity," 185.

12 It is unclear why the stranger switches here from *to on* to *ousia*. One is uncertain as to how to translate *ousia* in light of the change. Eva Brann resorts to "beinghood." Rosen argues that the stranger's *ousia* denotes the divine whole, while his *to on* denotes the formal principle being, *Plato's "Sophist,"* 212, 266. That is debatable. I shall treat *to on* and *ousia* as synonyms for being, without being confident that this is the right way to go.
13 Sayre, *Plato's Analytic Method*, 162.

unreal."[14] (Calling the Real the *same thing* as body looks like a definition of being to me but Sayre envisages a property, not a nature.) The boy denounces these giants as "terrible men," many of whom he has met during his [short] life. One wonders where he met them. Is Athens overrun by them? Has Theodorus been inviting them to his school? One also wonders why the mention of the materialistic giants triggers Theaetetus's emotional outburst. Is he offended as a geometer on behalf of the "real" plane and solid figures that are intangible and invisible? Is he outraged as a religious believer on behalf of the invisible gods whom the materialists blaspheme? Is he concerned about justice and natural right?

The opponents of the "giants" appeal to the invisible, forcing "true *ousia*" to be "certain thought-things and disembodied forms" (*noêta atta kai asômata eidê*, Eva Brann translation). In their speech, they break into small bits the bodies discussed by their enemies and also their truth, treating them as "carried-along-genesis." This might be how the stranger understands Socrates. Some modern scholars follow him in this assumption.

The stranger suggests that we now should obtain a fuller account from each party of what hey posit (*tithentai*) of *ousias*. It will be easy to get a statement from those who posit the ideas, for they are *hêmerôteroi* (gentler, tamer). However, it will be next to impossible to converse with those who violently drag everything down to body. We must try to make them better or, if that is impossible, improve them in our own speech (by which the stranger means that we ought to say better things than they would say, substituting our arguments for theirs). "For what is agreed to by better men has more authority than what is agreed to by worse men." The stranger, Socrates, Plato, and Aristotle all maintain that superior virtue guarantees superior insight. I am persuaded. However, Thrasymachus, Protagoras, Gorgias, Pericles, Alcibiades, and the great kings of Persia all might have subscribed to the same principle, touting themselves as the virtuous. We cannot know who the better men are or which judgments are superior until we know what genuine virtue is. The stranger has simply presumed that he and Theaetetus are the better men.

The stranger orders Theaetetus to assume that the materialists have improved, command them to answer, and interpret their replies. He wants to hear what Theaetetus supposes a better man would say. This will render

---

14 Sayre, *Plato's Analytic Method*, 164.

the materialists pliable, letting the stranger subdue them. The boy agrees
to play the assigned role.

The stranger asks the now agreeable materialists whether there is such
a thing as a mortal animal. Yes. The stranger inquires whether this animal
is a body with a soul. Again, yes. The improved materialists already have
made an admission that looks harmful to their cause. Modern materialists
would say no. However, the ancient materialists envisaged a soul that was
material and mortal: Theaetetus's answer would not infuriate them. Next
the stranger asks whether souls are just, unjust, wise and foolish because of
the presence of [an incorporeal] justice, etc. in them. The Greek materialists
could not stomach this. They would reject the proposition but Theaetetus
answers that they would be ashamed to deny the existence of the virtues
and vices or to call them bodies. It is Theaetetus who would be ashamed,
for reasons that he does not explain. We recall that in Theaetetus (185d–
86a), he said that the soul grasps being, likeness, beauty, goodness, and their
opposites directly, indicating a prior belief in immaterial realities and probably a wish to be good. Whatever his reasons, he hands the stranger an un-
earned victory over the materialists by imputing a fatal concession to them.
The stranger acknowledges this, saying that the materialists really are better, for those autochthonous men would have held fast to the doctrine that
bodies are the only realities. Now that Theaetetus has made the materialists
amiable, the stranger believes that they will have to recognize at least a tiny
particle of bodiless being. When this happens, the materialists will have
admitted that being is common to both the material and immaterial things
and identical with neither alone. Accordingly, they will have to tell us about
the "inborn nature" (*xumphues gegonos*, Eva Brann translation) common to
both. If they are stumped, perhaps they would agree that "being is" (*einai
to on*) the sort of thing that the stranger will now propose.

I shall offer two highly professional translations of the stranger's suggestion to the now bewildered materialists. The readings vary in subtle
ways but each can support the same pair of interpretations of the stranger's
intention, as discussed below:

> Whatever possesses any sort of power (*dynamis*) to alter any
> nature whatsoever, or to be affected in the smallest degree from
> the most trifling thing, and even if only once, all this is genuine

being (*pan toutos ontos einai*). For I fix as the boundary of the
beings (*horizein ta onta*) that it is nothing other than power (*hos
estin allo ti plên dynamis*)" (247d8–e4). (Rosen translation.)[15]

What possesses any sort of power (*dynamis*)—whether for
making anything at all, whatever its nature, other than it is or
for being affected even in the least bit by the meagerest thing,
even if only once—I say that all this *is* in its very being (*pan
toutos ontos einai*). For I set down as a boundary marking off the
things that *are* (*horizein ta onta*), that their being is nothing else
but *power* (*hos estin allo ti plên dynamis*). (Eva Brann translation.)

I offer the two translations because it is time to reconsider what the
stranger has done in his review of his predecessors and to think about what
he does now with his suggestion. Has he been looking for definitions of
being, expecting his forerunners to describe its nature precisely, saying what
it *is*, and is he now attempting the same feat himself? One could get this
impression from his uses of *tithentai tês ousias, xumphues gegonos, einai to on,
pan toutos ontos einai,* and *hos estin allo ti plên dynamis.* Or has he only been
seeking the property by which being can be recognized, as Sayre would
have it? Is that the force of his many uses of *einai*? Sayre relies on the
stranger's *horizein ta onta* (mark off, set a boundary of the beings) for his
interpretation. He has a point, but I fear that the matter is not quite as
clear as he supposes. *Horizein* might just be a synonym for "define." On the
other hand, the stranger's other phrases might be his synonyms for *horizein,*
to mark off or set a boundary.[16] Philology cannot settle the issue, so let us
explore each possible interpretation of the stranger's aim.

If we assume for the sake of argument that the stranger has been demanding and now is offering a definition of being, hoping to establish what
being *is*, I would say that his enterprise is invalid. Let us assume that being
has an essence, "X." If that is permissible, we also are entitled to suppose
that "X" has an essence "Y" and to inquire what it is. We can do this indefi-
nitely. (If the stranger says that "being *is* power," we are entitled to inquire

15 Rosen's translation, *Plato's "Sophist,"* p. 217.
16 Cf. Brown, "Innovation and Continuity," 192–93.

what *dynamis* and "a capacity for affecting or being affected" are, and so on endlessly.) An infinite regress seems unavoidable. This suggests that being is fundamental. It can be experienced but it cannot be defined. We only can give it synonyms, such as "existence" or "thereness" or "what is possessed by all things that are in any mode or respect." I realize that Aristotle held that it is the task of first philosophy to study being qua being, "what it is, and what the attributes are which belong to it qua being" (*kai ti esti kai ta huparchonta ê on*, *Metaphysics* 1026a). However, I cannot find a passage in which he clearly says what being qua being is. He talks instead about modes of being and what realities preeminently have being, apparently under the rubric of what "belongs" to being qua being. It is pertinent to add that Aquinas, Aristotle's commentator, concluded that being has no essence.

If we assume for the sake of argument that Sayre is right and that the stranger intends to identify a property most worthy of being classified as coextensive with being, that does not seem to be quite as hopeless a task as defining being's essence. The stranger's argument would be that his predecessors claimed that duality, unity, and materiality were the attributes most indicative of being, that their reasoning failed either because it was absurd or because there are beings that do not exhibit materiality, and that *dynamis* as he explains it fills the bill. Fair enough. Let us give the stranger the benefit of the doubt and infer that this is his intention. However, we have to be clear about what this implies. If we take Sayre at his word and agree that the stranger is trying to explain being but not define it, we cannot assert that *to on* is the *same thing* as anything. Rather than maintaining that being is the same thing as *dynamis*, we must say that being has power as a ubiquitous trait. (Similarly, we cannot claim that human nature is the same thing as rationality; we must argue that human nature possesses rationality as a ubiquitous trait.) In this view, being is more fundamental than power. Being is the source of *dynamis*, always somehow giving rise to it. All that might be so. However, I see a difficulty. If I advert to Aristotle's doctrine of potency and act, I can imagine a being that is pure act, that alters nothing, and that is affected by nothing. That would be a being not characterized by power if it existed. Power would be a property not of being but rather of most beings. Thus, *dynamis* might not be completely coextensive with being. If we put the idea of the Good aside, being might be the only reality that is perfectly coextensive with itself. Perhaps this is why Aristotle does not pick up on the stranger's *dynamis* doctrine in *Metaphysics*. He mentions Sophist four times in that treatise, saying that Plato was not wrong to declare that non-being exists in a sense (specifically, the sense that something is not a particular "this," 1089a15–30), but he either ignores the *dynamis* argument or radically transforms it.

On behalf of the improved materialists, Theaetetus accepts the stranger's marking off of the boundary of being as *dynamis*. That is fine with the stranger. However, he suggests that later some other explanation might occur to him, Theaetetus, and the materialists. He never disproves his *dynamis* argument explicitly so some contemporary scholars (such as Sayre) believe that it is settled Platonic doctrine. Given that additional proposals about being will follow, others think that the *dynamis* analysis is superseded or they concur in Heidegger's opinion that Plato averages his concepts of being. Paying attention to Plato's warning that he writes nothing concerning that about which he is serious, I do not choose sides in that debate.

The stranger now turns to "the friends of the *eidê*" for their statement that explains being. (*Idea* and *eidos* seem to be synonyms for him.) He appoints Theaetetus as their spokesman even though the boy is unfamiliar with them. The two agree that the thinkers whom we call idealists distinguish being (*ousia*) from generation, maintaining that we share (*koinônein*) in generation, which differs from moment to moment, by means of *aisthêsis* (perception, sensation) and in real being (*ontôs ousian*) [presumably any given *eidos*], which is always unchanged and the same, by means of the soul's calculation (or reasoning, *logismou*). It seems to the stranger that the sharing in both generation and "real being" (*eidê*) that the idealists perceive is either a passive affection or a positive act driven by some *dynamis* of which he just spoke, which has its origin in a coming together of things. This appears to contend that genuine being consists in the coming together of unidentified things, thus giving rise to power, which indifferently propels us toward participation in both generation and forms. It is hard to know precisely what to make of this but the stranger seems to want to insist that real being is not any of the idealists' changeless forms but a dynamic motion of generated bodies and forms that perhaps change at least insofar as they come together, empowering us to share in them. Hence, the coming together of things, both bodies and forms, whether the latter are unchangeable or not, and power as the stranger conceives it would be more fundamental than forms. This conception is un-Socratic. If Socrates replied to the stranger, he probably would posit a Form of power in which all instances of *dynamis* operating in the realm of generation (or becoming) participated.

The stranger reports that the friends of the *eidê* do say something close to that: generation partakes of *dynamis* but being does not. The stranger then inquires whether the idealists confess that the soul knows and that being is known. This seems correct insofar as we all are cognizant of being. Theaetetus says that the idealists do agree that the soul knows and that being is known but they deny that knowing and being known are either active or passive. The stranger strongly affirms the opposite position. He maintains that knowing is acting and that being known is to be "affected." Being is "affected" and "moved" (*kineisthai*) by being known, which could not occur if being were always at rest (or unchangeable, like the idealists' forms). The stranger's claim is dubious. Lesley Brown writes that G. E. L. Owen rightly acknowledged "the sheer prima facie absurdity of saying that coming to know anything changes it" and she argues that the truth is the other way around, that coming to know is to be changed, so that being affects and moves the soul when it comes to be known. Brown goes so far as to speculate that Plato does not endorse what the stranger has said.[17] Her argument is persuasive. I wonder whether the stranger himself might not accept her correction. He could maintain that being is still "changing" insofar as it is "doing" something by affecting the soul. That proposition is at least arguable, if not correct.

We come now to an extraordinary text. Heidegger claims that this passage "is the center and is decisive for understanding the whole ontological discussion."[18] It is important to get this impressively judged element right so I shall dwell on it at some length.

The stranger evidently is agitated by the idealists' contention that knowing is not active and that being known is not passive. This would imply what I believe is the case, that someone knowing being does not act on it and that being certainly is not moved by being known. In turn, this might imply that being is unchangeable, or that immutability is the one property coextensive with being. Thus, the stranger swears by Zeus, saying *"hôs alêthôs kinêsin kai zôên kai psychên kai phronêsin ê hradiôs peisêsometha to pantêlos*

17 Brown, "Innovation and Continuity," 199.
18 Martin Heidegger, *Plato's "Sophist,"* 333.

onti mê pareinai, mêde zên auto mêde phronein, alla semnon kai agion, noun ouk echon, akinêton estos einai." As with *archêgou prôtou*, English translations of this passage vary significantly. I shall offer the reader a representative sampling of professional efforts:

(1) Shall we be that easily persuaded that motion and life and soul and thought are truly not present in utterly complete being? That it neither lives nor thinks; but awful and holy, not possessed of mind, it stands there, not to be moved? (Eva Brann)

(2) Shall we let ourselves easily be persuaded that motion and life and soul and mind are really not present to absolute being, that it neither lives nor thinks, but awful and holy, devoid of mind, is fixed and immovable? (Fowler, in Loeb)

(3) Are we going to be convinced that it's true that change, life, soul, and intelligence are not present in *that which wholly is*, and that it neither lives nor thinks, but stays changeless, solemn, and holy, without any understanding? (White, in Cooper)

(4) Shall we be easily persuaded that change, life, soul, and intelligence are truly not present to what altogether is, that it neither lives nor thinks but, awesome and holy, lacking intellect, is unchanging and fixed? (Rosen)[19]

(5) Can we ever be made to believe that motion and life and soul and mind are not present with perfect being? Can we imagine that being is devoid of life and mind, and exists in awful unmeaningness an everlasting fixture? (Jowett)

(6) Are we really to be so easily convinced that change, life, soul, understanding have no place in that which is perfectly real—that it has neither life nor thought, but stands immutable in solemn aloofness, devoid of intelligence? (Cornford)

(7) We can scarcely believe that in what is *pantelôs*, in what completely, genuinely is, in beings in the most proper sense, there would not also be present movement, life, soul, knowledge. (Heidegger's first of two paraphrases.)[20]

---

19   Rosen, *Plato's "Sophist,"* 222.
20   Heidegger, *Plato's "Sophist,"* 333. Heidegger adds "solemn and sacred" later, 334.

Note that unlike translations one through four, five through seven do not render *semnon kai agion* as "awful and holy," an omission that is surprising because *semnon* also has a sense of holiness about it. Radically disparate inferences are drawn from these differing translations. The opposed parties agree that the stranger now has forced the idealists to accept his claim that being has life and, thus, moving power. However, they are at loggerheads about the means by which he has triumphed. Stanley Rosen remarks: "[T]he passage confirms . . . that the shift from precise to imprecise myth culminates in a theological ontology, or in what Heidegger and his followers call an 'ontotheology.'" Rosen maintains that the stranger has made *ousia* a changeable divine whole, almost like a deity of process theology.[21] His remark about Heidegger is somewhat premature. The term "ontotheology" is not included in Heidegger's lecture on the disputed passage in 1924–1925, cited just above. It appeared later. Rather, the early Heidegger understands Plato to refer not to being as divine but to "beings in the most proper sense," which might be ourselves. The omission of "awful and holy" enables this understanding. Kenneth Sayre seconds Heidegger. He contends that the stranger thinks only that intelligence, soul, and life are real,[22] meaning that the highest beings have life and therefore a power that is acted and acted upon.

It seems to me that the weight of the Greek favors Rosen's construction of the text rather than that of Heidegger and Sayre. The concepts "utterly complete being," "absolute being" "that which wholly is," "what altogether is," "perfect being," "perfectly real," and "what completely, genuinely is" (all renditions of *pantêlos onti*), in conjunction with life, thought, and holiness, all appear to entail a living being that resembles a Greek god or even the God of the Hebrew Bible, New Testament, and Aquinas, and perhaps also a deity of process theology that has been striving to become absolute and has done so, like Hegel's *Weltgeist*. Human beings do not have any such fullness of being. However, I suppose that a case can be made that the stranger envisages a being that has developed to its highest attainable point in us and which, accordingly, is "awe-inspiring and holy." We have reached another impasse from which philology cannot extricate us. Thus, it will be

21   Rosen, *Plato's "Sophist,"* 223. This is insightful, possibly correct, but uncertain.
22   Sayre, *Plato's Analytic Method*, 167.

useful to leave the dispute unresolved and to consider the consequences of each position.

If we suppose for the sake of argument that the stranger has tried to establish being as a changeable *dynamis* by conceiving of it as a living, thinking, moving, divine entity, we promptly encounter a difficulty. I cannot think of any way that being could be simultaneously an abstract capacity to act and be acted upon inhering in beings and a concrete, conscious, moving divinity. It would have to be admitted that Rosen's criticism is correct: "*There are two distinct ontologies at work in the Sophist*. The Stranger not only does nothing to reconcile these two ontologies; he never refers to the fact that he has introduced two distinct conceptions of being . . . the definition of being as power [and] the statement of being as comprehensive and divine."[23] Divinity would be one of the concepts of being better than power that the stranger said might crop up.

If we assume for the sake of argument that the Heidegger-Sayre interpretation is correct, Heidegger's presentation of the issue gives the game away. He has let slip that we are talking not about being but about "beings in the most proper sense." Under this rubric, *dynamis* cannot have even the rank that we previously observed Sayre trying to give it, that of a ubiquitous property of being. Now it can only be the essential characteristic of proper beings. Slipping back and forth between being qua being and beings confuses the reasoning, undermining it.

Although the stranger believes that he has defeated both the materialists and the idealists, I must note one more difficulty with his attempt to mark off the boundary of being as *dynamis*. To me it appears undeniable that he has endeavored to establish his case without serious rational argument. He cleared away the materialists' conception of being as body by making Theaetetus substitute the better man's opinion for the view of the terrible men. This involved no philosophic proof but, rather, an implicit flattery of himself and Theaetetus as superior in virtue that we need not accept without due consideration. He removed the obstacle presented by the idealists' notion of being as an unchangeable form by sheer bluster: "By Zeus, are we easily to believe that . . . ?" To which it occurs to me to reply: "Why not?" Being qua being could lack the life, motion, etc. that beings possess. It could be that in which

23   Rosen, *Plato's "Sophist,"* 223.

living beings participate. It might be just to suspect that the stranger's moves are sophistical rather than philosophic. At least, it would be fair to say that the state of the argument is not entirely satisfactory. One could excuse this by objecting that Plato would have had to use too much space to combat his antagonists adequately. However, if Sophist is his path-breaking ontology, why would he not give the fullest consideration to defenses against the most important challenges to his central thesis? As Socrates says in Republic (504c), measure that stops short of what is measures nothing at all.

The stranger finishes his treatment of the question as to whether perfect being has motion, life, soul, and mind by remarking: "Thus the outcome is, Theaetetus, that if the things that *are* are immovable, there is mind in nothing about nothing nowhere" (Eva Brann translation). He seems to be thinking that mind moves and, therefore, if we claimed that nothing moves, there could be no mind. At the same time, he appears to be arguing that because knowing something moves it, there could be no knowing of the forms and no mind if the forms were motionless. We have the impression that he has been trying to establish that the forms are movable or changeable, which would seem to imply that all things are in motion. However, the stranger suddenly reverses his course. He says that: "If we grant that all things are borne about and moving, we shall exclude, by that very account, this same mind from the things that *are*" (Eva Brann translation). Being in the same respect in the same way with regard to the same thing could never come to be unless there were rest. Without that, mind could not exist. It might be true that nothing can be known if neither mind nor the things it knows have stable self-identity. However, I am at a loss as to what things now exist in the same respect in the same way with regard to the same thing. The things of generation and the forms, being all of the things that *are*, were just forbidden to be immovable. What things, then, have now become immovable? Numbers? Is the nature of mind motionless? Or are generated things moveable and forms immoveable? Or is everything sometimes in motion and sometimes at rest? Without clearing this ambiguity up, the stranger tells Theaetetus to pray the prayer of children, "Whatever is immovable and moved," and to declare that being and the all [are] both together (*xunamphotera legein*).

Perhaps contra Sayre, this language seems to be tending back in the direction of defining being's essence. This might be why the stranger immediately runs into trouble. He congratulates himself and Theaetetus on having pretty well encompassed being in a *logos* (which according to Sayre means definition). Then he suddenly exclaims: "Alas!" The boy asks what is wrong. The stranger answers that they are still in the fullest ignorance of being. They can be asked the very same questions that they put to those who claimed that the all is hot and cold. If being is motion and rest, *to on* becomes a third over and above the two things of which they just said it consists. Given the stranger's previous assumptions about how to treat the terms, this is an eminently fair inference. However, it makes me wonder. How much of his thinking about being up to here has the stranger just repudiated? For example, the account of being as power has not been *explicitly* rejected. Does that mean that it still holds? Or does being "in the fullest ignorance" (*ev agnoia tê pleistê*) about being imply that all that has been affirmed about its nature is now disowned: the explanations of being as power, as a capacity to affect and be affected, as either a god with life, motion, soul, and thought or as life, etc. in the things that are most properly beings, and as both motion and rest? It appears that being "in the fullest ignorance" leaves nothing of the reasoning about what being is standing. As the stranger says literally (250d–e), we are in complete *aporia* about both nonbeing and being. However, the fact that we know nothing about being's nature or its essential characteristics does not necessarily subvert the stranger's original dictum. Without knowing what being is, we might still be able to assume that it is *megista archêgou prôtou*.

Abandoning the effort to say what nonbeing and being are, the stranger suggests that they should attempt a creditable account by steering between them. Then he abruptly inquires by what habit we call one thing many names (*pollois onomasi*). He makes it clear that he is talking about how "we speak" (*legomen*). For example, we give man many designations, such as "good." This practice is ridiculed by fools who argue that nothing can be both one and many, so that we must call good only good and man only man. We need to address everybody who has ever discoursed about being (*ousias*) by interrogating these people as well as the others. In our own *logoi*, shall we attach neither being (*ousias*) to motion and rest (*kinêsei kai stasei*) nor anything to anything but posit beings (*onta*) as unmixed, incapable of participating (*metalambanein*) in each other? Or shall we gather all (*panta*) together as capable of communing (*epikoinônein*) with each other? Or are some capable and some not? Theaetetus cannot speak for the respondents. For the moment, the stranger's question inspires me to reply with two of my own. (1) What are being, motion, and rest in this new argument? (2) Will an ontology now be deduced from how we speak?

The first question is motivated by the facts that we were just declared to be in the fullest ignorance about being and that we could no longer tell which beings were in motion and at rest, or when the unidentified things were in those states, so that we do not know to what motion and rest refer either. Contravening his announcement that we know nothing about being (*ousian*), the stranger simply presumes that everyone now understands what the word means.[24] He makes the same assumption about motion and rest. Someone might suggest that we are supposed to pick up cues about the meanings of these terms from the previous discussion. Well, earlier, the stranger spoke of his predecessors' *onta* in the sense of primary realities, or first things. He referred to the being of Parmenides as a physical thing with spatial dimensions. The materialists' beings were bodies. The beings of the idealists were certain *noêta atta kai asômata eidê* (thought things and bodiless forms) that evidently hovered in some ether. His own being was *dynamis*. Are being, motion, and rest any of those things now? The idea that they could be the *onta* of the unnamed ancestors or the One of Parmenides is quashed by the stranger's ridicule of their logical absurdity and his dismissal of his own being-motion-rest complex on the same logical grounds. True, the stranger has referred to being, motion, and rest as *onta* (beings, realities) but they cannot be *onta* in the sense of the ancients' first things. We still must wonder what they are. It also is clear that they could not be the materialists' bodies or the changeless forms of the idealists, especially not if the latter are both motionless and changing. Power seemingly has been eliminated by our total ignorance of being. So, again, what are the stranger's being, motion, and rest? This is a serious question that cannot be dismissed as illegitimate.

Responding to this query, Stanley Rosen observes that: "It seems to be quite clear that the Stranger introduces forms into the discussion at this point."[25] Well and good. Let being, motion, and rest be forms. My

---

24   Cf. A. L. Peck, "Plato on the *MEGISTA GENÊ* of the Sophist: A Reinterpretation," *Classical Quarterly* 2 (1952), 44.

25   Rosen, *Plato's "Sophist,"* 229.

question remains unanswered. For the stranger, what are forms? Without tackling that issue, we cannot proceed as if we knew what we were talking about. It appears that scholars generally assume that the stranger thinks of being, motion, and rest as the same sorts of entities that Socrates envisages when he speaks of Forms. For example, without calling attention to the fact, Sayre analyzes the stranger's forms as if they were continuations of the Forms of the earlier Platonic dialogues, Plato's notion of their properties having developed.[26] Kenneth Dorter says that: "Forms are the timeless aspect of changing things, the being of becoming."[27] This is a beautiful insight but it seems to be Dorter's concept of the Socratic Forms. We have no textual evidence that the stranger would agree that this describes his own forms.

Until such time as the stranger announces what he means by being, motion, and rest—a time that might not come—we must try to deduce their meanings from the only evidence: their context. We have the most information about being. We have learned that it seems to reside on the same ontological level as existing things (240b11–12).[28] It is superior to the Good. It is an *on* that might consist in the coming together of things that give rise to *dynamis*. It is changeable but perhaps also immutable. On all these grounds, we must judge it to be wholly unlike the being of Socrates. However, we also are in *aporia*. The stranger has negated every account of it, leaving its meaning unspecified. This prompts us to draw our own common sense conclusion that being simply is that in which all the things that are participate. The stranger might expect us to do that.

There is more to consider. Inasmuch as being, motion, and rest have been brought to the fore in conjunction with the subject of names and how we speak, I begin to believe that they are composite logical terms.[29] Being would be a category that embraces everything that is. It goes without saying

26 Sayre, *Plato's Analytic Method*, 169–70.
27 Kenneth Dorter, *Form and Good in Plato's Eleatic Dialogues*, 144.
28 Kenneth Dorter argues by relying on a grammatical analysis that the stranger preserves Socrates' two-world ontology, making being unmoved and the corporeal universe moved, *Form and Good*, 148–49. The Greek grammar also can be read in the opposite way; it is too thin a reed on which to support Dorter's conclusion, which is not shared by others.
29 Cf. Peck, "Plato on the *MEGISTA GENĒ*," 43.

that motion (*kinêsei*) must refer to change of spatial location and spinning on an axis. The stranger also has applied the term to thought. Theaetetus once supposed that motion encompassed the becoming and passing of all things. These are essentially different processes. They can be united under one name only by arguing that they all have beginning and end states and by ignoring the differences in what is happening. The stranger analyzes rest (*stasei*) as the opposite of motion so it must refer to the antitheses of all the things just listed. If being, motion, and rest are composite categories, as I suspect, they could not be Socrates' Forms. They could be nothing like the Beauty of Symposium, for example, one of the characteristics of which is that it is *monoeides* (211b1), one or singular in form rather than multifaceted. If my conjecture is right, this is another clue that the stranger is proposing an ontology that contradicts Socrates' teaching.

Given the probable assumption that being, motion, and rest are forms that are collective logical categories, it becomes possible for the stranger to draw conclusions about "the Real" (the term is Sayre's) by appealing to how we speak. If his forms "commune" in speech, they can be supposed to commune in reality. If *elegchos* shows that some cannot commune in speech, their communion cannot occur in the Real. *Logos* dictates metaphysics. I know that Heidegger denies this. He writes:

> The question of the *koinônia* of beings is clearly formulated at 251d: *pôs ta onta en tois par' hêmin logois tithômen* . . . "how should we posit the Being of beings in our *logoi*?" This way of questioning is clearly governed by the fact that *on* is interrogated thematically here as *legomenon*, as encountered in *logos*. But we must be careful not to say, on the basis of this connection, that the Greek theory of Being takes its orientation from logic. *Logos* in the sense mentioned is still very far removed from what was later called logic. The Greeks asked how *on* is present in *logos*, or, more precisely, how there can be a *koinônia* in *onta*.[30]

To me, it seems that Heidegger has offered us a distinction without a difference. His argument relies on his assumption that what is

---

30   Heidegger, *Plato's "Sophist,"* 354.

encountered in *logos* is *on* rather than conventional names with which we try to illuminate being, probably only with varying degrees of success. From this it follows inexorably that speech dictates ontology, whether or not it follows modern logic. I do not believe that Heidegger's argument is saved by Rosen's undoubtedly valid comments that the stranger purports to enjoy a direct intellectual grasp of forms, such that his "linguistic analysis is everywhere subordinate to the apprehension of the forms that makes discourse possible."[31] The linguistic analysis dominates to the extent that it is hard to avoid the impression that the stranger is drawing conclusions from definitions of words. So, to reiterate, I suspect that the stranger lets *logos* dictate ontology. If he does, this would explain why Plato or his later editor gave Sophist the subtitle *Ê Peri Tou Ontos: Logikos*. I think that the stranger's further reasoning will support my supposition.

Because Theaetetus cannot see his way through the problem that the stranger has raised, with its three proposed solutions, the stranger suggests dealing with the suggestions *seriatim*. As he does so, we finally will reach the crux of his argument.

Taking the proposals *seriatim*, the stranger suggests first that his respondents will declare that nothing has power to combine with anything. Then it is true that motion and rest will have no communion with being, is it not? Therefore, neither will exist, right? Theaetetus agrees. We can see that this has been a brief exercise in *elegchos*. The implicit reasoning is as follows: "Let motion and rest have no communion with being, which in our speech means that they cannot be. But we perceive that motion and rest exist. This is a contradiction. The assumption that motion and rest have no communion with being is false." Clearly, an ontological fact has been deduced from an "apprehension of forms" that is indistinguishable from a knowledge of the definitions of words.

Next up is the suggestion that everything can combine with everything. Theaetetus feels competent to reject this option. He says that, if it held, motion would be entirely at rest and rest would be in motion. The stranger replies that this would be impossible by the greatest

31 Rosen, *Plato's "Sophist,"* 247.

necessity. Again, there has been a direct apprehension of a verity about forms that is indistinguishable from a knowledge of the definitions of words. In this regard, I should point out that it would not have required an Athenian Einstein to observe that a person sitting on a moving cart is simultaneously in motion with respect to the ground and at rest with respect to the cart. Motion and rest combine in reality. True, I have just admitted that I am not referring to motion and rest with respect to the same things at the same times but this only highlights the facts that the stranger is arguing on the basis of the ordinary meanings of words. An object can be simultaneously in motion and at rest in reality. It is the definitions of motion and rest that do not admit of combination.

The third option is that some things commune and some do not. Given that it must be the case either that all things mix or none do or some do and that the first two alternatives have been found impossible, the third is proclaimed right by process of elimination. The stranger does not dwell on this result. He forges ahead, observing that his forms resemble letters of the alphabet, some of which fit together and some of which do not. He means that just as some forms mingle and some do not, vowels can be sounded with consonants while consonants (generally) cannot be sounded together. The vowels run through the consonants as a bond. Not everybody knows this. One needs the *technê* of grammar to discern which letters (sounds) mix with which. Similarly, some of the high and low sounds in music mingle and some do not. This means that some notes sounded together are harmonious while others are dissonant. One needs the *technê* of music to understand which notes can be combined. The stranger's analogies differ. The possibilities and impossibilities of pronouncing sounds together are universal across languages, depending on the permanent structure of the human palate, while the possibilities and impossibilities of combining notes shift from scale to scale, depending on thirds and other intervals, a fact known to Socrates (cf. Philebus 17d–e). Melody lacks vowels. The dissimilarity of the analogies is philosophically unimportant. Although the reasons why the stranger's forms, spoken sounds, and musical notes can and cannot mingle differ, thus weakening his analogies, I accept the alphabet and melody as illustrations of the fact that some things can combine and others cannot.[32] What is crucial is that the stranger has introduced his analogies as a transition to a point that he wants to make about his method.

The stranger maintains that, inasmuch as the kinds (*ta genê*), like letters, notes, and things in all other arts admit of combination in some cases but not in others, it is necessary for the man who intends to show which kinds harmonize and which kinds do not to have some knowledge of science (*epistêmê*). This is especially true if he wants to show that some of the kinds act in ways resembling vowels. Theaetetus affirms that such a person needs *epistêmê*, perhaps the greatest. The stranger asks what they should call this *epistêmê*. Giving Theaetetus no chance to reply, he then swears by Zeus and inquires whether they have not stumbled upon the *epistêmê* that belongs to free men without noticing it. Have they found the philosopher first while seeking the sophist? Theaetetus asks the stranger what he means. The stranger answers with a question of his own: Will we not maintain that it belongs to dialectical knowledge (*tês dialektikês epistêmê*) to divide according to kinds (*kata genê*) and not to take the same form as other nor the other as the same? Because this query has followed hard upon the previous ones, I infer that the stranger has defined the science of free men as philosophy, philosophy as dialectical *epistêmê*, and dialectical *epistêmê* as correct division according to kinds which does not mistake forms for each other.

A few lines later, the stranger adds that we will not attribute dialectical power to anyone who does not philosophize justly and purely. We will locate the philosopher in some such place if we eventually search for him. He is hard to see clearly but the difficulty of finding him differs from that of descrying the sophist. The sophist runs away into the darkness of non-being and he is hard to discern because of the darkness. The philosopher, in contrast, is always devoted through *logismôn* (account giving) to the look or idea of being (*tê tou ontos idea*) and he is difficult to see because of the brilliant light and divinity of the place.

Throughout this chapter and the previous one, I have been suggesting that the stranger's reasoning is certainly not Socratic and probably not Platonic. It is at this point that the strongest objections to my argument might be brought. It will be urged that the stranger associates being with light

32 For a thorough examination of the philosophic implications of the stranger's analogies, see Rosen, *Plato's "Sophist,"* 245–68.

and divinity, thus aligning himself with Socrates, and that the wish for philosophizing that is pure and just is completely identical with Socratic aspirations. It will be observed further that, in the Seventh Letter, Plato himself both associates philosophy with illumination and insists that a person who philosophizes must have a fine nature, with an affinity for justice and all that is fair (343e–44b). Surely, it will be claimed, this renders the stranger's arguments Platonic too. If other elements of the stranger's doctrine do not match Plato's earlier reasoning, this only goes to show that Plato could change his mind, which every philosopher has a right to do. Such is the position of those who maintain that Plato's thought "developed."

I offer these replies to my potential critics. First, it is true that Socrates associates being with light and divinity. However, he does so while treating education as the turning of the soul from becoming toward being, which permits it to look "at that which *is* and the brightest part of that which *is* (*eis to on kai tou ontos to phanotaton*). And we affirm that this is the good, don't we?" (Bloom translation, Republic 518c–d). This suggests that the light of being emanates from the Form of the Good, just as the light of the moon emanates from the sun. It also transpires that gazing at the Good *is* divine contemplation (517d). The stranger ignores the Form of the Good in his argument, letting being generate its own light. His position is not Socratic. Second, it also is true that the stranger and Socrates agree in demanding pure and just philosophizing. However, I have noted more than once that the same word often means different things to different speakers. For Socrates, knowledge of justice depends on the vision of the Good which the stranger slights. The stranger also has been at pains to convict Socrates of the injustice of sophistry. Plato called his friend Socrates the "most just" person of his time (Seventh Letter 324e). It appears evident that the stranger's concept of justice differs from those of Socrates and Plato. When we carefully avoid being charmed by words, his position looks neither Socratic nor Platonic. Third, Socrates never defined philosophy formally as anything, let alone as *epistêmê* that has divided according to kinds without mistaking one form for another. We also must remember that Plato decries the weakness of *logôn* in the Seventh Letter (342e–43a), a failing that prevents *logoi* from attaining to essence. It is very doubtful that Plato would have endorsed a word definition of philosophy. Fourth, Plato's Seventh Letter is approximately as late as his Sophist.

I would never deny that a philosopher has a right to change his mind. However, the chronological proximity of the Seventh Letter and Sophist does not seem to support the contention that Plato changed his thinking about the ultimate inadequacy of *logoi* in philosophy. It appears much more likely that Plato allows the stranger to set forth his own position, one that is neither Socratic nor Platonic. I believe that my potential critics have no case.

As an aside, I am curious as to why the stranger defines a dialectical *epistêmê* consisting in correct divisions according to kinds as "the science of free men." I understand that it would be slavish to be benighted enough to think that the definitions of motion and rest or of fish and fowl are the same rather than different. However, I doubt that many people are that stupid. It seems to be within the reach of every child who has learned a language to distinguish motion from rest. Yet, Socrates would not agree that everyone who can do this is free. For him, freedom consists in rational control of the appetites that dictates choices in light of the Good. Slavish individuals who cannot discern the Good are fully capable of distinguishing motion from rest and the same from the different. If I were to speculate, I would guess that the stranger thinks that his science is liberating because it involves a dialectical mastery of concepts that is intrinsically satisfying and that also furnishes means of control of one's environment.

In a passage that I skipped above, the stranger goes on to declare that whoever is able to divide *kata genê* and avoid taking one kind for another perceives adequately one *idea* extending through many each of which lies apart; many differing from one another embraced by one; one joined together by the union of many wholes, and many entirely separate. This, he maintains, is how to know (*epistasthai*) and distinguish which forms can and cannot share in another. I have not read a commentator who thinks that this statement is easily intelligible. Stanley Rosen states that: "It can be hardly an accident that Plato, who writes with such lucidity and in such detail on lesser issues, expresses himself as obscurely as possible" on the natures of ideas and dialectic in the paragraph just cited.[33] So, is the text esoteric? Kenneth Dorter offers a reasonable, plausible interpretation, warning that it has insufficient supporting evidence.[34] I commend his analysis

33   Rosen, *Plato's "Sophist,"* 259, 261.
34   Dorter, *Form and Good*, 154.

to the reader. Doubting that any interpretation of the passage could serve as a basis for confident conclusions or alter our understanding of what follows, I pass to the next topic.

The stranger suggests that it would be too confusing to examine all the forms (*tôn eidôn*) and that they would do better to concentrate on "the greatest" (*tôn megistôn*), thus initiating his famous discussion of the *megista genê* (greatest kinds). The greatest kinds turn out to be being, motion, and rest, closely followed by the same and the different. Stanley Rosen rightly observes that being, motion, and rest "are introduced by the Stranger, and accepted by Theaetetus, without any argument whatsoever."[35] This raises a pair of questions.

First, why does the stranger classify being, motion, rest, and (possibly) the same and the different as *megista* (greatest or most important), without explanation and without protest from Theaetetus? Rosen holds that this owes to the fact that these *eidê* or *genê* are the most pervasive, appearing most frequently in combinations and separations.[36] That is a good conjecture. I might add that these forms or kinds would appear to be self-evidently *megista* to an Athenian scientist who was simultaneously a geometer and an astronomer. The same and the different, if properly understood, also would be hugely useful to dialecticians like Socrates and the stranger, helping Socrates show people that their opinions are self-contradictory and helping the stranger discover grounds for separating like from like. These speculations will have to do.

Second, is the stranger's list of the *megista genê* exclusive? That is, would the stranger be open to including any other forms or kinds in the inventory of the greatest? Rosen thinks that he one and the many would make the grade.[37] That probably is right. However, I am especially concerned about the Form of the Good. Would the stranger admit it to the ranks of the *megista*? A critic of mine might argue that there is nothing in the stranger's reasoning to suggest that the five *genê* enumerated so far are the only greatest or most important ones, which I grant, and that his account is consistent with adding the Good as one of the very great kinds, not only alongside the others, but also potentially superior to them in intelligibility and power,

---

35 Rosen, *Plato's "Sophist,"* 366.
36 Rosen, *Plato's "Sophist,"* 264.
37 Rosen, *Plato's "Sophist,"* 264.

which I do not grant. The latter propositions are foreclosed by the stranger's classification of being as *tou megistou te kai archêgou prôtou* (243d1–2), which puts being in the place that Socrates reserves for the Good and establishes the superiority of being to the Good, if the Good exists for the stranger at all; by the stranger's statement that *diaeresis* distinguishes like from like, spurning distinctions of better from worse; by the stranger's assiduous avoidance of any mention of the Form of the Good, from which his entire argument prescinds, and by his curious allergy to use of the word good, at least in this dialogue. It seems to me that the stranger neglects to include the Good among the *megista* here not merely for reasons of analytic economy but, rather, because he intends to downgrade or eliminate it from consideration. His argument still appears un-Socratic.

The stranger asserts that being, rest, and motion are the greatest *genê*. Then he goes back over ground that he already covered, recalling that rest and motion cannot mingle with each other but that being can mingle with both of those. Therefore there are three forms, each other than the other two and each the same as itself. This deduction prompts the stranger to ask about the same and the other. Are they two new *genê*, always necessarily mingled with the other three, or must we say that either or both is the same as one of the first three? Still seeming to rely on meanings of words, the stranger points out that motion and rest are neither other nor same. Anything that we called motion and rest commonly could not be either of them because motion would be at rest and rest would be in motion. Nevertheless both motion and rest participate in same and other by virtue of being the same as themselves and other than the other. So, then, could same and other be the same as being? If same and being were the same, motion and rest would be the same, for both are. That cannot be, so same is a fourth form. What about other? The stranger says that it always is other in relation to an other. This could not be if being and other were the same for the other of the other is and therefore would be the same. Other must be a fifth form. The stranger adds that each form is other than the others not owing to its own nature but because it participates in other. For obvious reasons, this is a debatable point but I do not wish to spend time on it.

It seems more important to me to reflect a little on same and other. I said above that they could be helpful to dialecticians if properly understood. What is a proper understanding of them? I think that it must be recognized that, like the stranger's being, motion, and rest, same and other are unlike Socratic Forms because they are not and could not be *monoeides*. There are different kinds of sameness and otherness, for example, essential and inessential sameness and otherness. To put this another way, one cannot ever say same and other without specifying "with respect to what." Assume two horses, one large and one small. Or assume two objects, one of which has properties A, B, C, and D and the other of which has characteristics A, B, C, and E. Are they the same or different? The answers are plain. The stranger himself recognizes this tacitly in 256a–b when he observes that he has used "same" in different ways. Now, a dialectician, whether like Socrates or the stranger, must become adept at identifying the kinds of sameness and difference or the many "with respect to what" relations to be effective. One wonders whether the stranger has mastered his trade. Could an expert in kinds of sameness arrive at the stunning conclusion that Socratic philosophy is the same as sophistry in the most important respects?

The presentation of the stranger's basic ontology, which, in Heidegger's words, has been "governed by the fact that *on* is interrogated thematically here as *legomenon*, as encountered in *logos*," is now finished. We are no further forward with regard to the vexed question of what the stranger's *eidê* or *genê* are. We can be reasonably certain that these forms are unlike the Forms of Socrates insofar as they are not *monoeides*. Beyond that, I think that my guess that these kinds are composite logical categories that either represent or *are* the fundamental realities is as good as anybody's. The stranger now comes to the point of his metaphysical reasoning, which almost has been forgotten in the abstruse discussion of being, motion, rest, same, and other: the ontology has laid the groundwork for a proof that nonbeing is. This demonstration has four parts:

(1) Motion *is not* rest, being, the same, or other. Still it participates in being, same, and other. Therefore it *both is and is not* being, same, and other. Similar cases can be made for rest, being, same, and other. Therefore, nonbeing also is, being also *is not*, and all things are nonbeing and being at once. Being is many while nonbeing is unlimited in multitude.

(2) When we say nonbeing, we do not speak of the opposite (*enantion*) of being but only of other. The stranger says that we are bidding farewell to speaking of some opposite of being.

{260}

(3) Just as knowledge is one but has many parts (all the arts and sciences with their own names), the other is one but has many parts. "Non-" can be affixed to any noun or adjective such that, for example, both the beautiful and the non-beautiful *are*. Therefore, nonbeing is in all the interstices of being.

(4) Parmenides is refuted. We have shown not only that things that are not are but what the form of nonbeing is, namely the other. Theaetetus declares that this is "the entire and perfect truth."

It is not obvious to me that this is the entire and perfect truth. As I have observed above, I doubt that Parmenides had simple negation in mind when he forbade inquiry into nonbeing. It is more likely that he thought of nonbeing as the *nihil absolutum* or the widely proclaimed being of things apart from the one. The stranger has refuted a thesis that Parmenides probably did not maintain. The claim to have disproved Parmenides also masks a shift in the stranger's ground. Earlier, he had spoken as if he meant to demonstrate that the *nihil absolutum* exists. Now it has become clear that when he talks of the being of nonbeing his "nonbeing" means "not being that." This is somewhat misleading. As I have already protested, absences of being do not exist. They are not beings. Thus, the interpretation of nonbeing as otherness has come as a letdown. As an ontological theory, it is unimpressive. Holding the principle (non)*entia non sunt multiplicanda praeter necessitatem*, I reject the idea that every instance of otherness is a being of nonbeing.

From here, the argument proceeds by two steps—presented in more extensive detail than I shall report—to its conclusion. First, after a few more quibbles with people who like to play with semantic oppositions, the stranger tackles the issue of speech (*logos*). He observes that the complete separation of everything from everything would destroy speech and, hence, philosophy. For speech arises through the interweaving of forms. Speech is one of the *genê* of being and we must come to an agreement about it. Nonbeing [read otherness] is one of the classes of being too and we must inquire whether it mingles with opinion and speech. If it does not mix with them, all things necessarily are true. If it does mingle with them, false opinion and false speech come to be. If falsehood exists, deceit (*apatê*) exists. If deception exists, all kinds of *eidôlôn* (images), *eikonôn* (likenesses), and *phantasias* (phantasms, originally the productions of *phantasikên*) exist. It will be recalled that the stranger originally defined *eikastikên*, likeness-making, as the imitation of the exact proportions of originals, which appeared to imply that it had a certain veracity about it that would let it correspond to philosophic speech. Now *eikastikên* appears to have slipped into the realm of falsehood. That aside, the stranger says that the sophist has denied the existence of falsehood. Here it will be remembered that no sophist in the Platonic dialogues issues such a denial: the only "sophist" who does so is Socrates, when he treats Theaetetus's assumptions with reductios. The stranger's remark, which ignores Socrates' midwife role in Theaetetus, resumes the attack on Socrates.

So, what shall we say? Is there false speech or not? To get at this problem, the stranger discusses the nature of speech. He observes that it consists in interwoven nouns and verbs. Then he gives two examples of sentences: "Theaetetus sits" and "Theaetetus, with whom I am talking now, flies." Theaetetus thinks that the former sentence is true and the latter false. The stranger says that this is so because the former declares things about Theaetetus that are as they are, while the latter states things that are not about him as if they were. This is to say that falsehood exists in speech because speech sometimes affirms nonbeing, or things that are not [read things that are not that or things that are other than the case]. Opinion is the silent conversation of the soul with itself so false opinion can exist too. When nonbeing is understood as otherness, this reasoning is seemingly unexceptionable.

Second, the stranger recalls that he and the boy had divided *eidôlopoiikês* (image-making) into *eikastikên* (likeness-making) and *phantastikên* and that they had been uncertain as to which of these categories contained the sophist—and even more unsure about whether the classes were valid. Inasmuch as we have proved that false speech and opinion exist, we are allowed to choose one. However, the stranger does not immediately do so. Instead, he reverts to *diaeresis*, starting with his original separation of *technê* (art) into *poiêtikên* (production) and *ktêtikên* (acquisition) and proposing to divide *poiêtikên* to discover the sophist. This comes as no surprise, given that we have been talking about the production of images for some time now. It is another example of grasping our ever elusive beast with "both hands." It is not intended to repudiate the previous *diaereseis* that were based on acquisition. The hunting, competing, and commercial analyses are implicitly affirmed.[38] The sophist will be an individual who both produces and acquires.

Poiêtikês is divided into divine (*theion*) and human (*anthrôpinon*) production. After some meditation on the question of whether natural beings (such as people, animals, and plants) arise from a mindless nature or an intelligent god, Theaetetus chooses the latter alternative because he supposes that the stranger believes in it. This is not a Platonic testimonial to young Theaetetus's greatness of mind. Nevertheless, divine production is retained as a proper half of *poiêtikên* and not replaced by something like natural production, which the stranger has subtly introduced as a possibly valid alternative while ostensibly rejecting it.

Both sorts of *poiêtikês*, divine and human, have to be divided again. The new classes are "thing-itself-making" (*autopoiêtikon*) and *eidôlopoiikês* (image-making). This signifies that the gods make natural things and natural images such as shadows and reflections in water while men make artifacts out of natural things (beds, etc.) and images (paintings and poems). Now we come back to *eikastikên* (likeness-making) and *phantastikên* (phantasm-making). The stranger decides to divide *phantastikên*, so the sophist is a phantasm-maker, as we have long known. *Phantastikên* is split into one kind that is produced by instruments (*organon*) and another in which the maker of the phantasm is himself the effective instrument, using his own figure or voice to imitate some other being. One thinks of actors or epic poets who recite their works. These living instruments are engaged in imitation (*mimêsis*). Imitators, in turn, are of two sorts: Some act while knowing (*eidotes, gnôseôs*) that which they imitate. Others are unknowing (*ouk eidotes, agnôsias*). Those who know imitate by virtue of knowledge learned by inquiry (*epistêmês historian mimêsin*). The ignorant ones talk about justice and virtue, trying to make it appear that they know what they are saying but relying on mere opinion. They are attempting to imitate people who are well versed

---

38 Stanley Rosen wants to translate *ephantazeths* as "disguised himself" in a sentence in which most translators have the sophist "showing himself" as hunter, etc. *Plato's "Sophist,"* 311. This would imply that the stranger regards his previous *diaereseis* as wrong. However, I think that the usual translations are correct.

in these topics. It will not be lost on Theaetetus that Socrates is famous for frequent discussions of justice and virtue. Whether Socrates knows justice and virtue is anybody's guess in the view of non-philosophers, but he publicly confesses his ignorance.

Coining a neologism, the stranger calls the ignorant variety of imitating *doxomimêtikên* (translated by Eva Brann as the "opino-imitative art"). The practitioners of this art divide into a pair of types: some are deluded and think that they know what they are talking about. They may be classified as "simple" (*haploun*). The others suspect and fear that they have no understanding of their topics. Therefore, they become dissembling or ironic (*eirônikon*) imitators. Socrates, of course, is famous for his irony. The ironic kinds split into those who dissemble in long speeches to multitudes and those who work in private with short speeches that compel people to contradict themselves. The latter recall the competing *diaeresis* of Sophist V, bringing its malefactor back on stage. It is well known that Socrates forces men to contradict themselves with short speeches. The maker of the longer speeches is a demagogue. The other is the sophist.

FIGURE 9: PRODUCTION (SOPHIST VII)

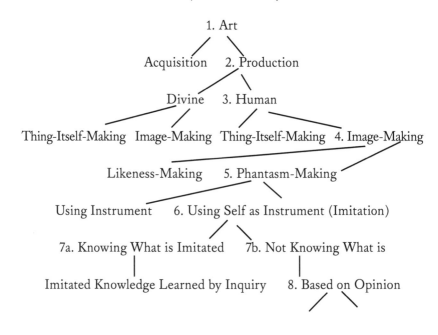

1. Art

Acquisition   2. Production

Divine   3. Human

Thing-Itself-Making   Image-Making   Thing-Itself-Making   4. Image-Making

Likeness-Making   5. Phantasm-Making

Using Instrument   6. Using Self as Instrument (Imitation)

7a. Knowing What is Imitated   7b. Not Knowing What is

Imitated Knowledge Learned by Inquiry   8. Based on Opinion

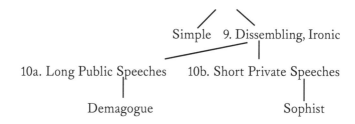

TABLE 9: PRODUCTION (GREEK) SOPHIST VII

1. *Technê –> poiêtikên, ktêtikên*
2. *Poiêtikên –> Theion, Anthrôpinon*
3. *Theion, Anthrôpinon –> Autopoiêtikon, Eidôlopoiikês*
4. *Eidôlopoiikês –> Eikastikên, Phantastikên*
5. *Phantastikên –> Organon, Mimêsis*
6. *Mimêsis –> Eidotes* or *Gnôseôs, Ouk Eidotes* or *Agnôsias*
7a. *Eidotes* or *Gnôseôs –> Epistêmês Historian Mimêsin*
7b. *Ouk Eidotes* or *Agnôsias –> Doxomimêtikên*
8. *Doxomimêtikên –> Haploun, Eirônikon*
9. *Eirônikon –> Makrois Logois Pros Plêthê, Idia te Kai Brachesi Logois, Enantiologein*
10a. *Makrois Logois Pros Plêthê –> Dêmalogikon*
10b. *Idia te Kai Brachesi Logois –> Sophistên*

     Summary: *Enantiologikês Eirônikou . . . Doxastikês Mikêtikon, Phantastikou, Eidôlopoiikês, Anthrôpikon, Thaumatopoiikon, Poiêseôs, Sophistên*

The stranger is at pains to declare that the sophist is not a philosopher but an individual who imitates the wise. Then, summarizing his *diaeresis*, he says that the man who practices the contradiction-making art of the dissembling part of the opining art of imitation, which belongs to the fantastic class of the image-making *technê* and is not divine but human, this being the wonder-working part of production (thus bringing the *goês* back into play), is the true sophist. Wonder-working was not part of the original *diaeresis* but it did figure heavily in earlier discussions. The summary reverses the order in which the terms of the original *diaeresis* appeared and it omits the distinction between the use of instruments and the use of the self as instrument. The sloppiness has persisted. The stranger remarks that whoever endorses this description of the sophist speaks the exact truth. His self-praise is an un-Socratic claim to knowledge: Socrates denied knowing anything but eros. The concluding definition of a sophist fits the popular image of Socrates to a T. Theaetetus agrees with it, thus voting to convict Socrates of sophistry.

Kenneth Sayre refers to this final *diaeresis* as one of three properly executed divisions in Sophist and he comments that, with it, the stranger's quarry is "finally bagged." As previously[39] noted, he thinks that proper *diaereseis* list all the necessary and sufficient conditions that make a thing be what it is. However, he does not believe that the stranger's real purpose was to find the sophist. Rather, he argues that Sophist was written to refute Socrates' denial in Theaetetus that knowledge is true judgment plus a *logos*. The "bagging" of the sophist is a bonus.

I have just shown that there is a discrepancy between the stranger's last *diaeresis* and his summary of it. Thus, as just mentioned, his practice of *diaeresis* has been consistently slovenly. However, the division/collection presents more important problems. One wonders whether the stranger actually has identified the necessary and sufficient conditions that coalesce to define the sophist. Also, I have pointed out above that Sayre has not overcome Socrates' objection that the disputed account of knowledge is circular. Sayre's favored definition of *epistêmê* reduces to the proposition that knowledge is true judgment plus knowledge of necessary and sufficient factors: this still does not say what the knowledge of the necessary and sufficient conditions is. As I have said, I doubt that Socrates supposed it possible to do that. His question intended *aporia*.

Let us ponder the more salient issue here, that of whether the stranger has identified the necessary and sufficient conditions of being a sophist. There are several difficulties in the crucial arguments that need to be mentioned.

I can condense this analysis by invoking the works of Stanley Rosen and Kenneth Dorter. Throughout his treatment of the stranger's doctrine of images, ontology, and theory of falsehood, Rosen keeps up a constant flow of criticism of the reasoning, offering well-considered objections of a

---

39   Sayre, *Plato's Analytic Method*, 215.

type not found in the more admiring commentaries. Gathering up strands of critique of the stranger's account of images that I myself have proposed, Rosen says that the stranger's equation of images, likenesses, and statements "makes sense only when the originals are spatio-temporal things (like the sitter for a portrait). It makes no sense at all in the case of pure forms, . . . facts, . . . or events. . . . It follows that there is no epistemically reliable refutation of the sophist."[40] With regard to the stranger's discussion of the *megista genê*, Rosen argues that his effort to present forms "in themselves" and "yet as independent of the form sameness" is unsustainable. "The fact is that the stranger's doctrine breaks down at this point."[41]

With reference to the stranger's celebrated discovery of the meaning of nonbeing, Rosen observes: "[The Stranger] has failed to capture the intuitive or plain sense of 'not.' He fails because he starts from the assumption that meaning derives from forms. This assumption will not lead us to an understanding of 'not' . . . [which] continues to refer to a primitive *absence of form* . . . . It is enough for us to see that the Stranger's doctrine will not work in its own terms."[42]

Alluding to the stranger's suppression of the idea of the Good and the distinction of better from worse, Rosen says: "With respect to the task of refuting the sophist, there is a fundamental defect in the Stranger's strategy. Even if he should succeed in 'persuading' us of his doctrine of forms, he would remain open to the charge that he is himself the most powerful of sophists. . . . If there is in any sense a 'proof' . . . it can only be in the comprehensive account of human life that this doctrine makes possible. But we compare accounts of human life, not with respect to the distinction of like from like, and hence not with respect to forms like the 'greatest kinds,' but with respect to the distinction between better and worse . . . . At this level, however, there is no technical refutation of sophistry."[43]

Touching on the same difficulty about images that Rosen noticed, which has much to do with the confused status of *eikastikên*, Kenneth Dorter maintains that: "If no image can perfectly represent the original, we can

40 Rosen, *Plato's "Sophist,"* 196–97.
41 Rosen, *Plato's "Sophist,"* 273.
42 Rosen, *Plato's "Sophist,"* 283.
43 Rosen, *Plato's "Sophist,"* 247.

understand why Plato extended the problem of falsity from overtly false images (semblances) to images in general . . . if the following discussion is to be successful, it must explain not only how sophistry is possible but also how philosophy is possible. We will see that this is not adequately achieved in the Sophist."[44]

It might be objected to Dorter that the stranger evades this critique by defining philosophy as the right discrimination of forms. However, the stranger offers no explanation of the method of right discrimination other than the counsel to divide through middles, advice that is confused by obviously equivocal concepts of middles. Referring, like Rosen, to the stranger's perfect silence about the idea of the Good and his definition of *diaeresis* as a method that does not distinguish better from worse, Dorter says that: "Unlike the Socratic pursuit of philosophy, then, the stranger's method does not discriminate better from worse. It is value free. That is why the stranger—once he has aligned himself with the pursuit of sorting like from like rather than the purificatory separation of better from worse— no longer has the means to distinguish the sophist from the philosopher."[45]

These quotations furnish a good sample of the difficulties in the stranger's reasoning that I also perceive. It would be useful to expand the criticisms and prove them right but this would require too much space. Perhaps it is not necessary to undertake that task. The critiques might commend themselves as self-evidently correct. In any case, it suffices to have shown that highly respected Plato scholars envisage such objections, thus raising serious doubts about whether the stranger's arguments are sound. It seems to me that one thing is indubitable. The stranger errs by trying to define sophistry as if it were a logical rather than an ethical phenomenon. The lies that sophists tell concern not definitions of forms but the good life.

It is time for a penultimate assessment of Sophist. Particularly, the moment has come for a provisional decision between two views of the dialogue. I have suggested that Sophist is a play in a seven-fold series in which Plato analyzes the reasons for Socrates' *Untergang*. Retracing the steps of Odysseus, Socrates has been cast into a situation that telescopes that hero's encounters with the Cyclops Polyphemus and Penelope's suitor Antinous.

44 Dorter, *Form and Good*, 139.
45 Dorter, *Form and Good*, 174.

The chief speaker in the drama, the Eleatic stranger, combines the roles of Polyphemus and Antinous and presents an ideological argument that attacks Socrates, weaving together assumptions and ideas that prevailed in Athens and caused people to see Socrates as a sophist who deserved execution. Philosophically, Sophist is Plato's exposition of sophistical logical reasoning about ontology that ineluctably leads to dead ends. Plato wants the reader to realize that being is a reality that he studies seriously. All such realities are ineffable. *Aporia* will arise in any attempt to construct a logical metaphysics.

The opposite view is that Sophist is Plato's philosophic breakthrough, a triumph of logic that permits him to transcend Socratic professions of ignorance and announce that he has finally attained to science after floundering throughout his career. The displacement of Socrates by the stranger symbolizes this change. The stranger's dialectical method (*diaeresis*) has been perfected, or nearly perfected, illustrating the right way to do philosophy analytically. His theory of images, his ontology, his analysis of false speech, and his definition of the sophist are masterpieces that perhaps have been superseded but that underpin our modern advances.

Some of the burden of my proposition that Sophist is an exposition of sophistical rather than Platonic doctrine has been carried by showings that the stranger offers un-Socratic and anti- Socratic reasoning. My stance undoubtedly has inspired resistance. It will be claimed that there are important similarities between the stranger and Socrates, such that the distance between them cannot be equated with that between Polyphemus and Odysseus.

Catherine Zuckert is one of the more balanced commentators who point out similarities between the stranger and Socrates. I shall address myself to her remarks. She writes:

> At first glance, Socrates and the Stranger have much in common. Both begin from Parmenides' insight that to be is to be intelligible. Both understand sophistry to be pretended wisdom. Both see dialectics as the defining feature of philosophy. . . . The Stranger, too, maintains not only that refutation is an art but also that it cures the greatest form of ignorance and so benefits its subjects. Like Socrates, the Stranger thinks that

believing that one knows what one does not know constitutes the greatest kind of ignorance. Further, like Socrates, the Stranger believes most people have to be freed from this sort of ignorance before they will be willing to learn.[46]

This appears to be an impressive array of similarities between Socrates and the stranger, constituting a match close enough to convince many that the stranger is Platonic. As Catherine Zuckert knows well, however, the similarities are in most cases merely partial or illusory. Yes, both Socrates and the stranger assume that being is intelligible—but to what extent? Unlike the stranger, who believes that the whole is knowable and that we fail to achieve a science of it only because we lack the time to master all of its variables, "Socrates thinks human beings can never achieve full knowledge (*epistêmê*) because the cosmos consists not only of eternally unchanging, hence purely intelligible entities but also of sensible, changing, and hence not fully intelligible things."[47] I would add that even "the purely intelligible entities" seem to be beyond a complete human grasp. In principle, the stranger does not recognize mystery. Socrates teaches that we are surrounded by it. Zuckert also knows what I have noted above, that the stranger defines sophistry as a *technê* while Socrates calls it an *empeiria*.[48] She is further aware that the two differ greatly over the nature of the wisdom to which sophists pretend. The stranger's sophists say they know correct classifications that do not confuse forms. For Socrates wisdom is attained only when the soul rises to the vision of the Good. The difference between the two kinds of wisdom produces disagreement about the nature of the cure of ignorance. "Unlike Socrates . . . the Stranger does not appear to think that virtue is knowledge. If it were, the cure for ignorance and vice would be the same (as it is, according to Socrates).[49]

The statement that both the stranger and Socrates regard dialectic as the defining feature of philosophy requires somewhat more complicated

46 Catherine Zuckert, "The Stranger's Political Science v. Socrates' Political Art," in the online *Journal of the International Plato Symposium* (Winter 2005), 1, 5.
47 Zuckert, "The Stranger's Political Science," 8.
48 Zuckert, "The Stranger's Political Science," 4.
49 Zuckert, "The Stranger's Political Science," 5–6.

treatment. This putative similarity conceals the following great dissimilarities:

— For Socrates, philosophy is more *erôs* than dialectic. *Erôs* for souls drives the dialectic. The stranger is silent about *erôs*. He claims that he will risk being judged mad because he cares about Theaetetus but this avowal rings hollow after his expression of indifference about whether Theaetetus might be replaced by young Socrates as his interlocutor.
— Unlike Socrates, the stranger does not tailor dialectic to the characters of interlocutors.
— Socratic dialectic is carried on by short speeches that are guided as much by the ideas of the interlocutor as by Socrates' questions, which channel the concerns of the interlocutor in directions calculated to free his soul to see truths for itself. The stranger agrees to question and answer dialogue with Theaetetus (and later with young Socrates) but he imposes his will on the conversation at every turn, guiding it toward conclusions that he wants to reach.
— As I mentioned in my previous chapter, Socrates calls for division of classes by natural joints (*kat' arthra, hê pephuke*) in Phaedrus (265e1–2), avoiding cleaving like a bad carver. He says that *erôs* is a sort of madness, that madness divides into two parts, human disease and divine release from ordinary habits, and that divine madness separates into four parts of its own, which are prophecy (inspired by Apollo), mystic (Dionysus), poetic (Muses), and Erôs. This taxonomy involves a pair of principles, that of collecting scattered particulars to make clear the definition of a thing and the other division by natural joints. The divisions look like what Socrates promised, natural sections of *erôs*. As also reported, in Philebus Socrates praises a method of investigation handed down by the gods. We must assume that in every case there is one idea of a thing, find it, and then search for two or three or some other number until we can learn not only that the thing is one and many and infinite but how many it is (16c–e). It seems for a time that he will explore kinds of pleasure but this does not immediately happen. Instead, Socrates undertakes to separate all things in the universe into four classes: the infinite, the finite, the combination of infinite and finite, and the cause of that combination. This appears to be as natural a *diaeresis* as that of *erôs*: it

certainly does not seem artificial. It genuinely attempts to discover how many parts something actually has. It also examines the whole from the viewpoint of a single principle. Now, when we turn to the stranger's divisions, in the present dialogue at least, the cuts look artificial rather than natural. There is a strange insistence on dividing by two, regardless of how many parts naturally are present. This imperative is abandoned without apology when it seems expedient. When it is heeded, the "halves" of the cuts sometimes are determined by "middles" that look like semantic opposites and sometimes by "weights" that produce numerically lopsided divisions. In addition to this, there is a problem that I did not discuss in the previous chapter. The principles by which the *diaereseis* proceed are not uniform throughout but change practically from one cut to the next. For example, in the angling *diaeresis*, divisions two, three, and four refer to means by which the activity that denominates the category are carried out. Cut five concentrates on the objects of the activity. Cut six focuses on the means of locomotion of those objects. Division seven returns to objects of the activity. Eight goes back to means by which the activity is carried out. Nine refers ridiculously to the times of day during which the activity ordinarily commences. Ten returns to its means. In the hunting *diaeresis*, after repetition of a number of cuts of the angling paradigm, division five invokes a conventional distinction, whether the object is wild or tame, with an aside that suggests that Theaetetus's choice between the results of the cut is unimportant. Six focuses on the means employed by the activity. Seven examines the venues in which the activity occurs. Eight touches on the question of who gives and receives benefits. Nine discusses the purported purposes of the activity, one of which is said to be pretended. Ten reports the nature of benefits received. I could go on like this about the other *diaereseis* but my point should be clear. None of this looks like the sorts of *diaeresis* that Socrates commends or does in Phaedrus and Philebus. I hope that I can say this without inserting book-length discussions of those dialogues here. What the stranger seeks is not natural cuts but apparently steps that promote his rhetorical intentions.

There is one additional aim that the stranger's divisions might have. He could be listing all the ways in which a thing or activity could be looked at, with a view toward enhancing human control of the environment. This exercise could be useful but it is not Socratic.

As for the common claim that Sophist is a triumph of Platonic logic, I wonder that anyone could believe this after taking note of the dialogue's logical defects. I need not rehearse them all here: it will suffice to summarize them briefly. The *diaereseis* are frequently garbled, they often contain ridiculous results, and their collections seldom tally with their divisions. The *diaereseis* reach their conclusions by equivocating on the meanings of words. It is not evident how many divisions are offered in the exchange *diaeresis* (or *diaereseis*). The epistemology, ontology, theory of falsehood, and final *diaeresis* proceed from the false premise that sophists generally deny the existence of falsehood. They obscure the distinction between the *nihil absolutum* and negation. They equate images with nonbeing by forbidding a definition of images that refers to our vision. They misrepresent the stranger's ancestors, especially Parmenides. They interpret myths literally. They are ambiguous about whether they are attempting to define being, which seems impossible, or to mark off some of its ubiquitous properties. They defeat the most serious challengers to the stranger's concept of being by illicit means. They might present two unreconciled metaphysics. They seem to deduce ontological conclusions by relying on common definitions of words. They do not justify their choices of the *megista genê*.

It seems to me that if Plato changed his mind about his philosophy of the so-called early and middle dialogues and offered Sophist as his serious reconsideration of his previous work, he should have been ashamed of himself for making all these sorts of mistakes. I do not believe that he was a philosopher who could have fallen into such a quagmire—unless all the errors amount to esoteric messages. Therefore, contrary to the weight of the scholarly tradition, I conclude that my reading of Sophist is correct. The stranger is Polyphemus-Antinous. Socrates is Odysseus. The stranger has been recruited by Theodorus to put Socrates on trial intellectually and to convict him of sophistry. His arguments are sophisms with that aim. Also, Plato has availed himself of the opportunity to show that an ontology founded on logic must end in *aporia*. Word definitions of image, being, nonbeing, and so forth that sophists in Athens purvey are followed fairly to their logical conclusions, which either are obvious technical tricks or do not make sense.

My conclusions about Sophist are stated strongly and definitely. However, I said above that they are penultimate and provisional. Why? The fact is that, although the stranger's work in Sophist cannot stand alone as great philosophy, Statesman might change the picture. The most severe critics of Sophist hold out this possibility. Stanley Rosen asserts that while Sophist is the stranger's refutation of Socrates, Statesman "is in effect the stranger's recantation." Thus, "Our account of the difference between Socrates and the Stranger is valid for the Sophist only. It is a separate task to understand the Statesman."[50] As noted previously, Kenneth Dorter believes that Parmenides, Theaetetus, Sophist, and Statesman constitute an experiment in which Plato outlines the epistemological problems of the Forms in Parmenides; tries but fails to explain knowledge without Forms in Theaetetus; brings Forms back in Sophist to solve the puzzles of Theaetetus, failing to illuminate the nature of the sophist because he prescinds from the Form of the Good, and in Statesman finally relates the Good to political order via "the mean," ultimately coming to an edifying end. The dialogues in the trilogy may be regarded as "an extended application of the method of hypothesis." On the basis of the final hypothesis of "the mean," the residual problems of Sophist (especially the *essential* difference between philosophy and sophistry) will be "more convincingly resolved."[51] We shall have to see whether Rosen and Dorter are right when we turn to Statesman.

Meanwhile, we must remember the function of Sophist in the drama of the *Untergang* of Socrates-Odysseus. In his role as Polyphemus, the stranger has brought a tremendous technical apparatus to bear in his effort to snare Socrates-Odysseus in his net of word devices. However, his casts of his word-net have missed Socrates again. Socrates is not a maker of phantasms that distort the true proportions of things. He is a seeker of truth who destroys the images to which people cling in his efforts to open their souls to illumination by the ineffable higher reality. His wrecking of popular phantasms is what causes Athenian hostility toward him. The Polyphemus-stranger has attempted to catch Socrates-Odysseus by construing various Socratic methods as the essence of sophistry. However, Socrates-Odysseus escapes the word-net because the real essence of sophistry consists in the resistance to the Good that the Polyphemus-stranger has exhibited.

50 Rosen, *Plato's "Sophist,"* 29, 25.
51 Dorter, *Form and Good*, 191.

6

POLITICIAN: ANOTHER EFFORT TO SNARE SOCRATES-ODYSSEUS

At the beginning of Plato's Politikos, the title of which I am now translating as Politician rather than as Statesman, Socrates thanks Theodorus for his introductions to Theaetetus and the Eleatic stranger. Theodorus replies that Socrates will be three times as grateful when the stranger has worked out the *politikos* and the philosopher for him too. Socrates affects to be shocked: he asks whether this is the word of the mightiest calculator and geometrician. Theodorus wonders what Socrates means. Socrates says that Theodorus has rated sophist, *politikos*, and philosopher at the same value even though they stand farther apart in honor than the proportion of his *technê* can express. Theodorus swears by Ammon, the god of his city, Cyrene, admitting that Socrates has spoken justly, catching his mathematical error. He vows to get revenge another time.

In what might have been the first good, serious book on Politician, Mitchell Miller reads these exchanges as friendly banter. Although he perceives a certain intellectual tension between Socrates and Theodorus, Miller seems sure that Socrates is among friends, that Socrates approves of the stranger's arguments, that the stranger takes up the task of teaching Socratic dialectic and philosophy to his young interlocutor, that he elaborates a Socratic political theory that is more or less consistent with what is written in Republic, and that he anticipates the trial of Socrates in a manner that acquits Socrates rather than convicting him. Young Socrates is the stranger's new interlocutor. Miller sees him as a probable historical personage, a member of the Academy. He thinks that the dialogue is directed at Plato's younger students, who are being taught not only the right method of dialectic but humility in the face of its limits. The young Socrates is a snapshot of these students, who tend to jump to conclusions and fail to practice the self-critical caution of the elder Socrates and Plato himself, faults that the dialogue seeks to combat.[1]

Modern scholars generally endorse Miller's interpretation of the drama and substance of Politikos. However, I should like to suggest that another reading of the dialogue is possible and that Miller might have written a first-rate treatise in pursuit of a thesis that is directly opposite to what Plato intended. In the drama, Socrates arguably is among enemies, not friends. As for the substance of the dialogue's reasoning, Miller seems to overlook several difficulties that indicate that the stranger advocates an un-Socratic philosophy and political theory that lead to *aporia* and that he subtly continues the intellectual prosecution of Socrates, convicting him of a crime much more conducive to death sentences than sophistry. Let us start with the drama.

If my analysis of the thrust of Plato's seven dialogues centered on the murder of Socrates has been right, and if my previous treatment of Sophist and the character of Theodorus has also been correct, Theodorus is no friend of Socrates. He is an intellectual refiguration of Anytus, one of Socrates' prosecutors in his political trial. He has been outraged by Socrates' refutation of his friend Protagoras and by his embarrassing failure to hold up against Socratic *elegchos*. His wrath has moved him to recruit the stranger to prosecute Socrates. The stranger is no friend to Socrates either. He refigures not only Meletus, another of Socrates' prosecutors, but also Polyphemus and Antinous, characters who attacked Odysseus. Under this hypothesis, in Politician he is trying to destroy a Socrates who refigures Odysseus descending into the underworld. If right, this scenario casts a light on the play's opening exchanges that differs entirely from Miller's.

To test the application of my thesis to Politikos, the first question to consider is whether Socrates thanks Theodorus for his introductions because he has been gratified by the stranger's arguments. As I have noted above, Socrates is unlikely to have been persuaded by reasoning that portrays him as a sophist. It is equally improbable that he is impressed by arguments that ignore the Good, suppress inquiry into the better and worse, and employ a dialectic that differs from his, especially when that dialectic fails to work on its own terms instead of improving on his earlier thought.

1   Mitchell H. Miller, Jr., *The Philosopher in Plato's "Statesman."*

It is much more likely that he is grateful for two reasons: Theodorus gave him a chance to convert a promising boy to philosophy. More importantly, he appreciates having been taught by the results of Sophist that he must face death at the hands of Athenian culture philosophically. His gratitude parallels that which he expresses in Apology to the jurors who sentenced him to a possibly better fate than he would have experienced had he been acquitted.

The next questions to ponder are these: What does Socrates' critique of Theodorus mean? Particularly, what does Socrates intend when he tells the mighty geometer that sophist, *politikos*, and philosopher stand farther apart in honor than the proportion of his *technê* can express? What *technê* does he have in mind? One tends to assume that the art in question is simple arithmetic. If one success pleases, three will be three times as delightful. However, it must be noticed that Theodorus's statement also obeys the stranger's demand for the suppression of considerations of worth in science. Louse-catching and philosophy would be honored equally in surveys of the arts in which they somehow fell into in the same *diaeresis*. To be sure, Socrates is telling Theodorus that arithmetic could never comprehend the natures of sophist, *politikos*, and philosopher but his reasons for saying so directly attack the stranger's position: worth and honor must not be ignored in philosophy. Theodorus accepts Socrates' critique because he is conflicted: he wants to support his friend, the stranger, but he also thinks of himself as a philosopher and he wants to be regarded more highly than sophists. The latter urge wins but his irritation at Socrates for backing him into yet another embarrassing dilemma inspires his desire for revenge.

Having uttered his threat, Theodorus exhorts the stranger not to give in to weariness but to continue with his presentation, choosing to analyze either the *politikos* or the philosopher as he sees fit. The stranger is raring to go but he has a solicitous question: Theaetetus might be tired. Should they replace him with the young Socrates [not with the elder Socrates, who would have been more interesting] as his interlocutor? Theodorus decides that Theaetetus needs a rest and agrees to the suggestion.

Socrates now makes his third and final speech to the stranger. The first was in Sophist, when he asked the stranger whether he preferred long speeches or dialectic and mentioned that he once had heard Parmenides use dialectic well. The stranger answered that he preferred speaking at length by himself unless he had an interlocutor who (literally) was "obedient to the rein" rather than "painful." If Socrates were not "legally" forbidden to speak while the prosecution's brief is presented, the stranger's reply still would suffice to explain why he and Socrates never get into a philosophic conversation. In the stranger's eyes, the inquisitive Socrates is a pain and anything but obedient to the rein. Socrates is the last person with whom he would wish to converse about serious things. Socrates would be equally averse to speaking with a man with that attitude.

The speech that Socrates now addresses to the stranger extends the previous ones in two ways that I shall consider in reverse order. First, Socrates does manifest an aversion to having a philosophic discussion with the stranger, agreeing that young Socrates should replace Theaetetus as the stranger's interlocutor. He also remarks that he will examine the boy himself on another occasion. This comment betrays the belief that he will not learn important things that he ought to know about the youth from the stranger's discussion with him. It is another sign that he does not view the stranger as a philosopher. Second, Socrates observes that he and Theaetetus have been said to look alike and that he and young Socrates have the same name, which implies some sort of kinship. We should always be eager to recognize our relatives, he says, through *logos*. Here, Plato has dramatically contrived that the stranger, who personifies *logos*, employs a personified image and a personified name who have only minimal, insubstantial relationships to Socrates to comprehend his nature (erroneously as a sophist and a detestable politician). This reminds us of the warning in the Seventh Letter that name, image, and *logos* are only tenuously related to being and do not produce the perfect knowledge in which the good-natured has communicated itself to the good-natured (although they might yield an imperfect verbal knowledge).

The stranger asks young Socrates whether he is willing to take Theaetetus's place. The boy agrees enthusiastically. He is much less cautious than Theaetetus, who already was obedient to the rein. This must please the stranger greatly. The argument of Politikos begins.

Having secured the co-operation of young Socrates, the stranger decides to work out the *politikos* next. I need to remind readers that this word has a double character. When translating it, I shall write either "statesman" or "politician" (pejorative) depending on what contexts appear to demand.

The stranger asks young Socrates whether the statesman should be numbered among the *epistêmonôn* (knowers, scientists). The budding geometer thinks so. This poses a problem. Whatever statesmanship is, it could not possibly be a science. Aristotle and long experience have taught us that political things are chancy. They exhibit no inexorable necessities, no adamantine laws, so no statesman could judge or act scientifically in the strictest sense. If we may relax our epistemological standards and consider knowledge of statistical probabilities science, statesmen could scientifically calculate odds about means-ends relationships, but they still never could know in advance whether means would produce desired ends in particular cases. Knowing generalities, they could not predict outcomes of specific initiatives that they undertook and about which they actually cared. The stranger also could be referring to experiential knowledge and the prudence (*phronêsis*) that might be founded on it. This would be a loose manner of speaking. Prudence is not science, valuable as it is in its own right.

It would appear that the stranger has started badly. However, his next question to young Socrates requires reconsideration of the point. He asks whether the *epistêmas* (sciences) should be divided in the same manner as they were in the previous case. When the sophist was sought it was *technê*, not *epistêmê*, that was divided. The stranger's query implies that he views *epistêmê* and *technê* as synonyms. This probably is how most Greeks thought too. If the stranger means that he is investigating a political *technê*, this is unobjectionable. I have suggested above that a *technê* is knowledge of the nature of a thing that allows treating it in ways ruled by its essential structure and limits. This is a partial knowledge that does not rise to the level of science because natures are subject to contingencies. There could be a political art. Socrates even lays claim to one, maintaining that he is the only practitioner of the *alethôs politikê technê* (true political art) in Athens (Gorgias 521d). He means that his *technê* of *erôs*, which is a care of individual souls in one-on-one conversations that aims at ethical improvement, *is* the *alethôs politikê technê*, or that the education of citizens (or at least leaders) to virtue is the only means to the reduction of evil in political life. As Politikos proceeds, it will become evident that his claim greatly endangers him.

When the stranger asks whether the sciences should be divided in the same way as they were earlier, young Socrates is unsure, whereupon the stranger abruptly decrees that they should be divided differently. He says that we must discover the statesman's path, "separate it from the rest, and imprint upon it the seal of a single class (*idean*); then we must set the mark of another single class (*eidos*) upon all the other paths that lead away from this, and make our soul conceive of all sciences as of two classes (*eidê*, 258c3–7, Loeb translation)." The paths to which he refers probably are *diaeresis* chains. His directive requires that my remarks about his method in earlier chapters be expanded. To do this, I shall avail myself of the analyses of a pair of scholars who already have considered the matter.

My previous comments require expansion because we no longer are dealing merely with arbitrary classifications that are rhetorically expedient. Harvey Scodel writes that the stranger is making *diaeresis* "remarkably poetic," meaning that the stranger creates *eidê* rather than finding them in the world, as witness his notion of the mind stamping impressions on things rather than receiving impressions from them. Scodel rightly observes that the ontological status of the *eidos* "all sciences other than statesmanship" is questionable.[2] Stanley Rosen agrees that the stranger turns *diaeresis* into a method of "concept construction." The "imprinting" verbs that the stranger uses usually refer to putting seals on wax or making coins. They connote "production." Rosen explains that: "We are engaged in the construction of cognitive artifacts by which to secure a grip on our prey." He tempers this account of the *diaeresis* as productive by arguing that the stranger's concept construction "follows and expresses the kind rather than creating it *ex nihilo*."[3] right insofar as "statesmanship" is an *eidos* that suggests its semantic negative complement, "all sciences not statesmanship." However, the latter formula is created as an *eidos*, as the language of "imprinting" and "making our souls conceive of two classes" makes clear. It now is evident that the stranger creates classes as a means of "securing a grip on our prey." This must be kept before our minds' eyes as we proceed. It will have a bearing on what the stranger means when he promises to make his students better dialecticians.

Initially, young Socrates is unwilling to follow the stranger's advice to stamp impressions on the sciences and make our souls conceive of them as

2 Scodel, *Diaeresis*, 25, 27. Scodel quotes L. Campbell, *The Sophistes and Politicus of Plato*, with regard to the *poiesis*.
3 Rosen, *Plato's "Statesman,"* 17, 19.

falling into the classes "statesmanship" and "all the others." He replies that this must become the stranger's work, not his. He probably fears that he cannot identify one thing that sets statesmanship apart from the others. The stranger retorts that the task must become the boy's too when the path has become plain. Young Socrates answers that the stranger speaks "beautifully" (or "nobly"). The prospect that he might be able to do the work himself enthuses him. However, the stranger ends up doing everything.

The stranger now begins his account of the statesman with a new *diaeresis* of *epistêmê* (or *technê*). He asks whether arithmetic and other related *technai* are "bare of practices," serving to acquire knowledge only. His question evokes a mental image of seeking mathematical truths for their own sake, without regard for their practical utility. This probably is what inspires the young Socrates to agree that some sciences are bare of practices. The other half of *epistêmê*, according to the stranger, is a technical kind that embraces carpentry and crafts in general, which produce objects that did not previously exist. He therefore advises young Socrates to divide "all sciences" (*sumpassas epistêmas*) into two parts, one practical (*praktikên*) and the other "only intellectual" or "only gnostic" (*monon gnôstikên*). As I observed earlier, this division of *technê* into practical and gnostic does not match the splitting of *technê* in Sophist into productive and acquisitive. It demonstrates that the stranger still is not dividing classes into natural parts. He is splitting them in keeping with the point of view that he wishes to adopt at the moment.

At this juncture, the stranger interrupts his *diaeresis* with what seems to be a digression. He asks young Socrates whether a *politikos*, a king (*basilea*), a master (*despotên*, that is, a slave owner or boss), and a household manager (*oikonomon*) are the same or different. Before the boy can answer, the stranger offers to help him by putting another question: If a private person is able to advise one of the public physicians, must we not call his *technê* by the same name as that of the public doctor? Young Socrates says yes. Well, the stranger continues, if a private person is clever at advising a king, should we not declare that he possesses the same *technê* as his advisee? The lad grants this too. So, the stranger asks, the science of a true king is kingly, and should not someone who possesses the science be called kingly whether he happens to be ruling or in private station? Young Socrates agrees.

At first glance, it appears that the stranger has raised two different issues. The question of the identity or non-identity of *politikos, basilea, despotên,* and *oikonomon* does not appear to have much to do with the issue of whether a person who possesses the kingly science should be called kingly even when not in office. Young Socrates' positive answer to this query might also have been too hasty. A man enjoying theoretical insight into kingship might lack the experiential knowledge that also would be required to make him kingly. One suspects that the purpose of the digression might be to inflate the status of Theodorus's friend Protagoras, who advised Pericles, or to claim a kingly distinction for the stranger himself, who will demonstrate with his reasoning that he possesses the kingly science although he is not in office.

Without denying those possibilities, second thought notices a way in which the stranger's pair of questions might be theoretically connected. Having established that a king and someone who knows the art of kingship are both kingly, the stranger inquires whether the *oikonnomis* and *despotês* are the same. Young Socrates says yes. Then the stranger inquires whether the outward form (or pretense or grandeur; *schêma*) of a large household and a small polis differ with respect to ruling. The boy thinks not. The stranger concludes, therefore, that with regard to his original question, *politikos, basilea, despotên,* and *oikonomon* share the same science, no matter whether one calls it kingship, statesmanship, or householding. His second question is theoretically related to the first insofar as the despot and the householder are not kings but are still kingly by virtue of their science. The stranger's argument merits two remarks. First, it misses Aristotle's objection that the four different kinds of authority have different final causes. It also ignores the practical problem that, unlike slave bosses and householders, all political rulers (including tyrants) have to satisfy their power bases and balance the forces exerted by numerous conflicting factions to hold their positions and get things done. Second, it appears calculated to make wealthy Athenians feel good about themselves. Oligarchical owners of slaves and households can regard themselves as kingly by virtue of their supposed science, at least for the time being.

Does the stranger's seeming digression into his questions about the identities, kingliness, and science of *politikos, basilea, despotên,* and *oikonomon* contribute anything to his *diaeresis* of *epistêmê*? This is hard to

fathom. However, the reasoning might not be digressive insofar as it fore-
closes the possibility that the category of commanding science that the
stranger will posit in a couple of steps would splinter into an unwieldy
multitude of branches.

The stranger resumes his *diaeresis* of *epistêmê* (or *technê*). He observes that a king can do little with his hands or body to keep his position as compared with what he can do with his soul. Therefore, he asks whether "the
king" is "more akin" (*oikeioteron*) to the gnostic or the practical side of
epistêmê. He and young Socrates decide that he is more akin to the intellectual. So, it is the gnostic branch that will be further divided.

The stranger asks his interlocutor whether he can discern a natural par-
tition (*diaphuên*) of *gnöstikê*. He cannot, so the stranger observes that they
previously had recognized *logistikê*, the calculating art. (They had not done
so, unless the stranger is defining *logistikê* as a synonym of *arithmêtikê*.) The
stranger states that the work of *logistikê* is to judge, separate, or discriminate
(*krinai*) numbers (such that the theorist is engaged in an unproductive form
of the *diakritikê* that was depicted in Sophist as a set of domestic tasks that
prepared wool for weaving). The stranger divides this activity from that of
the architect, who commands workmen without being a laborer himself.
Architecture is thus classified as *gnöstikê* because it acquires science and
gives orders without dirtying its hands. *Gnöstikê* is accordingly split into
judging (*krisei*) and commanding (*epitaxei*) halves. *Epitaxei* somehow does
not seem bare of practices, so it does not look like a natural category of
seeking knowledge for its own sake. Nevertheless, young Socrates agrees.

The boy's answer leads to a strange interlude. The stranger replies that
as long as he and young Socrates agree, they need not trouble about the
views of others. This is as much as to say that they need not worry whether
the contrary opinions of others are true. For example, it would not matter
if the elder Socrates disagreed with the *diaeresis*.

The stranger now raises the question of whether the kingly man practices *kritikê*, judging like a spectator, or *epitaxis*, acting like a ruler. The answer is obvious.

The stranger next divides *epitaktikê*, illustrating his *diaeresis* with an
analogy that revises a distinction that he made in Sophist. He suggests that
kings differ from heralds in the same way that *autopôlikoi* (people who sell
their own products) differ from *kapêloi* (salesmen who import and export

things made by others.)[4] Heralds are like *kapêloi* insofar as they transmit commands issued by others. They belong to a set of go-betweens that includes interpreters, boatswains (men who call cadences ordained by captains to warship rowers) and prophets. The stranger wonders whether the king should be placed in that class, which remains nameless, or in another for which they will coin the term "the *technê* of giving one's own orders" (*autepitaktikê*). Young Socrates puts the king in the category *autepitaktikê*. The nameless category appears to embrace speakers who do not know the whys and wherefores of what they are relating. It is hard to understand how they fit under the heading of *gnôstikên*. Rosen points out further that the stranger has just made merchandising a paradigm for *gnôstikê* and argues that this is absurd.[5] That aside, we now have a distinction between a nameless class of intermediaries who transmit orders and rulers who give their own orders, their art being called *autepitaktikê*.

Next the stranger inquires whether it is necessary to divide "this" (auto) if we can find a way of doing it. One assumes that he is speaking of cutting *autepitaktikê*. However, he reverts to the language of *epitaxei*, dropping the *aut*, thus introducing some confusion as to whether he is doing the *diaeresis* of *epitaktikê* over again or talking loosely, still planning to cut *autepitaktikê*. Whatever the case, he begins with the observation that rulers who issue commands do so "for the sake of some genesis." Final causes are controlling. "For the sake of" tips a balance. *Gnôstikê*, science "bare of practices," the purported guiding principle of the *diaeresis*, has been replaced as the dominant category by a scientific *praktikê* that intends production or genesis. The statesman is not, and never has been, inclined to seek knowledge for its own sake. He possesses or desires a science that enables him to give orders to others who will produce what he envisages.

All things that become, declares the stranger, are unsouled (*apsycha*, lifeless) or ensouled (*empsycha*, living). *Epitaxis* can intend "some genesis" with regard to either. So, "if we like," we may make a division of the part of gnostic

---

4   Scodel, *Diaeresis*, 45, alertly notices that the cut actually made in *Sophist* was between *autopôlikê*, selling of one's own, and *metablêtikê*, exchange. He remarks that "the stranger often displays a peculiar indifference to his own distinctions." Indeed.

5   Rosen, *Plato's "Statesman,"* 24.

science that commands. This perhaps inadvertent hint that the order of steps in a *diaeresis* depends on what we like rather than a logic intrinsic to the method is rather startling. Young Socrates is not startled. It is decided to divide *epitaxis* into parts that involve the genesis of lifeless and living things.

Which kinds of things will the *politikos* command, lifeless or living? Young Socrates is not sure which branch of the *diaeresis* to choose, probably because rulers' commands appear to embrace both. Pericles could call for the production of ships or the induction of citizens into the army and there would be a "genesis" in either case, of triremes or soldiers. (Of course, the ships would be financed and built by people.) The stranger assures young Socrates that "the science of the king" does not concern lifeless things but, rather, issues orders only and always in relation to *zôa* (living things). Hence, the king's science is "nobler" ("better born," *gennaioteron*) than the architect's. (The stranger has just violated his rule that his method should prescind from honor.) Young Socrates agrees that this is the right choice.

The phrase "some genesis" (*geneseôs tinos*) is vague. One wonders what it means with respect to living things. Surely, one supposes, the stranger thinks that the ruler intends to make his subjects "become something" or "do something" rather than "become" simply. However, this assumption misses the possibility that the ruler means to make certain types of "citizens" that did not previously exist become. The stranger's next remark also gives the impression that the ruler intends to get involved in the genesis of animals, including human beings, simply. He states that the genesis and nurture of living things" (*tên tôn zôôn genesin kai trophên*) is sometimes that of a single one alone (*idoi monotrophian*) and at other times "the common care of creatures in herds" (*tên koinên tôn ein tais agelais thremmatôn epimeleian*). He declares that the statesman is not the nurturer of a single one (*idiotrophon*). He is like the keeper of a herd of horses (*hippophorbô*) or a herd of cattle (*bouphorbô*). The next question is whether we should name the art of caring for many living creatures herd-tending (*agelaiotrophian*) or common tending (*koinotrophikên*). The boy answers "whatever." This is surprising because the former term appears to envisage animal husbandry while the latter could refer to nurturing of human beings. However, the stranger likes young Socrates' scientific detachment or his callousness, or both. Whichever name is picked, the stranger has divided *epitaktikê* into the bodily nurture of animals severally or collectively and has classified statesmanship as the bodily care of animals collectively. This diverges from the "true political *technê*" of Socrates, who, as we recall, cared for the souls of human beings individually.

The question of a name for the statesman's activity does not remain open for long. In the stranger's next breath, he asks young Socrates whether herd-nurturing (*agelaiotrophikên*), which now is doubled, can be halved. The boy promptly divides the category into the nurturing of man and that of beasts. The stranger scolds him for committing an error. The mistake is not that the distinction between man and beast is incorrect, for the *diaeresis* chain is headed in that direction. Rather, the error is to set a single small part off against many large ones, disregarding *eidê*. Thin cuts are not safe. It is better to proceed by dividing through the middle, for that way one is more likely to find *ideais*. Young Socrates inquires what the stranger means. The stranger replies that he cannot make the matter plain because that would be beyond the boy's capacity. Our curiosity about the puzzles in the stranger's method-ological statement (for example, why assume that cuts through middles yield *ideais*?) therefore will not be satisfied by the explanation that follows.

The stranger continues his scolding. He declares that it is much as if young Socrates had divided the human race into Hellenes and barbarians, making barbarians one *genos*. Again, it is as if he had separated a myriad (the number ten thousand) from all other numbers, making both sets *eidê*. It would be better to split number into odd and even and human beings into male and female, not confusing *meros* (part) with *genos* (kind, race). When there is an *eidos*, it must be a *meros* of an *eidos* to which it belongs, but not every *meros* is an *eidos*. Young Socrates' mistake when he separated man from beast was to remove a part (man) and conceive of the remainder as a *genos* because all the other animals could be given one name (beasts). Later he adds that young Socrates was brave but he behaved like the crane that, if it were rational, as it seems to be, would divide cranes from all other animals including man, giving the others the name beasts.

The stranger's rebuke calls for another comment on his method. We recall that at step six of the hunting *diaeresis* the stranger jumped directly from the category of tame animals to that of man. In terms of the present discussion, this was precisely to remove a part (man) and conceive of the remainder as a *genos* because the other tame animals could be classified as beasts. Young Socrates would be well within his rights to feel sandbagged. There also are many more examples of the stranger making "thin" cuts, citing one *eidos* and grouping the remainders as ontologically dubious *eidê*. It would be fair to argue that the entire *diaeresis* of *epistêmê* being done here has a thin cut as its premise. At the very beginning of this analysis, the stranger maintained that he and young Socrates had to discover the states-man's path, "separate it from the rest, and imprint upon it the seal of a single class (*idean*)" and "set the mark of another single class (*eidos*) upon all the other paths that lead away from this, and make our soul conceive of all sciences as of two classes (*eidê*)." This was to set one small part (the *epistêmê* of statesmanship) off against several large ones (all the other *technai*), declaring *politikê* one *eidos* and "all the other arts" another. There are other instances in Sophist. At 224c, the stranger divided the merchandising of lessons about virtue from the selling of lessons in all other studies, which were many and difficult. At 225b–c, he split *antilogikon* (argumentation) into eristic and business disputes that did not merit a name because they fell into divisions that were too small and *pantodapa* (miscellaneous). The stranger called the other debates an *eidos* despite their miscellany. At 229a, he argued that *amathia* was an *eidos* of ignorance distinct from "all others."

It might be argued that the stranger's scolding of young Socrates represents an advance in his conception of *diaeresis* insofar as it strongly reaffirms the necessity of cutting through middles and explains that this is more likely to lead to Ideas. The citing of odd/even and male/female is a very persuasive example of this probability. However, it must be remembered that the stranger has been extremely arbitrary about what he has portrayed as middles. Most of his cuts have been through "A" and "not A," as in the pair statesmanship/not statesmanship just cited. The concept of middle also shifted from the center of A/not A to equality of weight (*amathia*/all other forms of ignorance). To the best of my recollection, odd/even and male/female are the first examples of divisions into natural categories that the stranger has given. It remains to be seen whether he will continue this new practice or revert to the others.

It is important to note the stranger has denied that young Socrates has found natural *eidê*. That is the thrust of his Greeks/barbarians and myriad/other numbers examples and the point of his counterexamples of male/female and odd/even. This is surprising because the man/beast cut represents the natural division rational/irrational. Evidently, the stranger has depicted people as herd animals because he does not regard them as distinct from cattle by virtue of reason. Much like the crane, they merely seem rational. This creates the apparent problem that the stranger's *politikoi* could not be rational either, unless some means of elevating them above the herd could be found. The denial of human rationality also evokes a troubling image of statesmanship. The herdsmen of irrational beasts rules them not by appealing to their intelligence, reason, and moral sensibilities in order to persuade them, and not by seeking cooperation before resorting to force, but by a combination of punitive conditioning and feeding.

The bewildered young Socrates asks the stranger to explain how *meros* and *genos* can be recognized and distinguished. This is an entirely reasonable question, one that we readers would like to see elucidated. The stranger answers that the issue is too complicated to explain. He says only that when there is a class of anything, it must necessarily be a part of that of which it is said to be a class but not every part is a class. This does not tell young Socrates or us what we want to know.

Young Socrates is chastened by the stranger's scolding. When the stranger warns him to guard against his methodological mistake, he asks how. The stranger answers that they can guard against it by not dividing the whole *genos* of *zôa*. Young Socrates agrees that there is no need for that. It is ironic that the stranger already had committed this "error." It was he who declared that all rulers issue commands for the sake of some genesis, that there could be genesis of lifeless and living things, that *epitaktikê* gave orders to living things, and that the genesis and nurture of *zôa* separated into care of individuals and herds. Thus, if the *diaeresis* of the whole *genos* of *zôa* was a mistake, the fault was the stranger's, not the boy's. Also, it is not clear why dividing the whole class is an error. It seems that every step of every *diaeresis* done by the stranger up to here been a division of an entire class. The arbitrariness and opacity of the stranger's methodological rules are increasing, not decreasing. It seems probable that the stranger calls the *diaeresis* of the whole class of *zôa* a mistake at this juncture merely because young Socrates did a division that he did not want yet. He wishes to make a few more points before arriving at man/beast.

Purportedly retrieving his error, the stranger does what he has just forbidden, performing another *diaeresis* of the entire *genos* of *zôa*.[6] He says that

6   Cf. Scodel, *Diaeresis*, 61.

when the earlier error was committed, "all the *zôa* together" (*xumpan to zôon*) already had been divided into tame (*tithasos*) and wild (*agriô*). This is not true unless the stranger is referring to what he did in Sophist. Neither is the tame/wild cut exactly natural in the same sense that male/female and odd/even are. No animals are tame by nature. The young of domesticated animals would be wild if set free. There also is a political implication in the stranger's tame/wild division. If man is one animal among many, and if all animals are naturally wild, man is naturally wild. Theaetetus was mistaken in Sophist. The *politikos* must realize that even when man has been tamed he remains a treacherous herd animal.

Having introduced the tame/wild cut, the stranger repeats that they are seeking a science involving tame creatures in herds. He recommends that they start from the beginning by dividing *koinotrophikên* (common tending). That he equates *koinotrophikên* with the tending of animals is evident from the facts that he just referred to the part of *gnostikê* that gives commands as *tou zôotrophikou genous, agelaiôv mên zôôn* (263e), "the animal tending class, herd animals." He also continues to offer animal examples. One wonders what criteria he will use to divide tame herds with rationality out of the picture.

The stranger begins his answer to this question by bringing up the topics of "domesticated fish" (*tithaseiais tôn ichthuôn*) and "crane herding" (*geranobôtias*) in far distant countries, places that young Socrates has never visited. We live in a world in which anything is possible and some ancients might have managed to domesticate fish and herd cranes. However, it seems to me that the stranger is pulling young Socrates' leg. The images of domesticated fish and crane herding are so absurd that trying to visualize them provokes laughter. To be sure, it is possible that the Egyptians had farm-raised fish in pens and we know that ornamental goldfish can be conditioned over very long periods to rise to accept food from human hands. However, there is no sense in which these fish are "domesticated," as if one could open their pens to the sea, drive them out to "pasture," and expect ever to see them again. The stranger's foreign fish are no more tame than the salmon and trout in hatcheries that are stocked in our lakes and private ponds. As for cranes, these birds are raised in captivity only with the greatest difficulty. They breed in family groups in marshes. They are too behaviorally determined by instinct to herd. Plato is playing, alerting us, perhaps, to the fact that what is coming will be ridiculous.

The stranger tells young Socrates that he has mentioned the fish and the cranes because the nurture of herds partly has to do with creatures that live in water and partly with creatures that live on land. He asks the boy to agree to the division of *koinotrophikên*, the science of common nurturing, into water-nurturing (*hugrotrophikon*) and dry land-nurturing (*xêrotrophikon*). Young Socrates consents. The stranger seems to be repeating the error of his hunting *diaeresis*, in which he omitted the hunting of flying creatures. However, he can be excused on this occasion, for it is hard to imagine herding birds that travel mostly by air. Kingship, he goes on to say, clearly falls under the heading land-herding.

The "dry land nurturing of herd nurturing" is the next thing that the stranger proposes to cut. He suggests a division of "winged" (*ptênô*) and "footed," or "walking" (*pezô*). He adds that even the most irrational (*aphron-estaton*) would suppose that statesmanship must be sought on the "walking" side. This makes it necessary to divide "commanding by land" in half, "like an even number."

FIGURE 10: SCIENCE (STATESMAN I)

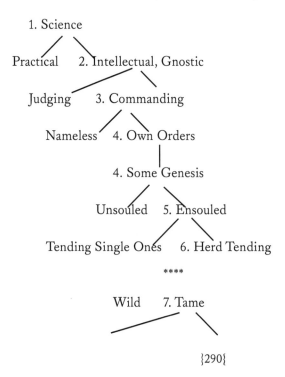

1. Science

Practical   2. Intellectual, Gnostic

Judging   3. Commanding

Nameless   4. Own Orders

4. Some Genesis

Unsouled   5. Ensouled

Tending Single Ones   6. Herd Tending

****

Wild   7. Tame

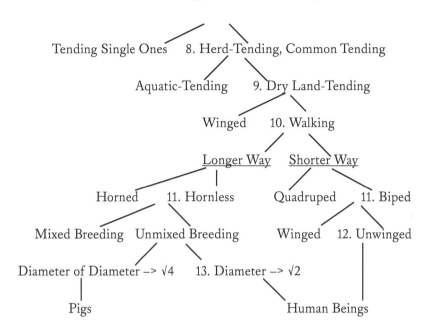

TABLE 10: SCIENCE (GREEK)

1. *Epistêmê –> Praktikên, Gnôstikên*
2. *Gnôstikên –> Kritikê, Epitaktikê*
3. *Epitaktikê –>* Nameless, *Autepitaktikê (geneseôs tinos)*
4. *Autepitaktikê –> Apsyche, Empsycha*
5. *Empsycha –> Monotrophon or Idiotrophon, Agelaiotrophikên*
6. *Agelaiotrophiken* **** *Agriô, Tithasô*
7. *Tithasô –> Idiotrophon, Agelaiotrophikên or Koinotrophikên*
8. *Agelaiotrophikên or Koinotrophikên –> Hugotrophikên, Xêrotrophikon*
9. *Xêrotrophikon –> Ptêno, Pezô*
10. *Pezô –>* Longer Way, Shorter Way

<u>Longer Way</u>

10. *Pezô –> Kerasphoron, Akerôn*
11. *Akerôn –> Koinogenous, Idiogenous*
12. *Idiogenous –> Diametrou Diametrô, Diametrô*
13. *Diametrô –>* Famous Joke, Pigs and Irrational Human Beings, Swine-herd and Statesman

Shorter Way

10. *Pezô –> Tetrapoun, Dipodi*
11. *Dipodi –> Pterophuei, Psilô*
12. *Psilô –>* Human Beings as Featherless Bipeds, Ruled by Statesman

Summary: *Epistêmê, Gnôstikê, Epitaktikon, Autepitaktikon, Zôotrophikê, Agelaiotrophikon, Pezonomikon, Akeratou,* three-fold division into *Epistêmê, Nomeutikon, Genosios Amiktou, Anthrôponomikon, Basilikon kai Politikon*

This is where things get comical. The stranger says that he sees two paths leading to their destination, one shorter and one longer. The former splits a relatively smaller part from a larger. This not only violates the rule that the stranger has just announced about cutting through middles but also directly contradicts his demand to divide the category of land-commanding in half "like an even number." Either the stranger knows this and is poking fun at the ridiculous nature of his argument or Plato is having fun making the stranger ludicrous. Young Socrates is oblivious to the absurdities. The longer way will go through a middle. The stranger advises the boy that they can take whichever path they wish, thus indicating again that the order of steps in a *diaeresis* depends on preferences. Young Socrates wants to take both paths. The stranger replies that both cannot be taken at the same time but suggests taking them consecutively, starting with the longer.

The stranger next asserts that tame walkers in herds divide "by nature" in two. This occurs by virtue of genesis of the horned and hornless. This *diaeresis* is as much or more a cut through an A/not-A center as it is a natural one. As Scodel observes, it also is arbitrary, for the stranger could have chosen many such middles.[7] Some would refer to natural phenomenal traits, such as fur/no-fur, wool/no-wool, tusks/no-tusks, and feathers/no feathers. Others would involve genera such as bovine/nonbovine. The horned/hornless choice might be a hint to the *politikos*. The stranger next maintains that the king clearly commands herds with "docked" or "mutilated" (*kolobon*)

7   Scodel, *Diaeresis*, 63–64n.

horns.[8] There is more than one way in which animals can become "naturally" hornless through "genesis." It might be advisable for the statesman to dehorn his treacherous human herd.

Pressing ahead, the stranger asks young Socrates how the dehorned herd should be torn up. Should they choose cloven-hoofed/not-cloven-hoofed or cross-breeding/non-cross-breeding? The latter option refers to the fact that horses and asses can interbreed but other herd animals cannot. This "fact" is not altogether true, for we know that dogs, which are pack animals by nature, can interbreed with wolves. Perhaps this is why the stranger soon denies that dogs are herd animals. His point depends on what dogs become when their natures have been repressed by domestication. The stranger is generating ideas in his student's mind about the relationship between breeding and taming. The interbreeding of horses and donkeys does not happen in the wild: it is engineered in domestic contexts. Although the stranger will assign the human herd to the non-interbreeding half of his next *diaeresis*, he will reverse himself later on when he discusses the interbreeding of people who differ in type by nature. Having sounded this theme here with a few notes, the stranger drops it and combines his two *diaereseis* into one: cloven-hoofed-interbreeding/non-cloven-hoofed-non-interbreeding. The statesman will govern the "privately breeding," which must be divided next.

The longer path is almost finished. The stranger says that there are only two species left to consider. Geometry shows the way. The division of unmixed breeding should be by the diameter and the diameter of the diameter. Rosen explains this well.[9] "Diameter" is "square root." Four-footed animals are compared with the square root of four and two-footed animals are likened to the square root of two, for the quadrupeds display two "feet" on each side of the "diameter" and the bipeds have one "foot" on each side of it. We are not yet told which quadrupeds the stranger envisages but he specifies that human beings are his bipeds. Everyone notices that equating man with the square root of two makes him irrational. The identity of the quadrupeds is established with what the stranger states would be a famous joke. The human race is joined by lot and runs along with the "noblest"

8   Rosen, *Plato's "Statesman,"* 33.
9   Rosen, *Plato's "Statesman,"* 34.

(best born) and laziest race. Young Socrates gets it and observes that the result is queer. The stranger replies that it is reasonable (*eikos*) for the slowest (*hustata*) to arrive last. Paul Shorey's note on the humor has convinced most scholars that the stranger is referring to the pig.[10] This conclusion is reinforced by the fact that the word for "slowest," *hustata*, appears to be a pun on *hus* (pig or boar), as if *hustata* were a superlative adjective meaning "most pig-like." For the stranger, the consequence is that the king appears "more laughable" running with his herd beside the man best trained for the lazy life (the swineherd). Probably, when the stranger scolded young Socrates for jumping too quickly to the man/beast division, he wanted to postpone that cut in order to depict man as an irrational cousin of the pig. The stranger observes that this is another instance of *diaeresis* paying no more heed to the dignified than the undignified.

Now the stranger negotiates the shorter way with a brief monologue. He asserts that they should have promptly divided walkers into biped and quadruped and biped into featherless and feathered. This makes "feathered" or "winged" appear as a lower subdivision of the rejected left-hand half of the *diaeresis* of dry land-tending into winged and walking. When this shorter way is added to the longer, we also get the result that man is an irrational featherless biped who is cousin to the pig. However, the statesmanlike, kingly (*politikon kai basilikon*) person is promoted. No longer simply laughable as a competitor of the swineherd (which he does not cease to be), he is to be recognized as a possessor of the science of the herding of human beings (*anthrôponomikês*), considered as a kind of charioteer, and handed the reins of the polis. This charioteer image has arrived from nowhere in the reasoning to end the *diaeresis* chain. However, readers of Phaedrus know from whence the image has come.[11] We must imagine that, in the prehistory of the drama, the stranger has met Phaedrus. He has heard about Socrates' myth of the soul as a team of horses harnessed to a chariot driven by the charioteer *nous* (reason). As a possessor of the science, the *politikos* has become more rational than the members of the herd whose nature he shares.

Young Socrates congratulates the stranger for having clarified the argument beautifully, as if he had paid him a debt with the methodological

---

10   Paul Shorey, "A Lost Platonic Joke," *Classical Philology* (1917), 308–10.
11   Scodel's insight, as usual, *Diaeresis*, 67.

digression thrown in as interest. The stranger decides that it is time to summarize the *diaeresis*. He declares that it went as follows: *epistêmê* (science), *gnöstikê* (intellectual science); *epitaktikê* (ordering); *autepitaktikê* (issuing own orders); *zôotrophikê* (animal-nurturing), *agelaiotrophikê* (herd-nurturing); *pezonomikon* (walking animal-herding); the *technê* of rearing or feeding (*threptikê*) the hornless (*akeratou*); a necessarily triple name, *epistêmê* (science), of *nomeutikê* (herding) of *geneseôs amiktou* (unmixed breeders); and *anthroponomikon* (herding human beings). This is what was sought, the kingly *technê* (*basilikon*) and statesmanship (*politikon*).

It is hardly necessary to mention that the *diaeresis* did not go that way. Animal-nurturing has replaced ensouled. The wild/tame, single animal/many animal, and aquatic-tending/dry land-tending divisions have been omitted. The shorter way has disappeared. The geometric joke has been omitted from the longer way. The *diaeresis* said nothing about the necessary triple name.

Now that it has been presented in full, the stranger's *diaeresis* of science requires comment. The needed analysis will look at the *diaeresis* as a whole and at its individual steps.

Examination of the *diaeresis* as a whole reveals that the logical sloppiness that pervaded the stranger's reasoning in Sophist has extended into the present dialogue. The two appearances of "winged" in the rejected halves of step 9 and step 11 of the shorter way and the failure of the summary to correspond to the course of the *diaeresis* are glaring examples. Even more jarring are the stranger's ad hoc announcements of methodological rules that he himself has been breaking all along and that he promptly violates again. This leaves one wondering what the rules truly are and whether the stranger cares about them. I am thinking here especially of the rules against thin cuts and against dividing whole categories.

As for the individual steps, most commentators agree that the *diaeresis* went astray at the very beginning. The stranger should have divided science into three parts, not two. The correct classes would have been "purely intellectual," "intellectual-productive," and "practical." Then the architect and the *politikos*, who do not precisely belong in either the purely intellectual or practical categories, could have found their proper homes in the intellectual-productive sector. This is what essentially happens anyway as the dialogue proceeds but the development occurs sub rosa.

At step six, when young Socrates tries to divide herd animals into beasts and men and the stranger scolds him, claiming that thin cuts are unsafe and that one should divide through middles because this is more likely to lead to Ideas, the reason why this benefit will be achieved is never explained. Mitchell Miller and Kenneth Sayre attempt to fill this lacuna, both by appealing to the male/female and odd/even examples. Miller declares that divisions through middles yield Ideas because: "Rather than a positive term and its indeterminate contradictory ('men' and 'not men'), they are reciprocally defining contraries. Thus each both excludes the other and yet is a definite, positive character in itself."[12] In a similar vein, Sayre asserts that: "When the first class posited (e.g., humankind) is divided into two independently characterized subclasses, a consequence is that each subclass (e.g., male) can be divided further in terms not dependent for their meaning on the identity of the other subclass (e.g., female)." This, Sayre contends, "opens up the possibility that the subclasses involved correspond to Forms," which are "entities that are what they are in and by themselves."[13] These apologies would be convincing if the stranger had developed these kinds of subclasses exclusively hitherto in Sophist and Politician, which he did not do, and if he also were to develop them exclusively throughout the remainder of this dialogue. He will not do that either. We soon come to divisions such as aquatic/land, flying/walking and horned/hornless, which do not satisfy Miller's and Sayre's conditions. The stranger has not overcome his tendency to define middles variously as the centers of "A/not A" and "equality of weights," with this new ad hoc focus on reciprocally defining contraries a third variant in the mix.

Starting with the movement from steps five to six and extending to the end of the *diaeresis*, the stranger gratuitously equates statesmanship with the tending of animal herds. One wonders what justification he has for doing this. Mitchell Miller argues that the stranger is referring in the first instance to the Homeric image of a king as "the shepherd of the people." What is envisaged is "a ruler who was 'father' and 'provider' to his subjects." Thus, the image originally generated the same kinds of warm feelings that Christians experience when they are informed that Jesus is

12   Miller, *The Philosopher in Plato's "Statesman,"* 21.
13   Kenneth M. Sayre, *Metaphysics and Method in Plato's "Statesman,"* 221.

the Good Shepherd and they are his sheep. Miller argues further that between Homer and Plato the image broke down, degenerating into the Thrasymachean claim that rulers are shepherds who strive only to fleece their sheep. Accordingly, the Eleatic stranger starts by making the statesman a herdsman because he intends to dispense with the metaphor later and replace it with something better.[14] We shall have to wait to see whether this occurs. Meanwhile, it is somewhat difficult to reconcile the stranger's image of the ruler as herdsman with that of the Good Shepherd because the latter does not go on to describe human beings as irrational featherless bipeds who are cousins of the pig. This image both misses and demeans the human essence.

Apologists for the stranger sometimes admit to these defects of the science *diaeresis*. They defend the stranger, however, by maintaining that our dialogue is deliberately structured as a self-correcting exercise, such that we must read to the end to learn what the stranger actually teaches. The early errors and later corrections are parts of a pedagogical strategy meant to overcome young Socrates' original deficiencies. So, we must wait to see whether both the idea of the herdsman of irrational, piggish, featherless bipeds and the mistakes of the science *diaeresis* will be surmounted. For now, one thing can be said certainly on the basis of a quick glance ahead. The troubling view of human nature will appear in a wholly new light in the next portion of the stranger's argument. Ultimately the stranger's opinion might not change but it definitely will be complicated.

When young Socrates declares himself satisfied with the argument, the stranger replies by suggesting that it is incomplete. It certainly is that. To be told that statesmanship is a science of tending irrational herd animals is to be told practically nothing about the content of the science. It also is a very unpolitical definition: We learn nothing about the aims and methods of the *politikos*. This is not yet to repudiate what the stranger has said as untrue. It is to indicate that something must be added. The boy wonders what that could be. The stranger says that we have found that there are many arts of herding, one of them being *politikê*, the *technê* of care (*epimeleia*) for one particular sort of herd. (The term *epimeleia* [care] did not appear in the summary of the *diaeresis* of *epistêmê*. It is, or is masquerading as, a synonym for the *trophikê* [nurturing] nouns that the stranger has been using.) Continuing, the stranger states that the argument defined *politikê* as the science of nurturing human beings in common (*anthrôpôn koinotrophikên*). But the king differs from other herdsmen. To see this, we must inquire whether anyone claims to be a fellow nurturer (*xuntrophos*) of his herd. Merchants, farmers, all grain workers, gymnastic trainers, and doctors—all ministers to bodily needs—immediately insist that they share in the nurturing care of human kind and even care for the rulers themselves. No one competes with the neatherd in this fashion. A herdsman is all things to his herd: physician, matchmaker, midwife, and musician. This is the first mention of music in the dialogue. It has come in connection with animals, not man. Music seems here to have not a spiritual but a physical function, that of soothing agitated organisms. It extends only to the nervous systems that are parts of bodies, not to souls. Thus, if the merchants, herdsmen, and others are fellow caregivers of the *politikos*, he cares only for bodies. The stranger again stands opposed to Socrates, who in his capacity as the only practitioner of the true political *technê* in Athens treats souls.

Our *logos* about the king, says the stranger, cannot be right if we pick him out as the only shepherd (*nomêa*) and nurturer of the human herd. We shall have only a sketch of the king until we separate him from his competitors, so that he stands purified of them. To neglect this work would be shameful. To save our *logos* from shame we must start over again from the beginning and travel by a different road. We must abandon *diaeresis* and engage in play, inserting a large part of a great myth into our discussion. After that we can return to *diaeresis*. I shall summarize the myth as it is presented and then go back through it again in an attempt to understand it.

The stranger declares that of the stories told by the ancients, many actually happened and will occur again, especially the one about the heavenly sign that appeared in connection with the conflict between Atreus and Thyestes. Young Socrates thinks that the stranger is referring to the sign of the golden lamb. The stranger corrects him. He means the account of the alteration of the courses of the sun and the other heavenly bodies. He also invokes the tales of the reign of Cronus and the birth of the ancients from the earth rather than from each other. All these myths, says the stranger, have their source in the same event, knowledge of which has been lost through the ages so that the tales have survived only as fragments. No one has ever related the event that unifies the pieces. The stranger will tell it for the first time now with a view toward explicating the king.

It will be helpful to become acquainted with the myths cited by the stranger. The first is a long story. Pelops was cut to pieces by his father Tantalus and served to the Olympians in a stew. This was the deed for which Tantalus was punished. Zeus put Pelops back together so beautifully that Poseidon fell in love with him and made him his catamite. Pelops also succeeded Tantalus as king of Paphlagonia. However, he was expelled by barbarians and migrated to the region of Elis, there desiring to marry Hippodameia, the daughter of King Oenomaus. The monarch did not want Hippodameia to marry, so he required her suitors to race chariots against his own invincible team driven by his loyal charioteer Myrtilus. A suitor who won the race could marry the maiden but a loser had to die. Pelops acquired a golden, winged chariot from Poseidon, won his bride, killed Myrtilus for ravaging her, succeeded Oenomaus as king, and subjugated the area now known as the Peloponnese. Atreus and Thyestes were two of his sons. Chrysippus was their brother. He was in line for the throne but was killed in an affair involving his abduction for use as a catamite. Atreus and Thyestes were suspected of complicity in this murder so they migrated to Mycenae. When the king of Mycenae was killed in battle, the city's nobles decided to choose either Atreus or Thyestes as their new sovereign. Hermes, angry about the slaying of Myrtilus, placed a golden lamb in the flocks of Pelops, which were held jointly by Atreus and Thyestes. Hermes wanted to stir up conflict in this way and his plan worked. The golden lamb belonged to Atreus by right of primogeniture but Thyestes seduced Atreus's wife, obtained the lamb, displayed it as proof of his preferability, and was declared king. However, Zeus favored Atreus. He reversed the course of the sun and stars as testimony to his choice and then switched them back when Thyestes abdicated in favor of Atreus.

In one old tale about Cronus, he was the Titan son of Uranus (Heaven) and Earth. Uranus threw the Cyclops into Tartarus. Earth urged the Titans to avenge this affront. Cronus castrated Uranus and became king. He married his Titan sister Rhea and fathered five of the gods who later became Olympians. Because there was a prophecy that Cronus would be dethroned by one of his children, he devoured the five as they were born. Upon next giving birth to Zeus, Rhea hid him. When he had grown, he approached his father disguised as a cup bearer and gave him an emetic. Cronus regurgitated his children, who with Zeus dethroned him and banished the Titans. Zeus became king.

Another account of the reign of Cronus is offered by Hesiod, in his song of the five ages of man. The stranger explicitly adapts this story to his own tale at 271c–d. Hesiod reports that first the immortals who dwell on Olympus made a golden race of men who lived when Cronus reigned in heaven. This is confusing, for the traditional myth that I just related has the Olympians lodged in the belly of Cronus during his reign, where they could not have created the golden race. Greek traditions varied. At any rate, Hesiod's golden people lived like gods, without toil, grief, and old age. They feasted on the fruits of the earth that sprang readily to hand. They dwelt in peace, rich in flocks and blessed by the gods. When they died, it was as if they had fallen asleep.

The story of the earth-born has it that the Athenians were autochthonous, having sprung up out of the soil of Attica. Their earth-born origin was their title to the land and explained why they always had inhabited it.

In the traditional Atreus-Thyestes myth, it was Zeus who changed the directions in which the heavenly bodies rose and set. The stranger does not mention Zeus in this connection, saying ambiguously that the miracle was performed by "the god" (*ho theos*). He also omits the account of Zeus's restoration of the original arrangement upon the abdication of Thyestes. In his version, the god's reversal of that order has endured, becoming our own order. He has taken liberties with the ancient myth, correcting it in keeping with his insight that permits him to relate the real story for the first time.

In this truer myth, "the god" (*ho theos*) himself accompanies *to pan* (the all, the universe) as a guide, helping it to revolve in a circle. However, when the cycles (*periodi*) have reached the measure (*metron*) of the time allotted to him, he lets it go. Then *to pan* turns of its own accord (*automaton*) in the opposite direction, for it is a *zôon*, a living animal endowed with wisdom or prudence (*phronêsin*) by the one who put it together (*sunarmosantos*) in the beginning. Notice that whereas the stranger first omitted Zeus and said that "the god" changed the courses of the sun and stars, he now has declared that the universe did this by itself. He adds that this occurred by a necessity of its nature (*ex anagkês emphuton*).

This innate necessity is explained by the fact that to remain always in the same condition and the same belongs only to the most divine things of all and body does not fall into this class. The stranger does not say what the most divine things are and it would be rash to assume anything about the matter.[15] What we call heaven and the cosmos has received many blessed things from the progenitor (*gennêsantos*) but it also partakes of body. Therefore it cannot be completely free from change. However, it moves to the best of its ability in the same place in the same way with a single motion and, consequently, it rotates in the reverse direction, this being the smallest change from its previous course. Now, to turn itself by itself forever is impossible except for that which guides all moving things (*tôn kinoumenôn au pantôn hêgoumenô*). That this should turn itself in one direction and then in another is contrary to divine law (*themis*). Therefore we must not say that the cosmos turns itself always or that it is turned by god (*hupo theou*) in opposite directions or that two gods opposing each other turn it (which also would be contrary to the nature of divinity). The only possibility is that sometimes it is guided by a divine cause (*theias aitias*), acquiring the power of living again and receiving renewed immortality from its demiurge (*dêmiourgou*) and at other times is left to its own motion, moving in the reverse direction through myriads of periods because it is extremely large, evenly balanced, and turns on the smallest pivot.

Young Socrates replies that all this appears very likely or reasonable (*eikotôs*). This gives the stranger an opportunity to connect the cosmology just related with the myths that he has cited. The reversal of the direction of the rotation of the cosmos, he declares, was responsible for all the events recorded in the tales. The reversal is the greatest and most complete change possible in the heavens. Accordingly, we must believe that it produced the greatest changes in those who dwell in the heavens. There was a great destruction of animals and only a small part of the human race survived. In keeping with Thomas Jefferson's skepticism about a biblical story, we marvel that every living thing was not thrown off the planet when the cosmos changed directions but that is a quibble. We accept that a remnant of humanity survived.

15   Some suppose that the stranger is referring to the Forms. There is no evidence for this.

This group immediately had a strange experience. Every creature first stopped aging and then started growing younger. Old graybeards descended through all the stages of their previous maturation until they became like newborn babes both in soul and body. (This appears to imply that knowledge could not be acquired and that memories, if they were formed at all, were lost with the passage of time.) Finally the creatures shriveled up and disappeared. The bodies of those who perished by violence also shrunk rapidly and vanished. Replying to a query from young Socrates, the stranger adds that our present mode of reproduction did not exist during that epoch. Animals and people grew out of the earth, thus giving rise to the stories of the earthborn race which were first transmitted to us by the survivors of the great calamity. The creatures that grew younger and ultimately disappeared fell into the earth like seeds and then sprouted up as the oldsters that grew younger until they vanished again. They all went through a number of such cycles except for a few whom god (*theos*) removed to another fate. (Who? Philosophers?)

Next young Socrates asks in which of the periods the reign of Cronus occurred, ours or the other. His question is inspired by the realization that both eras begin with changes in the course of the stars and the sun. He might be wondering how there could have been a golden age after the catastrophic destructions that initiated each period. The stranger replies that the reign of Cronus fell not in our period but the other. For then in the beginning the god (*ho theos*) took care of the whole revolution. Further, all the parts of the cosmos were divided among gods who ruled over them. The animals were distributed by kind and herd (*genê kai agelas*) among daimons acting as divine shepherds. No creature was wild, none ate each other, and there was neither war nor strife among them. God (*theos*) himself presided over them just as man, being of a more divine nature than the lower animals, now tends them. There were no cities, wives, or children for they all were born out of the earth with no memories of their previous lives. They ate fruits that sprang to hand from the earth without benefit of agriculture. They lived in the open air, needing neither clothing nor bedding, for the climate was mild and they could sleep on grass that served as soft couches. That was life in the age of Cronus, which differed from the lives that we know from experience in our period, which is said to be the age of Zeus. One can see how the god's care could have made for a golden age immediately after a great calamity.

The stranger asks young Socrates whether he can say which kind of human life was more blessed or happier (*eudaimonesteron*). He cannot. This is somewhat surprising, given that life in the age of Cronus appears to have been paradisiacal. Perhaps he is intelligent enough to wonder how reverse aging affected consciousness in the alternate human types of that era. The stranger offers to answer in the boy's stead. He says that if the foster children of Cronus, who had much leisure and the ability to converse not only with each other but with the beasts, made use of their opportunities with a view toward philosophy, talking with the others in quest of greater wisdom (*phronêseôs*), the people of those times would have been immeasurably happier than those of our own epoch. On the other hand, if those people merely sated themselves with food and drink and told stories about themselves such as those we tell now, it would be easy to decide the matter too. He breaks off there, saying that we have no information about the desires of those individuals with regard to knowledge and the use of speech.

Now it is time, says the stranger, to tell the reason for relating his story of the cycles and the age of Cronus. His first step in this direction is to spin a further tale about the transition to our period. He remarks that when the time of things was finished and the hour for change had come, and when the earthborn race had been used up, each soul having fallen into the ground and having been reborn the number of times prescribed for it, then the helmsman (*kubernêtês*) of the all let go of the tiller and withdrew to his observation post. Then the allotted and naturally innate desire of the cosmos altered its direction. All the gods who shared in the rule of the great daimon (*megista daimon*) abandoned their posts too. As the beginning and the end rushed in opposite directions, a massive earthquake and great destruction of living creatures occurred. After a time, things settled down and the world went on its accustomed course, caring for and ruling all within it, practicing and remembering the teachings of its demiurge and father (*dêmiourgou kai patros*). At first it did this more accurately and later more carelessly. The reason for the decline in care is that the all has matter in its composition, which of old was marked by great disorder before the present cosmos came to be. The world has received all fine things from its synthesizer (*synthetos*) but from its previous condition it has received everything bad and unjust under the heavens, transmitting them to the animals. As long as the cosmos nurtured the animals under the guidance of the helmsman (*kubernêtês*) it produced little evil and much good but when it grew forgetful in the course of time its original condition of disharmony eventually prevailed. When this occurred, the god who made the order of the cosmos (*theos ho kosmêsas auton*) feared that it might sink in the boundless sea of diversity. Therefore he took his place at the rudders, reordered the world and made it immortal and ageless.

When the transition to our period took place, people began to age, die, and reproduce as they do now. Just as the cosmos was autarchic, its parts had to govern and nourish themselves. Human beings were deprived of the daimon who had cared for them. They were ravaged by the beasts that had grown wild. They lacked the arts. Food no longer was offered to them gratis by nature so they could not provide for themselves. The gods intervened (once), Prometheus giving them fire, Hephaestus and Athena gave them the arts, and other gods gave them seeds and plants. From these things arose all that constitutes human life, for divine care had failed them and they had to take care of themselves, like the whole cosmos which they imitate and follow forever.

With this, the stranger says that his tale is finished and that they must use it to perceive the great error they made in the science *diaeresis*. Actually there were two mistakes, one greater and one smaller. The greater was that when they inquired about the king and statesman of the present cycle, they told of the shepherd of the opposite cycle, who was a god, not a mortal. A description of the smaller error can be left for later.

To understand the myth, it will be necessary to note one or two anomalies, clear up a few questions, and then comment on its important implications. One anomaly is that the stranger said at 269a that the unnamed god changed the rotation of the sun and stars to the present scheme in response to the quarrel between Atreus and Thyestes. This would place the dispute of the brothers in the cycle opposite to ours. However, the stranger also has stated at 271e–72a that strife, war, polities, and families did not exist in that epoch. Another anomaly is that the stranger remarked at 273a–b that after the dust had settled from the transition to our period, the cosmos governed itself and its creatures in an orderly way, caring for all within because it remembered the teachings of its demiurge and father. However, at 274a–b, he has declared that the human race was immediately in trouble, being ravaged by wild beasts and lacking the art to feed themselves. The

care that the cosmos lavished on its people must not have been very effica-
cious. It probably consisted only in its provision of the possibility that people could figure out how to defend and nurture themselves once the gods
had given them the gifts of fire, the arts, and seeds and plants, which they
evidently were incapable of acquiring by themselves. The first anomaly is
typical of the stranger: it shows that he is not particular about consistency
of detail as long as he can get his main points across. The second looks like
a deliberate contradiction that is more meaningful, as we shall see.

An issue that claims the reader's attention immediately concerns the
stranger's authority. If no one has ever told his myth before, how does he
know how his story goes? The only possible answer is that he just knows;
he is claiming a valid insight into reality that no one else has ever had.

A question that piques everybody's curiosity concerns the names "the
god," "the one who put [the all] together," "the progenitor," "the divine cause,"
"the demiurge," "the great daimon," "the synthesizer," "the one who guides
all moving things," and "the helmsman (or pilot)." Do the names refer to one
god or many? This does not become clear until the end of the tale. At 273d–
e, the stranger asserts that the god who ordered the cosmos, who surely is
the demiurge, resumes his place as the helmsman, who clearly is the god who
goes with the cosmos as it follows its circular course. The names all refer to
one divinity. Who is that god? He definitely is not Zeus. The only mention
of the Olympian king comes at 272b, when the stranger declares that our
present cycle "is said to be" the age of Zeus. He probably is not Cronus either.
Cronus was never a demiurge. The fact that the men of the reversed cycle
were his "foster children" means that they were somebody else's children
whom he neither created nor supplied with natures. Nowhere is it said that
Cronus reigns in the stranger's age of Cronus. The terms "age of Zeus" and
"age of Cronus" are pieties that the stranger utters to cloak himself in a veneer
of orthodoxy. The stranger's demiurge deity is not a traditional Greek god.

I return to another issue raised by the stranger himself. Were the alternate human beings of the reversed cycle inclined to philosophy or merely de-
sirous of gossip and stories? At 274d–275a, the stranger provides a clue when
he says that our science *diaeresis* erred by speaking about the god who governed the previous epoch rather than the human ruler of our time. If this is
so, the *diaeresis* also must have been speaking of the alternate people of the
other time when it concluded that the members of the god's herd were

irrational featherless bipeds who were cousins of the pig. Such men would have been incapable of philosophy. Their conversations with the animals might have consisted in mutually understood barks and grunts. Only in our age is there is a chance for human happiness and apparently only philosophers are able to seize it. This raises the question of whether the great mass of human beings of our time remain irrational featherless biped cousins of the pig.

The myth seems to have implications for cosmology, theology, and anthropology that the stranger intends to be true simply, not merely true for one of his cycles or the other.

Cosmology: In the beginning there was a boundless sea of diversity. Various fluctuating configurations of matter were the dominant elements and they were inherently resistant to order. A demiurge either stood to one side or swam in the sea. This demiurge had the power to impose order on the material chaos but he could not impose it permanently. He could not overcome the natural limits on the survival of order, for the disordering powers of matter are always ultimately stronger than his ability to order. All things made of matter irresistibly tend to disorder, striving to return to the sea of diversity. However, when all seems lost, the demiurge can summon up its strength and temporarily impose order again, so that a weaker ordering force is always in tension with a stronger disordering force. Thus the mythical oscillations of the cosmos, which reappear in our experience as real but lesser oscillations. Also, the superiority of the disordering powers of matter to those of the ordering demiurge means that the all is always more hostile than helpful to human beings. If the weaker ordering force were not always combating the stronger disordering force, somewhat countering the depredations of a cosmos that is unfriendly on balance, we would have been wiped out long since.

Theology. The only god who matters to the stranger can struggle with the material forces of disorder but is always weaker than they. This god is not a member of any Greek pantheon and is never present to our world, except when he blasts it at the ends of cycles. Ironically, Zeus and the other Olympians are also absent from our cosmos during the so-called age of Zeus. A few of them were present once and once only, near the beginning of human time. They intervened in our affairs with gifts that helped us avoid annihilation, aid that has not been supplemented since. All gods in our times are essentially irrelevant to us, for they have left us to fend for ourselves. There is no point to sacrificing or praying in hopes of securing divine help.

Anthropology. The alternate human beings of the mythical reversed world were irrational featherless biped cousins of the pig. It is not yet clear whether the stranger intends to assign that same status to the great mass of human beings of our real time who are incapable of philosophy. In any case, human beings are weak and often insufficiently intelligent creatures who must rely on the arts to defend themselves against the depredations of nature and their fellow creatures. They also must rely on their own efforts, for they are alone in the universe. They are intrinsically unjust and this impedes such striving.

I think that these cosmological, theological, and anthropological doctrines are the lessons that the stranger intended attentive audiences to find in his myth. They are asserted gratuitously and indirectly. We are never told why we should accept them. Their teachings about gods and men are un-Socratic. The theological doctrines are also inconsistent with the Athenian Stranger's retort to Protagoras that god is the measure. We are left in *aporia*, wondering how we might learn the truth of these matters.

As mentioned above, the stranger says at 274e–75a that his science *diaeresis* made two errors, one great and one small. We have covered the great mistake. The small one consisted in a failure to tell how the human statesman rules. Thus, the *diaeresis* was incomplete. That all is true. As he concludes his myth, the stranger also repeats that he narrated it in order to demonstrate that, with regard to herd-tending (*agelaiotrophias*), everyone disputes the statesman's claim to be solely in charge of human care (*epimeleian*). He also told the story with a view toward distinguishing the statesman from his competitors. As far as I can tell, neither of those aims has been realized. Perhaps the objectives will be achieved as the stranger draws further implications from his story. It is time to follow his reasoning into a new chapter.

Before we go there, let us recall the drama of the *Untergang* of Socrates-Odysseus. This story has not been much in evidence in the stranger's science *diaeresis* and his myth. However, as we shall see in the next chapter, these un-Socratic exercises have been laying the groundwork for an even more deadly attack on Socrates-Odysseus by the Polyphemus-Antinous-Stranger than was undertaken in Sophist.

7

SOCRATES IS CONVICTED
BY A JURY OF YOUNG CHILDREN

The stranger sets out to correct the errors that he has identified in his science *diaeresis*, namely, its confusion of the human *politikos* of our real time with the divine ruler of the human herd in the mythical reversed cosmos and its failure to tell the manner of the human statesman's governance. We must remedy the latter, smaller mistake by giving a full description of how the human *politikos* rules. As for the former, larger error, we must rectify it not only by doing the obvious thing, distinguishing the human statesman from the god, but also by keeping our former promise to differentiate him from the crowd of people like farmers and physicians who compete with him for the title of herd-tender (*agelaiotrophias*) or for possession of the role of care-giving tender of men (*tês anthrōpinês epimeleian exonta trophês*).

The distinction between the human statesman and the god may not be as absolute as we expected. The stranger says that the form (*schêma*) of the divine herdsman (*nomeōs*) is greater than that of the king, that *politikoi* today are by nature "much more like" those whom they rule, and that human statesmen share "much more nearly" their subjects' breeding and education. To be "much more like" and to "more nearly share" is not to be "entirely like" or to "entirely share." The stranger's formulas leave room for the chance that some real king will be "more divine" than his subjects in the same way that man excels animals, enjoying a much greater intelligence and education. A *politikos* would be a god to other men if he had the divine science. If that does not suffice to raise eyebrows, the stranger then asserts that today's statesmen must be sought whether their natures are like those of the divine shepherd or their subjects. This suggests that there could be a genuinely "divine" human king, a man who knew how to order his society, suppressing the forces of disorder within the limits of the possible.

To distinguish the real *politikos* from his competitors, the stranger suggests a return to an earlier point in his *epistêmê diaeresis* (figure 10, step six), the *technê* of giving one's own orders (*autepitaktikê*) concerning living things (*zōa*) and their common care (*koinê tên epimeleian*) that was herd nurturing (*agelaiotrophikên*). The stranger declares that we made our error around here—he does not say which one but he very well might have both the greater and the lesser in mind—and we missed the statesman, who slipped out of the *diaeresis* unnamed. All herdsmen other than the *politikos* feed or nurture (*trephein*) their herds. Hence, we needed a broader name that encompassed both herdsmen who feed or nurture their animals and those who do not. We should have called the common *technê therapeuein* (providing, caring) or *agelaiokomikên* (herd care) or *epimelêtikên* (caring). This would have yielded a term that did not connote feeding or nurturing, thus allowing for a later division (between steps eight and nine) between herdsmen who do and do not feed or nurture their herds. The name chosen is *agelaiokomikê*.

The next few cuts of the revised *diaeresis* putatively follow those of figure ten. Jumping over step seven to step eight, with the tame/wild distinction of step seven apparently presumed, the stranger decides to replace herd-tending (common tending) with *agelaiokomikên* (herd care). *Agelaiokomikên* is said to be divided as *agelaiotrophikê* was. However, step nine (the distinction between aquatic tending and land-tending) is omitted. Step ten is retained, the division between winged and walking. However, the former step eleven is garbled. The stranger claims that they had distinguished the herds that engage in unmixed breeding from the hornless (omitting the cuts of the shorter way). Actually, mixed breeding had been divided from the unmixed and hornless animals had been separated from the horned. Sloppiness still mars the stranger's *diaereseis*. The stranger says that we can divide *agelaiokomikên* by the same distinctions, evidently meaning that we can follow the remainder of the longer way of his science *diaeresis* down to the diameter and men. (This is a tacit reaffirmation of his opinion that human beings are irrational.) When he gets to men, he declares that no other art than kingship has a stronger claim to the art of caring for the whole human community and ruling all mankind. At first this statement looks imperialistic but it probably means that wherever men are found, kingship has the best claim to rule them.

FIGURE 11: SCIENCE (STATESMAN I), REVISED

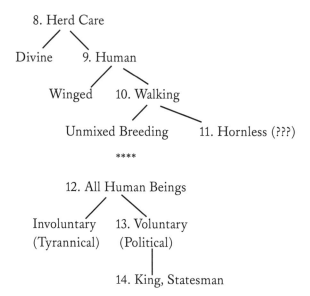

TABLE 11: SCIENCE (GREEK) (STATESMAN I), REVISED

8. *Agelaiokomikên –> Theion, Anthrōpinon*
9. *Anthrōpinon –> Aptêsi, Pezois*
10. *Pezois –> Amiktous, Akeratous*
11. *Amiktous, Akeratous **** Kata Pantōn Anthrōpōn*
12. *Kata Pantōn Anthrōpōn –> Biaiō (Tyrannikên), Hekousiō (Politikên)*
13. *Hekousiō –> Basilea, Politikon*

Perhaps forgetting what he had set out to distinguish from what, the stranger next declares that the change to *agelaiokomikên* embraced both the kingship of the present time and that of the age of Cronus. Reverting to his new step eight, he wants to divide *agelaiokomikên* again. It has divine and human halves. Then, rejoining the path of the longer way at its step fourteen, men, he extends it. The care of human beings must be divided in half: the rule can be either voluntarily accepted by the subjects or compulsory (or violent). Kingship (voluntary) must not be confused with tyranny (compulsory).

Young Socrates assumes again that the search for the statesman is finished. If he is right, we have been taught that the *politikos* is not a deity but a man who practices an art of giving his own orders with the purpose (not of feeding or nurturing but that) of caring for biped, walking, wingless, non-interbreeding, dehorned herds of irrational men who consent voluntarily to being governed by their ruler. Young Socrates is too eager to be finished and insufficiently thoughtful to understand why they are not. The new definition still says nothing about the aims or methods of the statesman's science, a fact of which the stranger is well aware.

The stranger squelches young Socrates' enthusiasm by telling him that their figure of the king is not yet complete. Like sculptors who make additions to their works that are too many and too large, thus impeding progress, they have used too much of their myth because they wanted to advance quickly and they thought that great paradigms (*megala paradeigmata*) were appropriate for the king. Evidently the error here, or at least part of it, was to describe the divine shepherd as the *politikos* of the earthly *polis*. The stranger's self-critique might be a little disingenuous. The divine shepherd might continue in some ways to be a paradigm of the human statesman. Also, I cannot think of any part of the myth that does not help to establish the cosmological, theological, and anthropological backdrops of whatever political theory the stranger will offer. Nevertheless, the stranger insists that their discourse has been too long. Still, it is salvageable. Like a picture of a living being, their product has been a good outline but it needs to be clarified by paints and mixed colors. If it is a good outline, the error has not been too egregious. The stranger adds that it would be more appropriate to portray any living creature with speech and argument than with painting. Young Socrates agrees, perhaps not realizing that this warning was meant for him.

Young Socrates asks the stranger to explain how their account has been inadequate. He is not concerned about whether he will get a *logos* or a painting. The stranger replies that it is hard to explicate any of the "greater" (*meizonōn*) [things?] without using paradigms (*paradeigmasi*), for it would seem that each of us knows everything he knows as if in a dream and then, when he is awake, he knows nothing of it at all. He appears to mean that people (such as young Socrates) think that they know things and might even actually know them in dreamy ways but cannot give a *logos* of them.

His assertion that they will have to resort to paradigms seems to indicate that he will accommodate the limitations of young Socrates by giving him a "painting" that is inferior to a *logos*. Whether this implies that we will get an inaccurate or incomplete picture of the opinions of the stranger is open to question.

When young Socrates asks what all this means, the stranger, somewhat mockingly calling the boy "blessed one," replies that [to explain] paradigm requires another paradigm. He says that when children begin to learn letters—but here the lad interrupts rudely. Perhaps he is offended by the stranger's condescension. The stranger ignores the discourtesy. So, when children begin to acquire knowledge of letters, they can recognize the letters (*stoicheiōn*) easily in short and easy syllables and make true statements about them but, when it comes to other syllables, they err with regard to the same letters and express mistaken opinions about them. The best way to solve this problem is to lead the children first to the syllables the letters of which they recognize and then to set these syllables beside the syllables the letters of which they do not recognize. By comparing the two sets of syllables, one can show the children that the syllables about which they had true opinions and the syllables that they do not recognize have the same natures, so that the children apparently acquire true opinion about the latter syllables too. Eventually, the pupils will be able to identify all letters in all syllables correctly. In this manner, the letters (of the easy syllables?) become paradigms. The stranger next provides a definition of paradigm: a paradigm comes to be when that which is the same in some unconnected thing is rightly compared with the first, so that both together form a "true opinion" (*alêthê doxan*).

Explaining the relevance of this definition to the inquiry into the statesman, the stranger first expands upon his comments about dreaming and waking knowledge. He says that our souls experience the same uncertainty about the elements of all things as the children did about letters. In some cases the souls enjoy true opinion about easy combinations of the elements but in other cases they are at sea when these same arrangements are encountered in difficult "syllables." The analogy between letters and the constituents of existential situations is not defended. It may not be sound. It is doubtful that human affairs exhibit "elements" that have the same eternal stability as letters and numbers, at least not more than a few. If they do, the sameness that is said to hold between any two existential elements could not be identity, as in the case of letters. More likely, it is metaphorical and, hence, constructed by the observer. At any rate, for the stranger the thing to do is to take a paradigm of a lesser thing and transfer it to the great reality of the king, showing that the lesser and greater things are the same. Then our dream knowledge will become waking.

There are a few ambiguities in the stranger's presentation that should be noted. First, it is not clear what situation the stranger envisages in his grammar school paradigm of paradigm. Is a child being commanded to spell "cat" and "catastrophic" and stumbling over the latter because of inability to recognize the similarity of the shapes of the "cat" syllables? Or is the child staring at writing and proving incapable of identifying the "cat" in "catastrophic" because the other letters in the word have confused him or her? The two cases differ. The spelling bee requires the child to put letters together. The reading test requires the child to pull syllables and their letters apart from the other letters. On the child's part, the spelling bee involves movement from a known to an unknown while the reading test entails movement from a known to another known that is not perceived as known. On the teacher's part, both cases involve movement from one well known thing to another well-known thing. The stranger is claiming that the teacher and he himself are in waking states. That is, he is presenting himself as wise.

Second, the stranger cited his myth as a possible paradigm of the king. This is a case of movement from a greater to a lesser. Can paradigm move both ways? If so, the person utilizing paradigm again knows the essence of what he wants to teach. He is wise.

Third, what the stranger has claimed for paradigm is the ability to produce true opinion, not knowledge (278c). An opinion cannot be pronounced true unless somebody knows the truth. The stranger himself points out that no one could start with a false opinion and arrive at any truth at all. So, paradigm must be an instrument that the wise use to lead the ignorant to true opinion. That being so, how does the stranger know the truth? Lacking this information, we are in *aporia*.

It is time for the stranger to choose a lesser thing unconnected with statesmanship which nevertheless has the same elements as statesmanship, so that the lesser can serve as a paradigm of the greater. Speaking as if he were picking up something at random, he decides to choose the art of weaving, the weaving of wool. He will make his case without the help of young Socrates.

He begins by saying that all things that we make or acquire are either *heneka tou poiein ti* (for doing something) or *tou mê paschein amuntêria* (for defense against suffering). "All things that we make or acquire" will be the primary category divided in the stranger's new *diaeresis* of weaving. It consolidates the categories of production and acquisition which were divided in the first *diaereseis* of the sophist. This is another illustration of the perfect malleability of the logic of *diaeresis*.

The stranger rejects "doing something" and divides "defense against suffering." Thus, we may assume that he is characterizing weaving and statesmanship as the same insofar as they aim not to do but to defend. This is a little odd insofar as weaving does something, as do statesmen, and also insofar as *politikoi* frequently inflict suffering on others.[1] However, an argument could be made that defense is the chief purpose of both weaving and statesmanship. This would not be a Platonic argument, or at least Aristotle would not have thought so. For Aristotle, and probably also for Plato, justice was the *telos* of politics.

The class of *amuntêriōn* (defenses) is divided into *alexipharmaka* (antidotes, spells) on the one hand and *problêmata* (defenses) on the other. The defenses can be either *theia* (divine) or *anthrōpina* (human). The divine are rejected and the human are retained. This eliminates the gods from participation in the preparation of the defenses created for human beings by weaving and statesmanship, just as the myth banished them from our era. Human *problêmata* are cut into *ta pros ton polemon hoplismata* (equipment for war) and *phragmata* (screens or fences). The war articles are rejected and the screens are chosen. This hints that *politikê*, the analogue of weaving,

---

1 Rosen, Plato's "Statesman," 84, adduces Napoleon as an example of a statesman, an odd choice in view of the stranger's ostensible equation of statesmanship with defense.

is a non-violent *technê* that erects screens between the citizens of cities and harmful forces. The *phragmata* are divided into *parapetasmata* (things spread out before one, such as curtains or veils) and *ta pros cheimōnas kai kaumata alexêtêria* (protections against heat and cold). Weaving does manufacture protections against heat and cold. However, likening this to statesmanship suggests that the *politikos* builds defenses chiefly against nature, thus soft-pedaling the myth's indication that both nature and human bellicosity threaten us. The division makes statesmanship seem more benign by turning attention away from the dangers that men pose for each other and the measures that must be taken to combat them.

The protections against heat and cold are split into *stegasmata* (coverings, possibly in the sense of roofs for houses) and *skepasmata* (coverings, perhaps for human bodies). *Skepasmata* are divided into *hupopetasmata* (things laid beneath one) and *perikalummata de hetera* (things to wrap around us). The analogy between weaving and statesmanship argues that one can be snug inside a *polis* qua other citizens wrapped around oneself. Wraps are cut into *holoshiota* (things that are whole, all of one piece) and *syntheta de hetera* (things that are synthesized). The stranger thus suggests that weaving and statesmanship synthesize. Their products are divided into *trêta* (stitched) and *aneu trêseōs sundete* (bound together without stitching). The latter are chosen. Indeed, it would be hard to imagine the citizens of cities stitched together. The stranger makes hair his analogue of human beings in the *polis*. Hair is virtually as inert as plants. To compare people, who are the "material" of politics, with hair is to make them as close to plants as possible while letting them remain animal. For present purposes, hair will be equated with wool. Hairy, woolen products are *ta hudasi kai gê kollêta* (bound together by water and earth) or *ta auta autois sundeta* (bound together by themselves). Wool is woven together by itself (warp and woof) and so, in the stranger's analogy, must be the citizens of cities. At this point, the model is becoming alarming, not only because the elements of woven wool are denied any say in how they are used, but because their tight binding and their inability to move freely inside their structures bode ill for the citizens of the stranger's city. We are reminded of Aristotle's warning in *Politics* against trying to make the *polis* too great a unity.

FIGURE 12: WEAVING

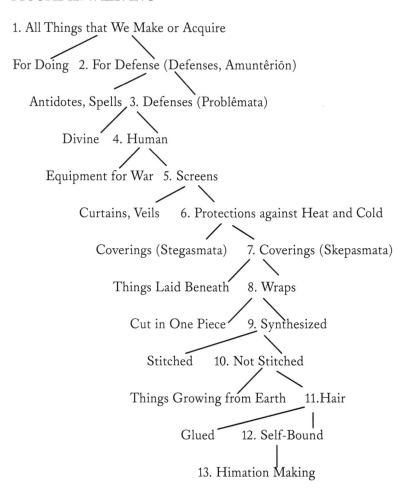

1. All Things that We Make or Acquire

For Doing   2. For Defense (Defenses, Amuntêriōn)

Antidotes, Spells   3. Defenses (Problêmata)

Divine   4. Human

Equipment for War   5. Screens

Curtains, Veils   6. Protections against Heat and Cold

Coverings (Stegasmata)   7. Coverings (Skepasmata)

Things Laid Beneath   8. Wraps

Cut in One Piece   9. Synthesized

Stitched   10. Not Stitched

Things Growing from Earth   11. Hair

Glued   12. Self-Bound

13. Himation Making

TABLE 12: WEAVING (GREEK)

1. *Panta hêmin hoposa dêmiourgoumev kai ktōmetha*
2. *Demiourgoumev kai ktōmetha –> tou poiein ti, tou mê paschein amuntêria*
3. *Amuntêriōn –> alexipharmaka kai 4, theia kai anthrōpina, ta problêmata*
5. *Problêmata –> pros ton polemon hoplismata, phragmata*
6. *Phragmata –> parapetasmata, pros cheimōnas kai kaumata alexêteria*
7. *Alexêteria –> stagasmata, akepmasmata*

8. *Akepmasmata –> hupopetasmata, perikalummasmata*
9. *Perikalummasmata –> holoschista, syntheta*
10. *Syntheta –> trêta, aneu trêseôs*
11. *Aneu trêseōs –> Ek gês, trichina*
12. *Trichina –> hudasi kai gê kollêta, auta autois sundeta*
13. *Auta autois sundeta –> himatiourgikon*

Summary *tōn heautois sundoumenōn, amuntêrious, and skepasmasi.*

The stranger collects the retained items of his divisions. He says that "to these defensive coverings produced from pieces designed to hold together by themselves we give the name of outer garments [himations]."[2] The Greek terms thus collected are *tōn heautois sundoumenōn, amuntêrious,* and *skepasmasi.* The other retained items are dropped. This is another instance of a mistake that, by now, we may judge intentional. This particular blunder reduces statesmanship, the analogue of weaving, to defense by means of the binding of citizens into something placed between themselves and natural threats.

The stranger next decides to call the *technê* of caring for himations himation-making, just as we formerly spoke of *politikê* with respect to the *polis*. This suggests again that cloaks wrap around bodies just as cities qua citizens wrap around individual persons. However, in the case of the *polis*, the citizens' "clothes" are the citizens themselves. The stranger concludes that, since the greater part of weaving is himation-making, we may say that weaving and himation-making differ in name only, just as *basilikê* (the royal art) and *politikê* differ in name only.

The discrepancies between the stranger's *diaeresis* of weaving and his summaries of it have become unremarkable. I shall not dwell on that issue further. It is time to turn to a new aspect of the stranger's combination of paradigm with *diaeresis*. It is not enough for the stranger to produce a paradigm of weaving by means of the *diaeresis* just reported. He must add material to the weaving paradigm-*diaeresis* to separate it from all like activities.

The stranger introduces his new tack by declaring that someone might mistakenly think that our description of the art of weaving is satisfactory.

2 Rosen's translation, *Plato's "Statesman,"* 104.

This person would not realize that we have not distinguished weaving from arts that are *xunergōn* (together-working, cooperative) even though it has been separated from *technai* that are *xungenōn* (congeneric, kindred). The paradigm of weaving has repeated another error but in this case it has done so with a pedagogical aim, to show that weaving, as a model of statesmanship, has to be divided from its competitors just as kingship must be distinguished from its rivals. The work of differentiating the king from his competitors now is scheduled to be advanced by the paradigm's lesson about the difference between *xunergōn* and *xungenōn*.

Before that can happen, young Socrates interrupts with a question: "What do you mean by congeneric *technai*?" The stranger replies by showing how his *diaeresis* has distinguished weaving from a number of other activities, including rug-making, the fashioning of clothing from flax, felting, the sewing of a shoemaker, leather-making, and carpentry.

Having said this, the stranger tells young Socrates that the case is not yet completely stated, for the man who is engaged in the first part of the making of clothes appears to do something that is the opposite of weaving. The process of weaving is a kind of joining together, but its first part, which is known as carding, involves a separation of things combined and matted together. The stranger then says "let us observe that there are two activities, division and collection, involved in all production." In the case of weaving, division, or carding is a contingent cause (*xuniation*); combination is the actual cause (*autēn aitian*). In general, the arts which do not produce the actual thing in question, but supply it with tools and materials, may also be called contingent causes; those producing the thing itself are causes as such. The stranger then shows young Socrates which are which, and concentrates on wool-working proper. Coming to a conclusion, he discusses the arts of twisting threads and intertwining them, i.e., the weaving of the warp and the woof. With this, the stranger has completed his analysis of weaving.

The stranger asks young Socrates why they did not simply say at the outset that weaving is the intertwining of warp and woof? Why did they make so many distinctions? Young Socrates, apparently believing that he has learned how to conduct a proper *diaeresis*, says that nothing of what was said seems to him to have been futile. The stranger worries, however, that the boy might change his mind, and so proposes to provide a standard of excess and deficiency in speech.

This leads to a discussion of the mean, which many scholars believe to be the most important section of this dialogue. Many of them, including the highly respected Kenneth Dorter, for example, also see the stranger as a friend of Socrates, or the voice of a more mature or realistic Socrates/Plato. They think that the stranger's concept of the mean is a way of introducing the concept of value into a discussion of the arts, including that of statesmanship, in a fully explicit way.

Dorter accepts his claim that this mean is both non-relative and substantive, and not merely mathematical, that "all creation is ultimately dependent on an absolute or divine standard," and that the goodness at which all arts aim explains their function as "the necessary essence coming into being."[3] He cautions, however, that no mean should be equated with the Republic's idea of the Good, nor be taken to be goodness absolutely; it is rather "a measure of the words and actions, and inseparable from them," and a measure of the words and actions of those who produce and consume works of art such as weaving and statesmanship. In this process, he argues, theory and praxis remain inextricably dependent upon one another; neither can function properly unless conditioned by the other, and what we know and what we do are inseparable.[4]

Dorter sees this concept of mean as a new and improved (subtler) version of the Socratic equation of knowledge and virtue. As production and acquisition have been reunited (or recombined), so too are knowledge and virtue, since knowing involves acquisition and doing is a kind of production. And so it is that Plato, speaking through the stranger, abandons his earlier tendency to apply principles in general and categorical ways, and joins Aristotle in the pursuit of practical wisdom (*phronêsis*), i.e., the capacity for discerning, given the limitations and constraints of practical situations, "the mean that embodies what is right and good."

In Dorter's admiring view, the stranger wants to replace the inadequacies of inescapably relative, mathematical reasoning with a new, improved version of higher-level moral reasoning, not one (the earlier Platonic tendency perhaps) that reduces the world and its multiplicity to a synoptic order informed by perceiving it in terms of forms or kinds or essences, over

3   Dorter, *Form and Good*, p. 203.
4   Ibid., p. 204.

and against individuals, but that inspired by myth, and empowered by the concept of the mean, somehow discerns the existence of essences springing from the good and the beautiful, and applies them to concrete judgments and decisions.

Dorter does well to avoid equating the mean with the idea of the Good. The two could not be identical because the mean comes into, and passes out of, being while the idea of the Good is eternal.

The problem with the way that both Dorter and the stranger relate this mean to the eternal Good is that the temporal good to which all human art and activity is said to aspire, is a "good" whose sense the text does not distinguish as other than entirely colloquial. It is not related to the Good beyond Being. But this opens the possibility that judgments and decisions in particular instances, limited and constrained as they will be, would be dependent on the non-specified moral calculi of ordinary, and very likely self-interested individuals. And it would also seem to justify the sacrifice of one good, that of justice, for example, to one or a number of other, competing goods, such as one's own life, one's family's happiness, or the city's harmony, i.e., arrangements or trade-offs against which Socrates in any of his versions or phases would most certainly protest. In any case, the stranger's discussion of the mean leaves us once again in *aporia*. We have been shown no non-arbitrary way of conducting a *diaeresis* that would lead to proper identification of the mean dependent on the Good, thus leaving matters subject to the application of highly subjective criteria.

At this juncture, the stranger raises a surprising question. He asks young Socrates whether their investigation has been undertaken for the sake of the particular subject of the statesman, or to make us better thinkers about all subjects. Young Socrates answers that it has been for the sake of all. The stranger replies that we must therefore endeavor to acquire the power of giving and understanding the rational definition of each thing, for immaterial things, which are the noblest and greatest, can be exhibited by reason only. He adds that our first and most important object should be to exalt the method of dividing by classes. This particular phrase has convinced virtually all analytic philosophers that Statesman is not a political text, but rather a methodological treatise. Let that be as it may. I repeat the criticism I have just made of the doctrine of the mean. I am in *aporia*, for I have been shown no consistent, non-arbitrary method of division by classes that adheres to consistent principles. The stranger has not taught me, at least, how to apply his method.

Having just denied that his investigation has been for the sake of statesmanship, the stranger will nevertheless continue using it as a model for the application of his method. He will take up his discussion of the art of a king where he left off the analysis of weaving. That is, he will try to separate from the *polis* the contingent and actual causes of statesmanship.

But here the stranger introduces yet another surprise. Throughout his presentation he has insisted upon dividing classes by two. Now, however, he says this will be impossible. He recommends dividing classes like an animal that is sacrificed by joints. He adds nevertheless that we must always divide into a number of parts as near to two as possible.

It should be noticed that the stranger has not just called for the division of classes by their natural joints, as Socrates did in Phaedrus. It should also be noticed that no explanation has been given for adhering as closely as possible to the rule of division by two. One could say that he changes the procedure of *diaeresis* from division by two to division by seven. Indeed, as Stanley Rosen has pointed out, the entire dialogue contains seven sets of divisions, five with either seven or eleven items, making for around forty-nine (seven times seven) stages.[5] This is an excellent piece of scholarship on Rosen's part, but nobody seems to know what the numerology means. I certainly do not.

The stranger resumes the paradigmatic comparison of weaving and statesmanship. He wants to cut away the contingent causes, leaving the actual causes, of statesmanship. He does this, strangely, by discussing possessions of the *polis*. He lists the following possessions: tools, receptacles, vehicles, clothing, most arms, defensive walls of earth and stone, ornaments, gold, silver, and materials for carpentry and basket-weaving, raw materials for production, food, and tame animals. The stranger then changes his mind, puts raw materials first on the list, also deciding to eliminate all property and tame animals except slaves because these things were included in the category of herding.

The stranger has excepted slaves because he prophesies that among them will be found those who will contest against the king for his power and art. All the other possessions, which we have called contingent causes,

5   Rosen, *Plato's "Statesman,"* 147.

have been removed. Now he examines the seven varieties of slaves and servants. The first four are relatively straightforward and uninteresting. They do work that is as vital to statesmanship as spinning is to weaving, but they do not presume to compete with the king. The fifth class is diviners or prophets who are thought to have a servant-like (servile, *diakonos*) science of interpreting gods to human beings. I think that this must be a sly, disrespectful reference to the Delphi Oracle and similar figures. The sixth category is priests, who are said by customary law to have a science of giving gods things that please them and asking gods for things that are good for us. These priests practice a servant-like (*diakonos*) *technê* too. Young Socrates is nervous about this assertion. Priests are grand officials of the *polis*. It could be dangerous to insult them by calling them servile.

The stranger presses ahead regardless. He declares that they are on the track of their quarry, namely, the free servants who are rivals of the king. He contends that the prophets and priests are very presumptuous (*phronêmatos*) and that they win great reputations owing to the magnitude of their projects. Certainly human history and literature are full of examples of power struggles and policy conflicts between prophets and priests on one side and rulers on the other. The stranger points to the encroachment of priesthood on the highest political offices of Egypt, where pharaohs must be priests, and of Athens, where the king archon must perform the city's sacrifices. Young Socrates is aware of these examples. The stranger therefore announces that we must look at them. But then he breaks this discussion off and never mentions the topic again. He could get in trouble by continuing, and it suffices that he has included prophets and priests in his list. In his political theory, religious figures are king's servants, not his superiors. Nevertheless, it should not be lost on us that he thinks that their work is as necessary to statesmanship as spinning is to weaving.

At this point, the stranger jumps the rails of his analysis. He suddenly sees a most unusual group of people heading towards him, one that appears to include lions, centaurs, and satyrs, and whose numbers keep changing forms from one to another. They are weak and yet wily. He says he knows who they are. They are sophists and *goêta*, (sorcerers who howl enchantments), and they must be separated from all genuinely statesmanlike and kingly men. In my view, one of the unnamed persons to whom these images are meant to allude is old Socrates himself, since the stranger almost certainly knew that Socrates had been called a satyr at Agathon's drinking party, was recently denounced as a Protean sophist and a *goês* in Sophist, often identified himself with the wily Odysseus, and claimed to be the only real *politikos* in Athens. In both its public and private effects, the stranger's inference seems clear: Socrates is a sophist, a sorcerer, and a dangerous rival of the king. He and others like him must be separated from real statesmen and kings, which is to argue that Socrates and others like him must be seen for the servile frauds that they are who lack the true *politikê epistêmê*, and must be separated from legitimate statesmen and kings. But wait. There is a problem with this. Socrates and other sophists have no legitimate place in a list of artists who stand to statesmen as spinners do to weavers. Whose servants are they? What could they possibly contribute to the real work of the city? They seem to be men whose intent is to harm or destroy, not serve it.

The stranger is subtle. He makes it appear that he is not talking about Socrates directly. He does this by going into a discussion of the forms of government, namely monarchy, oligarchy, and democracy. He asks young Socrates whether any of these forms could be the right one, and immediately answers no to his own question. Statesmanship is one of the sciences, and only a scientific government could be the right one. He argues that we must distinguish men who pretend to be statesmen from real statesmen, i.e., from real scientists. In this way he makes it seem that he has been talking about the leaders of the traditional forms of government, and not Socrates. However, Socrates is clearly one of the unscientific meddlers in the affairs of the *polis*.

Many Plato scholars maintain that this line of reasoning, and several more of the stranger's arguments, are essentially Socratic. I believe, on the contrary, that these arguments are not Socratic at all. They really are two types of un-Socratic thought: (1) lines of reasoning that are misinterpreted as Socratic because philosophy, love of wisdom, is confused with science or knowledge (*epistêmê*) and with wisdom (*sophia* or *phronêsis*) as such, and (2) arguments that are misperceived as Socratic because there are areas in which analyses of the problems of philosopher kingship and scientific tyranny happen to coincide. What I mean by this will become clear as I proceed.

The stranger's insistence that the only right criterion for classifying varieties of government is the ruler's possession or lack of *epistêmê* is not Socratic. In Republic, Socrates distinguished between philosophic and unphilosophic forms. "Philosophic" is not the same as "scientific." Socrates never claimed to have an *epistêmê*, never claimed to know. He always denied knowing anything other than his own ignorance. As I have observed elsewhere, he did say twice that he had a *technê* of eros that, at most, amounted to a kind of ignorant or incomplete knowing. This art of eros probably was the sum and substance of his political care of souls. Philosophy is literally the love of wisdom. The love of wisdom is aware that it is not wisdom. Its only wisdom is the knowledge that it is not wise. The stranger's *epistêmê* and *phronêsis* purport to be attained knowledge and wisdom. As such, they are the direct opposites of Socrates' philosophy and wisdom. Hence, to describe forms of government as philosophic or unphilosophic, and as scientific or unscientific, is to classify on different scales. Of course, another argument is that "Plato" changed his mind about all these things, redefining wisdom in his new spirit of retrenchment. I regard this as an arbitrary assumption, one less entitled to credence than my own view that the stranger is presenting an anti-Socratic doctrine.

The stranger continues his digression on the right criterion for classifying regimes by asking young Socrates whether multitudes could pass the sole test of statesmanship by acquiring the ruling science. The boy really does not have enough experience of life to answer this question. However, he has just been taught that the *epistêmê* is the most difficult to acquire so he faces pressure to reply with "no." Well, inquires the stranger, in a *polis* of a thousand men could fifty or a hundred acquire it? Young Socrates doubts that such a city could even produce that many good draughts players, let alone so many kings. It occurs to him at this point that he and the stranger previously had stipulated that he who has the kingly science must be called kingly whether he actually is a king or not. It may be that he does not want to seem to be foreclosing the possibility that the intimidating stranger who is interrogating him is kingly. The stranger praises his response and concludes: we must look for right rule in only one or two or a few men. Because Socrates himself expresses doubt, in Republic, that the many can become philosophic, the stranger's argument here often is said to be Socratic. It is not. The stranger and Socrates do agree that only a few persons could ever be considered as candidates for right kingship, but their reasons for taking these positions are not the same. As just shown, to declare that the many could not be philosophic differs from saying that the many could not be scientific. This is one area in which the arguments of

Socrates and the stranger are diametrically opposed and yet parallel. They are diametrically opposed inasmuch as they refer to totally different kinds of right kingship and qualifications for kingship. They are parallel to the degree that they both declare the many unfit for noble kingship.

The stranger feels a need to qualify his criterion for classifying regimes by saying what it is not. This requires a distinction between statesmanship and tyranny, which naive observers might confuse. The stranger asserts that the few men who rule rightly in accord with *technê* do so whether their subjects consent or not and whether they have written laws or not. They resemble physicians whom we call doctors when they treat us expertly in accord with *technê* by cutting, burning, and other painful ways as long as these make us better. There is only one right regime, that in which the rulers are truly and not only apparently scientific, whether or not (he repetitiously stresses) the subjects are willing and kings rule by written laws (thus nullifying his *diaeresis* at 274d–e.) If kings purge the *polis* by killing or ostracizing, or increase it in size by recruiting new citizens, they must be understood as ruling rightly only as long as they adhere to science (*epistêmê*) and justice (i.e., justice as seen through the lens of science). They are not tyrants. Other forms, whether they involve killing and ostracizing, or not, are illegitimate. As regime types, they do not even really exist. They have only a shadowy being as debased imitations of a true regime. Those said to have good laws imitate the true one for the better and the others for the worse. The stranger has sharpened his political theory by stressing that the essence of the genuinely political is scientific. The presence or absence of violence has nothing to do with that essence.

Many will say that these statements are Socratic. The designation of the scientific regime as the only right one, the demand for governance in accord with justice, and the comfort taken with measures such as killing and ostracism resemble arguments that Socrates made in Republic, e.g., his identification of philosopher kingship as the only right regime, his heavy emphasis on justice, and his endorsement of the expulsion from the city of everyone over the age of ten. While these may be prima facie similarities, however, the stranger's pronouncements are not Socratic. For one, Socrates only called for philosopher kings in the just city, and even more importantly philosopher kings and scientist kings differ fundamentally. And, for another, the same hermeneutic rules apply to the study of Republic as to the exegesis of Theaetetus, i.e., one must determine whether Socrates speaks for himself, or for Glaucon, when he suggests the deportation of everyone over age ten in connection with the education of guardians, and what he has in mind when he says that simply having a philosopher king would be enough to make a city beautiful. Finally, as I have previously noted, no one has ever commended any sort of regime without proclaiming its superiority in terms of justice. The important question is not one's commitment to justice, but his (or her) understanding of it, a matter to which the stranger has devoted no time or effort whatsoever.

Moreover, his neglect of the issue is compounded by a failure to consider the difficulty of improving people ethically by depriving them of the opportunity to make moral decisions for themselves and to participate in deliberations regarding the common good. Instead, on the basis of a "science" with no declared content beyond defining means, the stranger seems to equate justice with whatever is needed to defend the city, and to assure the survival of a fortunate minority therein. This is not a Socratic doctrine. His denial notwithstanding, the stranger has run up the Jolly Roger of a tyranny whose scientific ruler executes and ostracizes for utterly pragmatic reasons, and without restraint of any discernable kind. And so, it appears, we have another matter in which the recommendations of the stranger and Socrates are substantively opposed, although sometimes practically and even semantically parallel.

Young Socrates is leery of government without laws. This gives the stranger an opportunity for another digression, a discourse on the role of law in his political theory. The stranger agrees that lawmaking belongs to kingship (*basilikê*). He insists, however, that the kingly man of wisdom (i.e., science), not the law, should have power. In determining what is best (*ariston*) and most just for all, no single law could ever assure what would be best (*beltiston*) for diverse people under constantly changing circumstances. In effect, the rule of law attempts to do the impossible, forcing dissimilar cases into the same mold. Therefore, laws are not most right (*orthotaton*). We must ask, the stranger says, why legislation is necessary—a question that he does not get around to answering for a long time.

The stranger will ultimately concede the need for laws and legislation under special circumstances, but for the moment he continues stressing their absurdity. It seems ridiculous, he notes, that the Athenian trainers in charge of preparing athletes almost always ignore their individual differences (in physique, strength, and speed); they prescribe, instead, for majorities, and thus fail to order what is best for each individual. Lawmakers guiding herds in matters of justice and contracts do this as well, thus failing to identify or provide what might be appropriate for each individual. But no true possessor of kingly science or wisdom would allow himself to be hemmed in by common laws or other constraints. Again, if a physician or trainer had to go abroad, leaving his patients or students written instructions, and if, upon returning, he found altered conditions, he would issue new rules, denying the silly proposition that the old ones should never be violated. If laws were more rigid than medical or athletic regimens, it would be ridiculous. This could not occur in science or true *technê*. And so, in the stranger's view, in the regime of a truly wise (i.e., scientific) king, legislation actually would be both unnecessary and foolhardy. The real *politikos* would rule simply by giving orders. Indeed, one wonders why the stranger would even say that legislation belongs to *basilikê*, or exactly how the scientific statesman himself could manage to do what is said to be impossible for lawgivers, i.e., prescribing different best things for each one of a myriad of individuals. He would have to be not merely godlike but a god himself. The real statesmen of my own conception would not try to do what the stranger envisages. They would aim at goods that are actually common, good for everybody. True justice is one such good.

But the stranger is not finished, and offers an even more emphatic statement of a previous argument. He disapproves of people claiming that if anyone wants to improve on the laws he should persuade the city first. No one, he says, would ever consider unjust a physician who forced a patient to submit to a successful cure without persuading him. In the political *technê*, it is unscientific error that is baseness, evil and injustice. Thus, if people were forced, against the letter of customary law, to do more just, better, and finer things than before, one could hardly complain that an injustice had been done to them. Just as the pilot saves his sailors and passengers by applying his art rather than by writing laws, so the wise, good man will establish the right regime by making his *technê* more powerful than the laws. In this view, whatever intelligent rulers do will not be erroneous as long as they use reason and *technê* to dispense the greatest justice, i.e., preserve (or save, *sōzein*) the city, and make the citizens "better."

Again, one might think that these propositions are Socratic but they are not. Socrates would argue that the lack of attunement to the Good, not the lack of politically scientific acumen, is the root of all baseness, evil, and injustice. (The stranger still has not mentioned the idea of the Good.) While believing in the value and importance of a city, he would deny that its preservation was the greatest good, and would instead define as "better" something that made it worth saving or preserving, even as, in his own case, he would refuse to place his preservation above the city's. Socrates would agree that it is not unjust to forcibly prevent grossly evil acts, or to compel good ones under certain circumstances. He would disagree, however, that the forced performance of a good deed would make a person better. People are morally improved only if they do good of their own volition. The stranger regards his intentions in these matters as benevolent, but once again he advocates tyranny, and laws have no place in his dreamy, scientific regime. Only his godly and discretionary king can achieve the impossible, orders prescribing and assuring what is uniquely best for each of the individuals over whom he rules. The sway of laws arises only where no such kingly authority is to be found or acknowledged.

We learn when and where in yet another dialectical digression (222a–c), in which the stranger again suggests that regimes other than the true one are not real but imitations of it. Young Socrates asks for an explanation. The stranger replies that inferior regimes can save themselves by employing "the writings" of scientific ones, and severely punishing violations thereof. This amounts to a good "second choice," a regime in which the rule of law is rigidly enforced if, for some reason or reasons, the best regime is not feasible. Regimes ruled by one person, the few, and the many might all adopt arrangements of this sort, and they would all be examples of second-best regimes. Given their city's experience under the legendary lawgiver Solon, this line of reasoning would be of considerable consolation and appeal to conservative Athenians; their *polis* would surely qualify as at least a second-best regime, and its laws should therefore be obeyed and enforced without exception.

There are things about this that puzzle me. When and where has the one true regime existed? In what did its "writings" consist if its king only gave orders and wrote no laws? Where and how do second-best regimes get hold of these writings, and how are they to be used to generate new, inviolable laws if they were something other than laws? And, finally, what specific measures might the ruler or rulers of a second-best regime enact? Not surprisingly, the stranger offers no answers, although I might be forgiven for suspecting that a person, like him, though not actually ruling, fancies himself of kingly wisdom, might be persuaded to come to the aid of a second-best regime whose very preservation, and that of its privileged core, was being threatened by those challenging its laws.

Digressing further, the stranger embarks on a diatribe against the legal practices of the Athenian democracy, pleasing Athenian aristocrats and conservative democrats while alienating their foes. He seems to be addressing the question of what are acceptable and unacceptable rules of law in regimes that aspire to second-best status. The speech will appear to contradict what I just stated about Socrates, sympathizing with him rather than condemning him. But in the end it will reaffirm both the stranger's theory of law and Socrates' death sentence.

The stranger tells young Socrates that the best images to be kept in mind when discussing kingly rulers are those of a ship's pilot and a physician of great worth, and he then suggests that a number of the defining features of democratic life in Athens cannot but appear to be ridiculous: (1) that people should resent their treatment by pilots and doctors, decree that the nautical and medical *technai* may not rule, subject nautical and medical decisions to majority rule, inscribe the majority decisions on tablets, and demand that sailing and medicine be conducted in accord with those provisions forever; (2) that the rulers of the people who are selected in any manner whatsoever should govern in accord with such laws [and, therefore, not in accord with the scientific *technê* of *politikê*]; (3) that annual audits of pilots, physicians, [and rulers] should be held, with anyone [who is a nonscientist] being allowed to accuse those being examined of having not acted in accord with the laws; (4) that anyone who investigates the *technai* of piloting, sailing, and medicine contrary to the laws should be called neither a pilot nor a doctor but a stargazer and a sophist and be hailed into court on charges of corrupting the young, on grounds that nothing should be superior to the law; and (5) that these same rules should be applied to all *technai* without exception.

Young Socrates agrees that all this would be ruinous of the arts and of life generally. Such critiques of democracy are similar to those made by Socrates, and yet the allusion to one who is both a stargazer and a sophist is clearly an allusion to the parable of the ship in Republic and an attack on both philosophy and Socrates himself. In having the stranger say these things, Plato expects us to recognize both the perilous circumstances in which Socrates was caught up, and the not unrelated fact that he criticized Athenian democracy in similar terms. But it is the stranger, not Socrates, who is speaking, and he is as concerned with his own situation as he is with the philosopher who is the enemy of his *polis*. In Athens, the scientist who inquires into true *politikê* could run the same risks as do critical philosophers, however disdainful of such fanciful thinkers he might be. So here, again, we have a matter in which the stranger's science and Socrates' philosophy differ and yet generate parallel political judgments.

The stranger, moreover, is anything but indignant as to Socrates' fate. Indeed, his hearty approval is all too clear in a final (6th) indictment of (Athenian) democracy. Assume, he says to the boy, that the sciences have been placed under the authority of someone who is supposed to govern in accord with the law but knows nothing of it, takes bribes, and breaks laws, and thereby poses a worse evil than the ones previously decried. Sounding a bit like Edmund Burke, the stranger observes that the laws have been laid down on the basis of much *peiras* (experiment, trial, one could almost say "trial and error"), after having been considered by counselors and recommended to the people *charientōs* (gracefully, elegantly). To violate these laws, he says, would be a greater error and cause more ruin than the original mistake of having made them. Though its regime is only a second-best one, he lets the people of Athens know that their laws must be upheld, and those who defy them silenced and punished in exemplary fashion. And it will hardly matter to the city's aristocrats and conservative democrats that the stranger's argument has substituted trial, error, muddling through, and grace for *epistêmê/technê* as foundations for its system of justice.

The stranger's view of the role, nature, and basis of law in a second-best regime, although seemingly complete, turns out not to be, and he launches into yet another digression. Although earlier he had declared the six forms of government recognized by Greek civics teachers unreal, he now finds it advisable to rank them, and the standard on which he will do so will be science, or bits and pieces of it. The ranking starts with the observation that laws written by partially knowledgeable men imitate some portion of truth. Of course, the fully knowledgeable man, the *politikos*, would change his rules at will, whenever he saw a better course, and people lacking in *epistêmê*, be they rich men or the many, invariably imitate a true *politikos* badly. To minimize potential damage, the rulers of cities dominated by either the rich or the many must never do anything that transgresses written laws and ancestral norms based on *peiras*. Cities that take this advice will be lawful and rank higher; those that do not will be lawless and rank lower. Conservative Athenians will be glad to hear that their laws must not be broken. Lawful regimes that imitate the true one well will be called monarchies, aristocracies, and lawful democracies; the lax ones that do not will be known as tyrannies, oligarchies, and lawless democracies.

The popular tendency to confuse stern monarchies with tyrannies moves the stranger to seek criteria for defining them. He laments that both second-best and bad regimes have arisen because people do not believe that there are men worthy of the genuine king's power. That is, they do not think that there could be a person possessed of that power and capable of ruling with virtue (which the stranger appears to equate with knowledge) and *epistêmê*. They fear that someone with unfettered power would harm and kill arbitrarily. However, they admit that if the scientific man arose, they would welcome him with open arms and declare his regime most right-ful. And they would likely accept the harming and killing he might order if it seemed necessary for their city's, and their own, preservation. This is hardly what Socrates himself would argue. Instead, he would say that people should only accept such harming and killing as was necessary to the defense of institutions and practices in line with, and promoting the good, i.e., things that made a *polis* worth preserving. The stranger's *politikos*, in con-trast, whose "right" to rule rests on an allegedly scientific foundation of undisclosed content, and who forces into being perceptions of means, ex-cesses, and defects, is simply a tyrant who enjoys, and is likely to continue needing, the services of a good propagandist.

But, alas, the classification of the six unreal regimes is not quite com-plete. They must still be ranked vis-a-vis one another in terms of desirabil-ity, and this will not be easy, the stranger fears. The written laws and ancient customs on which most of these regimes are based are flawed, and many are essentially lawless, so that ranking them will require choosing among greater and lesser evils. In terms of relative desirability, moving from the more to the least acceptable, the stranger lists monarchy, aristocracy, lawful democracy, unlawful democracy, oligarchy, and tyranny in that order. The two democracies are placed where they are because they are weak, and for better or for worse, incapable of doing anything great for good or ill. This means that relative strength is the principle that differentiates the three second-bests from one another and from the three worsts. Of course, the seventh regime, led by a politically wise ruler, would be best of all, but it is set apart from these others as the gods stand apart from man.

Reflecting on the absolute undesirability of the six unscientific regimes, the stranger draws a conclusion: those who participate in them are not *politikoi* but *stasiastikoi*, seditionists—traitors to the true scientific regime and combatants in the power struggles of their own cities. Harking back to the morning's conversation, the stranger asserts that because they preside over the greatest images, these politicians are the greatest imitators and thus the greatest sophists. Although the stranger is referring to political partisans of the six regimes, we know from his earlier allusion to Socrates that he intends to include him in his condemnation. Socrates is a *goês* who engages in the city's affairs in his own way. He is a Protean sophist, a faux-purifier who wrongly claims to do the statesman's work of making people better and who has openly confessed to knowing nothing. Although he is not a ruler or a partisan, he is a member of the class of unscientific political sophists in question. Following the stranger's reasoning, we are entitled to deduce that if the scientific man is a king whether he is in office or not, the most sophistical unscientific meddler in the business of the city is a seditionist whether he grasps for power or not. Moreover, Socrates is a seditionist who, unlike the reigning authorities, stands outside the law and therefore merits death. Perhaps in order to clinch this judgment of old Socrates, the stranger reminds young Socrates that he has been discussing a troop of centaurs and satyrs that he saw. He has been working very hard to separate this class of slaves [and thus, Socrates, who has claimed to be the only true *politikos* and therefore the king's rival] from the statesman. We can be forgiven for having forgotten this *diaeresis* of the seventh class of slaves from the king, for we had thought that it was finished. Evidently, all of the excursions into political theory that seemed to be digressions were, on the stranger's account, steps of that division.

The seven classes of causes of *politikê* just divided from it were not the only ones in need of such treatment. They were alien, incompatible impurities like earth mixed with gold. Still remaining to be "smelted" away are the "precious metals," the arts of rhetoric, generalship, and judging. These *technai* are absolutely indispensable to *politikê*. The practitioners who perform them take orders from the king who gives them, deciding when, how, and for what purpose they are to be employed. The stranger does not say so but it seems to me that a *politikos* could not give the right instructions and supervise his practitioners unless he knew the arts. So, for example, if he does not serve as his own Minister of Propaganda and Truth, he would still have to tell his minister what the "truth" is, and this will require finding the words in which to couch such a clarification. Similarly, to direct the generals in war he would have had to study war, and to run a successful regime he also would have to tell his judges what his orders mean, interpreting laws that are not laws, and thus doing their work.

With these preliminaries complete, the stranger finally is ready to discuss *politikê* as weaving. This requires an introductory discourse on the virtues, but it will rest on a clearly un-Socratic premise. Socrates regularly postulated the ultimate unity of the virtues in wisdom. For example, courage was not courage if it had no sense of what should be feared and what not. *Sōphrosunê* (sane self-control, moderation) was not *sōphrosunê* if it had no inkling of what was just right, insufficient, or excessive. Justice was not justice if it was not guided by reason. In contrast, the stranger sees the virtues in a condition of hostility (*echtran*) toward one another. He comes to this view by depicting courage as a kind of mindless impetuosity and *sōphrosunê* as an equally mindless daintiness that ends in lethargy, such that the courageous will risk everything stupidly, while the moderates will venture nothing (307e–08a). As for justice, he ignores it altogether, undoubtedly because he sees no just men among the tame animals making up the citizen body, and defines wisdom as the king's science.

The stranger maintains that it is the statesman's work to weave the brave and moderate parts of society together. In saying this, however, he greatly oversimplifies society. Surely there is more than one social scale and there are more than two types or options on any one of them. But he is anxious to move on and asks young Socrates whether any "synthetic science" voluntarily composes its works out of good and bad materials. The young boy answers "of course not." And so it apparently follows, just as the weaver directs a fuller to remove impurities from wool, the king who supervises political fullers will order them to eliminate social elements who are neither courageous nor moderate. Newborns would be taken, school-age children would be seized and sent off for re-education, and unsuitable citizens will be dishonored, enslaved, exiled, and even killed (309c–e).

Taking the mindlessly courageous and moderate as his warp and woof, the stranger's *politikos* weaves them together. He does so in three ways, all in an effort to do the common tending of the *polis* with which he has been charged. He first impresses his own, true opinions regarding virtue on each of the materials he has at his disposal, exercising the function of rhetorician, and uses his political power to ensure that his rhetoric will be spread. In doing so, he will push the mindlessly brave in the direction of gentleness and the mindlessly temperate toward wisdom and prudence (making them more venturesome). Secondly, he mixes the pure varieties of courageous and moderate citizens on official boards and in positions of authority, which he imagines will draw the citizens together in friendship, perhaps because their basic inclinations no longer clash (a thin basis for friendship). Finally, thinking that virtues could be more readily inculcated through therapeutic and eugenic breeding practices, he arranges marriages in a dubious effort to blend normally hostile virtues in individual souls (310a–e).

In the minds of the stranger and his admirers, then, the following ultimate picture of the scientifically-run *polis* emerges. The scientist *politikos*, functioning somewhat like a philosopher king in Republic, controls education, teaching true opinion to all the citizens, officers and boards that he has perfectly balanced between excessive gentleness and courage. Informed by the true opinion they have been taught, these citizens and bodies make correct decisions concerning the defense of the *polis*. There is justice for all and no harm could possibly come to an innocent like Socrates. Scholars like Sayre and Miller contemplate this image with satisfaction. Sayre says that: "This accomplishment brings to completion the finest product of the statesman's art, a civic fabric held together by this rule and direction." In this he essentially repeats Miller,[6] who sees (pp. 111–12) the stranger playing a "mediative" role between Socratic philosophy, for which young Socrates, and the many with whom he stands, is clearly not prepared, and

6   Sayre, *Metaphysics and Myth in Plato's "Statesman,"* 133; Miller, *The Philosopher in Plato's "Statesman."*

a second-best course, the rule of law, for which the stranger's weaving-based notion of statesmanship is at least intelligible and pleasing. In Miller's view, the stranger's closing portrait of the statesman is a "thoroughly Socratic mediation," and the one approving of it as "beautiful" and "complete" is *not* young Socrates, with whom the stranger has been in sustained dialogue, but his elder, would-be mentor, who breaks a long silence to indicate his, and presumably Plato's, approval. In a related footnote, no. 52, Miller notes that while most editors (F. Schleiermacher, 1836, A. Dies, 1956, and J. B. Skemp, 1952) believe that the elder Socrates makes this final speech, others (L. Campbell, 1867, Burnet, 1900, A. G. P. Taylor, 1956 and 1961, and P. Friedlander, 1958 and 1969) insist that it is young Socrates. Miller quotes Friedlander as saying that the elder Socrates would have found the stranger's exposition notably deficient. I agree.

The proposed assessment by Sayre and Miller is flawed in every respect. It is a misnomer to speak of the philosopher in Plato's Statesman. No philosopher is there. A philosopher king would not be content to leave his citizens in the hands of a so-called scientist who dispensed true opinion, trusting that to regulate the *polis* properly. He would be ready to guide those citizens who merited further attention higher than true opinion, preparing to introduce wisdom into the deliberations of the *polis*. The primary reason for this is that he knows that true opinion inevitably breaks down. If he behaved like the stranger's scientist, he would be faced with the necessity of replacing broken parts of his system every day. It also is doubtful that the application of true opinion to practical political questions automatically leads to just results. Wisdom is needed to adjust true opinion to the particular situations of each moment. The stranger continues to prescind from the Good. Finally, Socrates would not be saved by the fine functioning of the well-balanced boards. These boards consist only in persons judged fit for the *polis* by the "fullers." He would have been eliminated long since as a man not measuring up to the stranger's standards of persons meriting retention in the *polis*. This recalls our attention to the turmoil constantly roiling beneath the serene surface of the stranger's creation. We are left in *aporia*, wondering how the problems of a *polis* like the stranger's could be solved.

Just prior to this section, the stranger offers a final definition of *politikê*. He said it is the *technê* that rules the arts, and cares for the laws and virtually everything else in the city, weaving them together most correctly. This directly conflicts with his previously stated view that true statesmanship neither required, nor could tolerate, the constraints that general laws would impose. And yet it won the hearty approval of Socrates the younger, who praised it as most beautiful and complete. Sayre and many others argue that it is Socrates the elder who says this. I think not for several reasons. First, as noted in chapter two, the trajectories of Plato's dialogues on the life and death of the philosopher Socrates make it highly improbable that he would have considered the stranger's performance as either truly beautiful or complete. His standards for the truly beautiful were much too high, and he was well aware that in Athens he was regarded as both a nuisance and an enemy of their democracy by many powerful Athenians. Moreover, in each of the three dialogues we are examining, it is always a young man, either Theaetetus or young Socrates, who responds to the stranger's questions and assertions. And thirdly, in this particular dialogue, a sophistical politician fabricates a pseudoscientific, philosophically impoverished, but rhetorically brilliant rationale for condemning Socrates. As such, the drama is an analysis of the political culture that was at least partially responsible for the philosopher's murder. In terms of the third dramatic trajectory of the complete series, i.e., all seven dialogues,[7] Politician is a play in which the Antinous-Meletus-Polyphemus-stranger prosecutes Socrates before a jury of children, winning another vote to convict.

There remains a final intellectual issue to consider: the epistemological status of paradigm. According to the stranger himself (277c), the paradigmatic method can only produce true opinion, not knowledge. This is quite an admission. There is no science in the stranger's scientific politics.

One also must raise the question of whether the stranger's choice of a basis for his paradigm obscures rather than illuminates politics. The stranger could have chosen one of the activities he discussed in the *diaereses* of Theaetetus or Sophist, e.g., art, exchange, hunting, angling, science, or competition; or he might have selected religion, farming or war. But instead he chose weaving, an activity characterized by a pacifistic concern for defense against a variety of threats. He never explains or justifies his choice, but surely he had in mind its quasi-universality, widespread agreement as

7   See above, Chapter two.

to its seemingly straightforward purposes, its considerable dependence on material resources, and its emphasis on defense.[8] These features must have seemed an attractive starting point from which to reflect on a more complex and multi-faceted activity like political leadership, in which a lack of consensus as to goals and purposes was the cause of ongoing conflict and instability, but might justify the placing of overarching priority on defense. And so, rather predictably, he develops a defensive vision of politics in which the leader is [intent] on the safety of the whole, and on any and everything that appears instrumental thereto, including the re-education of citizens deemed insufficiently courageous or, failing that, their enslavement, exile, and elimination.

The oversimplified character of such a notion of leadership is a consequence of the use of weaving, a relatively simple, one-dimensional human activity, as a model for a more complex, multi-dimensional human activity requiring ongoing judgments and choices that turn on conflicting values and ethical questions of purpose. This is not to say, however, that an appropriately modeled study of politics or political leadership cannot produce useful pieces of knowledge regarding it. The stranger's "analysis," in contrast, produces, predictably, a one-dimensional theory of political behavior, one whose resulting vision of political leadership misses the enormous complexity of the "weaving" that real statesmen actually have to do.

Socrates, on the other hand, is a philosopher, and has no theory of politics. He does have a political *technê* which involves the care of individual souls. As for the reasons why ordinary politicians succeed or fail, he would say these are complex things about which he knows nothing. Instead, he is interested in understanding what true political leadership might be, and what real political leaders should be doing, not what most of them are doing.

The conclusions of my study affirm my hypotheses.

Theaetetus, Sophist, and Politician are all aporetic dialogues. Against the objection that Plato would not have written so much for the purposes of casting doubt on it, or tearing it down, I reply again that Plato never did anything else.

In the dialogues discussed, Socrates definitely plays the roles of

---

8   One could argue that his image of weaving is deliberately contrived to better set up the kind of political leadership he favors.

Odysseus and himself. He is prosecuted by Theodorus and the Eleatic stranger, who have assumed the roles of Anytus and Meletus.

It is my belief that these three dialogues have hindered the proper understanding of Plato for millennia. I also think that Plato scholars have missed the heavy irony with which Plato has written, especially in the deliberate mistakes he has factored into the *diaereses* and other arguments with the antagonists of Socrates.

BIBLIOGRAPHY

Aristotle. *Aristotle IV: Physics, Books I–IV*. Trans. P. H. Wicksteed and F. M. Cornford. Ed.

G. P. Goold. Loeb Classical Library. 1929. Reprint, Cambridge: Harvard University Press, 1980.

_____ *Aristotle V: Physics II, Books V–VIII*. Trans. P. H. Wicksteed and F. M. Cornford. Ed.

G. P. Goold. Loeb Classical Library. 1934. Reprint, Cambridge: Harvard University Press, 1980.

_____ *Aristotle XVII: Metaphysics I–IX*. Trans. Hugh Tredenick. Ed. G. P. Goold. Loeb Classical Library. 1933. Reprint, Cambridge: Harvard University Press, 1989.

_____ *Aristotle XVIII: Metaphysics X–XIV. Oeconomica. Magna Moralia*. Trans. Hugh Tredenick and G. Cyril Armstrong. Ed. G. P. Goold. Loeb Classical Library. 1935. Reprint, Cambridge: Harvard University Press, 1990.

Austin, Norman. *Archery at the Dark of the Moon: Poetic Problems in Homer's "Odyssey."* Berkeley and Los Angeles: University of California Press, 1975.

Barnes, Jonathan. *The Pre-Socratic Philosophers*. Vol. 1, *Thales to Zeno*. London: Routledge and Kegan Paul, 1979.

Benardete, Seth. *The Being of the Beautiful: Plato's* Theaetetus, Sophist, and Statesman. Chicago: University of Chicago Press, 1984.

_____ "Eidos and Diaeresis in Plato's *Statesman*." *Philologus*, 107 (1963): 193–237.

Berger, Jr., Harry. "Plato's Flying Philosopher." *The Philosophical Forum* XIII:4 (Summer 1982): 385–407.

Blitz, Mark. *Plato's Political Philosophy*. Baltimore: Johns Hopkins University Press, 2010.

Bostock, David. *Plato's "Theaetetus."* Oxford: Oxford University Press, 1988.

Brandwood, Leonard. *A Word Index to Plato*. Leeds: W. S. Maney and Son, Limited, 1976.

Brann, Eva. *Homeric Moments: Clues to Delight in Reading the Odyssey and the Iliad*. Philadelphia: Paul Dry Books, 2002.

Brann, Eva, Peter Kalkavage, and Eric Salem (trans. and ed.). *Plato's Sophist: the Professor and Wisdom*. The St. John Review, vol. 55, 1 (Fall 2013).

Brecht, Arnold. *Political Theory: The Foundations of Twentieth-Century Political Thought*. Princeton: Princeton University Press, 1959.

Brown, Leslie. "Innovation and Continuity: the Battle of Gods and Giants," *Sophist*, in Jyl Gentzler (ed.), *Method in Ancient Philosophy*.

Brumbaugh, Robert S. *Plato on the One: The Hypotheses in the Parmenides*. New Haven: Yale University Press, 1961.

Burnyeat, Myles. "The Philosophical Sense of Theaetetus's Mathematics," *Isis*. History of Science Society, 489–513.

_____ *The Theaetetus of Plato*. With a translation of Plato's *Theaetetus* by M. J. Levett, revised by Myles Burnyeat. Indianapolis: Hackett, 1990.

Bury, J. B., S. A. Cook, and F. E. Adcock. *The Cambridge Ancient History*. Vol. VI. *Macedon 401–301 B.C.* Cambridge: Cambridge University Press, 1933.

Chappell, Timothy. *Reading Plato's "Theaetetus."* Indianapolis: Hackett, 2005.

Cooper, John M. *Plato's "Theaetetus."* New York: Garland Publishing, 1960.

Cornford, Francis MacDonald. *Plato's Theory of Knowledge: "The Theaetetus" and "Sophist" of Plato,* translated with a running commentary. New York: Liberal Arts Press, 1957.

Desjardin, Rosemary. *The Rational Enterprise: Logos in Plato's "Theaetetus."* Albany: State University of New York Press, 1990.

David, Amirthanayagam. "Plato and the Measure of the Incommensurable." *The St. John Review*, 46:1 (2000).

Dorter, Kenneth. *Form and Good in Plato's Eleatic Discourses: "The Par-*

menides," "Theaetetus," "Sophist," and "Statesman." Berkeley: University of California Press, 1994.

_____ "Three Disappearing Ladders in Plato." *Philosophy and Rhetoric*, 29:3 (1996): 279–99.

Fine, Gail (ed.). *Plato 1: Metaphysics and Epistemology*. Oxford Readings in Philosophy. Oxford: Oxford University Press, 1999.

_____ *Plato 2: Ethics, Politics, Religion, and the Soul*. Oxford Readings in Philosophy. Oxford: Oxford University Press, 1999.

_____ *Plato on Knowledge and Forms*. Oxford: Clarendon Press, 2003.

Fowler, D. H. *The Mathematics of Plato's Academy: A New Reconstruction*. Oxford: Clarendon Press, 1987.

Goethe, Johann Wolfgang von. *Wilhelm Meisters Wanderjahre*. Goethes Werke: Berlin Ausgabe: Romane und Erzählungen. Bd 9–12. Intelex Past Masters. The quotation is found on main text page 691.

Goldstein, Rebecca. *Incompleteness: the Proof and Paradox of Kurt Gödel*. New York: W. W. Norton, 2013.

Gooch, Paul William. "Vice Is Ignorance: The Interpretation of *Sophist* 226A–231B." *Phoenix*, 25:2 (Summer 1971): 124–33.

Graves, Robert. *The Greek Myths*. Complete and unabridged edition in one volume. Mt. Kosco, New York: Moyer Bell Limited, 1988.

Guthrie, W. K. C. *A History of Greek Philosophy*. Vol. 5, *The Later Plato and the Academy*. Cambridge: Cambridge University Press, 1978.

Heathe, Thomas. "A History of Greek Mathematics." Vol. 1, *From Thales to Euclid*. Oxford: Clarendon Press, 1921.

Hegel, Georg Wilhelm Friedrich. *Vorlesungen über der Geschichte der Philosophie. Georg Wilhelm Friedrich Hegels Werke: Vollständige Ausgabe*. Vol. 14. Ed. Philipp Marheineke. 2d ed. Berlin: Duncker und Humblot, 1842.

Heidegger, Martin. *The Essence of Truth: On Plato's Cave Allegory and "Theaetetus."* Trans. Ted Sadler. New York: Continuum, 2002.

_____ *Plato's "Sophist."* Trans. Richard Rojcewicz and André Schuwer. Bloomington: Indiana University Press, 2003.

Hobbes, Thomas. *Leviathan: Or the Matter, Forme, and Power of a Commonwealth Ecclesiasticall and Civil*. Ed. Michael Oakeshott. Oxford: Basil Blackwell, 1960.

Homer. *The Iliad*. Trans. A. T. Murray, revised by William F. Wyatt. 2 vols. Ed. G. P. Goold. Loeb Classical Library. Cambridge: Harvard University Press, 1999.

⎯⎯ *Odyssey*. Trans. A. T. Murray, revised by George E. Dimock. 2nd ed. 2 vols. Ed. G. P. Goold. Loeb Classical Library. Cambridge: Harvard University Press, 1995.

Howland, Jacob. *The Paradox of Political Philosophy: Socrates' Philosophic Trial*. New York: Rowman and Littlefield, 1998.

Kant, Immanuel. "Von einem neuerdings erhobenen vornehmen Ton in der Philosophie." Vol. 3, *Werke in sechs Bänden*, ed. Wilhelm Weischedel. Wiesbaden: Insel Verlag, 1958.

Kato, Shinro. "The Role of *Paradeigma* in Plato's *Statesman*." Ed. Christopher J. Rowe. *Reading the* Statesman: *Proceedings of the III Symposium Platonicam*. Sankt Augustin: Academie Verlag, 1995.

Klein, Jacob. *A Commentary on Plato's "Meno."* Chapel Hill: University of North Carolina Press, 1995.

⎯⎯ *Greek Mathematical Thought and the Origins of Algebra*. Trans. Eva Brann. Cambridge: Massachusetts Institute of Technology Press, 1968.

⎯⎯ *Lectures and Essays*. Ed. Robert B. Williamson and Elliott Zuckerman. Annapolis: St. John's College Press, 1985.

⎯⎯ *Plato's Trilogy: "Theaetetus," the "Sophist," and the "Statesman."* Chicago: University of Chicago Press, 1977.

Knorr, Wilbur Richard. *The Evolution of the Euclidean Elements: a Study of the Theory of Incommensurable Magnitudes and its Significance for Early Geometry*. Dordrecht, Holland: D. Reidel Publishing Co., 1975.

Lakoff, George, and Rafael E. Nuñez. *Where Mathematics Comes From: How the Embodied Mind Brings Mathematics in Being*. New York: Basic Books, 2000.

Lane, Melissa S. *Method and Politics in Plato's "Statesman."* Cambridge: Cambridge University Press, 1998.

McDowell, John. *Plato, "Theaetetus": Translated with Notes*. Oxford: Clarendon Press, 1973.

Marquez, Xavier. *A Stranger's Knowledge: Statesmanship, Philosophy, and Law in Plato's "Statesman."* Las Vegas: Parmenides Publishing, 2012.

Miller, Mitchell H. *The Philosopher in Plato's "Statesman."* The Hague: Martinus Nijhoff, 1980.

Parmenides. *Parmenides: A Text with Translations, Commentary, and Critical Essays.* Trans. and ed. Leonardo Tarán. Princeton: Princeton University Press, 1965. The quotation that forbids positing the being of nonbeing is in fragment vii.

_____ *Fragments*: A Text and Translation. Trans. and ed. David Gallop. Toronto: University of Toronto Press, 1984. The quotation that forbids positing the being of nonbeing is in fragment 7.

Payne, Thomas. "The *Crito* as Mythological Mime." *Interpretation*, 11:1 (1983): 1–23.

Peck, A. L. "Plato on the *MEGISTA GENÈ* of the Sophist: a Reinterpretation." *Classical Quarterly*, 2 (1952).

Pindar. *The Odes of Pindar.* 2nd ed. Trans. Richmond Lattimore. Chicago: University of Chicago Press, 1976.

_____ *Pindar.* 2 vols. Trans. William H. Race. Ed. G. P. Goold. Loeb Classical Library. Cambridge: Harvard University Press, 1997.

Planinc, Zdravko. *Plato's Political Philosophy: Prudence in the "Republic" and the "Laws."* Columbia: University of Missouri Press, 1991.

_____ *Plato through Homer: Poetry and Philosophy in the Cosmological Dialogues.* Columbia: University of Missouri Press, 2003.

Plato. *The Collected Dialogues of Plato, Including the Letters.* Ed. Edith Hamilton and Huntington Cairns. Bollingen Series. New York: Random House, 1961.

_____ *Complete Works.* Ed. John M. Cooper. Indianapolis: Hackett, 1997.

_____ *The Dialogues of Plato.* 2 vols. Trans. B. Jowett. 1892. Reprint: New York: Random House, 1920.

_____ *Plato.* Ed. G. P. Goold. 12 vols. Loeb Classical Library. 1914–1935. Reprint, Cambridge, Harvard University Press, 1982–1992.

_____ *The "Republic" of Plato.* Trans. Allan Bloom. New York: Basic Books, 1968.

_____ *Republic.* Trans. Joe Sachs. Newburyport, MA: Focus Publishing/R. Pullins, 2007.

_____ *Theaetetus*. Trans. Joe Sachs. Newburyport, MA: Focus Publishing/R. Pullins, 2004.

Platon. *Werke*. Ed. Friedrich Daniel Ernst Schleiermacher. 6 vols. Berlin: Akademie Verlag, 1984.

Platonis. *Platonis Opera*. Ed. John Burne. 5 vols. 1901–1907. Reprint, Oxford: Clarendon Press, 1995.

Polansky, Ronald M. *Philosophy and Knowledge: A Commentary on Plato's "Theaetetus."* Lewisburg, PA: Bucknell University Press, 1992.

Rhodes, James M. *Eros, Wisdom, and Silence: Plato's Erotic Dialogues*. Columbia: University of Missouri Press, 2003.

_____ "Politikos," in Karl-Heinz Nusser, Matthias Riedl, and Theresia Ritter (eds.), *Politikos: Vom Element des Persönlichen in der Politik. Festschrift für Tilo Schabert zum 65. Geburtstag*. Berlin: Duncker und Humblot, 2008, 51–66.

Rosen, Stanley. *Plato's "Sophist": The Drama of Original and Image*. New Haven: Yale University Press, 1983.

_____ *Plato's* Statesman: *The Web of Politics*. New Haven: Yale University Press, 1995.

Rowe, Christopher J. (Ed.) *Reading the Statesman: Proceedings of the III Symposium Platonicam*. Sankt Augustin: Academie Verlag, 1995.

Salmon, Wesley C. (Ed.) *Zeno's Paradoxes*. Indianapolis: Hackett, 1970, 2001.

Saltis, John. *Being and Logos: Reading the Platonic Dialogues*. Bloomington: Indiana University Press, 1996.

Sayre, Kenneth M. *Metaphysics and Method in Plato's "Statesman."* New York: Cambridge University Press, 2006.

_____ *Parmenides' Lesson. Translation and Explanation of Plato's "Parmenides."* Notre Dame, IN: University of Notre Dame Press, 1996.

_____ "Plato's Dialogues in Light of the Seventh Letter." *Platonic Writings, Platonic Readings*. Ed. Charles L. Griswold, Jr. New York: Routledge, 1988.

_____ *Plato's Literary Garden: How to Read a Platonic Dialogue*. Notre Dame, IN: University of Notre Dame Press, 1995.

Schleiermacher, Friedrich Daniel Ernst. *Schleiermacher's Introductions to the Dialogues of Plato*. Trans. William Dobson. New York: Arno Press, 1973.

Scodel, Harvey Ronald. *Diaeresis and Myth in Plato's "Statesman."* Göttingen: Vandenhoeck und Ruprecht, 1987.

Sedley, David. *The Midwife of Platonism: Text and Subtext in Plato's "Theaetetus."* Oxford: Clarendon Press, 2004.

Shorey, Paul. "A Lost Platonic Joke." *Classical Philology*. 1917: 308–10.

Stern, Paul. *Knowledge and Politics in Plato's "Theaetetus."* Cambridge: Cambridge University Press, 2008.

——— "The Rule of Wisdom and the Rule of Law in Plato's *Statesman*." *American Political Science Review* 91 (June 1997): 264–77.

Strauss, Leo. *The City and Man*. Chicago: University of Chicago Press, 1964.

——— *Natural Right and History*. Chicago: University of Chicago Press, 1953.

——— *Persecution and the Art of Writing*. Chicago: University of Chicago Press, 1952.

——— *Studies in Platonic Political Philosophy*. Chicago: University of Chicago Press, 1983.

Tschemplik, Andrea. *Knowledge and Self-Knowledge in Plato's "Theaetetus."* New York: Lexington, 2008.

Vlastos, Gregory. *Platonic Studies*. Princeton: Princeton University Press, 1973.

Voegelin, Eric. *Anamnesis*. Trans. Gerhart Niemeyer. Notre Dame, IN: University of Notre Dame Press, 1978.

——— *Anamnesis: Zur Theorie der Geschichte und Politik*. München: R. Piper, 1966.

——— *The Collected Works of Eric Voegelin*. 34 vols. Columbia: University of Missouri Press, 1989–2004. Especially vol. 12.

——— *Order and History*. 5 vols. Baton Rouge: Louisiana State University Press, 1956–1957, 1974, 1987. Especially vol. 3.

White, David. A. *Myth, Metaphysics, and Dialectic in Plato's "Statesman."* Burlington, VT: Ashgate, 2007.

White, John. "Imitation," in Plato, *Republic*, trans. Joe Sachs, 323, 325.

KNOWLEDGE, SOPHISTRY, & SCIENTIFIC POLITICS

White, Nicholas P. *Plato on Knowledge and Reality*. Indianapolis: Hackett, 1976.

Zuckert, Catherine. *Plato's Philosophers: The Coherence of the Dialogues*. Chicago: University of Chicago Press, 2009.

_____ "The Stranger's Political Science v. Socrates' Political Art," in the online *Journal of the International Plato Symposium* (Winter 2005).